SEMANTIC POLARITIES AND PSYCHOPATHOLOGIES IN THE FAMILY

The gap between psychotherapeutic practice and clinical theory is ever widening. Therapists still don't know what role interpersonal relations play in the development of the most common psychopathologies. Valeria Ugazio bridges this gap by examining phobias, obsessive-compulsions, eating disorders, and depression in the context of the family, using an intersubjective approach to personality. Her concept of "semantic polarities" gives a groundbreaking perspective to the construction of meaning in the family and other interpersonal contexts. At no point is theory left in the wasteland of abstraction. The concreteness of the many case studies recounted, and examples taken from well-known novels, will allow readers to immediately connect the topics discussed with their own experience.

Valeria Ugazio, PhD, is the Scientific Director of the European Institute of Systemic-relational Therapies, Milan, Italy and is Professor of Clinical Psychology and Coordinator of the Clinical Psychology Doctorate program at the University.

SEMANTIC POLARITIES AND PSYCHOPATHOLOGIES IN THE FAMILY

Permitted and Forbidden Stories

Valeria Ugazio
Translated by Richard Dixon

Routledge
Taylor & Francis Group

NEW YORK AND LONDON

First published in English 2013
by Routledge
711 Third Avenue, New York, NY 10017

Simultaneously published in the UK
by Routledge
27 Church Road, Hove, East Sussex BN3 2FA

Routledge is an imprint of the Taylor & Francis Group, an informa business

First published in Italian by Bollati Boringhieri 2012

Library of Congress Cataloging in Publication Data
  Ugazio, Valeria. Permitted and forbidden stories : semantic polarities and
  psychopathologies in the family / authored by Valeria Ugazio. — 1 [edition].
  pages cm Includes bibliographical references and index.
  ISBN 978–0–415–82306–7(hardback) — ISBN 978–0–415–82307–4 (paperback)
  1. Personality disorders—Complications. 2. Psychology, Pathological—Case studies.
  I. Title.
  RC554.U33 2013616.85'81—dc23
  2012039336

ISBN: 978–0–415–82306–7 (hbk)
ISBN: 978–0–415–82307–4 (pbk)
ISBN: 978–0–203–55238–4 (ebk)

Typeset in Galliard
by Swales & Willis Ltd, Exeter, Devon
Printed and bound in Great Britain by
CPI Group (UK) Ltd, Croydon, CR0 4YY

CONTENTS

Introduction

CONTENTS

FIGURES

FIGURES

ABOUT THE AUTHOR

Valeria Ugazio PhD is a clinical psychologist and psychotherapist. She lives with her husband in Milan where she is director of the European Institute of Systemic-relational Therapies (www.eist.it), which she founded in 1999. She is Professor of Clinical Psychology at the University of Bergamo, Italy, where she runs Clinical Psychology Doctorate courses. She is currently interested in developing systemic therapeutic approaches specific to the four psychopathologies—phobic, obsessive-compulsive, eating disorders, and depression—to which this book is devoted.

ACKNOWLEDGMENTS

Ideas grow from encounters. And the ideas of a psychotherapist first arise through interaction with patients. I thank them before all others for the extraordinary professional and human experience I have had with them and for the trust they have put in me. I am also grateful to them because almost all have allowed me to record the whole therapy and have taken part in the follow-up, sometimes even several years after the end of their therapy experience. Thanks to their generosity, the European Institute of Family Therapy in Milan, where I carry out my clinical activity, now has an archive of more than 10,000 video-recorded psychotherapy sessions of mine from which I have taken the 220 psychotherapies on which I have based my model. They are family, couple and individual psychotherapies, chosen due to the presence of phobic, obsessive, eating or severe mood disorders in the family. At the moment when the therapy began, these 220 patients showed prototypical patterns of one of the four psychopathologies mentioned and there were no diagnostic doubts nor could additional diagnoses of other psychopathological disorders be formulated. They have been chosen for this, and this alone.

Three people with whom I have had direct contact have been of crucial influence in my intellectual development and in the elaboration of the psychopathological model which I present in this book. First of all, Mara Selvini Palazzoli. I was barely twenty when I first met her, and I wasn't at all sure that psychotherapy was the right thing for me. Listening to her lectures in Milan I felt the joy I feel when I finally discover something that engages me unreservedly. Many years have passed since then but my therapeutic and scientific interests remain substantially in keeping with the horizon that Mara Selvini Palazzoli initially opened up for me, even though I was very soon to find my own directions (in keeping with my character). I am grateful to Mara Selvini Palazzoli, for it is also through her teaching that I have continued to work with undiminished passion.

When I met Vittorio Guidano, I had already developed an interest in the semantic aspects of communication, and in the conversational processes through which family members build up their own subjectivity. At the end of

1986 a mutual friend organized a meeting between the two of us at the Consiglio Nazionale delle Ricerche (National Research Council) in Rome. The meeting was to prove very important: From that time on, the psychopathological model elaborated by Guidano was to become a fundamental point of reference for me. Moving beyond the "black box" model, which was then characteristic of the Milan Approach, had opened up for me the problem of subjectivity, but I lacked the instruments and concepts that would enable me to analyze the subjective experience. Psychoanalysis, which was custodian of the inner world, could not be the point of comparison, especially at that time. For those like me who were looking at it from the outside, it still seemed to be based firmly on assumptions that I could not share. Guidano's model, which I still regard as one of the most interesting proposals for interpretation developed outside psychoanalysis, fitted much better with my own point of view.

When I met Alessandro Biral in 1991 I had lost interest in the philosophical and political debate for some time. I couldn't seem to find any handles in that debate that would help me to understand the changes that I felt both within and around me. His courageous and striking article, *Per una storia della sovranità*, left a profound impression on me. It made me consider new and disquieting hypotheses, pose questions about points of view that I hadn't thought I needed to be concerned about, and pushed my research in unexpected directions. A result of these explorations was also the discovery of Louis Dumont; I did not have the chance to know him personally but he had a great influence on me. When I discuss the cultural premises underlying the psychopathologies examined, one can hear the echo of this influence.

The psychopathological model discussed here is also the result of long discussions with colleagues at the Family Therapy Centre in Milan. I have discussed many aspects with Luigi Boscolo and with Gianfranco Cecchin, Maurizio Viaro, Laura Fruggeri, Peter Lang, Martin Little, Umberta Telfener and Mario Garbellini, and received most valuable stimulus from them. To Luigi Boscolo and Gianfranco Cecchin I feel a particular gratitude. I have learned a great deal from them and, over the years, thanks to them, I have been able to enjoy a relational context—created around the Milan centre—that has been intellectually lively, stimulating and above all open. It was this fruitful context that led to the creation of the family semantic polarities model, especially in its first version produced in 1998.

From the first publication of the model up to the present day, there has been a particularly intense exchange with Harry Procter. The reason is simple: our theories converge on many points, even though they were created entirely independently and from different traditions—Kellian constructivism in his case and systemic psychotherapies in mine. His encouragement, as well as that of Tim Parks, was a crucial stimulus for the translation of the book into English. My discussions with Tim Parks have also been extraordinarily enriching. His application of the semantic polarity model to the works of D. H. Lawrence and

Thomas Hardy prompted conversations that have given me important ideas for the activities of the clinic itself. I have always thought that literature and psychotherapy are two worlds that have much to offer each other, but thanks to Parks I have been able to put this into practice.

I must give particular thanks to my university students and above all to a small group of my doctorate students, now colleagues who immediately after the first publication of the model suggested testing out one of its central ideas. This led to research that is still continuing—a long and complex task due to the difficulty in empirically validating clinical concepts. In order to test the hypothesis that the semantics of freedom, of power, of goodness and of belonging characterize the conversations, respectively, of patients with phobic, eating, obsessive and mood disorders, we have constructed an ad hoc instrument—the "Family Semantic Grid", which we have applied to the transcripts of 120 sessions. The reader will find some of these studies referred to in this book, while others are yet to be published or still running. Lisa Fellin, Attà Negri, Daniele Castelli, Roberta Di Pasquale, Roberto Pennacchio and Emanuele Zanaboni have worked with me as key figures in the research program and in the necessary task of clarifying concepts. Ferdinando Salamino, Stella Chiara Guarnieri, Gabriella Gandino, Marta Sconci, Michela Scramuzza and Guido Veronese have also taken part in this program in various ways; every aspect of the model has been examined and discussed with them. I also wish to record my gratitude to David Campbell whose death, in 2009, was particularly sad for me. While he helped us to construct the Family Semantic Grid, he was so enthusiastic about the model that, together with a Groenbaeck, he made an interesting application of the model to organizations.

A fundamental contribution to *Semantic Polarities and Psychopathologies in the Family. Permitted and Forbidden Stories* has been made by the students and lecturers of the European Institute of Systemic-relational Therapies (EIST) in Milan, which I founded in 1999, and which provides a four-year training course in individual, family and couple therapy. I have discussed with them every aspect of the model I have developed. I have found their ideas, appreciation and encouragement, as well as their critical observations, extremely useful. My gratitude goes to them. I cannot name the students and former students who have made a contribution as there are so many of them, but I would like to mention the lecturers with whom my discussions have been so intense, including Laura Colangelo who extended the model to the borderline personality disorders, Carmen Dell'Aversano whose critical analysis of Margaret Edson's play "W;t" was inspired by this model, Roberta Di Pasquale, Miriam Gandolfi, Manuela Genchi, Elisa Gusmini, Enrico Molinari, Ferdinando Salamino and in particular Maurizio Viaro, whose critical observations and suggestions have been of great assistance.

I have received valuable advice, especially with regard to our attempts at empirical verification of the model, from Robert A. Neimeyer and Guillem

Feixas, Carlos Sluzki and Manuel Villegas. I am particularly grateful to Robert Neimeyer and to Tim Parks, and also to Harry Procter, Arlene Vetere, Peter Stratton and Nick Wood for having encouraged me to translate this book into English and for having supported its publication.

My gratitude to Stefania Baccanelli, Roberto Pennacchio, Daniele Castelli, Lisa Fellin and Gabriele Melli for their help in putting together the bibliography.

I would like to thank Richard Dixon who has translated this book with his usual remarkable competence and to Peter Greene for reading and commenting on the final translation. I am also very grateful to David Noonan for his help in finding translations for certain technical terms for which there were no previous codified expressions in this area.

Heartfelt thanks to all the staff of Routledge Mental Health, and especially to Marta Moldvai for having believed in this book and for the enthusiasm and extraordinary dedication with which she has pursued its publication.

I am grateful to my husband, Carlo Erminero, for having shared this experience with me, for reading the text and encouraging me to improve its form and to clarify its ideas, and above all making it a subject for conversation, at times serious, between us.

INTRODUCTION

1

THE CONSTRUCTION OF PSYCHOPATHOLOGICAL DISORDERS IN INTERSUBJECTIVE CONTEXTS

1.1 Four Stories and Several Questions

Her parents and sister watched in amazement: Natascia was crying, she was tense, her face was grim, her hands clenched, her arms rigid inside a dark sweater on a hot summer's day. Natascia was wracked by many disturbing emotions. She asked the therapist to help her overcome her bad thoughts; she feared they had gotten the better of her. Summer frightened her; she couldn't spend it at the seaside as her family would have liked. She had to go "somewhere cold where I can stay covered and closed up, talking to no one, studying and nothing else." We were dealing with the onset of an obsessive compulsive-disorder in an 11-year-old girl. Natascia, a model child until three months earlier, was now devastated by the eruption of emotions she couldn't cope with: she called them "temptations." She wanted to look pretty and she thought about using make up. She had thoughts about kissing boys; she felt an urge to get on to tables and dance; she had even complained that her parents didn't argue like they used to. She no longer cared about anyone else and wanted to do as she pleased. There was a "bad" part in her that she couldn't control, not even with the "superstitions" to which she devoted herself for hours. Her parents were astonished: Natascia was changing before their eyes. Even her voice had changed. No one, they emphasized, had ever pushed her to work particularly hard at her studies. She had always been more conscientious than she needed to be. No one had ever stopped her going out with her friends. On the contrary, Natascia had always enjoyed more freedom than other girls, such as her younger sister who, unlike her, was lively and gregarious.

What should have been a trip with friends to Amsterdam—and a fairly wild one, as they had already planned to smoke hashish—turned into a nightmare for Alessandro:

> I felt separated from my body ... A terrible scare! I said to my friends: "hold on to my body because I'm leaving, I'm going off." I thought I was dying. As soon as I began smoking it was like a flash: a load

3

of pictures appeared before me, the strangest sensations. I felt really frightened. I was terrified, my heart was beating like mad. I thought I was having a heart attack or worse—I'd smoked before but nothing like this had happened.

Alessandro ended up in hospital. Two years had passed since then, but the fear had never disappeared. Once discharged from hospital he returned to London where, a few months later, with the help of a grant, he had begun university. He did all he could to stay there. It had been his dream to live abroad ever since he was a child, when he used to listen to his parents' tales of wonderful weekends spent on their scooter in Brittany, where they had moved just after they got married. From this experience in London he had hoped to start off his career in an international aid organization. He also had a relationship in London that was important to him: This time he was in love. So he tried to carry on. When panic prevented him from going out of the house, he had to give in. Alessandro returned to his parents' home in Italy. He felt better at first, but when he tried to leave home, travelling just a few kilometers, the panic attacks and feelings of depersonalization returned. As his stay with his family dragged on, he became depressed and suicidal. He ended up in hospital several times. "What sort of illness have I really got?" he asked. It was a phobic disorder, but Alessandro was convinced he had something much more serious. His feelings of depersonalization experienced during the onset of symptoms, and later when trying to leave his parents home, had convinced him that he was suffering from a psychosis. And this idea had naturally frightened him more.

She didn't want to start therapy. Her parents and sisters had practically forced her. And it showed: Sabina had her arms crossed, her head bowed. When she looked up, her gaze was imperious and hostile. There was no doubt about it: she didn't wish to cooperate. There was no point asking questions: she wouldn't answer. Over the previous two months this 15-year-old girl had lost 12 kilos and had no intention, it seemed, of stopping there. She had also gradually withdrawn from her family with the same obstinate silence with which she was resisting therapy. No one could communicate with her any longer, not even her mother or her older sisters with whom Sabina had been very close. She had stopped talking to her whole family, including her grandparents. And everyone was worried about what they saw as this girl's relapse into anorexia. Two and a half years earlier, Sabina had dropped to an alarming weight just as quickly but had recovered in less than a year. When she and her family returned to Milan, she had literally re-blossomed and was once again cheerful and lively. On their departure from the Persian Gulf area, where her father's work had taken them, all the family thought Sabina's problems were finally over. So no one had worried about her any more. Her mother had noticed she had recently become introverted and sometimes sad, but had attributed the change of mood to her first periods, which had begun late: her sisters had matured earlier. Everyone, except Sabina, was alarmed and confused. Why, for example, her father asked me, did Sabina now refuse all outside help, contrary to what had happened during the first anorexia? But was she really suffering from anorexia? her mother asked. Sabine was less mature than other girls her age. Unlike many of her friends and her younger sister—who had had a string of boyfriends since primary school—she had never taken any care over her appearance or been bothered about enjoying herself. She still hadn't shown any interest in boys. This relapse, unlike the first anorexia, hadn't begun with a diet.

After being left by her partner, with whom she had begun to re-plan her life after the breakdown of her marriage, Giulia's mental balance, which had already been unstable for some time, had deteriorated. She felt she couldn't carry on; she was wracked with insomnia; she was extremely anxious and agitated. Her life: a mass of mistakes! And she was seething with pain and anger. Giulia felt lost: she couldn't live alone; she could no longer look after her child. She was well aware of it:

> I felt a howl which rose from my toenails up to the ends of my hair. I wanted to go up a mountain, on top of the world and cry out. Let me cry out like a child, I need to cry out! My body needs to howl, physically. I want to howl myself away. But I can't. What would my four-year-old son see? No, no, I can't … But who will look after me and my child?

In the presence of the psychotherapist, Giulia phoned her parents, who have been separated for many years. Her father came into her life for the first time and took care of the child, whom he had seen only three times until then. "My mother won't take even me in. 'My girl,' she says, 'I'm worse off than you, I can't help you.' I realize then there's no way out, I have to get treatment. I'm the one who decides." Giulia was in the clinic for only a short time, eight days, just enough to regain a little control over her emotions. Then she went into a community: she left it after a while, stopped taking the medication and went off to India. These were the most dramatic months of her life. She risked ending up badly. But in the end, her will to live prevailed. She returned and gradually tried to re-establish some emotional stability as well as rebuilding her relationship with her son, who had been left for almost a year with her father and his partner. When I met Giulia, a little over two years had passed since her return from India. She had started several psychotherapeutic treatments and had broken them off immediately. But it was now essential for this 30-year-old woman, who had a lively intelligence and was emotionally wild and seductive, to regain her mental stability, or risk losing custody of her son, now seven. Giulia loved him and didn't want to lose him. Her ex-husband had begun proceedings to take the child: he had serious and well-justified reasons. There was a diagnosis of bipolar disorder, made during her medical treatment, and there was her abandonment of her child during her time in India. And Giulia was also alone in therapy. No one in the family had been prepared to take part in the therapy with her. Perhaps it was for this reason that just before the end of the initial consultation session she stopped, looked at me in surprise, and said: "Would you believe it! I'm telling you things I've never told anyone: you're already my therapist!"

Natascia, Alessandro, Sabina, and Giulia suffered respectively from obsessive, phobic, eating and depressive disorders, the four psychopathologies examined in this book. What had triggered off the first appearance of symptoms? In Giulia's case the inciting event seemed to have been an abandonment. But what happened in the intersubjective context of Natascia, Alessandro and Sabina? Natascia's parents were stunned: family life during the six months up to the onset of Natascia's symptoms had been happier than ever before. After years of difficulty, in which the family had risked splitting up (the reader will have the full story later), the atmosphere had changed: everyone was calm and positive. Having won a grant to study in London, Alessandro had achieved his dream and had also fallen in love. Sabina's relapse was equally puzzling. Her parents, mindful of the anorexia from which she had just recovered, had consulted Sabina over all important decisions. They had also complied with her wishes, including her going to Art College, which had involved the family in complicated arrangements.

Giulia's abandonment itself did not resolve the question of why her symptoms first appeared: if anything, it raised others. Giulia had already had to face other abandonments. Why did the ending of a relationship which, all in all, was less significant than others, lead her into depression? And why should a normal experience like abandonment, however painful, cause such a serious depression in a young woman who, until a few years before, had always been the first to be invited to parties and social events?

Why did Natascia develop an obsessive disorder while her younger sister seemed free from psychological problems? Both Alessandro and Giulia had brothers who were happily married, with good jobs and full social lives. And why did two parents, like Sabina's, of normal weight who had never ever thought of dieting, have two out of four children with eating disorders? In addition to the anorexia, for which they sought therapy, there was the obesity of their second daughter, which began shortly before the emergence of Sabina's symptoms and remained unchanged. Was there something in this family's conversation that had favored the development of an eating disorder as opposed to some other psychopathology? Can we identify relational events in the history of these patients and their families, or ways of "co-positioning" each other?[1]

Neither biochemistry, nor genetics, nor psychopharmacology have provided answers that render these questions obsolete. At least for obsessive, phobic and eating disorders and for depression, the biochemical and genetic hypotheses advanced in biological psychiatry have received no definite confirmation. Even for depression, on which biological psychiatry and psychopharmacology have focused particular attention over the past twenty years, no result has emerged that cancels out the relevance of the role of emotions and interactive experiences in the origin and persistence of this most widespread mood disorder. The model that sought to equate depression with an organic illness, similar to diabetes, has been brought into question, especially in the last ten years (Greenberg, 2010; Healy, 2004; Horwitz & Wakefield, 2007; Kirsch, 2010; Moncrieff, 2008; Shorter, 2009) shown to be a marketing operation (Lane, 2007; Whitaker, 2010). In particular, the idea that depression is caused by a shortage of serotonin that can be corrected through ad hoc drugs, the Selective Serotonin Reuptake Inhibitors (SSRIs), has been challenged. As we shall see in Chapter 6, only a quarter of depressed patients seem to present low levels of serotonin (Horwitz & Wakefield, 2007). And no empirical evidence has demonstrated what Kirsch (2010) calls "the myth of the chemical imbalance." Up to today, no study has established that serotonin is the one-directional cause of downward mood swings. On the contrary, the research carried out by ethologists since the 1980s on our closest relatives—the non-human primates—demonstrates exactly the opposite: Monkeys increase their levels of serotonin and other neuro-chemicals connected with depression when they become dominant in the group and lose them when they suffer a loss of status.[2] The data causing the greatest outcry relates to Prozac and other SSRIs. Meta-analyses—including those carried out on the research results provided by the pharmaceutical companies themselves to the U.S. Food and Drug Administration to obtain approval for these drugs—have demonstrated that SSRIs certainly produce effects, but more or less the same as those of the placebo (Kirsch, 2010). But, unlike the placebo, they are accompanied by disturbing side effects, which include sexual dysfunction, headaches, insomnia, nausea and vomiting, to cite the most common of them. Paradoxically, these very drugs, advertised as the solution to depression, have been found to cause an increased risk of suicide at least in children, adolescents and young people up to the age of 24 (Hammad, Laughren, & Racoosin, 2006).[3] And the genetic component certainly doesn't seem to play such a role in depression as to marginalize the influence of interaction with the environment. The percentage effect of the genetic factor, studied with longitudinal research on identical twins and on adoption is estimated to be around 30–40 percent (Sullivan, Neale, & Kendler, 2000). The most recent research using more accurate measures, thanks to the remarkable developments in genetics, tends to reduce this estimate, as we shall see.[4]

I have mentioned depression because it is still the favorite pathology of biological psychiatry and pharmacology. For serious anxiety disorders (including those in the phobic spectrum), what happened in Freud's time is valid today:

Drugs alleviate the symptoms but do not eliminate the "illness." This is also the case with eating disorders, where drugs generally do not alleviate even the symptomatology.

It is therefore surprising that over the last twenty years scarce attention has been paid by family therapists and other relational therapists to the role played by interpersonal relations in the development of some of the most common psychopathologies, including those which I will be considering here. On this question the scientific literature, from the 1990s onwards, is indeed limited. The recognition of the oft-repeated truism that understanding (not necessarily treating) the majority of psychopathologies requires "a bio-psycho-social approach" seems to have inhibited therapists in making their contribution to this joint task, as happens in many group phenomena where collective responsibility develops into lack of commitment.

This book breaks the silence and seeks to fill a hiatus created over the last twenty years between psychotherapeutic practice and clinical theory. Many of the questions I have raised still guide the practice of relational psychotherapists, whether cognitivists, systemic therapists or psychoanalysts. They are difficult to avoid since they are questions that the patients and their families themselves raise and direct towards their therapists.

1.2 An Intersubjective Perspective to Psychopathology

The intersubjective perspective on the phobic, obsessive, eating disorders, and depression developed here is in tune with the extraordinary developments in neuropsychology. These have demonstrated the importance of social interaction in the development of the very structure and functions of the brain, not just in childhood but throughout our whole lives (Cozolino, 2006; Siegel, 2012). This perspective also offers a way out of radical subjectivism and relativism which, in the name of two truths—the individuality and uniqueness of every person and the self-referential nature of all knowledge—has imprisoned a large proportion of relational therapists inside the individual case, precluding them from all possibility of making vital, albeit provisional, generalizations. Moreover, it helps in avoiding the fragmentation of psychopathologies in the *DSM*, which is the subject of much criticism especially among psychotherapists (Bentall, 2009). It is, in fact, evident that a classification system, limited to single symptomatic behaviors taken out of context, inhibits the understanding of the psychopathology itself and is of use solely for the administration of medication (indeed it is not even useful for the prudent administration of medication).

The central thesis of the book is that people with phobic, obsessive and depressive organizations and eating disorders have grown up and are still part of conversational (usually family) contexts where specific meanings predominate. The identity of those who participate in the conversation ("identity" meaning the repertoire of self and life narratives available to each subject), and the ways in which the people in these families build and preserve the relationships and values, are marked by characteristic meanings. For example, in contexts where we find people with phobic disorders, there prevails what I have called the "semantics of freedom" which, as we shall see, is fuelled by the emotional polarity of fear-courage. In contexts where there are people with obsessive or eating disorders or depression, other semantics predominate—respectively, the semantics of "goodness," "power," and "belonging"—each marked by other emotions and other ways of feeling.

The semantics I have mentioned can be seen as a necessary condition, but are certainly not sufficient for establishing what I suggest to be the corresponding psychopathologies. There are many families, for example, where the semantics of "freedom" predominates but no one has any kind of phobic psychopathology, even though various members of the family develop narratives about self, ways of relating and values similar to those who develop agoraphobia. *A crucial role in the transition from "normality" to psychopathology is played by the particular positions mutually assumed within the critical semantics by the subject and by those family members who are significant to him or her.* These positions, which will be described in detail, *may* induce one of the subjects involved to experience a situation of conflict in relation to the critical meanings. The conflict is similar to the "strange loop" described by Cronen, Johnson, and Lannamann (1982) and shares many characteristics of Feixas's "implicative dilemmas" (Feixas & Saúl, 2004; Feixas, Saúl, & Àvila-Espada, 2009) if attention is limited to the subject who experiences it. When this happens, the subject *may* no longer be able to maintain a stable positioning within the predominant semantics, and may waver between mutually exclusive positionings. Those who find themselves in this position develop complex ways of feeling and relating, marked by conflicts and tensions in relation to the dominant meanings in their relevant contexts, but not necessarily a psychopathology. The writer Tim Parks (2009) in applying this model in a literary analysis, has pointed out how the semantics of "freedom" is central in Thomas Hardy and D.H. Lawrence. The characters in their novels, as well as their own personal lives, are dominated by freedom/dependence and by the corresponding polarities of security/vulnerability/weakness, as well as by fear and courage, the emotions at the care of these meanings. The stories told by these writers seem to describe a conflict they were experiencing in their own lives, especially when it is sex that triggers off fear and calls for courage. But however conflictual their positionings might have been in the semantics of freedom, neither of them—so far as we know from their biographies—ever developed a full-blown phobic disorder. The conflict seems instead to have stimulated their creativity.

Generally it is only when conflict in the predominant semantics is so intense that subjects are no longer able to find any "co-position" for themselves that the first symptoms appear. One pragmatic effect not to be ignored in the symptomatology is to allow the person, who is now a patient, to find a "co-position" with conversational partners, however precarious and awkward.

The thesis I have outlined here is based on certain hypotheses about the origin of meaning that can be summed up in the concept of "family semantic polarities," to which the first chapter is dedicated. This concept has important similarities with Procter's "family constructs" (Procter, 1981, 1985, 1996, 2007)[5] and it is consistent with the shift of attention from the family as a whole to the "co-positioning" of the individuals in the family. It takes account, in fact, of the specific nature of subjects as well as their interconnection with the other members of their relational system. The constructionist viewpoint, which underlies the concept and, through it, the psychological model presented, goes beyond the individual/family dualism that has been a characteristic of family therapy literature for many years. Individual and family are empty abstractions outside the pattern that connects them: individuals, when separated from the communicative relationships of which they are a part, break away and the family no longer exists, except as a "co-positioning" of individuals.

The proposed model is also based on the Positioning Theory (Bamberg, 1997; Harré et al., 2009; Harré & Van Langenhove, 1999). The assumption is that every member of the family, within a shared semantics, has ways of participating in the conversation, relating with others and constructing the reality that are often quite different and incompatible with those of the others. These, however, are consistent with the particular position that the subject occupies in the family's semantics and are interdependent with those of the other members of the group. Emotions, aims, basic ideas, and belief systems are, in this respect, some aspects of how each person "co-positions" him or herself with other members of the group.

By embracing, in accordance with the Positioning Theory, a conception of self as a position in the conversation, I certainly do not intend to associate myself with those who equate the self as no more than a "peg," to quote a metaphor used by Goffman (1959), on which are hung the clothes of the infinite positions that it can assume.[6] An assumption of this type clashes with the clinical experience one comes across every day with the difficulty, experienced especially by patients with chronic psychopathologies and their families, in modifying positions that are by now crystallized, and the source of great suffering. Generally speaking, the self cannot assume an endless number of positions. Being born into a particular family and into a particular culture, as well as the history of previous relational experiences limits the possible positions through which individuals can "co-position" themselves with others. And it is this very limitation that confers reality on the self. The same feeling of instability and fragility of the self, a modern-day characteristic, is a result of relationships having become less stable than in the past and certainly does not mean that the self is a "nothing" which can easily pass from one position to the other. The concept of family semantic polarities anchors individuals to their history, as we shall see. New semantics can be learned by subjects over the years; others may dominate the conversation in which they are involved: but, at least initially, certain meanings, those dominant in their own family at the time they are born—and not others—will guide the construction of their world.

Some of the hypotheses put forward in this book have been empirically verified over recent years. The idea that the four psychopathologies mentioned here are connected to the four semantics I will be illustrating has been confirmed by various studies carried out by myself along with several colleagues (Ugazio, Negri, & Fellin, 2011, 2012; Ugazio et al., 2007). During these studies we used the Family Semantics Grid that we have specially devised for this purpose (Ugazio et al., 2009). Other researchers, using different instruments, have provided significant confirmation of this hypothesis.[7] It provides partial confirmation of the overall proposition that will be put forward here, based on my own therapy practice for families, couples, and individuals.

Before reaching the heart of the argument I will deal with a preliminary matter: the links between psychopathology and meaning. The model I will be presenting implies a conception of psychopathology closely connected to meaning, which I have borrowed from certain cognitivist psychotherapists. The implications and limits of this borrowing need to be clarified.

1.3 Psychopathology and Meaning

A very important contribution to understanding human personality and psychopathology in terms of meaning comes from cognitivist therapy. Kelly's psychology of personal constructs (1955), with his attention on meaning, anticipates the reasons that brought about the birth of the cognitivism revolution a few years later. As Bruner states (1990, pp. 1–2),

> That revolution was intended to bring "mind" back into the human sciences after a long cold winter of objectivism. [...] It was, we thought, an all-out effort to establish meaning as the central concept of psychology—not stimuli and responses, not overtly observable behavior, not biological drivers and their transformation, but meaning.

This same intent is at the base of the psychology of personal constructs. For Kelly, individuals actively construct the world in which they live through bipolar semantic patterns: personal constructs. Without these patterns people would be incapable of giving sense to their experience, and the world would appear as a series of undifferentiated stimuli. Ordinary people, no less than scientists, need to give meaning to events, to construct their own points of view, to elaborate constructs that resemble theories, so that they can control and predict the course of events. All the constructive activity is based on bipolar semantic contents and has characteristics peculiar to each subject. There is no single way of constructing events: there are as many different ways as there are people. Kelly, by adopting the metaphor of the "person as scientist," as well as giving priority to the need to give sense to the events, suggests there is a natural tendency for all of us to put the truthfulness of our constructs to the test. In accordance with his "constructivism in solitude," Kelly (1955) gives a restrictive meaning to the concept of falsification. According to his theory, invalidation is "the incompatibility (subjectively construed) between a personal prediction and the observed evidence."

The concept of falsification plays an important role in the explanation given by the psychology of personal constructs for the origin of psychopathology. Psychological disorder is identified by Kelly with "any personal construction which is used repeatedly in spite of consistent invalidation" (Kelly, 1955, p. 831). It is therefore a sort of "repetition compulsion." Nevertheless, in Kelly's work as a whole his interest in the psychopathology, and above all in the psychopathological organizations, is marginal. The object of the theory of personal constructs is to outline the fundamental processes underlying the ways in which people construct experience and to set out a new method of clinical analysis and psychotherapy.

Psychopathology and its relation with meaning are, however, central to the psychopathological models elaborated many years later by Guidano and Liotti (Guidano, 1987, 1991; Guidano & Liotti, 1983) and by other cognitivist psychotherapists (Arciero & Bondolfi, 2009; Bara, 1996, 2005; Neimeyer & Raskin, 2000; Villegas, 1995, 1997, 2000, 2004). Guidano (1991) in particular equates psychopathology with a "science of meaning." This comparison enables him to overturn a central concept of clinical psychology, derived from psychoanalysis, namely the idea that there is a single path from which both "normal" as well as psychopathological courses of development (identifiable with the various syndromes) take form.[8] For Guidano there is no single path. On the contrary, from the very beginning, there are parallel courses of development—personal cognitive organizations—consisting of quite different personal meanings that can evolve towards psychopathology or towards normality.

By personal cognitive organization, Guidano means the combination of cognitive processes, whether tacit or explicit, which "gradually emerges in the course of individual development. Each individual, though living in an 'objectively' shareable social reality, actively constructs at a higher level of perceptual experience his/her own and uniquely private view from within" (Guidano, 1987, p. 91). What gives unity to cognitive organizations is *personal meaning*, shaped by emotional patterns ordered according to personal semantic contents. As well as making every aspect of the subject's mental activity idiosyncratic, Guidano regards personal meaning as organizationally closed, a sort of "epistemological constraint."

It is through these two notions that Guidano (1991, p. 59) considers psychopathology to be a "science of meaning." The main psychopathological disorders, according to him, are derived from as many cognitive meaning organizations, structured on the basis of different development paths and attachment patterns. He describes four of these, whose pathological developments give rise to the four psychopathological disorders examined in this book (phobic, depressive, obsessive-compulsive, and eating disorders). Guidano's attention is directed towards the psychopathological disorders, but nevertheless each organization is assimilable into a personality structure that can evolve in a normal, neurotic or psychotic manner. Let us examine, by way of example, a depressive personal meaning organization. This, according to Guidano, is characterized by a personal meaning that oscillates between "anger/ aggressive and provocative behaviors" and "helplessness/sadness" and by themes of loss and loneliness. Subjects with this organization oscillate between a sense of loneliness felt passively—(despair)—and a condition in which separation from others is experienced actively (anger and aggression). This emotional circularity is present in the normal condition, in the neurotic state and also in the psychotic state (manic-depressive psychosis). In the normal condition—unlike what happens in the psychopathology—the recursiveness between anger and aggression on the one hand, which produce conduct aimed towards establishing interpersonal contact, and despair on the other, which brings a return to separation and personal withdrawal, generally does not go beyond the critical limits. The experience of loneliness is therefore elaborated positively or even creatively.

Even though Guidano considers that the four personal cognitive organizations identified by him do not extend to cover all possible dimensions of meaning, he is nevertheless convinced that the organizations must be finite in number. He states (1991, p. 34):

> The number of possible basic *personal meaning organizations* should be relatively small, probably between four and six, at most nine or ten. Indeed, if we assume that personal meaning reflects the pattern of emotional and psychophysiological organization, and we bear in mind the relatively small number of fundamental emotions that human beings can experience, we can see how the possibilities for combination and recombination which can produce reliable self-perception matched by an acceptable level of self-esteem must be rather small.

I have briefly described the principal assumptions in this model because, in my view, it constitutes one of the most interesting attempts so far to explain psychopathology in terms of meaning. And it is from Guidano that I have drawn the hypothesis that each of the four psychopathologies examined here constitutes a way of organizing meaning characterized by specific emotions.

Apart from this loan (which is considerable), the distance between us is great, and relates above all to his genetic and evolutionary hypotheses.

Guidano and the other cognitivist therapists I have mentioned follow Bowlby's theory (1969, 1973, 1980). The various psychopathological diseases are traced back to dysfunctional attachment patterns. This dyadic explanation, as I will argue later, is unable to account for certain crucial characteristics (pointed out by these therapists themselves) in the way that subjects order and construct reality. Furthermore, as is now well documented, the attachment patterns envisaged by Bowlby, insofar as they are described in his theory, are not specifically connected to any psychopathology—on the contrary, they are to be found in more than one disease.[9] The reconstruction that I propose here of actual and original intersubjective contexts for phobic, obsessive, depressive organizations and typical of eating disorders, is therefore put forward as an alternative.

The other areas that separate us are the consequences of a different point of view: My work is guided by a constructionist approach whereas the cognitivist therapists I have quoted follow a constructivist approach. Our differences are also the result of varying clinical practices, which in my case includes family therapy, whereas my cognitive colleagues have generally concentrated on individual treatment. These differences relate above all to the way in which meaning is conceived. For these authors, meaning is something that relates essentially to the individual. The concept of family semantic polarities, on the other hand, regards it as a shared enterprise in which at least three interacting subjects cooperate.

What is more, these psychotherapists postulate a closure of personal meaning organizations after adolescence, which risks leading them into the shallow waters of a determinism which psychoanalysis itself now rejects. According to Guidano (1988, p. 20)[10]:

> A complex knowing system is therefore *organizationally closed*, as it will not admit alternatives to the "experiential order" (personal meaning) on which are based the continuity and coherence of its sense of self, and it is *autonomous*, since in order to maintain and renew that order, it needs nothing else but to constantly refer to itself.

The environment, from this point of view, is just a source of unsettlement and the individual adapts "by preserving its own inner coherence at the expense of the environment, even if it means producing irreversible changes in the latter" (Guidano, 1998, p. 21).[11] In Guidano's view, the process of differentiating new emotional schemas, when it occurs after adolescence, does not lead to any change in the personal meaning of a cognitive organization. On the contrary, it further stabilizes the inner coherence of the subject (the personal meaning) because it becomes possible to explain an ever more complex and changing reality with the use of few unchanging principles. For example, the construction of meaning for a person who has developed a depressive cognitive organization will always be dominated by "helplessness-sadness"/"anger-outbursts of aggression." This emotional circularity which, as we saw just now, constitutes the personal meaning of a depressive organization is, for Guidano, an "epistemological constraint" from which the subject will no longer be able to escape. Subjects can better articulate this recursiveness and thus avoid oscillations that are too rapid and intense. At best they will be able to perceive the underlying theme of loss as a category of human experience, rather than as a personal destiny marked indelibly by rejection and loneliness. The model not only excludes the possibility of subjects abandoning this dimension of meaning—it would be the same as losing personal identity—but also of their being able to organize their own experience within other meanings reducing the importance of re-dimensioning the critical dimensions. On the contrary, according to Guidano the orthogenetic progression during the life span makes the dimension of meaning resulting from the process of growing up increasingly consistent and monothematic.

I also differ from these psychotherapists in respect of the transition of a personality organization from the condition of normality to that of neurosis and/or psychosis. According to the cognitivist psychotherapists I have referred to, a decisive role in this transition is played by syntactic aspects. For Guidano, the semantic dimension of each personal organization of meaning is the unchanging aspect, whereas the syntactic rules of flexibility, concreteness/abstraction and integration are what determine the normal or pathological way in which meaning is expressed. The pathology therefore seems to be defined by formal components, whereas the position of the patient in the semantics (which for me is of great importance) is ignored.

One last aspect of difference that I would like to emphasize is less central for practical therapeutic purposes. These therapists, though recognizing the historicity of meaning, are interested more in the evolutionistic bases of human beings, in their being part of a natural evolutionary story that links them to the higher primates, than in the cultural dimension of meaning. They consider cognitive organizations as eternal conditions of "human consciousness," connected to certain basic emotions, seen as unchanging aspects of human existence.

Instead, in the model I present here, the emphasis is on the cultural definition of meaning and psychopathology. Indeed, I put forward the hypothesis that each of the psychopathological organizations examined in this book is an expression of one specific family conversational context and of one equally particular position that the patient and the other members of the family assume in relation to the critical semantics, but at the same time it expresses certain implicit assumptions of a wider cultural context. At the center of phobic, obsessive-compulsive, anorexic-bulimic and depressive organizations it is possible to identify (as I will try to show in the chapters dedicated to each of these organizations) respectively, *the ideas of freedom as independence from relationships, of "abstinent" goodness, of equality as removal of differences, and of belonging irrevocably to a group of relationships.* These "ideas" have a precise history in the wider cultural context and play a fundamental role. The families within which these psychopathological organizations are developed, make such ideas particularly relevant.

From this point of view I am following the path indicated by Bateson (1971) in *The Cybernetics of Self: A Theory of Alcoholism.* In this essay, Bateson overturns the way in which alcoholism is commonly conceived, and at the same time reconnects this pathology to specific premises of Western culture. The alcoholic's problem, according to Bateson, is not intoxication but soberness. The "error" or pathology is to be found in the conditions that guide his state of sobriety. Intoxication, on closer examination, is a correction of the meaningless premises that guide the alcoholic's conduct when he is sober and which are reinforced by society.

The alcoholic fully expresses the epistemology of self-control, but, precisely because his symmetrical pride leads him to the extreme consequences, a *reductio ad absurdum* comes into play. He shows, entirely unwittingly, through his vain struggle against the bottle, that self-control is absurd and furthermore doesn't work.

However ineffective it might be, the epistemology that supports the alcoholic is conventional in the West. The Westerner believes there exists a specific agent, the "self," which carries out "finalistic" actions on objects. Western culture tends in fact to confirm the idea that one part of a system can operate a one-way control on the system as a whole; and it is this idea that guides the conduct of the alcoholic. For this reason, according to Bateson, alcoholism expresses the difficulty of a particular way in which an individual "co-positions" himself within a specific micro-social context and at the same time highlights a series of assumptions that are problematic for a culture as a whole. Something similar also happens for the psychopathologies examined in this book. They express the meanings and the culture of the family in which subjects have grown up, but these meanings and this culture are infused with beliefs and theories that we find in a wider social context. These are, of course, implicit theories.

Part I

THE THEORETICAL MODEL

2

FAMILY SEMANTIC POLARITIES

Thus one portion of being is the Prolific, the other the Devouring. To the Devourer, it seems as if the producer was in his chains; but it is not so, he only takes portions of existence and fancies that the whole.

But the Prolific would cease to be Prolific unless the Devourer, as a sea, received the excess of his delights.

(...)

These two classes of men are always upon earth, and they should be enemies: who ever tries to reconcile them seeks to destroy existence.

William Blake,
The Marriage of Heaven and Hell

2.1 A Conversational Definition

The family is a "co-positioning" of differences. Within a single group there is a confrontation between individuals who are so diverse that it often seems, to use Blake's words, they should be enemies.

Dostoyevsky's *Brothers Karamazov* is a classic example. Mitya, like his father Fyodor Pavlovich, is sensual, full of a lust for life. Alesa is a saint. Ivan, the enigmatic protagonist of Dostoyevsky's masterpiece, is in the middle: his heart is noble, touched by the suffering of the world, but he is capable of wickedness. He needs to believe in something in order to live, but cannot do so. Pride and arrogance lead him to the abyss of nihilism until he becomes morally responsible for the murder of his father.

And what about the grim family business in Dickens' *Dombey and Son* (1848)? It is hard to imagine greater differences than those that set the main character against his two children. Dombey is arid, insensitive, fiercely strong-willed. Paul, the expected heir of Dombey and Son, has an autumnal temperament. Crushed and overwhelmed by a series of illnesses that afflict him one

19

after the other, Paul seems to have had no other wish than to rejoin his late mother. Long before depriving the family firm of its male heir through his early death, Paul is as much an alien to his strong-willed father as his sister Florence. The kindness, charity, and devotion that Florence continues to give her father, despite the abuse she receives, make her just as much of a stranger to Dombey.

Many married couples are polar opposites, but Christina Stead's couple, the Pollits (in her novel *The Man Who Loved Children* 1940/1979), are something else: their opposition goes to the very root of their relationship. Conversation after conversation, episode after episode, we watch impotently, amazed and open-mouthed, as do their many children, at the frightening abyss separating Sam and Henny. When we meet them, they have already spent years waging a civil war that has produced devastation. But Sam's blue eyes, along with his idealism, still brighten the family setting, just as Henny with her mass of raven black hair and powerful theatrical scenes infuses dramatic pathos into their home. As the family gradually slides into degradation and misery, Sam's idealism turns into a hypocritical denial of reality and the scenes where Henny spews out everything become grotesque. He takes refuge in the company of his brats, who he keeps madly begetting to avoid facing reality, while she pushes her nose ever deeper into the garbage of the world. When tragedy arrives it is a liberation for everyone, for over ten years we have seen their two worlds move not one single step closer to each other: they remain poles apart from beginning to end.

The actors placed on stage by these fictional families are profoundly different, as are the meanings interwoven into the narratives. Naked power, the will to dominate, episodes of submission, humiliation and class pride dominate the stage in *Dombey and Son*. For the Karamazovs, it is good and evil, guilt and innocence, that drive the central episodes of the novel until Ivan is led to accuse himself of a parricide he has not committed. Events in the Pollit family are no less dramatic than those affecting the Karamazovs. Louie, Sam's daughter by his first marriage, would have more reason than Ivan Karamazov to accuse herself of her stepmother's death. But the only time she does so, all she wants is to force Sam to face reality, just as Henny had done. In this novel there is no trace of guilt. The help that Louie gives her stepmother to get her out of her plight is a painful gesture, an act of compassion. Henny only wants to be free from herself. Her game is over and we have all had enough of her scenes, of watching her shame, her ravings and her threats. Commiseration and contempt, sadness and jollity, are the dominant emotions of Stead's novel.

The Karamazovs, the Pollits, and the Dombeys belong to different cultures and historical periods, so it comes as no surprise that they each have different significances and that even the same events should produce different emotions. The families I meet in clinical practice all live in the same period of time, they often come from the same background, and yet they are each different from the other. Those things that one whole family fights, rejoices or despairs over are entirely irrelevant for another. Meanings and feelings change from one family to the next. Equally frequent are the polar differences that place the various members of a family into conflict with one another. I have often come across a sensitive, cerebral child with athletic, down-to-earth parents, or an active, dynamic wife with a thoughtful, gloomy husband. I often meet siblings who are opposites: one with many intellectual pursuits, the other interested only in football and girls; a loyal sister who is so frank as to be tactless, with a brother who is diplomatic or even a skillful liar.

I have found myself reflecting on these differences within families and between families, particularly when practicing family therapy. Patients in individual therapy also talk about wives, siblings or parents who are sometimes profoundly different from themselves, but their stories are narrated accounts. It is quite a different matter to have parents and children, siblings, husbands and wives physically there in front of you. Their differences stand out and strike you. I am therefore surprised that the literature describing the practice of family therapy has so often focused, from the very beginning, on holistic concepts such as the family myth or paradigm (Anderson & Bagarozzi, 1989; Andolfi, Angelo, & De Nichilo, 1989; Ferreira, 1963, 1966; Reiss, 1981) that give us a monolithic vision of families. These concepts are capable of showing the similarities between the various members of each family—similarities which certainly exist—but they ignore the perhaps greater differences within families, as extensive studies on siblings has shown. "Children raised in the same family—researchers agree—are more often different from one another than they are similar" (Walsh, 2003, p. 618). And it is the very fact of living in the same family that makes siblings different rather than similar, a surprising discovery as it alters the perspective that has traditionally been applied to the family's influence on development.

The concept of semantic polarities to which this chapter is devoted offers an explanation of this unexpected finding. It provides a constructionist approach to meaning that captures the differences as well as the similarities inside the family as in any other group.

According to this concept, conversation within the family, as in every group with a history, is organized between opposing polarities of meaning such as just/unjust, good/bad, closed/open, attractive/repugnant. This follows the idea—an ancient one as we shall see—that meaning is constructed through opposing polarities, applying to it a constructionist approach, whose background is the Positioning Theory of Harré and colleagues (Harré & Moghaddam, 2003; Harré et al., 2009; Harré & Van Langenhove, 1999).

Polarities are not considered as something in the mind of each individual, but as a discursive phenomenon. These are identified with certain qualities of conversation. Let us now examine three of these.

1) A Shared Plot of Semantic Polarities

Each member of the family constructs conversation within certain specific semantic polarities made prevalent by the discursive practices of that family. Those polarities form a kind of shared plot that generates specific narratives and storylines.

Polarities define what is relevant to each group. They indicate, in the face of the incessant and multiform flow of experience, what will be constructed through joint action as an episode, the minimum unit in which the discourse is articulated (Harré & Van Langenhove, 1999).

One family, like any other intersubjective context, acquires its own identity and specific nature insofar as those who belong to it construct the episodes through which conversation is articulated in a different way from other families. Within each family only certain semantic polarities present in the cultural context prove to be salient. Naturally, everyone understands the main meanings constructed by people in their own culture, even if it is an abstract understanding. In fact, each person is able to interact only within discursive practices that present at least *some* semantic polarities already experienced in their own relational contexts.

In short, *a family is a family inasmuch as those belonging to it have a shared plot, formed by a certain number of semantic polarities and by the narratives that these polarities feed.* The similarity between members of the family is limited to this sharing of a plot of semantic polarities which is derived from the conversational history of the family. This plot circumscribes the repertory of narratives and storylines within which the episodes will be constructed.

2) Inevitable Positioning

All members of a family, as in the case of any other group with a history, *must* necessarily take a position inside the relevant polarities within their group.

Here one of the key hypotheses of Positioning Theory is applied to the concept of semantic polarities, according to which we inevitably find ourselves taking a position in the conversation. This hypothesis recalls a well-known axiom of the *Pragmatics of Human Communication* (Watzlawick, Beavin, & Jackson, 1967): the impossibility of not defining the relationship.[1] Taking a position is a two-way process:

> Whenever somebody positions him/herself, this discursive act always implies a positioning of the one to whom it is addressed. And similarly, when somebody positions somebody else, that always implies a position of the person him/herself. In any discursive practice, positioning constitutes the initiator and the others in a certain way, and at the same time it is a resource through which all persons involved can negotiate new positions.
>
> (Harré & Van Langenhove, 1999, p. 22)

22

This discursive practice is not semantically empty: people always take a position in relation to some meaning present in the conversation. I will be able to feel and behave as someone who is "full of energy" only if the polarity "full/lack of energy" is relevant to the context in which I am (or have been) a part; otherwise I will experience other emotions and feelings. Even if my conduct might resemble that of someone who appears to be full of energy, I will feel "curious" or "lively" in a situation where, as well as those who are similar to me, there are others who are "apathetic" or "sad."

In short, positioning does not occur within unpredictable meanings. On the contrary, this process takes place within a repertoire of meanings that is pre-defined, though flexible and changeable. Conversational partners position themselves and are positioned within the semantic polarities that appear relevant in a given moment in a specific context, as a result of the discursive practices of their own families (and other groups to which they belong or have belonged). Naturally, the relevance the conversation assigns to each semantic polarity is continually negotiated. In the same way the possibility of the conversation developing new meaning is always open. The whole process is spontaneous and to a great extent unintentional.

3) Semantic Polarities and the Interdependence of Multiple Selves

Conversational partners, positioning themselves with others into the plot of semantic polarities relevant to their own intersubjective contexts, anchor their own identity to those of the other members of those groups. *Shared subjectivities are consequently assured by the polar structure of meaning.* Moreover, in all families (as in all other conversational contexts), *more than one polarity is relevant,* so that *the number of selves become as many as the positions generated by each polarity.*

This property of conversation ensures that the organization of meaning according to opposing polarities *creates an interdependence between the identities of the members of the family,* as with any other relational context with a history. Individuals, co-positioning themselves into the relevant semantic polarities of the social groups to which they belong, assume a specific position within the shared narrative plot: they can position themselves as "just," "loyal," "reserved," but in order to occupy these positions others will have to position themselves as "unjust," "untrustworthy," "theatrical." The identity of each partner thus crucially depends upon how many people, occupying different positions, allow the existence and continuity of discursive practices that generate the meanings on which his/her identity is built. That is why, when someone in therapy tells me: "I am a good person," I immediately ask: "Who is the bad one in your family?"

I use the term identity to refer to two fundamental aspects of the self that express both its singularity as well as its multiplicity. In accordance with the Positioning Theory, singularity is experienced subjectively "as a continuity of our point of view" and expressed in conversation through the use of such discursive mechanisms as the first person. Multiplicity, on the other hand, is ensured by the variety of positions occupied by the conversational partners. Each person is thus a single self but also a "plurality of persons" (Harré & Van Langenhove, 1999), at least as many as the relevant semantic polarities within his/her relational contexts.

If, for example, the polarity "intelligent/dim-witted" is relevant in a family—in other words, if it constitutes a semantic dimension around which conversation is organized—the members of this family will position themselves with people who are intelligent or very intelligent but will also be surrounded by people of limited intelligence or who are actually dim-witted. They will marry people who are intelligent, bright, stupid or clueless. They will strive to become intellectually brilliant or will help those who are unfortunately less bright to become so. They will fight and compete to ensure that their intellectual abilities are recognized, they will end marriages and friendships or, alternatively, develop new relationships when intellectual problems arise. Some members of the family will be intellectually brilliant, or regarded as such, while others will prove to be intellectually lacking. One thing is certain: everyone in this family will have to "co-position themselves" into the polar dimension in question and each member, in order to maintain their own identity, will have need of those positioned at other points in this semantic dimension.

In other families, though belonging to the same cultural background, the semantic dimension "intelligent/dim-witted" will be irrelevant and the conversation will be organized instead around episodes, for example, in which the theme of "giving and taking" is central. These people will "position themselves" at work, socially, in their private life, with people who are generous, very generous, and in some cases lavish or, on the contrary, with selfish, mean people. They will form friendships and fall in love with people capable of giving and being altruistic. They will end relationships and friendships when they realize they are being exploited by people who they had trusted or when they realize their partners or friends are concealing an underlying selfishness. Their children will be generous, sometimes even too disinterested in themselves and their own interests or, on the contrary, capable only of taking. They will suffer for the prodigality of some people and the incapacity of others to take into account the needs and rights of others. Conflicts, relationships, alliances, break-ups, and reconciliations will all be played out around problems of "giving and taking." In reconstructing the history of these families, there will certainly be people who are admired for their generosity, while others will be ruined by their prodigality, as well as perhaps someone who was driven by selfishness towards acts of cruelty and those who, thanks to their avarice and greed, have built up fortunes. One thing is certain: all members of these families will position themselves according to the polarity of generosity/selfishness.

In other families different polarities are relevant, and *all families have more than one relevant polarity*. For this reason, the organization of meaning into opposing polarities, besides making identities interdependent, guarantees the multiplicity of the self.

I will be examining other aspects of the concept of family semantic polarities below, but two points should be clarified straightway.

First, the organization of meaning into opposing polarities, as set out above, guarantees, *from the outset*, "intersubjectivity,"[2] in other words, a community of interconnected identities. As soon as children encounter meaning through their emotions, they immediately take a position in the family's shared plot of semantic polarities by constructing their own position in relation to the others, and, through this position, their own subjectivity interdependent upon that of the others. The concept of semantic polarities thus excludes the idea of a subjectivity which, being constructed outside social relationships, has to be coordinated *at a later time* to that of others. This idea, supported by much of modern and contemporary philosophy, including the phenomenological tradition from Husserl to Sartre, reflects its individualistic assumptions. The concept of family semantic polarities is, instead, in keeping with the more recent developments in philosophical thinking that have seen a radical rethinking of individualism (MacIntyre, 1981; Taylor, 1991; Zahavi, 2001). These developments overturn "that singular 'error'," as Elias (1939/2000) described it, by which man is identified as something "internal" and separated from other people "outside." Once that was accepted, "thoughts steers helplessly back and forth between the Scylla of positivism and the Charybdis of apriorism" (Elias, 1939/2000). The concept I have set out here likewise presupposes a "primary" or "nuclear intersubjectivity," as suggested by Trevarthen (Trevarthen, 1979; Trevarthen & Aitken, 2001; Trevarthen & Hubley, 1978) and Stern (1985, 2003) and validated by numerous studies on the interaction between adults and children (Beebe et al., 2005; Bråten, 2007; Meltzoff, 1995; Meltzoff & Moore, 1977, 1999) and also by recent neurobiological studies, including the celebrated discovery of "mirror neurons" (Gallese, 2001; Rizzolatti, Fogassi, & Gallese, 2001).

The second point I wish to clarify is that family semantic polarities are constructed from the emotions. Many family semantic polarities are expressed entirely or mainly through non-verbal conversational patterns. In line with social constructionism (Harré, 1986; Parrott, 2003)—and in agreement on this point with Kelly (1955) who was the first to overturn the idea of a fracture between emotion-cognition—there are no purely cognitive meanings, just as there are no emotions without cognition. Even a semantic polarity such as "intelligent/stupid" is emotionally significant. Our perception of ourselves as intelligent or stupid, at the moment when we feel it, is inseparable from our emotions of personal effectiveness or, alternatively, of helplessness, in the same way as it often produces pride or dejection, especially in relation to other

25

people. Semantic polarities play an important role in our understanding of psychopathology precisely because they are connected to emotions. This is the central theme of the book, which I shall develop over the following chapters. I will now show, using a clinical example, how belonging to a group of people living together and the consequent sharing of the same plot of semantic polarities contributes towards differentiating the individuals who belong to it, and how any symptoms or problems of one or more members are connected to the specific semantics of that group.

2.2 A Clinical Example

"Shy, fragile, a disaster with girls," his father tells me in a preliminary phone call, "I'd always known these things about my son. But crazy, no!" It was only when his third child had developed a limp three months earlier that the father, an engineer with little sympathy for psychotherapists, finally accepted what doctors had been telling him for several years. Armando had serious psychological problems: his son had to be persuaded to undergo psychotherapy. This 24-year-old architecture student had been consulting psychiatrists, osteopaths, orthopedists, cardiologists and other specialists for five years. He suffered pains throughout his body. There wasn't a bone, a muscle, an organ or a tendon in his body that hadn't given pain at some point. The absence of any physical complaint, confirmed by no fewer than three hospital admissions, had failed to alleviate Armando's concerns about his health. Those fears had indeed reached more disturbing levels over the past year. Haunted by anxiety, he had woken his parents several times during the night—once because he thought his knee-cap had "come out" of his knee, once because he felt he was about to have a heart attack, and on another occasion because he felt he was having a stroke. His father was alarmed by these episodes, as well as by the psychiatric diagnoses made by doctors on Armando's discharge from his periods in hospital for observation. But he had continually rejected the idea of consulting a psychotherapist: "because it is hard to know when my son is acting and when he is telling the truth … Bear that in mind," he warned me during the telephone conversation that preceded the first family consultation. "Armando is a semi-professional actor." The family had found out about this talent unexpectedly three years before, when he had invited them to a performance at a local theatre. "I'm playing the main character!" he had told them excitedly. And they had all laughed, thinking that he was joking as usual. He was so timid that it was impossible to believe him. Yet Armando performed for an hour and a half in front of an audience of 200 people. "Unbelievable, a disaster like him!" his father commented. It was a comedy, and from then on the young man earned money to get himself through university with comedy performances for adults and children.

I immediately recognized Armando when I met the family, even though there were four children in all—natural, adopted, and fostered—three of them male. Armando, short and thin, was sitting in a very strange position: head, legs, arms, neck seemed to be connected on different planes. But there was a center, and it still held: an ironic and likeable expression that gave a comic air to the anxiety emanating from such lack of coordination.

Armando's symptoms were easy to place within the semantics of his family. We shall concentrate on examining two polarities that emerged during the first two consultations before therapy and were more obviously connected to the patient's psychopathology. Within Armando's family, those who were fragile, as well as sensitive, aristocratic in manner, and delicate in health, had co-positioned themselves for at least three generations alongside strong people, who had robust health and coarse manners. Armando was tiny, exactly like his mother and, like her, was sensitive and aristocratic in manner, while his father and the eldest child, Elisabetta, were energetic, well-built and rather coarse, as was Pietro, a 17-year-old whom they had fostered four years earlier. But none of them could be described as being the personification of strength and good health. That position was held by Alberto, the second child, the "gentle giant" adopted at the age of three, and the polar opposite of Armando. According to this family, with its taste for exaggeration, Alberto had never ever had flu, had had various exceptional sporting successes, was so strong that on several occasions he had been found with the fridge door or a doorhandle in his hand, and had saved a child from drowning. I looked at him. He really did seem to be of a different breed. He was tall, strong, and solid. In a family where everyone was reactive, he was the only one who remained imperturbable. And most importantly Alberto felt no pain, an astonishing fact in this family in which the mother had never spent a single day without complaining of pain, and in which the history of fear of illness went back three generations. In the case of the father's family these illnesses were imaginary. Their paternal grandmother was clearly a hypochondriac who had spent her life consulting doctors and despairing over physical afflictions for which there was no objective evidence. On the maternal side the illnesses were real. One sister suffered from muscular dystrophy and her father had suffered throughout his life from injuries suffered during the Second World War.

The genetic influence upon these differences was unquestionable, but the family dynamic had plainly contributed towards amplifying them. Let us focus on Armando and Alberto. The centrality of the strong/weak polarity, combined with health and illness, had given Alberto a fine opportunity to excel at something. He was adopted by the couple, who thought they were unable to have any more children after the disastrous delivery of the eldest child, and was in a pitiful state when he entered the family at the age of three. He rapidly recovered but worried about his performance in comparison with that of his sister, who was two years older, and his brother, who was born a year after his adoption. His school results were poor. Unlike his siblings, he couldn't play a musical instrument and couldn't draw. It was his physical performance that gave him an advantage in the family. Even though they teased him with various nicknames—"the giant," "the hulk"—his siblings respected him for his strength and envied his excellent health. Right from primary school Armando relied upon his protection. Alberto fought any classmates who mocked his brother for his weakness or, worse still, attacked him. He waited for him or went to collect him from junior school and carried his satchel when it was too heavy. Later he also protected his elder sister when she grew up and became particularly attractive. It was the admiration he received from the family for his sporting successes that helped him overcome his difficulties. His parents said that Alberto changed from the age of ten, when he had started playing football and going to the gym. This gave him a position of respect within the family and the self-confidence that enabled him to graduate, to set up a successful business and eventually to start a family of his own. Alberto had been married for two years, was awaiting his first child and still went regularly to the gym. Armando had always kept clear of anything for which he wasn't genetically suited, presumably also because of the comparison with his brother, who had a physical advantage. He never went to a gym, never practiced any sport—despite pressure from his father—and even managed to get exempt from gymnastics at school. Instead of sport he preferred to read newspapers. "When he was eight," according to his parents, "Armando used to read newspapers and discuss politics, at least within the family; outside the home, due to his shyness, he couldn't even look someone in the eye." While Alberto had improved his physical abilities, Armando had cultivated his own weakness. The genetic difference between the two brothers—made relevant by a family history in which the strong/weak polarity was at the center of the conversation—had led both of them to maximize their own natural qualities. The parents naturally played an active role in this process. Alberto's sporting successes had filled his father with pride and brought him closer to this son, with whom he identified because both of them, unlike his wife, were "born poor." Armando, with his fragility, strengthened his alliance with his mother. The eldest child had complained during the session that their mother had always defended him by protecting him from her husband's sometimes rather harsh educational methods. On the other hand Armando had reacted very powerfully on the only two occasions when his father had slapped him: his lips had turned purple and he had cried all night.

The meanings we have considered so far, which can be summarized in the strong/weak semantic polarity, produced and were nourished by fear and courage. These emotions were clearly present in conversations with the family and were apparent in the episodes that were gradually presented. The story of the paternal grandmother's hypochondria, for example, ended with a bitter and alarming memory: when she developed cancer, everyone assumed it was just another of her imaginary illnesses and they only began to understand the seriousness of her illness shortly before her death. Just as the mother herself was giving accounts of her own exaggerated perception of grief, showing a certain courage as she did so, her husband interrupted to recall the ten operations she had had over the past five years, thereby prompting a concern among all of them. These accounts, along with others that emerged every now and then in the conversation, brought about a sudden unspoken doubt: "Was it really true then that Armando was a hypochondriac? Can they be sure that Armando didn't have an undiagnosed illness?"

As Armando's purple lips suggest, this family's conversation also brought into play a fear and courage that differed from those arising from the fragility of the human condition and the dangers to which we are exposed. It is the fear and courage experienced through the harsh and open conflict between human beings fighting for supremacy. The conversation in the session continuously presented episodes in which the father, but also the eldest child and Pietro, attacked, provoked, aroused or lashed out at someone or something, while the mother, Armando and Alberto sought to avoid confrontation by withdrawing in various ways. Armando had two escape strategies. He revealed nothing about himself. In a family in which everyone knew everything about what was happening to the others, no one knew whether he had ever had a girlfriend, or which of his many acquaintances were his friends, or what were his political ideas. He had built what the family called "his fence," which he defended from outside attack firstly through his fragility and then through his symptoms. Armando's second escape strategy was to use comic wit to play down and deflect more difficult moments of confrontation, such as the move that his father made to end the first session. Up until that moment he had been extremely cordial, at least with me. As we were about to say goodbye—looking me straight in the eye—he warned me quite unexpectedly that he had been forced by the seriousness of his son's symptoms to seek the help of our team:

> Unlike priests, our family doesn't like psychotherapists—not because we particularly like priests, whose limitations we are well aware of through long experience, but because, being all of us religious, we consider them to be the representatives of God. I don't think the same can be said of psychotherapists.

And he ended in a serious, dramatic manner: "however we are all here willing to collaborate." It was at that point that Armando gave me a worried nod as if there was something above my head: "Take it, doctor, take it." While I was having difficulty in understanding what he was referring to, the young man added: "It's the sword of God, if you don't grab it, it will fall on your head and, instead of treating me, we will all end up in hospital together!" Everyone laughed and the tension broke. Not a bad ending for the first session.

2.3 Origin of the Concept in West and East

The idea that meaning is based on opposing polarities is certainly not a new one. Kelly's psychology of personal constructs (1955)[3] is based on this premise,[4] as are the repertory grid and the semantic differential (Osgood, Suci, & Tannenbaum, 1957), the two main instruments that we still use for the empirical measurement of meaning.

Psychologists had used the concept of polar opposition even before then.[5] Freud used it as the foundation for the dual-instinct theory (1915–1917/1963, 1920/1955, 1923/1961, 1940/1964) that led him to suggest that Eros and Thanathos were the two leading principles in the life of the psyche. Jung also made it a key concept of his analytical psychology.[6] However, the difficulty in fitting this concept within the paradigms of empirical research and the tendency of clinical psychologists themselves to avoid the problem of meaning have contributed towards pushing it into the background among the psychological sciences.

The concept of polarity has in fact a very much older history than its role in psychology. In Western culture, it dates back to pre-Socratic thought. In the words of Lloyd (1966, p. 7): "Few of those who study early Greek thought can fail to be struck by the recurrent appeal to pairs of opposites of various sorts both in general cosmological doctrines and in accounts of particular natural phenomena."

The principal cosmological theories, such as the Pythagorean Table of Opposites, are based on opposites. Anaximander, Parmenides, Empedocles, and Heraclitus also place forms of polar opposition at the basis of everything. Heraclitus stands out among the other pre-Socratic philosophers for his more radical affirmation of the interdependence of opposites:

> What opposes unites, and that the finest attunement stems from things bearing in opposite directions, and all things come about by strife. (fr. 8 D.-K.)

> They do not apprehend how being at variance it agrees with itself: there is a connexion working in both directions, as in the bow and the lyre. (fr. 51 D.-K.).

And also:

> And as the same thing there exists in us living and dead and the waking and the sleeping and young and old: For these things having changed round are those, and those things having changed round again are these once. God is the night, winter, summer, war peace, surfeit famine (fr. 67 D.-K.).

Even specific physical phenomena such as the distinction of sexes in the mother's womb were explained by the pre-Socratics through the concept of polarity.

It was also an accepted principle of Hippocratic medicine that health consisted of balancing opposing elements in the body. We find this same principle of yin and yang in Chinese medicine. Specific diseases were often attributed to the effects of an opposite, and the cure itself involved the skillful use of opposites. As one of the Hippocratic treatises succinctly states: "Opposites are cures for opposites."[7]

Plato and Aristotle used opposites in the same way as their predecessors, but each of them introduced a new element, of a different kind, that was to change the whole question.

Until Plato, opposites were used as constituent—and therefore explanatory—principles of the physical world and of nature. Early cosmologies were founded upon them. The interest of the pre-Socratics focused on nature, or rather, the pre-Socratics had a conception of nature as an external reality, already complete, independent of man and his knowledge.

Plato overturned this idea of a *physis* external to man and his interrogation of himself, and opens the way to a new way of thinking. The turning point is powerfully expressed in one of the central passages of the *Phaedo*.[8] Socrates, the kindest, mildest, most good-hearted man in all Athens, is about to pay the penalty imposed on him by his city. He reviews the direction and significance of his research as he awaits his death in the company of his closest friends. It is precisely the claim by his predecessors to explain nature with reference to polarities of a "physical" kind—hot, cold, water, fire—that distanced Socrates from them. Even Anaxagoras has disappointed him: in the end, he too, like the other philosophers, invokes air, ether, and water. What is the point of an enquiry that excludes the enquirer? Why construct a nature from which man is removed? What value can there be in "objective," "neutral" knowledge that excludes the search for better things? Or to put it in terms that are even more congenial to our present discussion, what is the point of knowledge without meaning?

Unlike the typically pre-Socratic approach to "nature," which confuses means with causes and describes as causes those things that are at most concomitant causes, Plato proposes a quest that leads man to examine what is best in himself. It is a quest that inevitably also leads him to confront the worst of himself "because knowledge of the best and the worst is one and the same."[9] The object of this quest is no longer what is hot, cold, dry or wet but polarities concerning such matters as what is beautiful, just, good, and their opposites. We can therefore say that Plato shifts attention on to semantic dimensions that are similar to those we will be examining over the course of this and subsequent chapters.

Aristotle's approach to the problem of polar opposition is entirely different, and equally crucial. It takes the form of a restriction of the explicative value of this concept, a consequence of Aristotle's tendency to attribute greater reality to the individual substance. In contrast with the pre-Socratics, who focused their attention on constituent principles—opposites—Aristotle places at the center of the process of becoming the "substratum"—the individual substance—to which "privation" and "form" apply.

The lesser importance given to polar opposition after Aristotle is also a result of the specific formalization that he gives to the question, as well as the impulse given to logic in Greek thought, and subsequently in Western thought, thanks to his contribution.

I have so far referred to polar opposition as if it were a single construct. That is not the case. There are various forms of opposition. These are not mere variations on one simple basic relationship. On the contrary, the concept is intrinsically multifaceted. Aristotle was the first to set out a typology of forms of opposition that can be summed up in four categories: correlatives, contraries, terms of privation/possession, and contradictories.[10]

This typology remains fundamentally important, even though it has been the subject of much revision over the centuries. For present purposes, it is important that the reader should consider one apparently surprising aspect that has been highlighted by various commentators. Aristotle does not explicitly set out the criteria for bringing together these four classes of very different phenomena, nor does he attempt to define what we might call "the basic relationship" of opposition, nor does he attempt to clarify whether the opposition has inherent and distinctive aspects. Instead he takes the concept as already established and sets out the various types of opposition. In short, the various kinds of opposition are identified but, as Needham (1987) points out, the fact that the various forms of opposition all contain a shared pattern (present always in all of them) is hardly considered.

The *connection* between opposites—which constitutes the distinctive, inherently relational feature of this concept, as we shall see more clearly below—is apparent only in one of the four classes under examination, namely in the correlatives, which are those opposing terms where each of the two is what it is in relation to the other (for example, double and half, previous and subsequent, etc.). For the others, Aristotle's analysis—particularly through the principle of non-contradiction—focuses on the conditions that separate the opposites. If its central nucleus is ignored, the concept of polar opposition loses many of its heuristic capacities.

Aristotle's decision to move attention to the conditions separating opposites is neither casual nor unmotivated. The pattern connecting each opposite and all opposites is an enigma in terms of formal logic. Needham (1987), in his rigorous and lucid monograph on the concept of opposition, reaches the conclusion that, unlike similar concepts of symmetry and transitivity, opposition has no intrinsic logical form; it is not a formal concept. The heart of the concept of opposition—in other words, the form of relationship that characterizes each opposite and all opposites—involves the *idea of connection*, but this idea leads us to problems regarding the very structure of meaning. We will examine these later but for the moment it is enough to say that the concept becomes less important with Aristotle. This is because Aristotle adumbrates this core idea (the "basic relationship" that is always present in all oppositions), and also because of the central position that formal logic begins to take, thanks to him.

After Aristotle the concept has certainly not been banished from Western thought, but it has been reassessed. Like all concepts that resist logical formalization, it is viewed with suspicion. This tendency—which prevailed for a long time—has been called into question:

> Formal logic, to be sure, represents an idealization of the conditions of communication and an abstraction from certain features of it: but much actual communication depends on conditions and assumptions to do with the context of discourse that are themselves not captured by Aristotle's—or by anyone else's—formal logic. Thus, on this score, the tendency to criticize pre- or non-formal uses of oppositions as symptomatic of a pre- or non-logical stage of thought represents a fundamental misconception of the pragmatics of communication.
>
> (Lloyd, 1991, p. 32)

These considerations help us to understand why the idea of polar opposition was, and still is, more relevant in the East than in the West. The East has certainly been more able to face up to the "authentick obscurity"—to use the words of Sir Thomas Browne (1646/1835)—of the concept. The complementary, interdependent nature of opposites lies at the center of Eastern mysticism and of Chinese philosophical doctrine.

This was certainly not achieved by mysticism using the instruments of reason. Mystical experience—in the East no less than the West—arises from the need to silence reason in order to reach a direct intuition of reality. As we know, mysticism, of marginal importance in Western culture, has assumed a central role in the East. Hinduism, Buddhism and Taoism are philosophical systems, but above all they provide different ways of achieving "liberation," as well as an attempt to go beyond conceptual understanding and its limitations. Underlying this distrust of reason is the awareness that every aspect of reality is related to its contrary, and that opposites can exist only in relation to one another. So long as each person places his trust in reason and sensory perceptions, his view of himself and the world seems to be guided by the dualism of polar oppositions. Eros and chastity, life and death, heroism and cowardice, joy and sorrow are, however, so closely bound together that they become one in the eyes of the sage. Oriental mysticism has developed many techniques—from yoga to archery—for reaching a state beyond ordinary awareness through which to experience union with the surrounding environment and the unity of opposites.

In the *BhagavadGītā* (Trans. 1979), an epic poem and one of the best loved sacred texts of Hinduism, the god Krishna, disguised as a charioteer, warns Arjuna against "intellectual distinction" and urges him: "Trascend it, Arjuna, free from opposites" (II, 45).

In Buddhism, liberation also requires the overcoming of opposites. In the words of Suzuki: "The fundamental idea of Buddhism is to pass beyond the world of opposites, a world built up by intellectual distinctions and emotional defilements, and to realize the spiritual world of non-distinction, which involves achieving an absolute point of view" (1968, p. 18).

Mysticism's distrust of reason is found even more clearly in Zen Buddhism. The teaching that leads the follower towards illumination (*satori*) is done by the master of the Rinzai school almost entirely through *koans*. These are often paradoxes, which Bateson et al. (1956) have compared with double bind pathogenic relationships.[11] One of the best known *koans* was spoken by the Sixth Patriarch to the monk Myo who fervently wished to obtain illumination: "Show me your true face before your father and mother conceived you and you will enter the truth of Zen." *Koans* share many of the ingredients of the double bind: the pupil who tries to do what is requested by the *koan* finds himself trapped in a series of contradictions; at the same time the emotional importance that the relationship with the master has with the follower makes it difficult for him to escape from the pattern imposed by the *koan*. The Zen master is generally, of course, very different from a pathogenic parent; the double binds that he intentionally imposes form part of a religious framework of meaning shared with the pupil. The purpose of these experiences, however disturbing and difficult they may be, is to bring the disciple face to face with the inconsistency of the dualism between intellectual abstraction and sensory perception. In the words of Suzuki: "The *koan* is only a piece of brick used to knock at the gate, an index-finger pointing at the moon. It is only intended to synthesize or transcend—whichever expression you may chose—the dualism of the senses" (1969, p. 106).

The frequency with which the texts of sages and commentators refer to the dualism between thought and the senses, with their deceptions, suggests that awareness of the polar relationship that links opposites has contributed to producing that distrust in reason which is the first step on the way towards mystical experience, and so important throughout the East. Reason and sensory perception itself are in fact unable to detect the underlying unity implicit in polar opposition.

Recognition of the interdependency of opposites in the East does not relate just to the mystical requirement to transcend phenomenic reality, as is shown by the *I Ching*. This classic text, developed over thousands of years, whose role in China might be compared with that of the Bible in the West, is essentially a reflection on the interdependency of opposites. But unlike much oriental mysticism, in this work phenomenic reality with its polar oppositions is not rejected, and it does not teach any way of transcending the world of opposites. The purpose of the *I Ching* is pragmatic: with divine help, man can behave in accordance with the requirements of the moment and can master change.

Hard and soft, yang and yin, are represented respectively by a continuous and a broken line which, when combined together in various ways, produce the sixty-four hexagrams comprising the present version of the work. Each hexagram describes a situation that is considered as exemplifying the possible, ever-changing conditions in which people might find themselves.

Underlying this work is an idea of change similar to that of Heraclitus. All that is real is subject to change: yang—light, heat, masculinity, activity, odd numbers, creativity—is transformed into yin—darkness, cold, femininity, passivity, even numbers, receptivity—and vice versa. The sixty-four hexagrams indicate as many states of movement destined in turn to change in the direction indicated by the so-called moving lines. But precisely because it is possible, with divine guidance, to identify the situation in its *statu nascendi*, man can find the appropriate form of behavior at any specific moment and therefore take an active part in his own destiny: "As long as things are in their beginnings they can be controlled, but once they have grown to their full consequences they acquire a power so overwhelming that man stands impotent before them" (The *I Ching*, trans. 1951, p. 53).

The reflection upon the interdependency of opposites that we find in the *I Ching*, which forms the expression and at the same time the origin of pragmatism in Chinese culture, remains external to mysticism, but it is nevertheless the product of a culture that distrusts reason, or rather speculation unanchored from experience. As Lloyd (1991) observed, the Greek philosophers were prepared to follow the *logos* and reasoning wherever it might lead them, even if it meant accepting extreme, radical, even counter-intuitive positions—as in Parmenides' denial of the existence of change and plurality. It is true that in Greek debate, unlike what happens in modern philosophy, importance was placed upon tradition, and upon the authority of those with greater skill and experience. Generally speaking, however, preference was given to the theory that could be most rationally justified. Chinese attitudes were different: although they had no shortage of methods for evaluation, they placed clearly defined limits and conditions on the pure dictate of reason. The practical utility of what was stated by reason had to be proved: theory for theory's sake did not fit in with that mentality. If reason supported an opinion that ran contrary to ordinary experience, then it was reason rather than experience that had to be rejected.

The *I Ching* highlights another difference between the two traditions. The East has given much greater importance than the West to the intermediate position of polar opposition, the Middle Way. This work views with suspicion all forms of "excellence" resulting from phenomena of polarization. Instead, it favors the middle position. One of the main purposes of the *I Ching* is to avoid processes of polarization. The Great Treatise asserts: "It is the great virtue of heaven and earth to bestow life. It is the great treasure of the holy sage to stand in the right place" (p. 328).

And the right place is generally identified as a balance between opposites, between hard and soft, between *yang* and *yin*, but also between the position and nature of each line, between the relationship of each line with the others and finally between each line and the whole context.

The idea of the "Middle Way" is further developed in Taoism, where all excess is harmful. The Taoist sage is neither good nor bad because:

> He avoids extremes, excesses and complacency (*Tao Te Ching*, XXIX).

> He is sharp but not cutting, pointed but not piercing, straightforward but not unrestrained, brilliant but not blinding (*ibid.*, LVIII).

> The Sage does not do attempt anything very big, and thus achieves greatness (*ibid.*, LXIII).

Ancient Greek thought also placed great value on the middle position. Plato and Aristotle identified virtue with the "golden mean." Modern Western culture, on the contrary, is more inclined to value extremes.

2.4 Polar Opposition and Intersubjectivity

I have described the ancient origins of the concept of polar opposition in order to point out that the "new" idea I am proposing is certainly not the polar nature of meaning. Instead, as I suggested in the first paragraph, it is the hypothesis that *meaning, by virtue of its polar structure, contributes towards establishing "intersubjectivity."* The studies I referred to earlier on intersubjectivity have documented the existence of pragmatic mechanisms in personal interaction that ensure interconnection between individuals and, especially, between adult and child. The hypothesis I put forward earlier is that a similar interconnection is assured by the polar structure of meaning. *The semantic contrasts present in all languages constitute a "universal" characteristic whose function is to render individuals interdependent at a semantic level as well as a pragmatic level.* It is precisely because the structure of meaning is polar that individuals cannot position themselves or be positioned as "generous" or "intelligent" unless there is at least one other individual in their relational context who occupies the opposite position of "selfish" or "stupid." In this way, however, their position, and that part of their identity which is fuelled by that position, come to depend on those who position themselves in complementary positions.

This hypothesis clearly differentiates what I call "family semantic polarities" from the personal constructs described by Kelly (1955). Kelly also considers the polarity of meaning to be a "universal" characteristic. Kelly, however, believed that the duality that characterizes meaning is the expression of a law governing the functioning of the mind. Kelly asks: do people really think in dichotomic terms? His answer is that "dichotomy is an essential aspect of thought itself." That answer is consistent with the Kantian origin of his constructivism,[12] which we also find in the work of other authors from other backgrounds.[13]

Semantic polarities, however, do not express either laws or tendencies in the way that thought functions. They are not mental representations. They are properties of conversation. From this point of view, the polar structure of meaning provides a basis that offers positions within which interdependent identities are constructed, maintained, and deconstructed in the conversation. The duality arising from the concept of family semantic polarities does not therefore relate to human cognition but is an attribute of the conversational matrix within which individual identities take form.

The conversational interpretation of the concept of polar opposition that I am proposing here is in keeping with the metaphor underlying the etymologies of word opposition in many languages: The face-to-face position in conversation. The word used by the ancient Greeks to describe opposition was *antios*. It was used by Homer to describe the face-to-face situation, generally between individuals, but also between opposing armies or natural phenomena: two promontories, for example, facing each other at the mouth of a harbor. Similarly, the German word *Gegenteil* originally referred to social confrontation: the opposing parties in a legal dispute (Grebe, 1963). In Sanskrit, the word "opposition" clearly equates with the face-to-face position in a conversation: the adjective *pratipaksa* is made from *prati*, which means face-to-face, and *paksa*, position.

The very structure of the concept of polarity is relational. Needham (1987), in his brilliant monographic work on the concept of polar opposition, poses a central question: what is the shared feature in all the various forms of opposition? That question, as we have seen, was avoided by Aristotle, whose analysis focused on the conditions that separate opposites. Needham believed that the factor that links opposites and makes them a single construct is complementarity, a construct that cannot unfortunately be examined using the tools of logic and is indeed paradoxical from the point of view of logic. When Sir Thomas Browne (1646/1835) stated that "contraries [...] are yet the life of one another," or when Romano Guardini (1925) stated that each polarity can only exist in the other, they were referring to this type of complementary relationship, one which doesn't necessarily relate to the mystical idea that opposites are the same thing. On the contrary, according to Guardini (1925), *every polarity, although it cannot exist without the other, remains only and always itself*. The polar relationship consists simultaneously of a related exclusion and inclusion. This is the source of its paradoxical as well as its relational nature. The polar structure of meaning is therefore organized in such a way that each meaning exists in relation to another which opposes it. In other words, meaning would seem to be the joint activity of two polar terms that are indispensable precisely because one is essential to the other.

But why has the structure of meaning been so organized as to require the collaboration of two polar extremes? What advantage does our species gain from an organization of meaning that is so relational?

The psychology of personal constructs provides an answer. According to Kelly (1955), dichotomy increases man's capacity for foresight. The availability of polar constructs enables a person to widen the construction of possible horizons in much the same way as the increase in information from binocular instead of monocular vision: new dimensions open up.

The answer I propose is different. As I have already indicated, the semantic contrasts we find in nearly all languages may constitute a "universal" characteristic whose function it is to make individuals interdependent also in terms of meaning.

This answer is consistent with the constructionist perspective within which the concept of family semantic polarities has developed, and one which I think is plausible, given the social nature of man. In a species such as our own, in which each individual can only function within group structures, *the fact that semantic opposites bind individuals to one another represents an advantage from an evolutionary point of view.*

The idea that "intersubjectivity" is based upon the organization of meaning into opposing polarities explains, among other things, why profound differences and conflicts can exist within the family, as in every other group with a history, and why such differences do not necessarily cause its destruction. The conflict, however severe it may be, does not lead to the break-up of a group *if it lies within the same narrative plot.* A conflict is of this nature where it opposes individuals who are positioned at the extremes of the same semantic polarity. Since they both share the same plot, their disagreements and conflicts, however acrimonious they might be, assist in maintaining the conversation and the continuity of each individual identity. This is why Blake, in describing the Prolific and the Devourer, which are taken as symbolizing the differences that divide and oppose men, as well as affirming their interdependence, added: "These two classes of men are always upon earth, and they should be enemies: whoever tries to reconcile them seeks to destroy existence."[14]

In many Italian working-class families during the first half of the twentieth century, central importance was placed upon the semantic dimension of "good/bad," expressed in terms of bigoted religiosity and a total fear of sex. In some of these families with large numbers of children, where it was common for one or two children to enter religious orders, there was always another who was described as a "libertine." This expression was not used to mean a free-thinking follower of Enlightenment philosophy but rather a member of the family, generally a brother, whose life was dissolute, or at least regarded as being so. His presence—which I have often encountered while tracing back three generations in the history of families and individuals I have seen in therapy—has been important in making the family more cohesive. Let us imagine Christmas time in one of these families. As soon as the brothers and sisters meet up there will be a fast flow of communication. In response to the lowered eyes and the disdainful glances that the religious brothers cannot fail to direct towards him, the libertine will certainly respond with sneers and comments in doubtful taste, inciting the clerics to step up the game by adopting sanctimonious attitudes. The conversation will bounce backward and forward. They all speak the same language, though from different positions. But if we look closely, the libertine's conception of sex must not have been all that different from that held by his prudish brothers and sisters. For all of them, sex will have been something sordid, and it is for this reason that the libertine indulged himself while the others abstained. Even the identities of the siblings will be strengthened by the encounter. The libertine's vulgarity and corruption will inevitably have confirmed the clerics in their choice of the path of abstinence, just as the evident attitude of mortification emanating from the brothers who had chosen the path of the priesthood will have further convinced the libertine that his enjoyment of the pleasures of life, even though he risks the flames of hell, has been well worthwhile.

As this example shows, the concept of family semantic polarities regards polar opposition as a matrix for the construction of individual identities. *The duality is in the matrix, not necessarily in the individual identities and in the mental representations of the individuals.* The clerics in our example can construct themselves as good, even without possessing mental constructs that oppose good against bad; they can consider themselves to be pure and unsullied even without concealing "bad" parts and emotions. They may also have been unaware (wittingly or unwittingly) that their identities had been constructed and maintained in relationship to their libertine brother. The fact that they could rely on polar mental representations of good and evil is not excluded from the concept of family semantic polarities but nor is it necessary. The interdependence of opposites that this concept entails has to do with conversation which, according to Vygotsky (1934/1962), is more primitive than thought both phylogenetically and ontogenetically. Semantic polarities call into being opposite positionings in the conversation, thus helping to orientate mental representations of the subjects; but they themselves are not representations.

To summarize: the concept of family semantic polarities is in many ways different from and complementary to Kelly's concept of personal constructs. The two concepts refer to different phenomena. They have two different underlying conceptions about meaning. Kelly's personal constructs express a constructivist conception of meaning, "privileging the individual construer" (Stam, 1998) as is also recognized by such therapists as Procter (1981, 1985,

2009; Procter & Parry, 1978), Stojnov and Butt (2002), who have offered relational interpretations of the psychology of personal constructs, and underlined by social constructionist (Gergen & Gergen, 2004). Semantic polarities are, instead, consistent with human beings' social constructionist conception.

2.5 A Conversation With Three Positionings

The idea of opposition immediately evokes two polar terms that constitute its essence. In reality, however, the concept of family semantic polarities involves three positions. It uses the metaphor to which many etymologies of the word "opposition" refer—the face-to-face position—and essentially identifies three positions in the conversation: the two polar extremes, and a series of possible intermediate positions that can be summarized as the middle position.

Family semantic polarities are a class of triadic constructs in formal terms as well. They are represented, with a few exceptions, by contrasts that give rise to a range of intermediate terms between the two extremes. For example between love and hate there is a range of intermediate sentiments that Ogden (1932) encapsulates in the middle point of indifference.

Even those few family polarities that would seem to exclude any middle position, derived as they are from opposites that admit no intermediate states, are still triadic. This is true of the case of "honest/lying." We might suppose that this polarity, originating as it does from true/false, would respect the principle of *tertium non datur*—no middle possibility—and that it can therefore only give rise to two relational positions. But conversation, and the realities that conversations create, do not necessarily follow the rules of logic. As well as those who are honest and those who are liars, there is a third position that is taken by those who avoid being honest and yet do not want to lie. When people in therapy place themselves in this position, I immediately ask them: "Who are the honest members of your family and who are the liars?" knowing that I am on the right track. There is never an honest person without a liar. No one ever thinks of describing themselves as honest unless they have to deal with someone who is false. And it is inconceivable for people to lie unless there is someone to discover them: at most, they will be fanciful, creative or shrewd. But when a liar and an honest person come into contact and conflict, a third position inevitably opens up: *someone who is neither honest nor a liar*. Those who occupy this position have experienced in their family context that honesty can offend, can create friction, and can be personally damaging, but also that lying and deceit can dangerously compromise personal integrity and relationships with others. Taking part in a context where the polarity honest/lying is relevant, in fact, gives semantic meaning to the positioning "neither honest/nor lying" which, from a purely logical point of view, given its relationship with true/false, might seem nonsensical. But in the realities created by conversation, and the situations arising from it, there is sometimes a *tertium datur*.

Because of its triadic nature, the concept of family semantic polarities also fits well into the systemic tradition. The use of triadic forms of explanation has been one of the distinctive features of systemic psychotherapy from the very beginning. As early as 1967, Haley identified the triangle as the primary unit of analysis in nascent systemic psychotherapy. Since then, recognition of the importance of the transition towards the triad in order to understand human behavior has been an important step forward in the conceptualization of systemic therapies. Triangles and triangulation are in fact at the center of clinical developments among the pioneers of family therapy (Bowen, 1966, 1978; Minuchin et al., 1967; Selvini Palazzoli et al., 1978, 1980; Zuk, 1969). It was, however, only through the work of Fivaz-Depeursinge and Corboz-Warnery (1999) that empirical evidence emerged to demonstrate the capacity for all of us, at a surprisingly early age, to be aware of two conversational partners at the same time. These authors have shown, through "Lausanne triadic play," how many three-month-old children are already able to alternate their gaze between their two parents, and that at nine months almost all children are capable of complex triadic interactions. As Stern (1999, 2008) pointed out, the results of this fascinating program and the research it led to[14] have transformed the traditional vision of development, which presumed a dyadic to a triadic development for the child, and now indicate a need to rethink many developmental problems within triadic conceptual frameworks. These results are important in terms of the hypothesis I have set out here because they demonstrate that as soon as a child enters meaning he/she is capable of performing tacit positionings that take into account two partners at the same time.

The concept of family semantic polarities moreover provides a therapist with criteria with which to approach a problem that in systemic psychotherapies remains unsolved, namely: in order to understand the context creating the problem, to what extent must we enlarge what used to be called the range of observation and what, in constructionist terms, we would call the field of inference.

Systemic therapists, unlike colleagues who follow other approaches, tend to extend their analysis to older generations. Some go back three generations in family therapy sessions. Often the first generation is not directly involved in the consultation but is taken into account during the therapy. Furthermore, certain therapists, such as Seikkula and Arnkil (2006) still use forms of network therapy. Even when the therapy is limited to a single patient, as in individual systemic therapy, the therapist must choose the extent to which, through questions, to help patients expand the context in order to attribute meaning to their emotions and conduct and those of the people who are most important to them.

The observation by Watzlawick et al. (1967) that "a phenomenon remains unexplainable as long as the range of observation is not wide enough to include the context in which the phenomenon occurs" (pp. 20–21) is still shareable,

41

but it does not give us any ways of identifying in which of many possible contexts a phenomenon acquires meaning. It is certainly not always advantageous in therapy to expand the field of observation. It is impossible, in fact, to receive information without at the same time giving it: the process is two-way. By involving older generations, relatives or representatives of other bodies (schools, communities, etc.) in the session, the therapist inevitably modifies, albeit temporarily, the confines of the family group—a move that can have negative effects, even though these can be counteracted during the therapy. Expanding the field of inference may not be appropriate, even when it does not mean involving people outside the family group in the session. The more the therapist extends his/her analysis to older generations or relatives, the less time is available to examine the emotions, feelings, expectations, and beliefs of members of the family group itself. The field of inference should therefore be expanded as far as is necessary to understand and deal with the problem. No further.

The concept of family semantic polarities suggests that we *extend the analysis at least to include the positions at the two extremes of the semantic polarities that are considered important for the interpersonal situation we intend to analyze.*

In many family groups we find positionings at both extremes of the most important semantic dimensions, at least for the purposes of understanding the problem for which therapy has been requested. These are families in which we find the presence of opposing individuals within the family—as in the Karamazov, Dombey, and Pollitt families, as well as in the family described in Section 2.2. In these cases, it is possible to limit our attention to the family group, precisely because it contains the opposing positions of each polarity. It therefore provides a sufficiently broad context in order to give meaning to events.

Where, however, the positionings of all members of the family are *within the same extreme* of the crucial semantic polarities (even though each family member has developed their own personal position that is different from the others) focusing on the nuclear family may be misleading. In these cases, the psychotherapist will have to understand the patient's symptoms and the family's emotional dynamic by including in the analysis members of the extended family (or other contexts outside the family group) where people are generally found who have constructed their own positioning and identity by placing themselves at the opposite extremes of the polarities. That is what happened in the following case.

What most disturbed and appalled the parents of Filippo, a bulimic adolescent, was finding the kitchen, which they had left spotlessly clean, strewn with blobs of jam, chicken thighs, chocolate spread, and banana skins. Not only was Filippo unable to prevent himself from eating enormous quantities of food at the most unlikely hours but, horrified by what he had done, he fled from the kitchen as soon as he regained control, in order to vomit what he had eaten. He couldn't return to the scene of his "food crime," not so much through fear of another attack but to avoid the unbearable humiliation of facing up to what he had done. It was not difficult to understand his family's dismay when they discovered the aftermath of Filippo's binge. Everyone—parents as well as children—seemed so "restrained," "measured," "active," and "determined." This was true of Filippo as much as his older sister. Their father, a respected intellectual, regarded determination and understatement as a philosophy of life. His wife shared his lifestyle and reflected it in every aspect: in her character, voice, and clothes. There was a striking resemblance in this married couple: they shared the same elegant, neutral manner of moving and speaking, the same quiet tone of voice, the same simple style of dressing. They were both slim and fit. The children resembled their parents in build and character; like them, they had always been frugal, determined, and restrained. Prior to Filippo's bulimia, where in this family could we find the unrestrained devourers, those driven only by their impulses? It was useless looking for them inside the family group where everyone—though with notable differences, was positioned at the same pole in terms of determination and control. The polar opposites were in the father's family. Filippo's grandmother, an attractive and likeable woman, who had been widowed at an early age, was reckless and excessive in everything: in her spending, in her generosity, in her rash love affairs, in her garish clothing. As a result of her impulsive manner, very little remained of the substantial fortune her husband had left her. The uncle, on the other hand, was the opposite of his brother, Filippo's father. He was temperamental, enjoyed parties and the high life, was an astute businessman, alternating moments of success with lapses into alcoholic binges.

It may also happen that the couple or other more important members of a family place themselves in a *middle position* on all or some of the semantic polarities most directly connected with the problem for which therapy has been sought. In cases such as the one I am about to describe, the problem must then be put into a context that includes the two extremes. The three poles of the crucial polarities will therefore become the subject of the therapeutic exchange.

"I want at least five children!" Costanza had told Guglielmo when they first started going out together. Guglielmo could hardly believe it: he had found the woman of his dreams. Unlike other people of his age, he too couldn't wait to have a large family. So they got married immediately, at the age of twenty. The fact that they were both still at university was not going to stand in their way. When Guglielmo was eighteen, he had received a large inheritance from an uncle and Costanza also came from a well-to-do family. Alessandro's birth, eighteen months after their wedding, therefore filled them both with great joy. And yet I had great difficulty in getting them to remember this happy beginning. They sat there humiliated and disillusioned, as if to ask me: "Can you help us understand how we could have produced such a child?" One thing was clear, even though they lacked the courage to admit it even to themselves: they both dearly wished they could turn their backs on this child, Alessandro, who had destroyed their plans for the future. The idea of a large family had been forgotten and Guglielmo and Costanza were no longer considering even a second child. What disturbed Alessandro's parents was his aggressive and demanding behavior. It was visibly clear that he was a difficult child: he stood erect, with the direct and imperious glare of a little tyrant. He wandered around the therapy room, every now and then pushing a book or a piece of paper across the floor so that I too would understand who I was dealing with ... His parents told me that the teachers at the nursery school had complained that Alessandro wanted to control the other children, would hit them if they failed to do what he wanted, got his way through violence and was even aggressive towards the little girls. The contrast with his parents could not have been clearer. Costanza and Guglielmo were affectionate and gentle with each other. They had the appearance of mild, thoughtful, rather dreamy and romantic children. Alessandro and his parents didn't seem to have anything at all in common. Genetics must have played a role, but it was certainly insufficient to explain such aggressive behavior in a five-year-old child. Costanza and Guglielmo were doubly upset because they had taken personal care over Alessandro's education. They had not left him with grandparents or babysitters, they explained immediately. They had looked after him personally, sharing responsibilities on an entirely equal basis.

Working with them on their relationship as a couple, I quickly became aware that it was useless looking for conflicts between them: they had never had any arguments because they shared the same ideas, the same interests and most importantly of all, as they explained, neither of them enjoyed *commanding or obeying*. Perhaps it was for this shared characteristic that they chose each other; certainly, according to what they told me, this was the secret of their relationship. And it was also the reason why Alessandro's behavior left them so helpless and impotent.

It was precisely this similarity in the couple that gave us an insight into how to understand and deal with the problems they were experiencing with Alessandro. For Costanza and Guglielmo "command/obey," "dominate/submit," "impose/succumb," were polarities that had played and—when I met them—continued to play a central role in the construction of their subjective position and an important part in their identity. No one describes themself as someone who neither commands nor obeys unless they have lived in a context in which someone dominated and someone else submitted. When, in fact, I asked Alessandro's parents who dominated and who submitted in their own original families, much suffering and pain emerged—even Alessandro stopped his provocation and took part in the session, giving me a drawing which showed, as he explained, an enormous grandpa lion and a tiny grandma mouse. Both Costanza and Guglielmo had a family history in which one of the parents was aggressive while the other submitted. There were commanders and subordinates, at least in their narrated stories. On these matters, there had been serious conflict and drama in their families, and their plans for the future had been developed precisely because of what had happened to their parents.

They had imagined themselves as parents with a large family in which no one commanded and no one obeyed. But their plan for a large family did not relate to the future but to the past: to show their parents how they should have behaved towards their children. A family like the one they had dreamed of could only exist in relation to their original families, as shown in Figure 2.1. And at first they had constructed their family in this way. For the first two years, Alessandro had caused no difficulty, and the young couple had behaved with their son in the same way that they wished their own parents had behaved with them when they were children. Whenever they interacted with him, they were speaking at the same time to their own parents, even though their parents were not physically present. Alessandro was therefore the apparent receiver of their communications. To paraphrase T. S. Eliot (*The Waste Land*, 1922/1962), he might have asked his parents, "Who is the third who walks always beside me?" Although no one seemed to realize it, the parent–child field of inference always included the grandparents as well.[15] Was Alessandro, through his behavior, expressing all of his anger because his parents were not actually talking to him? Was he challenging their "middle identities," forcing them towards more resolute behavior that their conflict with their own parents prevented them from assuming? By making them fail as parents, was he compelling them to deal with their unsolved problems as children? We can leave it to therapy to answer these questions; here it is enough to underline that a family like the one Alessandro's parents had dreamed of could only exist in relation to their original families, as shown in Figure 2.1.

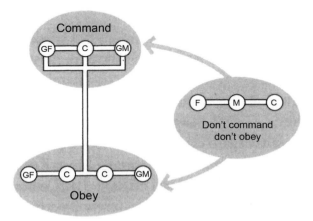

Figure 2.1 An "egalitarian" triad in a middle position (as Costanza and Alberto had dreamed of and achieved during Alessandro's first two years of life)

45

In the next section I shall examine in more detail the middle position, which is crucial for the positioning of subjects with obsessive-compulsive disorders, to which the fourth chapter is devoted. For now it is sufficient to observe that the middle position is defined in relation to *both* extremes. Costanza and Guglielmo could not bear to be aggressive or even merely assertive or resolute but nor could they yield or simply accept Alessandro's behavior.

2.6 Harmony and Excellence: On the Edge of Disaster

Let us now examine the conversational processes between people occupying the various positions on relevant semantic polarities: the two opposing extremes and the middle position. Such processes contribute towards constructing the various identities of the conversational partners. Occupying a position in a conversational context means having to hand a range of verbal and non-verbal communication strategies as well as a series of emotions, assumptions, ideas, belief systems, and objectives that are consistent with that position.

> A subject position incorporates both a conceptual repertoire and a location for persons within the structure of rights and duties for those who use that repertoire. Once having taken up a particular position of one's own, a person inevitably sees the world from the vantage point of that position and in terms of the particular images, metaphors, storylines and concepts which are made relevant within the particular discourse practice in which they are positioned.
>
> (Harré & Van Langenhove, 1999, p. 35)

Precisely because each person occupies a limited range of positions (as many as the semantic polarities relevant to that person), a number of stories will be permitted, in the sense that they are easy to construct and live, while others will be more difficult, unavailable, or even forbidden.

The concepts of symmetrical and complementary interaction and of schismogenesis, help us to understand how the two extreme positions are constructed. I describe them here for the reader who might not be familiar with these basic concepts of the systemic approach by referring to their first formulation in *Naven* (Bateson, 1936/1958), prior to the beginning of systemic psychotherapy during the mid-twentieth century.

One of Bateson's great intuitions, which anticipates a central theme in Positioning Theory, is that the individual traits that contribute to what, in ordinary language, we call "character" are at least partially the product of interactive processes, in particular of symmetrical and complementary schismogenic interactions.

In his studies of the Iatmul, a New Guinea tribe which until a few years earlier had been head hunters, Bateson (1936/1958) was struck by the rigid opposition dividing the lives of men and women. Men carried out spectacular, dramatic, and violent activities that centered around the ceremonial house, a magnificent building compared with the simplicity of the huts around which the life of the women was organized. The women were responsible for gathering and cooking food and raising children. The men were proud, theatrical, and superficial; they spent much energy asserting themselves and blended pride with histrionic self-esteem. They moved about feigning a prestige that in fact they did not have: The Iatmul were highly individualistic and had no fixed hierarchy. Arrogance, boastfulness, and buffoonery were accepted as normal, respectable behavior. Their conversation was noisy, irascible and sometimes ironic. Their most admired verbal demonstrations were a display of erudition and violence. Much of the discussion involved their totemic system. There were men who knew by heart between ten and twenty thousand names of ancestors, each name of several syllables, and their erudition was a source of pride to the whole village. Other speakers relied on the tone of their discourse, rather than expertise: they peppered their speeches with expressions of contempt and threats of violence towards members of other clans, and interspersed them with obscene danced mimes. Apart from those speakers who were articulate and those who were insulting, there were nervous, timid ones whose contributions to the discussion were dismissed as almost worthless. The discussions were always highly animated and all the activities in which men took part were marked by deep rivalry.

The women, unlike the men, performed their activities privately and quietly. Every morning they rose early and went, each in their own canoe, to set up nets to catch fish, then returned home to carry out domestic work and look after their children. They were lively and good humored; in personal relationships they were spontaneous, cooperative, and relaxed. Every four days the Iatmul women from the villages met women from the forest tribes at the market, where they traded fish for sago. Trading was carried out easily and cheerfully. The women did not seem to place too much importance on business. Bargaining was rapid and they chattered a great deal about recent events in their villages. There was a marked contrast between the rapid, calm negotiations among women and those among men. The women generally took care of business, but for particularly serious negotiations—such as buying a canoe or a sleeping bag—the men took over, assuming a darkly taciturn air in order to get the better of their adversary. The proceedings became lengthy and complex and in most cases the deal was not concluded. While the men behaved as if life were a magnificent theatrical performance, a drama in which they always took center stage, the women generally behaved as if life were a cheerful routine in which the business of providing food and looking after their children was enlivened by the exciting and spectacular activities of the men.

Bateson analyzes these opposing forms of behavior between the sexes and the relative uniformity of behavior among each sex through the concepts of complementary and symmetrical interaction and schismogenesis, seeking to demonstrate the interdependence of the behavior and attitudes that characterized the community. The arrogance, pride, theatricality and much of the psychology of the male Iatmuls were constructed upon the admiration that these forms of behavior produced among their women. There is no theatre without an audience.

The attitudes and behavior of the women also tended to adapt to those of the men, without which they lost meaning. The simplicity, humility, undramatic cheerfulness of the Iatmul women were a response and way of dealing with the imperious needs for self-assertion and the quarrelsome behavior of their men. Similarly, the women's spirit of observation, their curiosity, their willingness to be enchanted and to show admiration were encouraged by, and encouraged, their men's exhibitionism.[16]

What rendered the character traits of Iatmul men and women so obviously interdependent, according to Bateson (1936/1958), was a specific interactive pattern to which he gave the name of schismogenesis. According to Bateson schismogenesis was a process of differentiation in individual behavior resulting from cumulative interaction between individuals. This was a potentially progressive process that could occur in complementary interactions as much as in symmetrical interactions. In the case of complementary schismogenesis the two interacting subjects or groups exhibited increasingly opposing forms of behavior:

> If, for example, one of the patterns of cultural behavior, considered appropriate in individual A, is culturally labeled as an assertive pattern, while B is expected to reply to this with what is culturally regarded as submission, it is likely that this submission will encourage a further assertion, and that this assertion will demand still further submission. We have thus a potentially progressive state of affairs, and unless other factors are present to restrain the excesses of assertive and submissive behavior, A must necessarily become more and more assertive, while B will become more and more submissive; and this progressive change will occur whether A and B are separate individuals or members of complementary groups.
>
> (p. 176)

In the case of symmetrical schismogenesis, the subjects involved, whether they are individuals or groups, exhibit increasingly similar forms of behavior:

> If, for example, we find boasting as the cultural pattern of behavior in one group, and that the other group replies to this with boasting, a competitive situation may develop in which boasting leads to more boasting, and so on. This type of progressive change we may call symmetrical schismogenesis.
>
> (p. 177)

Through schismogenic processes, individuals maximize certain character traits to the detriment of others. In the case of the Iatmuls, the men for example became increasingly exhibitionistic and the women became increasingly passive spectators. Bateson was well aware of the many risks to psychic balance caused by the polarization of individual traits through schismogenic processes, as can be seen in various examples described in this work from his early years. Nevertheless, his attention at the time was focused on the dangers that these phenomena pose in terms of the cohesion and stability of a social group and, in particular, on the tools developed collectively to control and counteract those processes. The central theme of his book was in fact the enigmatic naven ceremonies, which, according to Bateson's interpretation, served the purpose of reducing the tension produced in the community by schismogenic processes. In his later writings, borrowing the language of cybernetics, Bateson (1958) compared the navens to self-correcting circuits.

I have referred to the first formulation of these concepts because a clear attention was given in *Naven* (Bateson, 1936/1958) to the semantic contents to which they are applied, although they were considered in an overall and summary manner through the concept of *ethos*. Moreover, *Naven* contains many references to the role of interactive processes in the formation of character. In later years, Bateson (1972) and the Palo Alto school focused increasingly on the interactive process in the here and now, ignoring its semantics as well as the relationship between interactive processes and individual identity. In order to understand the process of construction of identity in conversation, attention must be focused on the temporal dimension and meanings.

Returning to Bateson, we can say that when a semantic dimension is salient in a particular context, the relationship between members occupying opposing poles of that dimension will be complementary—based on the exchange of opposing communicative behavior: one commands and the other obeys; one teaches and the other learns; one complains and the other comforts, and so forth. Among those who place themselves at the same polarity, however, the relationship will be symmetrical, based on equality: one shows off and the other shows off; one commands and the other commands; one complains and the other complains.

There is nevertheless also *a middle position* that Bateson and his colleagues ignored. In studying the Iatmuls, Bateson was particularly struck by the polar type who was most admired. He was violent and was enthusiastically described as "having no ears," in other words that he did not listen to the advice of others and recklessly followed his own impulses. However he noted that the natives also approved of men who were more reasonable and prudent. Indeed it was they who were the holders of esoteric information. While the Iatmuls admired the more violent types, they feared that these people, lacking self-control, might inadvertently reveal important details of their secret knowledge to their adversaries. They therefore entrusted this knowledge to those who could remain calm during discussions and could therefore judge when it was appropriate to reveal a certain secret to the other side or when, instead, it was sufficient to make some cryptic allusion, which would be interpreted as a threat of possible revelations. Bateson, however, did not consider these individuals as representing a specific middle position. Even the comparison with Bali, which occurred after he had written *Naven*, did not prompt him to consider a middle position. And yet Bali in the 1930s was a classic example of an Eastern culture that preferred to organize itself around the middle position rather than at the extremes. Bateson understood the radical difference that separated the Balinese culture from that of the Iatmuls, as well as those of the West. Nevertheless, having constructed the concepts of symmetrical and complementary interaction and schismogenesis upon a dyadic idea of the concept of polarity, Bateson interpreted the culture of Bali and the character of its inhabitants as the result of interactive processes that tended to avoid any form of schismogenesis (Bateson, 1949). Bateson interpreted Balinese culture in a subtractive way, as can be seen from the very construction of the essay which is entirely centered around the statement: "*In Bali no schismogenic sequences have been observed.*"[17] Certain patterns observed and reported by Bateson in this essay are, on the other hand, at least in my view, examples of communicative maneuvers that are typical of the middle position.

The theory I propose to put forward is that the middle position does not simply derive from the extremes. It has its own specific status because *it is constructed by conversational processes that are different from those that produce the two opposing polar positions.*

The difference is not immediately clear. The conversational processes that produce the middle position are apparently similar to the processes that construct the two polar opposites. The relationship between those who place themselves in the middle position inside a particular semantic dimension and those who are diametrically opposed is complementary, since it is defined by difference. Similarly, relations between those who occupy the middle position are symmetrical, inasmuch as they are based on equality. These analogies, however, are superficial. The complementary relationships that fuel the middle position have very different characteristics from those that compete in the construction of the two extremes. We can define them as *oscillating complementary relationships* because they are the result of continual *balancing* processes: the alliances, conflicts and collaborations with those who occupy the two extreme positions are always partial. As a result, they express a certain withdrawal from the interaction.

But, above all, *the conversational processes of the middle position differ from those relating to the other two poles in their effects upon identity*. While the relationships fuelled by opposing polar positions produce an *externalization* of individual qualities—regardless of schismogenic processes—the relationships that construct the middle position, whether they are oscillating or symmetrical, give rise to an opposite process, which I describe as *centralization*.

Let us examine both of these processes, illustrated in Figure 2.2. The individual, placed at one of the two extremes—by "co-positioning" him or herself differently to those at the opposite pole or similarly to those at the same pole—*externalizes* specific qualities. Precisely because his attention is focused on the other, he acquires an increasingly specific individuality: there is no "I" without a "Thou"—as Buber put it (1923/1958). *The positions at the extremes imply a full recognition of the conversational partner as equal and similar, or as different and opposite.* They are the product and, at the same time, fuel alliances and collaborations as well as conflicts and fights in which the other is central in his position as ally or antagonist.

The relations fuelled by the middle position—whether oscillating or symmetrical—trigger a process that is the opposite of externalization: *centralization.* Through this process, the middle position is constructed and maintained through a continual balancing in relation to those positioned at the two extremes. For example, in a family context divided between weak and strong

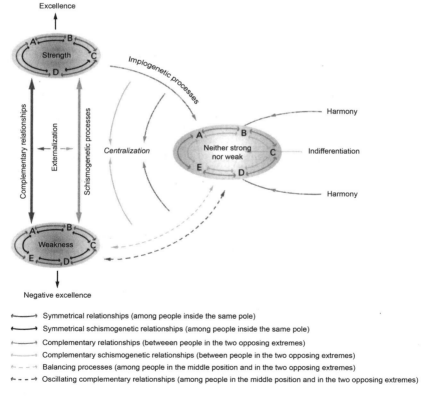

Figure 2.2 The conversational processes which fuel the three polar positions

51

members, there is someone who tries to keep a balance between strength and weakness. This member rejects strength because he regards it, say, as tantamount to violence and abuse, but decries weakness. The person in this position, by supporting or opposing those occupying the extremes, moves noticeably towards one pole and then towards the other, but these shifts are restricted and balanced by adjustments in the opposite direction over a relatively brief span of time. As his attention is focused primarily on keeping a balance in relation to the two extremes, and therefore *in his own position* in relation to the two polar positions, the person in the middle position acquires a lesser degree of specific individuality in the semantic dimension to which the process is applied than happens to those who place themselves at the extremes. Precisely because his "co-positioning" is only partial in terms of alliance, conflict, or collaboration with the other, the definition of self with respect to this relevant semantic dimension will also be partial.

Likewise, relations between those who share the same middle position—relations that are symmetrical inasmuch as they are based on equality—have a very similar effect upon identity: The more that people are balanced between the two poles, the more equal they will be, and they will therefore *be defined very little (or not at all) in terms of the semantic dimension within which they have placed themselves.*

The processes of externalization and centralization are maximized when phenomena of polarization occur.[18] Through the concept of schismogenesis that we have examined, Bateson studied one type of polarization involving two extremes. The outcome of this process upon the identities of those involved is *excellence*: People maximize the trait brought into play by the polarity on which the schismogenic interaction takes place, developing a sort of hyper-specialization. If the dimension in question is, for example, "strength/weakness," some will learn how to become stronger, while others will become skilled in weakness. As Bateson and systemic psychotherapy have shown, this is a risky process in terms of individual and social adaptation. Those who position themselves inside the culturally approved extreme of a relevant semantic dimension will develop a genuine excellence, because they will maximize a socially valued quality: courtesy, generosity, beauty etc. They run the risk, however, of being one-dimensional: *Every excellence is accompanied by some deficiency.* In order to maximize certain qualities, a person has to neglect others. Hyper-specialization in one conversational context makes people unsuitable to take part in other types of conversation. As a result, participation in "specialized" forms of conversation that processes of polarization lead to, reduces their capacity to deal with changing circumstances and situations in life. Suffice it to consider those situations that maximize semantic dimensions that can only be fully achieved in youth, such as beauty or physical fitness. The very passing of time may become problematic. *All languages are in fact multidimensional* from the semantic point of view and the individual who tries to reach fulfillment in a single dimension—the "pure type", to use Guardini's terminology (1925)—ends up over the edge in disaster. It is what we learn from many myths in various cultures and from the experience of daily life itself.

The dangers are obviously even clearer for those who find themselves in a position with a negative cultural connotation. These people also externalize clearly defined qualities. Their position demands a considerable outlay of energy and much specialized learning. One learns to be passive in the same way as one learns to be active. Being bad can be just as hard as being good. It takes a certain determination to be ugly in the same way as it does to be pretty. But if a person positions himself at the negatively viewed extreme, as well as being exposed to the same risks as his polar opposite he also receives a negative self-valuation: his excellence has a negative value. Nature obviously helps to produce differences but it leaves the game open, as research on monozygotic twins has shown (Plomin et al., 2001).

Phenomena of polarization also affect the middle position. They are the product of *implogenetic* processes through which centralization becomes extreme. *These processes result in harmony*, but also in *undifferentiation*, a lack of individual specificity. When centralization in relation to one semantic dimension is at its maximum, the individual is perfectly balanced inside the dimension in question. If a person takes this position inside all relevant semantic dimensions then he/she will be harmonious and multidimensional but, for this very reason, runs the risk of being undifferentiated.

Polar contexts produce three areas of risk, not two, as Guardini had suggested, albeit in terms of an exclusively philosophical interest. As well as the risk posed by the two extreme polar positions—"the disaster area of the 'pure type'"—there is another hazard: "the disaster area of perfect harmony." Guardini observes:

> The experience of opposites as a form of life is besieged at the extremes and assailed at the center by a basic impossibility. Nevertheless, these impossibilities are, at the same time, the perfect forms of life itself. In perfect fulfillment there is destruction.[19]
>
> (1925, p. 205)

Excellence is risky because it is unilateral, but harmony also contains risks of disaster of another kind.

Being perfectly balanced within a relevant semantic dimension is the same as withdrawing from conversation. The individual, so far as that semantic game is concerned, is no longer a conversational partner. As there cannot be a me without a you, if this borderline positioning (more conjectural than real) is taken by the individual within all relevant semantic dimensions, he/she will have to face the worst conceivable threat: the annihilation of self.

That is what happened to Jean-Baptiste Grenouille, the product of Patrick Süskind's (1985/2001) literary imagination. In the eighteenth century, when smell must have had an importance that we can scarcely imagine today, Grenouille is born without any bodily odor. He keeps in touch with the world, however, through his extraordinary sense of smell, becoming a genius in the fleeting realm of perfume. His wet nurse, horrified at his lack of odor, rejects him. Later, others who are not forced into such close proximity simply fail to notice him. His is not an external condemnation, at least not in the way the expression is generally understood. To emit an odor means to "co-position" oneself between those who are fragrant and those who stink. But Grenouille, due to the dramatic circumstances that mark him out from his very first whimper, cannot accept any "co-positioning" with others and for precisely this reason is unable even to recognize himself. The whole plot of this fantastical and chilling story is organized around two inescapable and irreconcilable "choices": the obstinate wish to live that prevents Grenouille from quietly leaving the stage, choosing the direct route between birth and death, and the equally stubborn determination of this soul to remain sealed, to give nothing to the world, not even his own odor.

Implogenetic processes, in Grenouille's case, express a condition in which the individual is unable to define himself because the other person cannot even be recognized as an object of hatred. More frequently, these processes are the outcome of relationships in which a conversational partner fears that, by moving from the middle position towards one of the extremes, he might harm or even destroy those positioned at the opposing poles, or might be harmed and overwhelmed by them. I think that Bowen (1978), with his concept of "undifferentiated family ego mass," was referring to something of this kind. His theory is based on emotional triangles and the difficulties individuals experience in defining themselves and differentiating themselves within the context of the complex network of emotional interdependence brought into play by triangular relationships within the family. One typical case is that of a child who cannot ally itself with one parent—not even in certain areas and for a limited period of time—without the other parent feeling hurt or even devastated by that alliance.

I am referring to borderline conditions to which oscillating relations do not necessarily relate. They imply for the most part a partial equilibrium in relation to the two extremes: the individual in the middle position is continually moving towards one or other of the two extremes, and by reason of these moves he takes part in the conversation and defines himself as a partner. Indeed, his partial alliances, as well as limited conflicts, give him a semantic multidimensionality that someone positioned at the extremes does not have. When, however, implogenetic phenomena prevail, and there are also difficulties in partial forms of participation in the conversation, the middle position becomes the chosen area for dramatically pathogenic conversational patterns, which systemic psychotherapy has described as disconfirmation\disqualification, tangential responses, etc. These are communicative maneuvers, which Laing (1961, 1965, 1969) has described brilliantly, that go in the direction of producing the message: "You do not exist." These conversational patterns are not necessarily an expression of psychopathological contexts and can be observed with a certain frequency in cultures that tend to prefer the middle position. Bateson (1949) describes some that he observed in Bali in the 1930s. For example, when Balinese mothers and their child became intimate, absorbed or excited in their interaction, the mothers would suddenly divert their attention. If the child responded to this behavior by becoming upset or crying, the mother would look at it with an air of indifference or amusement. Even if the child became aggressive, the mother did not react or respond, for example, by getting irritated. She would limit herself to fending off the attack. Moreover, in the Bali that Bateson studied there was no conversational pattern—which is common for us—in which the person talking receives special attention for a certain period from listeners, and therefore exerts a sort of one-directional influence on those he is talking to. Patterns of this type were discouraged even before they could occur because the listener would immediately look elsewhere. To expect somebody's continual attention was inconceivable for a Balinese. The Balinese whom Bateson met also told stories, but the person who began the story would stop after a while, expecting questions and comments, and the whole story would wander about and become strongly conversational.

To summarize: families or groups with broader histories that value the extremes and in which processes of externalization prevail—such as the Iatmul in the first half of the twentieth century, but also many other Western cultures—tend to encourage the differentiation of individuals or (to use a term from psychoanalysis) "individuation." Differentiation implies, by its very nature, developing certain qualities to the detriment of others. However, only when the processes of schismogenic polarization prevail in a conversational context is there a drastic reduction in the number of relevant semantic polarities, even though no family organizes its conversation around one single semantic dimension: as we have already stated, in every group with a history there are always several relevant semantic dimensions. Schismogenic processes, by reducing the semantic dimensions at play, and therefore the number of positions available, encourage the construction of identities focused on few maximized traits. In this context, we can reinterpret the term "character." As used in everyday language, it seems to indicate a person who, having grown up in schismogenic contexts, is defined by a limited number of characteristics.

Conversely, families and also cultures—for instance, the Balinese that Bateson observed and other Eastern cultures—which value the middle position and in which processes of centralization prevail, encourage the development of multidimensionality. As a result, the identity of individuals who place themselves in a middle position can become close to an ideal of harmony. When, however, implogenetic processes prevail there is an increase of messages of disconfirmation and self-disqualification that threaten the very reality of the subjects as conversational partners. There is, however, a certain intrinsic degree of withdrawal from interaction in the middle position and, as a result, individuals who place themselves in this position are less differentiated in comparison with those who place themselves at the extremes of the relevant polarities.

2.7 Constructing a New Conversational Position

How does a child become part of the shared plot of its family's semantic polarities? The conversational definition of this concept that I proposed in the previous paragraphs excludes the possibility that family semantic polarities are learned—consciously or unconsciously, in childhood or adulthood—in the same way that schemes, belief systems, or other mental constructs are learned. What children learn—obviously with the assistance of other members of the family—are ways of positioning themselves with family members into tri-polar semantic contexts.

But how do children "co-position" themselves with other family members? By establishing what the literature calls "bonds of attachment."[20] So far, nothing new. What I want to emphasize is that *the bonds of attachment are different according to the relevant semantic polarities in the particular family of which the child becomes a part.*

Let us consider a fairly ordinary episode in the life of a family group: A father comes home to find his infant child of a few months old crying alone in its cot. Contrary to what he expected, neither the babysitter nor his wife are at home. His wife returns fifteen minutes later. It was she who had let the babysitter leave earlier than usual. On her way home from the office there had been more traffic than usual and the baby had therefore been alone for half an hour. Different fathers might react in different ways to a situation like this, depending on the way they interpret the situation, on their own personality, on the type of relationship they have with their wife, on the cultural models of the family's social context, and so forth. But also those fathers who react, through their manifest behavior, in a very similar way have a different influence on a child, and on bonding processes, if such reactions are an expression of different family semantic polarities.

In one case, for example, a father might feel in his baby's cries a terror of being left alone in the face of a thousand dangers, and will immediately take it in his arms. While he seeks to give the child a sense of protection, reassuring her/him with gestures and words that he is back, that there is no longer anything to fear, at the same time he will be thinking about the dangers to which his child had been exposed. As soon as the baby has calmed down and the situation is back under control, he will begin worrying about his wife: What has happened to her? Is she ill? Has she had an accident? But just as his worries are beginning to increase, his wife returns home, explains what has happened and everyone relaxes. Another father, when faced with the same situation, will see in his baby's eyes the despair of feeling abandoned, and will hear in the baby's tears the distress of being left alone. This father will also pick the baby up and hold it in his arms, he too will comfort it, he will tell it that daddy will never leave it, he will always be there, and mummy will be back soon ... Once the infant has calmed down he will start to feel angry. Why has his wife left their baby alone? Does she really love the baby? And does she love him? At this point, the man might begin to feel lonely, and perhaps more or less distinct thoughts of abandonment might come to mind. But at this point the wife hurries in, full of concern; the husband's anger and worries are transformed into joy: Nothing has actually happened.

Why was the baby crying? Perhaps because it was alone; perhaps because it was hungry. It is more interesting to ask: What did the baby feel throughout this episode? If the baby was small it felt very little, but nevertheless it felt something. In the first case, it will certainly have felt its father's fear, his anxiety, and the change in the emotional climate as soon as the mother returned and the family group was back together. In the second case, it is presumable that the child would have felt, though perhaps not distinctly, its father's anger, and his joy when his wife returned. The emotions are gradually learned through empathy; one of the first manifestations of this phenomenon is the crying that resounds around neonatal wards: one baby cries and others immediately follow in response.

This episode, through these embryonic emotions, has contributed towards the father/child "co-positioning" and therefore towards creating a new conversational position. The "co-positioning" in both cases is different, according to the different meaning attributed to the episode by the adult. In the first case, there is a bond of attachment to the father in which the baby is regarded as fragile, vulnerable to danger, and the father is the protector. In the second case, the pattern of attachment involves an abandoned infant, left alone by its mother, and a father who consoles it, offering himself as a vicarious emotional partner.

Other meanings can be attributed to this episode. What I seek to emphasize is that the construction of a new relational position is the outcome of attachment processes that differ according to the semantic polarities present in the family. Attachment is not a purely behavioral phenomenon, even during the first few months of life, as Bowlby's attachment theory (1969, 1973, 1980) would seem to suggest. Our species cannot ignore meaning. Also, for that reason, it cannot favor a single model of attachment.

As is well known, the hypothesis of a universal model of attachment, implicitly advanced by Bowlby, has been demonstrated empirically. This began with Ainsworth's studies, through the identification of a series of behavioral patterns in the child, defined as "secure" attachment, correlated with certain kinds of behavior by the mother, and regarded as the *biological norm*. According to Ainsworth, "Securely attached babies have developed normally, i.e. along species-characteristics lines" (1979, p. 45). The other forms of empirically observed attachment were therefore considered as deviant patterns—they have been defined as "anxious/ambivalent," "avoidant" or "disoriented/disorganized" attachment patterns.

This theory is difficult to support, even from a biological point of view. Hinde (1982), following the findings of a research project by Grossmann and Grossmann (1981), which showed that the number of "securely" attached children was much lower in Germany than in the United States and England, pointed out that, because of profound differences between the human societies, natural selection must have favored the transmission of a flexible range of relational strategies, and *not* of a single model of attachment. Indeed, on the basis of a biological argument that ignores the problem of meaning, the suggestion that there exists a universal model of child attachment can hardly be supported. On the contrary,

> mothers and babies will be programmed not simply to form one sort of relationship but a range of possible relationships according to circumstances. So we must be concerned not with normal mothers and deviant mothers but with a *range* of styles and a capacity to select appropriately between them.
>
> (Hinde, 1982, p. 71)

The theory of a universal model of attachment proves to be misleading in the context of the more characteristic aspect of our species—meaning making.[21] Children establish bonds with members of the family, they "co-position" themselves with them according to a range of strategies that are consistent with the semantic polarities relevant in their family context.

Some of the countless episodes through which attachment bonds are established relate directly to the position of the child. For example, when a young girl holds her hand out to her mother, this gesture is ambiguous like most of the actions of young children. It is therefore open to a variety of semantic interpretations. One mother will say: "Look how sweet you are; do you want to stroke me?" Another will joke: "Well then, what do you want? Are you going to scratch your mummy because she won't pick you up? Look how pushy you are!" Yet another will turn round to look at the poster behind her saying: "How clever you are ... you already want to know what that big animal is called? Yes, that's a lion ... it has a mane and people call it the king of the forest," or she will turn to her husband and say: "Look how she's flirting ... she wants you ... she's already trying to seduce you."

All of these mothers are attributing a meaning to the behavior of their child by "co-positioning" themselves with her according to various patterns that reflect specific semantic dimensions. But they are also behaving as if their child had assumed a specific position within a particular semantic context.

Episodes that involve the position of the child less directly are equally significant. For example, let us consider a typical everyday episode between a mother and a child who, this time, is a rather older child attending nursery school. We might give this episode the title: "Why not invite one of your friends here tomorrow?" In this situation one mother will say: "Why not invite Francesco? He's so well behaved ..." Another might say: "What a good idea! Yes, let's invite Antonio: He's so talkative, straightforward, enthusiastic; I really like him." Yet another might say: "How about inviting Matteo? He's bright, he knows a lot of games and so much else ..."

All of these mothers try to guide, or simply comment upon the choice of a playmate for an afternoon game with their child. Even if they do not openly refer to their son's position in relation to his playmate, they still provide the semantic polarity within which the child will construct his own position in relation to his playmate and to the larger context of playmate–mother–other family members.

One aspect links these examples together. In all of them, it is always the adult who attributes meanings to events. *At a semantic level there is not the adult–child two-way influence that is instead present, from birth onwards, in the interactive exchanges.* In terms of behavior, the child "socializes" the adult no less than the adult socializes the child, in the sense that there exists an adult–child loop in which both partners, though they have different roles, are equally active.

On a semantic level, the situation is different. As we know, all adults, when interacting with small children, behave "as if" the children had intentions or aims that presumably they do not have, and treat children as fully-fledged conversational partners even though they are not. Adults over-interpret children's behavior, attributing a significance where there is none (Kaye, 1982). This phenomenon, well known to developmental psychologists, also occurs with household pets. Anyone who has a dog or cat ends up talking to it, and believes their animal understands much more than ethologists are prepared to accept. Every adult, however, favors certain semantic polarities and not others. In this way, adults provide children with what, to paraphrase an expression used by Bruner,[22] we can call a "semantic scaffolding" within which children will begin to "co-position" themselves with members of their family, thereby defining their own position. This process is therefore not two-directional, nor does the adult exercise a direct, linear, deterministic influence on the child.

Let us return to an example introduced earlier. The fact that a mother "co-positions" herself with her daughter, frequently interpreting the child's behavior as "aggressive," and responding to the child in a way consistent with this interpretation, does not mean that the daughter constructs her own position in these terms. Instead, it indicates that the semantic polarity of "aggressiveness/

gentleness" will be relevant for the child, together of course with other polarities. Her positioning in the group as "gentle," or alternatively as "aggressive," will depend instead upon the alliances and the more complex configuration of relations within the family. As the child grows up, she will contribute more actively to this configuration, which may change, and indeed will change, in directions that are hard to predict. In later chapters I will examine some changes of position within the critical semantic polarities characterizing the development of individuals with phobic, obsessive-compulsive, eating disorders, and depression. However, reversals of position within a semantic dimension are common and this phenomenon is a direct consequence of the polar organization of meaning. That is the reason why a hardened sinner can convert and become a religious ascetic, as is seen in the stories of so many saints, while a man ruled by pride can experience humiliation. In the words of Blake: "shame is pride's cloak."

These last observations bring us to the question of change, on which I focus in the next section by asking a question that I imagine must already have concerned readers who share my constructionist approach. Once an individual has "co-positioned" himself within the plot of his family's semantic polarities, are his possibilities to change limited to shift inside this plot? Does the introduction of meaning, (albeit within a polar dialectic that certainly assures each person a degree of liberty), compel us to reject the idea of an individual as an open system upon which the Palo Alto school established its position in the world of psychotherapy, offering a new approach that sweeps away the narrow vision of the "compulsion to repeat"? Does the idea of a shared plot of polarities enclose individuals in a cage, however large it might be and however many people it might contain? The introduction of meaning undoubtedly returns the individual to his/her history.

2.8 Changing Through Enigmatic Interactions

The questions I raised at the end of the previous section need to be answered. Certainly, being born into a particular family and into a culture, as well as the history of previous "co-positionings," restricts the possible positions with which each individual can "co-position" himself or herself with others. But it is precisely this restriction that gives substance to each individual. By accepting a conception of the "I" as a position in the conversation, I certainly do not mean to associate myself with those who regard "I" as no more than a "peg" onto which to hang the clothing of the infinite positions that it can assume. The positions that an individual can occupy are not infinite. The feeling of the I's precariousness and fragility—a characteristic of modernity and a result of social relations being seen as temporary and unstable—does not actually mean that the "I" is a "nothing," that it can move easily from one position to the other, as MacIntyre (1981) underlined and as clinical experience teaches us.

The concept of semantic polarities does not confine an individual within single semantics, as Guidano's post-rationalist cognitivist model would suggest (1987, 1991). It suggests that individuals have a plurality of semantic games into which to position themselves with others. Even in the most schismogenic contexts there will be a great number of relevant semantic polarities. As people gradually construct their positions within their family, they nevertheless learn that they have a series of conversational practices, and emotional and cognitive abilities that make it easy for them to "co-position" themselves with individuals with a repertory of compatible capacities insofar as they have grown up in contexts with similar semantic polarities. On the other hand, these same capacities will make it difficult for them to "co-position" themselves with others who have constructed themselves within different semantic polarities. The phenomenon is even more evident when individuals have developed in schismogenic contexts and therefore have "specialized" capacities.

Furthermore, the concept of semantic polarities is compatible with the explanations for change suggested by systemic psychotherapy and by other psychotherapeutic approaches. If anything, it introduces the idea that changes are generally restricted to a pre-established semantic scaffolding. The concept also allows for the possibility of people making changes that enable them to "co-position" themselves within new semantic games, within semantic polarities previously unknown. I believe that this type of change is stimulated by "enigmatic episodes" and by "enigmatic relations."

For anyone to enter into a significant relationship with a person who does not already belong to their particular environment, they must share one or more semantic games. "Defenseless" people who move into a new organizational environment, such as a company, school or college, will find themselves revealing quite spontaneously and simply what they are, forming alliances with other "helpless," "defenseless" colleagues, being protected by someone who is "warlike," or becoming the targets for attacks from a more experienced "veteran" who sees them as an easy target for their warlike temper. In much the same way, liars who join a new group will find themselves quite inadvertently "co-positioning" themselves with those who are naïve or gullible, or with people who are honest and can see through their deceptions. Each identifies the other even before they are aware of it: liars immediately catch the eye of someone who is innocent and ready to be duped, in the same way as honest people cannot fail to notice that moment of hesitation, that tiny contradiction that betrays a liar. Such behavior is hardly noticed, of course, by someone whose history has been constructed inside different semantic contexts.

A relationship between work colleagues, friends or lovers therefore always starts off on the basis of a semantic game that is familiar to both partners. Since, however, each has constructed their identity in contexts in which there was more than one semantic polarity, sooner or later the two will find themselves facing enigmatic episodes that put the future of the relationship into difficulty.

That is what happened to Franz and Sabina, two of the main characters in the four-sided love affair around which the plot of *The Unbearable Lightness of Being* by Milan Kundera (1984/1999) is arranged. Their relationship is marked from the very beginning by enigmatic episodes: Kundera calls them "words misunderstood" and develops a short glossary of them. Let us recall a few of them.

Sabina asked Franz at a certain point: "Why don't you sometimes use your strength on me?" Franz replied: "Because love means relinquishing strength." And Sabina realized two things: first, that Franz's words were noble and just; second, that with these words Franz disqualified himself in her eyes as a sexual partner.

Franz often told Sabina about his mother, perhaps with a sort of unconscious calculation. He imagined that Sabina would be attracted by his capacity for faithfulness and thus would have been won over by him. Franz did not know that Sabina was attracted by betrayal, and not by faithfulness.

When Sabina told him once about her walks in cemeteries, Franz shuddered with disgust. For him, cemeteries were "bone and stone dumps," but for her they provided the only nostalgic memory of her country of birth, Bohemia.

Franz admired Sabina's homeland. When she told him about herself and her Czech friends, Franz heard the words prison, persecution, tanks in the streets, emigration, posters and banned literature, and Sabina appeared even more beautiful because behind her he could glimpse the painful drama of her country. Hopes of revolution in that country had faded some time ago, but there remained what Franz liked most about revolution: life put at risk on a grand scale, courage, and the danger of death. Sabina felt no love for that drama. Prison, persecution, banned books, occupation and tanks were ugly words to her, devoid of the slightest romantic intrigue.

Both of them closed their eyes during the most intense moments of lovemaking. Were they finally on the same wavelength? At the instant in which he felt pleasure flood through his body, Franz stretched out and dissolved into the infinity of his own darkness, becoming himself infinite. Sabina also closed her eyes: she did not want to look at Franz's closed eyes and so she also closed hers. That sight was unpleasant to Sabina. For her, darkness did not mean infinity but rather the negation of sight, the refusal to see.

Here, with the help of a literary example, am I describing one of the many dramas of intersubjectivity (this time with the meaning given to it by individualistic modern philosophy)? Are Franz and Sabina unable to escape from their aprioristic shell, from the niche of their self?

It does not seem to me that Kundera recounts in these terms the abyss—to use his word—that separated Franz and Sabina. Certainly that is not how I read it.

Franz and Sabina come from different cultural environments. Franz is a university professor with a very respectable academic career in the quiet, sanitized city of Geneva. Being highly intelligent, he had already planned—since his student days in Paris—to spend his life within the walls of university libraries, lecture halls, and study rooms. Even then, however, the idea gave him a feeling of suffocation. Sabina is a Czechoslovak refugee artist. She studied at the Fine Arts Academy in Prague during the period when so-called socialist realism was still compulsory. At school they painted portraits of statesmen and party secretaries.

Even the family environments in which they were brought up give rise to very different meanings and positions. Franz loved his mother deeply, from his childhood until the day he accompanied her to the cemetery, and was still in love with her memory. This gave him the idea that faithfulness was the most important virtue. Faithfulness gives a unity to our lives that would otherwise shatter into thousands of fleeting impressions. Above all, impressed upon Franz's mind was something that had happened when his father left his mother. They had gone together into the city that day and, as they left the house, Franz had noticed his mother was wearing two different shoes. He was confused. He wanted to tell her but was afraid to hurt her feelings. And so he spent two hours walking around the city with her and for the whole time he could not tear his eyes away from her shoes. For the first time, at the age of twelve, he had understood the meaning of suffering. For Sabina, the word faithfulness reminded her of her father, a provincial puritan, who on Sundays painted vases of roses as a hobby and ridiculed contemporary art. He sent her first of all to church but then, out of fear, he made her join the Communist Youth movement. Once again out of fear, this time of pregnancy, he forbade her to go out for a year when he realized that his teenage daughter had fallen in love with a boy her age. Ever since she was a child, her father and the school teacher had taught her that betrayal is the worst thing you can do. To her, betrayal meant breaking ranks and setting off into the unknown. And Sabina could think of nothing better than setting off into the unknown. When she betrayed her father by going off on her own, life opened up before her as a long road of betrayals: each new betrayal attracted her like another victory. She would not stay in the ranks! She refused to remain with the same people and the same ideas! She could not stay still: the idea of her escape ever coming to an end was intolerable.

Even though their backgrounds were very different, Franz and Sabina did share at least one semantic game: "betrayal/faithfulness." It is on this dimension that the two of them began a relationship at opposing polar positions. And it is clear that if their "co-position" had been limited to this semantic game, the plot of the story would not have led them to learn new positions. This is what happens.

But how could Franz and Sabina have achieved a "co-positioning" that would induce them to try new positions? How could they have overcome the enigmatic episodes that I have described?

63

A number of post-Piagetian studies offer some suggestions. Doise, Mugny, Carugati, and Pèrez[23] have shown that change—important change that entails a transition from one stage of cognitive development to another—is triggered off by interactive situations that have some comparison with the enigmatic episodes we have examined.

Children who, prior to testing, showed that they still lacked certain crucial notions of concrete operational thinking—for example, the understanding of distance or quantity conservation—and who were therefore still at the stage of intuitive thought, acquired these notions in the course of interactions during which they were involved with a partner in finding a shared solution. Not all social encounters were effective in terms of learning. Only certain interactions, similar to our enigmatic episodes, were capable of bringing about improvements. These were interactions where what Doise et al. call "socio-cognitive conflict" was created between the two interacting subjects. For this to occur, two conditions were necessary:

1) those involved in the interaction had to produce diverging responses to a shared task. The divergence could be caused by contingent factors (for example, the differing physical positions in which the children were placed during the experiment) or by a differing level of competence between partners in constructing the notion upon which the experiment focused;

2) those involved had to be induced—either by virtue of the experiment itself which encouraged them to reach an answer, or simply for the pleasure of sharing—to find an agreement that was substantial and not just superficial.

In short, for the interactive situation to generate cognitive advances, it was necessary to create a situation of conflict between the partners and, at the same time, a desire to overcome the difference.[24]

Enigmatic episodes, in order to become an opportunity for learning new semantic games, must also be accompanied by emotions that induce those involved to continue their interaction. It is these emotions—which do not derive from the enigmatic episodes but from other episodes—that allow the partners to overcome the impasse: both partners, in attempting to continue the interaction, experience emotional states that allow them to "co-position" themselves on the basis of a semantic polarity that was previously unknown to both of them, or, as more often happens, one of the partners develops ways of feeling that allow him/her to "co-position" themselves with the other. When this happens, one or both of the partners learn a new position in the conversation. Experiments in socio-cognitive conflict also involve emotional aspects such as *the joy of sharing*, hitherto little focused on also among social emotions studies. Emotional involvement is certainly crucial to the change in which we are interested. The divergences we observe in enigmatic episodes, which are important for constructing and breaking bonds and for the identity of each conversational partner, are mainly emotional.

Let us return to Kundera's novel. Are Franz and Sabina unable to understand each other's point of view? Not exactly: "Although they had a clear understanding of the logical meaning of the words they exchanged, they failed to hear the semantic susurrus of the river flowing through them" (Kundera, 1984/1999, p. 88).

To put it in less literary terms, as their relationship gradually evolved, Franz and Sabina were faced with episodes that produced in them incompatible emotions. Enigmatic episodes are, in fact, situations in which the partners create emotions that do not enable them to "co-position" themselves. In order to overcome these diverging emotions, they must be accompanied by other emotions generated by the relationship.

The relationship between Franz and Sabina had been finished for a long time. But there was an emotion connected to a memory—nostalgia—that enabled Sabina to overcome the abyss that had opened up between her and Franz from one of the many enigmatic episodes that had marked their relationship.

> Suddenly she missed Franz terribly. When she told him about her cemetery walks, he gave a shiver of disgust and called cemeteries bone and stone dumps. A gulf of misunderstanding had immediately opened between them. Not until that day at the Montparnasse Cemetery did she see what he meant. She was sorry to have been so impatient with him. Perhaps if they had stayed together longer, Sabina and Franz would have begun to understand the words they used.
>
> (*ibid.*, p. 124)

As this passage suggests, the relationship with Franz has nevertheless introduced changes in Sabina's identity. Relationships studded with numerous enigmatic episodes are generally brief. A substantial number of experimental studies tell us that people examine the facts in order to confirm their hypotheses and not to falsify them.[25] Similarly, we prefer to "co-position" ourselves with people and in interactive situations that do not place our identity in doubt. "Co-positioning" ourselves within semantic dimensions that are unknown to us involves significantly modifying our position and therefore our identity.

Since change is not necessarily a value, there are probably perfectly good reasons for our preference for relationships offering "confirmation." Some relationships, however, are necessarily enigmatic. This is the case with the therapeutic relationship which, by definition, seeks to change the patient. If a therapeutic relationship fails to provoke enigmatic episodes then it produces dependency or, at best, adjustments within a plot of semantic polarities that remains the same. But precisely because it must provoke enigmatic episodes, this relationship must occur in a context that is emotionally significant for the patient. All therapeutic settings—if they are to produce change—produce intense emotions. The systemic therapeutic approach has focused less than other approaches upon the emotional dynamic between patient and therapist, simply because the prevailing practice for this model is provided by family therapy. This form of treatment, which involves the patient together with the other most important people in the patient's life, arouses such powerful emotions between members of the family as to reduce the centrality of the emotional exchange with the therapist. When patients, during the session, find themselves in front of their mother, father, partner or children, their emotions towards the therapist stay in the background.

2.9 Difficult Positionings

A Dilemma Between Self and Relationships

As I suggested in the introduction, each of the four psychopathological organizations examined in the following chapters is characterized by the prevalence of certain semantic polarities. I have called the meanings that typify each organization the "semantics of freedom," of "goodness," of "power," and of "belonging" because the polarities typifying each organization, though presenting appreciably different meanings, are *fuelled by the same emotions. They therefore make up a single configuration of meanings which the processes of polarization render predominant.* All members of the family are involved in the predominant semantics but generally speaking only one of them shows a psychopathological organization. What seems to characterize those who develop a psychopathology is the *position they assume within this semantic.* In order to understand difficult positionings in which those who develop phobic, obsessive, depressive or eating disorders find themselves—positionings that will be described in detail in the chapter dedicated to each psychopathology—we must examine the process of construction of meanings, which is hierarchical, operating on several levels.

Bateson, as we know, was the first to introduce the idea that communication—and most interestingly for us, the construction of meaning—is organized hierarchically. In 1952, while he was watching monkeys playing in the zoo at San Francisco, he noticed that they exhibited behavior more or less identical to what they would use during a fight. And yet it was evident, both to the human observer as well as to the monkeys taking part, that this wasn't a fight. He concluded that biting and other behavior in the sequence that suggested an attack (content level) must be accompanied by other messages—of a higher hierarchic level—which signaled the way in which they should be interpreted: "This is a game" (relational level). Since communication is not limited to representing social reality but creates it, there must be several hierarchical levels. Cronen, Johnson, and Lannamann (1982), and later the *Positioning Theory* (Harré & Van Langenhove, 1999), as well as many other constructionist authors, suggest that, in addition to the content level of every message and the relational level of the meta-message, which indicates what meaning must be attributed to a message, there are *the episode, the relationship between the communicants, the self or personal life script* and the *cultural patterns.*[26] All of these levels are constructed during the course of the conversation and are organized hierarchically. In other words, the meaning of a message is defined not only from the meta-message, but also from the episode of which it is part and from the relationship between the partners, as well as the respective selves and the cultural models. And each message, of course, contributes towards creating all these levels.

The messages are normally contextualized from higher levels which represent the "contextual force," in the terminology of Cronen, Johnson, and Lannamann (1982). So long as this happens, the nature of the episode, the type of relationship between the partners, the concept of self of the individuals involved, and the cultural models are confirmed by the message. But it can, and does, happen that the "implicative force" (which pushes upwards from below) prevails. In this case a single message reverses the nature of the episode since it becomes the context within which meaning is given to the episode. An episode can, in turn, become the context in which to interpret a relationship, and a relationship can function as a context for the self. One word, one glance, can bring about an "exchange of confidences between friends" in a "moment of sexual intimacy." And the episode can modify the relationship—from being friends, the two can become lovers. If, moreover, the two protagonists are a black and an Afrikaner in a South Africa that has just emerged from apartheid, their love affair will help to change cultural patterns in their country.

Generally speaking, the reversals that see the implicative force become a contextual force relate to levels of meaning that involve message-metamessage-episode. But there are plenty of episodes that can change the nature of a relationship, the selfhoods of the protagonists and even cultural patterns. Literature offers us numerous examples. Think of the climactic moment in Ibsen's *A Doll's House* (1879/1992), which caused such a scandal and stirred passionate debate at a time when the first feminist campaigns were hitting Europe. Torvald Helmer discovers the trouble into which Nora—moved by the noblest intentions but alas inexperienced in the world—has put both of them. This, as the reader will recall, was the signature that Nora forges to spare her dying father's pain, and to obtain a loan that she uses to organize a journey to restore her husband to health. Nora does all she can to prevent her secret being discovered, hiding her anxieties and her forced economies with a crescendo of chatter and frivolity, designed to confirm in Helmer's eyes the carefree life of a "doll-wife." But she was sure her Torvald would have assumed all responsibility if the whole business were ever discovered. Her fears about revealing the trap into which she had fallen were of quite another kind. When her friend advises her to confess everything to her husband, she says:

How painful and humiliating it would be for Torvald with his manly independence, to know that he owed me anything! It would upset our mutual relations altogether; our beautiful happy home would no longer be what it is now.

(Act I)

In effect, the discovery of the "secret" changes the couple's relationship irreversibly, but in an unexpected way. Helmer becomes angry, shouts, throws insults: his little squirrel, his little lark, becomes a miserable creature, a liar, a hypocrite, even a criminal. What upsets Helmer is not the injury to his male pride. It is the effect it might have upon his reputation and his career that makes him furious. His aim is to prevent a scandal at whatever price.

This behavior which, in Nora's eyes, seems cheap and squalid, and the very ease with which Helmer passes to joy and to forgiveness on discovering that the danger is over, become the context through which Nora reinterprets all the important relationships in her life. Firstly her relationship with Torvald and with her father:

You have never loved me. You have only thought it pleasant to be in love with me. [...]

When I was at home with Papa he told me his opinion about everything, and so I had the same opinions; and if I differed from him I concealed the fact, because he would not have liked it [...] And when I came to live with you. [...] You arranged everything according to your own taste, and so I got the same tastes as you—or else I pretended to. I am really not quite sure which—I think sometimes the one and sometimes the other. When I look back on it, it seems to me as if I have been here like a poor woman—just from hand to mouth. I have existed merely to perform tricks for you, Torvald. But you would have it so. You and Papa have committed a great sin against me. It is your fault that I have made nothing of my life.

(Act III)

Even her relationship with her children is contextualized by the episode in question:

The children have been my dolls. I thought it great fun when you played with me, just as they thought it great fun when I played with them.

(Act III)

The episode does not end at the relationships level, but goes as far as involving Nora's self and the cultural patterns of the society of which she is part: Nora decides that she must first of all become a person, "free and alone." When her husband reminds her of her duties as wife and mother, she replies:

> I have (…) duties to myself (…) I believe that before all else I am a reasonable human being, just as you are—or, at all events, that I must try and become one. I know quite well, Torvald, that most people would think you right, and that views of that kind are to be found in books; but I can no longer content myself with what most people say, or with what is found in books. I must think over things for myself and get to understand them.
>
> (Act III)

And when Helmer justifies himself protesting: "but no man would sacrifice his honor for the one he loves," Nora answers: "it is a thing hundreds of thousands of women have done," which drew applause from women in audiences half way across Europe. The implicative force of the critical episode, developed quietly over months of exhausting economies, subterfuges, lies, and strained cheerfulness, magnified by Helmer's unexpected reaction, has become the context in which Nora elaborates her new positioning marked by a feminist awareness.

I have lingered over the central episode of Ibsen's Nora because it has the power of reversing the protagonist's positioning in relation to all levels of social construction. In fact it is preceded by many episodes that have loaded the implicative force with new meanings until it become contextual. Nora's decision to borrow money from a usurer to save her husband without telling him about it, from which the drama develops, suggests a Nora who is strong, self-assured, which has little to do with her positioning as a "doll-wife." There was also a moment, though Ibsen only hints at it, where Nora had oscillated between conflicting meanings. It is intuitively clear that when the implicative force is about to become a contextual force the reflexivity may, at times, be greatest: the participants oscillate as to the interpretation to give to the episode or the nature of their relationship.

The difficult positionings which, as we shall see in the next chapters, characterize the position of subjects who develop a phobic, obsessive, depressive or eating disorder, relate to two levels of the social construction of reality: the self and relationships. Between these levels the reflexivity can reach a maximum and the individual oscillates between two irreconcilable perspectives.

Strange Reflexive Loops and Implicative Dilemmas

Distancing themselves from Bateson and his double bind theory (Bateson et al., 1956), Cronen et al. (1982) take the view that reflexivity as such is not an element that upsets the communication process. On the contrary, it is one of its normal and essential components. It is worth recalling that:

Reflexivity exists whenever two elements in a hierarchy are so organized that each is simultaneously the context for and within the context of the other. We can identify a reflexive loop in a system when by moving up or down in a hierarchical system we find ourselves back where we started.

(ibid., p. 94)

Reflexive loops are an intrinsic part of social interaction according to Cronen, Johnson, and Lannamann. If individuals, pursuing a unity of meaning from top to bottom and vice versa, never found themselves back at the point where they began, then no change would ever be possible. The experience of reflexivity—which forms the basis of double bind messages[27] that Bateson considered pathogenic—is, according to these authors, a sine qua non for change, growth and development.

Let us return to Bateson's analysis of monkeys at play, an analysis that led him to suggest the existence of a *contextual force*—"this is a game" (relational level)—which modifies the meaning of the bite (content level). In order for the episode to turn into a fight, as in fact it frequently does, there has to be a certain degree of reflexivity between the contextual force of the bite ("this is a game") and what the authors call an *implicative force* ("it's an attack"). Normally during the game the contextual force prevails. As a result the aggressive behavior exchanged between the monkeys is redefined as inoffensive behavior. Even though the contextual force is uppermost, during the game there is also a weaker implicative force operating from the bottom upwards, which defines the aggressive behavior as an attack (Figure 2.3). And in the process, of varying rapidity, that leads the monkeys to pass from play to fighting, the implicative force will become increasingly powerful until it is transformed into a contextual force. During this process there will be a moment—which may last just a fraction of a second—in which the reflexivity will be total: the two

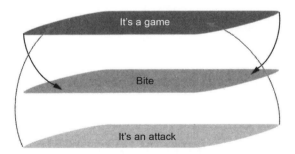

Figure 2.3 Contextual force and implicative force during an episode of monkeys at play

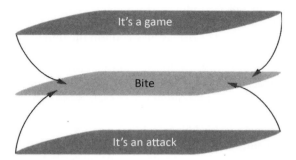

Figure 2.4 Reflexive loop during an episode of play: contextual force and implicative
force become equal

forces—implicative and contextual—will have the same power. The ambiguity between the monkeys at this moment will be at its greatest and, in giving meaning to the events, they will oscillate between two irreconcilable views: "It's a game" "it's an attack" (Figure 2.4).

The fact that reflexivity is a normal attribute of communication processes does not mean that it has nothing to do with the pathology. In addition to *"charmed loops,"* which are not problematic, there are, according to Cronen et al. (1982), *"strange loops"* which create difficulty and, at worst, psychological pathologies. These are the kind of loops in which people with a phobic, obsessive or depressive organization or with eating disorders, eventually find themselves entangled.

The concepts of *transitivity* and *intransitivity* make it possible to distinguish the two types of loop:

> Two levels of social meaning have a transitive relationship when each can be the context for the other without changing the meaning of either. Two levels of meaning have an intransitive relationship if each *cannot* be the context for the other without changing meaning of either.
>
> *(ibid.,* p. 109)

The transitivity or intransitivity between levels of meaning is defined in the subject's experience by *meta-rules,* which are the product of cultural and family patterns and of the particular position that each individual occupies in his or her personal contexts of belonging. These vary between cultures and between individuals in one and the same cultural context. *No message therefore exists to which the characteristics of a strange reflexive loop can be universally attributed.* For example, one-step reflexive loops such as "This statement is false" are problematic for a Westerner, who has always regarded language as an instrument for organizing phenomena and obtaining control over them. But for many Eastern cultures who regard language as an obstacle to enlightenment, such loops are charmed insofar as they confirm the unreliability of language.

To clarify the nature of "strange" loops I will use two examples, the first of which is take from Cronen, Johnson, and Lannamann (1982).[28] It concerns the stage at which two young people, Jane and Bob, are developing a relationship. When the couple were interviewed their relationship was already well-established but, despite this, Bob had difficulty in describing the episode and said he felt deeply troubled by it.

It was their third date. Their relationship, according to Bob, was developing fast and was beginning to seem like an "intimate and serious relationship." In this situation, Bob expressed his own feelings and invited Jane also to make a verbal commitment to which she responded with a polite joke. Bob was surprised and confused. If he started from the assumption that his relationship with Jane was serious and intimate, then he could interpret the joke as meaning "we are already so sure of each other we can joke about it." But could he be sure, on their third date, that Jane too had already defined the nature of their relationship as serious and intimate? Bob wasn't at all sure and thought: "If the joke is an attempt to cool down the atmosphere and distance herself, then it means this is just a casual flirt."

Why is this reflexive loop problematic for Bob? At the "relational" level, the alternatives for Bob were: this might be a "serious and intimate relationship" or just a "casual flirt." But he was not sure whether to treat the episode as an attempt by Jane to cool the atmosphere and distance herself or as confirmation ("we are already so sure of each other we can joke about it").

To understand the strange reflexive loop in which Bob found himself, it should be remembered that a new relationship does not already exist before the individual episodes but has to gradually emerge from them and function *then* as a context in which to give meaning to past and future interactions. Bob did not know whether what he was experiencing had to be treated as the context for his relationship with Jane or vice versa. If Bob was sure that their relationship was developing as "serious and intimate" then the episode would not have caused him problems because he would have interpreted it in the context of this definition. But he did not have that certainty.

Moreover, at the moment when the episode occurred, Bob had presumably *felt* that the relationship he was constructing with Jane was serious and intimate and for this reason expressed his own feelings, and had also felt *emotionally* that the girl's reply was a distancing tactic. At the level of "story experienced," the alternative was therefore between "this is a serious and intimate relationship" and "this is taking distance." And for Bob, this alternative constituted a strange reflexive loop: the two levels of meaning could not exchange their respective hierarchical positions without the meaning of one of them being changed (Figure 2.5). Bob's culture and his experience had imposed a

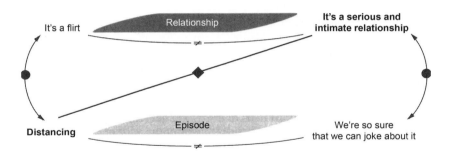

It's a flirt

Relationship

It's a serious and
intimate relationship

≠

Distancing

Episode

We're so sure
that we can joke about it

≠

≠ Exclusive disjunction
◆ Strange reflexive loop
● Charmed reflexive loop

Figure 2.5 The strange reflexive loop that involves mainly the "episode" and "relationship" levels. The significant emotional alternatives ("stories experienced") are in bold

meta-rule by which there is intransitivity between an episode of distancing and a serious and intimate relationship.

But would anyone finding themselves in Bob's position have experienced a strange reflexive loop? Many, yes, but not everyone. Even restricting attention to Western culture, for many people the reflexive loop could have been charmed and not problematic. Our culture allows for a serious and intimate relationship to develop through the alternation of episodes of confirmation and distancing. A relationship that proceeds in this way is not a model example, but nor is it anomalous. Many people with a phobic organization, as we will see in Chapter 3, proceed this way in forming relationships—their partners, who have to deal with episodes like those experienced by Bob, do not necessarily end up entangled in strange reflexive loops. If Bob had been able to think that a serious and intimate relationship can also develop through phases of distancing, then he would have had no difficulty in interpreting Jane's reply to his declaration. Jane's joke would have seemed an attempt to temporarily diminish the intensity of the emotional climate within a serious and intimate relationship that was developing.

Let us take an example from literature that brings into play all the levels of context mentioned. The episode actually took place, at least as a story that became the talk of the Berlin salons for a whole season. Theodor Fontane used it as the inspiration for his masterpiece *Effi Briest* (Fontane, 1895/1967), which Thomas Mann judged to be one of the six finest novels in German literature.

"Where did the letters come from?," Instetten asked the maid. Untying the red tape around them, Geert Instetten (Baron von Instetten) learns about the adultery by his wife, Effi, with Major Crampas. The affair had taken place six years before, or earlier still, when the couple were living at Kessen.

We are in imperial Berlin during the second half of the nineteenth century. The discovery, as we shall see, produced in Instetten a full-blown strange reflexive loop: for several hours the Prussian officer finds himself floundering between oscillating and mutually exclusive perspectives. By calling on Privy Councilor von Wullersdorf, Instetten came out of the loop at the cost of irreversibly changing his life and that of the other main characters in the story.

Even today the discovery of an adultery can bring a relationship to an end but, as we shall see, an event of this kind, in our society, cannot produce a strange reflexive loop such as that experienced by Instetten. Let us examine it, starting from Instetten's answer to the Privy Councilor's question:

> "Do you really have to do it? Do you feel so injured, so insulted, so enraged that one of you must disappear, he or you? Is that how it is? [...]"

> "No, that's not how it is [...] It's just that I'm infinitely unhappy. I'm humiliated, I've been shamefully deceived and yet in spite of that I have no feeling of hatred at all, or even a thirst for vengeance. And if I ask myself why not, then the first reason that comes to me is merely—the lapse of time. People always talk about an unforgivable sin and in God's eyes this is wrong, but not in man's eyes. I should never have believed that time, purely as time, could have such an effect. And then the second thing is that I love my wife, yes, strange to say, I still love her and however frightful all these things appear to me, yet I'm so much under her spell, she's so lovable and so gay, she has such a special charm all of her own, that, in spite of myself, I feel tempted, in my heart of hearts, to forgive her."

> (*ibid.*, p. 214)

Despite what he would have expected, Instetten doesn't feel any sense of hatred or vengeance. His unhappiness, the injury for the deceit he has suffered, seems to be on a level that is more explicit than implicit, more the "story told" than the "story experienced." There is no intransitivity between the adultery and his relationship with Effi. Episode and relationship form a "charmed" reflexive loop. Instetten feels he loves his wife. A few hours after discovering the adultery he talks about her fascination and her particular charm; her adultery has not deprived Effi, in her husband's eyes, of the qualities that had endeared her to him. "Deep down in my heart, despite all my thoughts," says Instetten, I feel an urge to forgive.

Why then does he end up in what he himself describes as a blind alley? Why does he leave that note for Wullersdorf, knowing that it will thereby preclude him from the possibility of forgiving, as the transitivity of the loop would seem to suggest?

> It's now ten o'clock. Six hours ago, I'll grant you this in advance, the cards were still in my hand and I could have done one thing or another, there was still a way out. But not any longer, I'm in an impasse. I've only myself to blame; if you like, I should have been more guarded and shown more self control, have kept everything to myself and fought it all out in my own mind (...) I went to your place and wrote you a note and by doing that the game passed out of my hands. From that moment onwards, there was someone else who knew something of my misfortune and what is more important, of the stain of my honor; and as soon as we had exchanged our first words, there was someone else who knew all about it. And because there is such a person, I can't go back.
>
> (*ibid.*, p. 215)

Instetten describes Wullersdorf's involvement almost like an *acting out*, dictated by an unendurable sense of confusion. The drama takes place earlier. It is in the hours leading up to the delivery of the note to Wullersdorf that Instetten experiences an agonizing dilemma (Figure 2.6).

> To forgive, let things continue, allow the adultery to be forgotten about, as his feelings towards Effi suggest, means despising himself; to end the marriage and fight a duel with Major Crampas means destroying his own life, going contrary to his own feelings.

Fontane seems to suggest that Instetten's anxiety is derived from his own emotions, from that absence of hatred or thirst for revenge, which casts doubt upon his sense of belonging to his world. Not conforming to the laws of his own social world, for Instetten, means putting in doubt the unity of his own self; it is the same as no longer having a fixed point of view from which to judge events. Until he decides to leave the note for Privy Councilor von Wullersdorf, Instetten feels a rift between his "social self" and his "individual self" so that the one cannot contextualize the other; he oscillates between two alternatives that are equally worrying because they undermine the unity of the self. If the relationship with Effi contextualizes his self, he will be urged to forgive, he will follow his most intimate feelings ("I love my wife"), but he will destroy his own self-image, which is inextricably linked to belonging to his social world. Later he will say to von Wullersdorf:

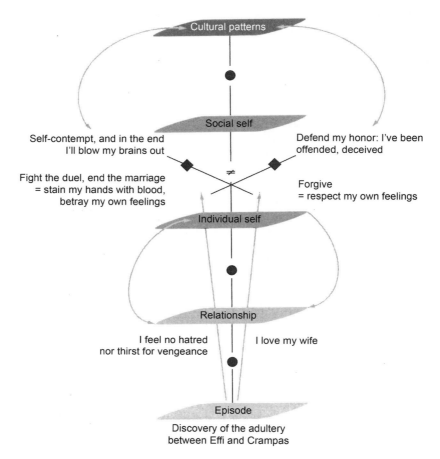

Figure 2.6 The strange reflexive loop involving the higher meaning levels in which the main character in *Effi Briest*—Teodor Fontane's masterpiece—was entangled

With people living all together, something has evolved that now exists and we've become accustomed to judge everything, ourselves and others, according to its rules. And it's no good transgressing them, society will *despise* us and finally we will despise ourselves and not be able to bear it and blow our brains out.

(*ibid.*)

Instead, selfhood is contextualized by social patterns, Instetten has to defend his honor, he has to fight Crampas and bring an end to his relationship with

Effi; but this choice means going against his own feelings, staining his hands with another man's blood.

During the terrible hours when the maid and the daughter hear him pacing up and down, Instetten, trapped between two continually shifting alternatives, feels he no longer has a point of view from which to judge events. The note to Wullersdorf marks his emergence from this state of indecision. Instetten, through this action, perceived as an impulsive, uncontrolled act,[29] operates a forced hierarchization between "social self" and "individual self." Later he will say to Wullersdorf:

> I've turned this thing over and over again in my mind. We're not isolated persons, we belong to a whole society and we have constantly to consider that society, we are completely dependent on it. If it were possible to live in isolation, then I could let it pass (…) But with people living all together, something has evolved that now exists and we've become accustomed to judge everything, ourselves and others, according to its rules. And it's no good transgressing them (…) So once again, there's no hatred or anything of that sort and I don't want to have blood on my hands merely for the sake of the happiness I've been deprived of, but that *something* which forms society—call it a tyrant if you like—is not concerned with charm or love, or even with how long ago a thing took place. I've no choice, I must do it.
>
> *(ibid.)*

That "I must do it" indicates the distance from the modern state of things. Even today, partners can bring an end to even a long-term relationship because of adultery, but they cannot find themselves in a strange reflexive loop similar to that experienced by Instetten. If their feelings towards their partner have not changed as a result of the adultery then they cannot feel that the unity of their own selfhood is under threat: their social world is not in danger of collapsing once they realize that they feel neither hatred, nor a thirst for vengeance, and that they still love their partner. For present-day cultural patterns, the relation between adultery and marriage is transitive. That "I must do it" also prefigures a change in cultural patterns. Instetten is a Prussian officer, and being a Prussian officer in nineteenth-century imperial Germany means having a certain status, in the same way as being a public school headmaster or an explorer in Victorian England. In these figures, role and personality are combined much more than generally happens. Yet despite being a figure, Instetten feels an inner rift during the hours in which the reflexive loop lasts: his self splits into a "social self" and an "individual self." He no longer has a narrative plot that allows him to give unity to his inner life script.

Must we therefore conclude—in spite of what constructionism suggests— that Instetten finds himself facing the eternal conflict between individual and society, between individual ahistorical needs that are always identical with his own, and social rules? Not at all. The quandary experienced by Instetten is the result of a particular social situation in which cultural patterns are changing. When this occurs, people feel social rules to be a weight, a burden, and experience an inner rift between what they feel to be personal needs and what society requires of them. I have given the name "individual self" to the implicative force that pushes from below and fuels those emotions in Instetten that would urge him to forget about the adultery, because the protagonist experiences this force in these terms. In reality, this self is not individual (in the ahistorical sense); it originates from other social practices, carriers of needs that will be accepted in the future as part of cultural patterns. A hundred years earlier Instetten would have felt hatred, bitterness, and thirst for revenge. And only thirty or forty years later he would have let it pass without such terrible heartbreak. That "I must do it" shows that Instetten and his social world are at a half-way point: the meta-rule which makes an act of adultery in the couple's relationship intransitive is still valid, but it is placed in doubt. Instetten, in fact, talks about a "tyrannical" society; he describes killing Crampas as "staining his hands with blood." Even though the values of imperial German society prevail, they are no longer capable of *fully* contextualizing his selfhood.

The two examples I have given involve different levels. In the case of Jane and Bob the strange loop concerns principally the episode/relational level, whereas in the case of Instetten the reflexivity involves higher levels of meaning. Cronen et al.(1982) suggest that the degree of harm produced by the unresolved strange reflexive loops is greater when the levels of meaning involved are higher. In these examples the reflexivity is overcome within a relatively short space of time. But if it persists and begins to involve the self, then the individual—as well as being placed in a state of indecision—is no longer able to establish a firm point of reference from which to give meaning to events. This is what I suggest happened to Instetten, even if only for a few hours.

Instetten's difficult positioning can be interpreted, not only as a strange loop. If we limit our attention to the protagonist's subjectivity, it can be considered similar to one of the implicative dilemmas described by Feixas and his colleagues (Feixas & Saúl, 2004; Feixas et al., 2009), a consequence of which is to paralyze the action. Both poles of the construct "forgive, forget the adultery/vengeance, fight Major Crampas" have negative implications because they involve Instetten in defining his self within poles of other conflicting constructs, and therefore (to use the concepts developed by Feixas) far away from the "ideal self." To "forgive" in fact implies "self-contempt," but "vengeance" means "staining his hands with blood" and therefore committing a real crime, not just violating his own feelings ("deep in my heart I feel an urge to forgive").

The position of subjects with a phobic, obsessive-compulsive, anorexic-bulimic or depressive organization within the dominant semantics also assume the form of an implicative dilemma or of a strange recursive loop which involves the levels of selfhood and the relationship, as it did for Instetten. This, at least, is the hypothesis I will be putting forward in the following chapters. *Two essential requirements for the human being—to have rewarding relationships and maintain an acceptable self-esteem—become mutually exclusive precisely in relation to the central meanings for the conversational context of which the subject is part.* This dilemma regards all four organizations, even if, in each, it assumes specific characteristics, as we shall see.

Recursive loops or implicative dilemmas are not the only conditions that can make the positionings of individuals within the predominant semantics problematical. For example, all semantic polarities make positions available in the negatively considered extreme. A position in the positive pole does not assure a problem-free future for the individual. "Active" people, for example, may never be able to relax or may find themselves in the unpleasant situation of having to complete tasks which others—the "passives" in the family—should have carried out. Those who are "generous" may become easy prey to "selfish" people who exploit their capacity to give. Those who are "strong" may feel weighed down by too many "weaklings" who rely on them. Those positioned in the negative extreme may at times reap advantages from their positioning. Thanks to their selfishness, some may have created or conserved the wealth and honors they enjoy, in the same way as others by virtue of their weakness may have obtained help and favors they would never otherwise have received. Nevertheless, in families where the positive pole is valued, it is a disadvantage to be considered "passive" rather than "active," "selfish" rather than "generous," "weak" rather than "strong": such people receive a definition of self that undermines their self-esteem. "Selfish" people can proudly counter "generous" people's capacity to give by boasting their own skill in looking after their own interests (sometimes to the advantage of the family as well as themselves). But if the generosity polarity is valued in a family, they have to acknowledge that the latter have a moral superiority.

To be positioned in the negatively valued pole, though a source of suffering, is not a pre-requisite for all psychopathological conditions. Of the patients whom we are concerned with here, only the depressives seem to have a history of exclusion and rejection in a context where belonging is particularly valued. Anorexic patients or bulimic patients of ideal weight are positioned during the period prior to the onset of symptoms in the winning end of the critical semantic polarity and remain there, though ambiguously, even during the course of their "illness." Obsessives, however, are in a median position and phobics, prior to the development of the pathology, are often positioned in the "freedom, independence" pole—a positively valued position in their context—into which they are generally moved during adolescence. It is the illness, if anything, that moves them into a humiliating position of dependence. In short, receiving a negative definition of self does not seem to be a condition that necessarily favors the development of a psychopathology. The onset of symptoms, at least for the psychopathological organizations we examine here, seems connected not so much to traumatic experiences as to a positioning that threatens to deprive subjects of the narrative structure within which they can position themselves, as we shall see in the following chapters. The problem—at least in the period before entering the pathology—is not that certain stories are forbidden while others are permitted, but that the very possibility of co-positioning themselves within a narrative structure is precluded. It is the onset of the disease that gives back a positioning to the individual, but at the price of becoming a patient.

Part II

SEMANTICS AND PSYCHOPATHOLOGIES

3

SEMANTICS OF FREEDOM AND PHOBIC DISORDERS

3.1 A Conversation Dominated by the Semantics of Freedom

Like the Brangwen sisters in the opening pages of D.H. Lawrence's *Women in Love* (1920/1996), phobic people feel themselves "confronted by a void, a terrifying chasm." They are constantly dogged by a feeling of alarm, similar to that of the Brangwen sisters when faced with the prospect of change in their lives through unforeseeable events. This is why it is so important for them to have points of reference: a marriage, a parent, a work routine, social conventions. Even the newsagent or barman they see each morning can be an anchorage. But though points of reference provide reassurance, they are seen as barriers, and people with a phobic personality would like to leap beyond these limits, exactly like Gudrun and Ursula Brangwen, to escape from an inner space that is regarded as limiting.

Fear in the face of a world construed as dangerous and, at the same time, the urge to be rid of protective anchors and refuges, has a history behind it. As I will show, it is the result of a particular positioning in a family conversation ruled by a homogeneous group of polarities that I call the "semantics of freedom."

Its main polarities are "freedom—dependence" and "exploration—attachment." Individual selves, the ways in which relationships are constructed, and the values in which members of these families believe, become intertwined with meanings created by these two polarities and by *fear/courage*, the emotions that fuel these polarities (Figure 3.1). As a result of dramatic events that have actually happened in the family history, or for reasons that are less clear, the outside world is seen as threatening. The very expression of emotions is seen as a source of danger. Precisely because reality arouses fear, family members are perceived as sources of protection and reassurance. They are nevertheless free precisely because they are able to face a dangerous world alone, without the guidance, protection and help of others. It has to be emphasized that freedom and independence are understood in this respect as freedom and independence *from* relationships and *from* their restraints.

By virtue of the relevance of these semantics, the conversation in these families is organized preferably around episodes where fear, courage, the need for protection and the desire for exploration and independence play a central role. As a result of these conversational processes, members of these families will feel, or be defined as, fearful or cautious or, alternatively, courageous, even reckless. They will find people who are prepared to protect them or will meet up with people who are unable to survive by themselves, who need their support. They will marry people who are fragile or dependent, but also individuals who are free and sometimes unwilling to make commitments. They will suffer for their dependence. They will try in every way to gain their independence. In other cases they will be proud of their independence and freedom, which they will defend more than everything else. Admiration, contempt, conflict, alliances, love, and hatred will be played out around issues of freedom/dependence.

The more that these polarities dominate the conversation, the more probable it is that there will be processes that Bateson (1936/1958) described as schismogenetic, with the consequent polarization of identities within the family. In the same family we will therefore have globetrotters as well as people who have never moved away from the district where they were born. And there will be those—like agoraphobic patients—who are so dependent and in need of protection that they will require someone to accompany them in dealing with the most ordinary situations in daily life, and those who, on the other hand, will be so independent as to seem self-sufficient.

In the families of all phobic patients I have encountered in my clinical practice, there are those who express independence in the most extreme manner, even if the nature of such independence varies from family to family, depending on the inevitable presence in the family of other polarities apart from this critical one.

Francesco, for example, placed *both* parents—not just one as usually happens—in the "freedom" and "exploration" pole of the critical semantics. In the case of his father, Amedeo, it was the freedom to stick to his own choices in the face of those who sought to control him. This independence was unfortunately to become emblematic: during the Fascist period it cost him his life. He also remembered Eleanora, his mother, for her exceptional independence. The beautiful, intelligent daughter of landowners in a small Piedmont town, she moved among the most highest intellectual circles in Turin during the 1920s, first as a student of philosophy and then as a brilliant academic. For a long time she remained true to her decision to live free and alone in order to pursue her studies in philosophy. Amedeo was the only one who managed to persuade her to accept a more "normal" married life, which turned out to be happy, though tragically short. At least, this is the reconstruction of the patient who is a sort of prototype of the phobic condition. Francesco was 62 years old when I began the therapy with him and his wife. He had been phobic since he was 17. No less interesting was the positioning of his wife, Elena. She belonged to a family of actors and had been used to travelling and a life of freedom since she was a child. She had had to reorganize her career and her way of life because of her husband's symptoms. But as soon as her husband improved and could cope with her going away, she was finally able to take part in exhibitions of her design objects and to indulge freely in her passion for travel, which she also enjoyed doing alone. The couple sought therapy because the wife, now almost sixty, didn't wish to make any further sacrifices. Her husband either had to overcome his problems and accompany her or would have to stay at home without her. She had no more time to delay her plans.

In the family of Raniero, another phobic patient, only one member, as more often happens showed a marked independence. It was the "cold" autonomy of narcissistic self-sufficiency of his father. At the age of thirty-five, Raniero's father, who was physically attractive, a tireless worker, and had spent his younger days in dance halls, had married the daughter of his business employer. It was a marriage of convenience. His future wife was kind, an enthusiastic worker, but ugly and with no feminine charm. It took him seven years to think it over and finally make up his mind. After the marriage he treated her more as a work colleague than a wife. He was regularly unfaithful in escapades of an entirely sexual nature. In Raniero's view, at least, his father felt no need for affection. He had no friends and women interested him only for sex. His wife was no more than a useful work companion. He had no contact with his original family. He never referred to his parents and siblings, and seemed to have forgotten all about them. His siblings had also gone off in their own directions without maintaining contact—one of them had joined the Foreign Legion and they had lost all trace of him.

Among my cases of agoraphobic patients there is even a husband who was a professional explorer. Romeo was an anthropologist, a documentary film-maker and author of scientific publications. When he went to live among one of the world's last "savage" communities, he remained there for weeks and sometimes for two or three months without any contact with his wife and children. It was a job he had wanted to do since he was a child. To leave the known world and venture out into the unknown gave him a new lease of life. He had never even considered other job opportunities. When Ermia, his wife, developed serious panic attacks during his absence they were both extremely upset. Romeo's journeys were his great passion but were also the family's source of economic support.

Eleonora, Amedeo, Elena, Raniero's father and Romeo are each different. Even the type of independence that they express is dissimilar, and yet all of them are symbols of a large degree of independence *from* relationships.

I have drawn the reader's attention to "freedom" and "exploration"; the opposing poles of "dependence" and "attachment" are obviously just as important, and around them specific identities are built up. Raniero's mother, for example, was anxious, possessive and overly protective towards her son, and never left the family home. Her whole life was spent inside the grounds of the family's business premises, which contained her parents' old villa, where she and her husband now lived, and the new villa built for Raniero and his family. She had been born there, had always worked there, had met her husband and started her new family there. For her, leaving that perimeter fence meant venturing out into a world in which she felt lost and inadequate. She tried to avoid it at all cost, preferring not even to take holidays. Equally housebound, anxious and controlling was one of Francesco's paternal aunt's who had been a second mother to him. When her nephew married, she followed him, moving into an apartment next to the young couple. Francesco was therefore able to have a secure base and Elena could continue to live the free and independent life to which she was accustomed without even being aware of her husband's problems. Only after the death of this aunt was she forced to change her way of life.

The greater space that I have allowed for "autonomy" and "exploration" is justified by the need to combat an opposite tendency. The literature has often provided a description of family contexts in which phobic disorders are developed entirely out of the need for protection and a rejection of the outside world. There are, indeed, very few voices of dissent (Holmes, 1982). Instead, it has been said time and again—as we shall see later—that parents of people with phobic disorders describe the outside world to their children as being dangerous, that they are hyper-protective and limit their children's freedom.[1] My cases also confirm these observations. The detailed reconstruction, which I will present later, of the interpersonal context within which the phobic organization is set out, shows how important the "attachment" and "dependence" poles are. However, this is only one side of the coin.

There is also another reason for drawing attention to "freedom" and "exploration." In the conversation of families of those with phobic disorders, they are regarded—though often ambivalently—as the positive poles. When, for example, Romeo's wife Ermia developed serious panic attacks during her husband's absence, they were both very upset. Not only were his explorations important to Romeo, but they were also the pillar upon which Ermia based her great admiration for her husband. She loved Romeo for his courage, for his love of risk. To transform him into a sedentary individual, Ermia repeated, would mean losing the man she loved. She wasn't playacting. Ermia really was distraught. Even though she found it difficult to cope with the consequences, she saw a positive value in her husband's choice. The semantics of these families in fact expresses a moral order in which freedom, independence and exploration are construed as values, while the bonds of attachment and the company of others are regarded as an expression of the need for protection from a "dangerous" world and are consequently associated with a certain degree of humiliating dependence. The members of these families consider friendship, love and other forms of attachment partly in negative terms because they construe them as being forms of dependence. While episodes in which the individual manages to deal alone with situations are regarded as expressions of freedom and independence. All of the values indicated in Figure 3.1 are seen in this way. Even those in the family who position themselves as courageous and strong do not scorn security and stability; they consider them to be values of lesser importance. Freedom, change, novelty and even risk stir admiration, even on the part of those members of the family who keep themselves well away from such things.

Francesco, whose parents I described earlier, had always unreservedly admired his mother, Eleanora, for her independence and freedom of thought. He loved and respected her throughout his life. Her memory would not be marred by the many reconstructions and deconstructions of family history that Francesco was repeatedly encouraged to make during his psychotherapy experiences. He could not imitate her autonomy, but emulated her passion for study and knowledge, and her lack of conformity. This man, who for most of his life could not freely move about outside a radius of one kilometer from his home, always demonstrated an unusual freedom and independence of thought. Francesco also admired his wife Elena. Although her curiosity, her passion for

VALUES	
FREEDOM	DEPENDENCY
EXPLORATION	ATTACHMENT
RISK	SAFETY
CHANGE	STABILITY
DEFINITIONS OF SELF / OTHERS / RELATIONSHIPS	
FREE	DEPENDENT
RISK TAKING	PROTECTED
UNPREDICTABLE	RELIABLE
COURAGEOUS	TIMID
STRONG	WEAK
WAYS OF RELATING	
KEEPING DISTANT ⇄	GETTING CLOSE
BREAKING FREE	DEPENDING ON OTHERS
EXPLORING	ATTACHING
FRIGHTENING	REASSURING
EMOTIONS AND FEELINGS	
COURAGE	**FEAR**
DISORIENTATION	CONSTRAINT

Figure 3.1 The semantics of freedom. The detailed grid is set out in Ugazio et al., 2009

travel and her independence created anxiety and disorientation in Francesco, these same qualities made her attractive to him.

Raniero, similarly, though he felt humiliated by his father's arrogant, often contemptuous treatment of him, had always admired him. The wounds that his father inflicted were many and deep. He had always belittled him until he took over the family business. He had sexually assaulted his daughter-in-law and, even during the therapy itself, had made indecent advances towards his 13-year-old niece. At one tense moment during the therapy, his wife said:

> Now you [Raniero] hate your father. After forty years you have rebelled, you treat him badly and he is suffering ... Despite every-thing, even now—I know—you love your father. I have seen my husband cry only once, when he found out how his father had behaved with Laura [referring to the indecent advances towards the niece]. Your father has totally disillusioned you ... But for you he is still a god, you have always seen him as a god."

To summarize: because the semantics of freedom prevails in these families, people who are free and independent, sometimes self-sufficient, oppose and co-position themselves with members of the family who are dependent and in need of support and protection from others. And, above all, those who place themselves within the positively-valued pole are admired, or sometimes hated, but seem to belong, in the eyes of agoraphobic patients, to other dimensions of being—the world of these members of the family has nothing at all in common with theirs, they are ontologically different, as if they were semi-divine.

This semantic, as for the others, even if constructed jointly with all conversa-tional partners, does not have the same importance for all. For some members of the family other semantics will be more important. The same semantics of freedom will not be equally dominant in all families with phobic members. It will tend to monopolize the conversation in families where it has been present for several generations, whereas in others they will be less pervasive. In all my phobic patients' families, at the time when symptoms first appear in one member of the group, the semantics of freedom are relevant and the symp-toms amplified their importance. Imagine you have a brother or a father who, because of a phobic disorder, has had to turn down an interesting job oppor-tunity that would have required him to travel to other countries on business. He fervently desires to travel but has to be satisfied each year with holidays no further than a hundred kilometers from home, and for long periods needs to have someone with him to carry out everyday tasks. Having to deal each day with a member of the family with these problems, you too would end up placing considerable importance on your capacity to manage alone, and your independence would become the most important asset. This is what happened to Francesco's daughter. From early childhood, she had been particularly inde-pendent, curious, and active. When I met her she was a television journalist.

She had travelled throughout the world, had had various relationships and had only recently, at the age of thirty-five, agreed to settle down with somebody for the first time.

3.2 A Dilemma that Threatens a Narrative Plot

The semantics of freedom must be present, but this is not enough for phobic psychopathologies to develop. I have met many families during my clinical practice who have been dominated by such semantics even though no member has ever developed a phobic disorder. What is more, all members of the family generally contribute towards constructing the semantics of freedom in their conversation but only one will develop a phobic organization. It is the positioning that subjects assume within this conversational context that has a decisive impact on the development of the disorder. Mere participation in a conversation dominated by the semantics of freedom does not seem to be sufficient to explain the development of a phobic disorder. All my phobic patients—though different in terms of background, age, professional status, and personality—found themselves at the beginning of therapy in a position in the semantics of freedom that induced them to experience a particular dilemma.

As we shall see, the patient's position in the semantics of freedom is obviously a *relative position* and other members of the family, as well as the phobic subject, play a role in its construction. For the moment I would like to focus attention on the phobic patient alone and the dilemma experienced in relation to these critical semantics. This narrative strategy enables me to stay closer to the stories of the patients, who tend to focus attention on themselves, undervaluing the *relative nature of their own positionings*. Furthermore, I can more easily emphasize my points of convergence with cognitivist authors who are more concerned with the individual than with his or her context.

According to Guidano, Liotti and other cognitivists (Glauber, Copes, and Bara, 1996; Guidano, 1987, 1991; Guidano & Liotti, 1983; Lorenzini & Sassaroli, 1998; Sassaroli, Lorenzini, & Ruggiero, 2005; Villegas, 1995), phobic subjects try to find a balance between two equally unassailable necessities—the need for protection from a world perceived as dangerous and the need for freedom and independence. It is difficult for them to find a compromise between these two needs. Attachment and exploration are in fact regarded as irreconcilable. Since subjects see reality as threatening and see themselves as affected by some presumed form of psychological or physical weakness, they need relationships with figures who provide reassurance. Every time they are physically or psychologically distanced from such figures they risk finding themselves at the mercy of their own fragility and weakness. On the other hand the continuance of a close relationship with protective figures is accompanied by a painful sense of constriction and limitation. At the base of these patients' problems is the dilemma: whether to explore freely, finding themselves alone, at the mercy of dangers they cannot deal with, or whether to be suffocated by the reassuring protection of family and other protective havens.

Using Feixas et al.'s implicative dilemma concept (Feixas & Saúl, 2004; Feixas et al., 2009) the "free" pole of the free-dependent construct implies "being alone", whereas the "protected" pole of the protected-up against the odds construnct implies "dependent". In my view, this dilemma—which the above-mentioned cognitivists rightly regard as central to phobic organization—shares the characteristics of a strange reflexive loop affecting the self and the relationship. I will try to clarify this point. The problem for this type of disorder is not just the protective aspect of the relationship. The very possibility of building and maintaining emotional bonds is regarded as limiting. Phobic subjects regard love, friendship, and all ties as being forms of dependence. The relationship as such becomes, at least in part, intransitive with those aspects of self connected with self-esteem. For these people, having a relationship that is enjoyable and satisfying means being protected, being able to rely on someone being close at hand in order to help them deal with fear, but it is translated into a humiliating dependence that produces a negative self-image. On the other hand, to acquire a positive self-image, it is necessary to be autonomous, independent of others, alone. A task of this kind is impossible for those who have grown up in the belief that the world is dangerous and they are weak.

When specific interpersonal episodes and situations maximize the reflexivity of the strange loop, such individuals no longer have a narrative plot into which to "co-position" themselves: Their position is entangled in a series of irreconcilable and sliding perspectives. If they seek to maintain the relationship and therefore feel protected they are suffocated by a humiliating dependence; if they seek to become autonomous and consequently to obtain self-respect, they are overcome by fear because they feel themselves to be at the mercy of a dangerous world (see Figure 3.2). I take the view that the episodes of depersonalization, which are so frequent to be included by *DSM-IV* among the symptoms characterizing panic attacks,[2] express this moment of maximum reflexivity.

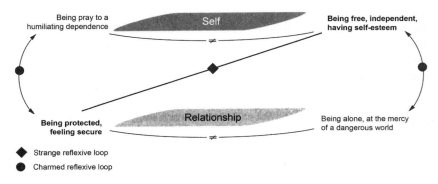

Figure 3.2 The strange reflexive loop of phobic organizations

This is what happened to Emilio at the age of fourteen, when his brother was born. For reasons that will become clear when I describe his family history,[3] the event was a great shock for him. Continuing to maintain his relationship of dependence upon his mother after the birth of his little brother was an unacceptable attack on his self-esteem, but he felt it impossible to distance himself from his mother. His mother, who had just returned from hospital with the baby, involved Emilio in the countless problems posed by the arrival of a new child. Perhaps she had noticed him becoming increasingly silent and moody and realized how much he was suffering and was trying to make him feel part of what was happening. Perhaps, on the other hand, she simply needed the help of her elder son. Her husband, despite these difficulties, had gone off to help his sister who was worried about her daughter's serious health problems. It is in this context that Emilio experienced his first episode of depersonalization.

> At a certain point my mother asked me to change my brother's nappies. I well remember the disgust, the smell ... wanting to be sick. I clean him, I change him. I feel ill, I have to get out, I cannot stay in that house any longer. Just as I am about to leave, in the lobby, I don't know why, the proportions of the room seem different to me ... I look around. At that moment I look into the mirror: I don't know what is happening, I do not recognize myself. It's a horrible feeling. I feel frightened, a terrible anxiety.

Generally it doesn't quite reach that point. When the reflexivity of the strange loop reaches high levels, the appearance of traditional phobic symptomatology makes it possible to reduce the reflexivity to within acceptable limits, so as not to trigger such dramatic mechanisms as depersonalization. With the development of symptoms, individuals maintain their protective relationship but this no longer constitutes an unacceptable attack on self-esteem. Dependence upon the relationship is now justified by an "external," unintended and uncontrollable event: the "illness."

Raniero was twenty-two when he had his first panic attack. Even though he was at university, he was still under the firm control of his family when at home. A ten-minute delay was enough to worry his mother, who wanted to know where he had been and with whom. She was continually warning him about his friends, reminding him that if he wasn't careful—naïve as he was—he would end up in trouble. His father criticized him less than in the past, perhaps because his relationship with Raniero had recently become closer. It was now his mother and aunt who annoyed him. They ruled him with a rod of iron as if he were their servant.

As generally happens with people with a phobic organization, Raniero tried to position himself at the positively-considered extreme of the critical polarity ("freedom, independence").[4] He had changed. He went out with his friends, did well at sport, and at university, where he was studying engineering. He was therefore furious when he discovered his aunt had already booked their annual summer holiday at the usual hotel at Canazei. Being unmarried, she found it convenient to take him along as company. Raniero had a row with his mother: his friends were going on holiday with their girlfriends, not with their aunt. He wanted to go off with several friends from university. He had already told his family the previous year that he wouldn't be going on holiday with his aunt again.

Raniero lost the battle. His mother, who was very close to her sister, had persuaded him with tears and threats to go with his aunt. At Canazei he seethed with anger, so much so that his aunt, an imperious career woman, kept him under tight control. It was here, against the magnificent backdrop of the Italian Dolomites, that Raniero had his first symptoms in grand style. His panic attacks forced him to return home, then to have treatment for over a month in a clinic. When he was discharged he felt better, had calmed down, but was no longer himself. The smallest thing was enough to send him into a state of anxiety. He had to have someone with him when he travelled away from his home town. He no longer felt safe even going out alone at night. Sometimes he was too frightened to drive. In short, he had become a patient. The family attributed the crisis to too busy a life over recent years. He wanted to do too much and had had a breakdown. In reality, he had never been so well as during the years immediately prior to the onset of symptoms, but even Raniero ended up accepting this version. Whatever the reason, his symptoms forced him to reduce his plans for the future. He stopped playing football and moved from engineering to architecture, which he considered to be a second-rate course. But above all—and this is what I wish to emphasize—the symptoms made him more tolerant of the restrictions imposed upon him by his family: he had to accept them because he was no longer self-sufficient.

In this respect I think it is necessary to re-interpret the tendency, reported by many authors, for phobic subjects "to assume an (...) attitude towards [themselves] in which feelings and emotions are regarded as external to the self" (Guidano, 1987, p. 169).

For Guidano and other cognitivists, this tendency is a consequence of the habit of excessively controlling personal emotions and internal states. In my view, however, it also enables phobic subjects to attribute their needs for protective ties to reasons that are external, "objective," and inescapable: somatic occurrences, which include emotions and feelings, are generally construed by phobic subjects as physical events. As these are external and inescapable forces, self-esteem is less compromised.

The construction of emotions and feelings as events external to the self also facilitates that exasperated control of interpersonal relationships which is one of the characteristics of this organization. In order to limit the degree of reflexivity of the strange loop, the subject must maintain the relationship but must at the same time feel unfettered. Attempting to exercise unidirectional control over the other is a necessity in these circumstances. Haley's brilliant suggestion (1963) that symptoms have the function of manipulating the course of relationships fits perfectly with the phobic organization. The entire interpersonal phobic strategy is manipulative because it is a concealed—and perhaps intentional—attempt to induce the other person to become involved and always amenable, without the subject committing him or herself in the same way to the relationship. For this reason, in defining the relationship, the subject prefers to rely on non-verbal forms of behavior, which include the symptoms. This approach takes on its most extreme forms in sexual relationships, where the emotional involvement is more intense and where it is clearly not easy for the subject "to have a reference figure at his/her disposal, while at the same time being careful to avoid feeling dependent and limited in one's freedom of movement" (Guidano, 1987, p. 148). The commitment is often accepted only so long as the other person becomes controllable. Only in this way does the relationship not compromise self-esteem.

3.3 Permitted Stories and Forbidden Stories

When therapists meet people with phobic disorders in clinical practice, the degree of reflexivity of the strange loop is always high. The symptomatology has reduced it at the cost of placing the subject in a state of precarious equilibrium, marked by uncontrollable emotional states.

Prior to the development of their psychopathology, most of my phobic patients were well adapted to their environment. The subsequent reconstruction[5] of the lifestyle and personality prior to the onset of symptoms has shown that patients lived in a variety of entirely normal ways but with specific limitations and possibilities: for these people, certain stories were "permitted," in the sense of being easily experienced, while others were "forbidden," in other words problematic, generating anxiety if not symptoms.

Simplifying greatly, it is possible to attribute the range of lifestyles prior to the onset of symptoms that I found in my cases to a continuum with two strategies at their extremes (Figure 3.3). I will call the first of these, *a strategy of emotional distancing*, and the second *a strategy of limiting closeness*. I have found the first of these more frequently in subjects in which claustrophobic symptoms prevailed, and the second in subjects with agoraphobic symptoms.

Subjects with *a strategy of emotional distancing* felt themselves to be, and were regarded by others as free, independent people capable of managing alone. They positioned themselves, prior to the onset of symptoms, at the positive end of the semantics of freedom and seemed to have fairly high self-esteem. During the years prior to the outbreak of symptoms, in order to maintain this position, they had avoided being emotional in their behavior, or limited it as far as possible. The underlying fear was that emotional involvement would

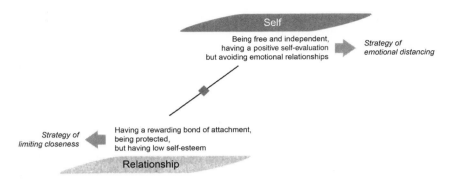

Figure 3.3 The adaptive strategies of *emotional distancing* and *limiting closeness*

have led them to see themselves as dependent upon others and, as a result, to lose their positive self-evaluation. Self-esteem and equilibrium seemed to be maintained at the price of avoiding emotional involvement, which was seen as being destructive and limiting to individual, functional capacities. Intimacy aroused positive emotions in them and was considered as gratifying, in contrast to what happens, for example, to narcissistic personalities. Emotional ties, however, were nevertheless regarded as interfering with personal functioning and therefore with self-esteem, even before the onset of symptoms. To summarize: "forbidden"—dangerous, difficult, enigmatic—stories, for these people, were those that involved emotional involvement, whereas situations in which they could express their own autonomy formed part of the stories that were easily experienced or "permitted."

People with this strategy were never without ties, including emotional relationships, unlike the situation so often found with narcissistic personalities or depressive organizations. They generally had various emotional relationships "kept at a distance." A feature of this strategy, however, is difficulty in maintaining adequate levels of effectiveness and competence in emotionally disruptive situations such as falling in love. Various patients of mine with this strategy have had many superficial relationships. The possibility of developing more stable commitments was generally postponed.

The frequent tendency of these subjects to have many short-term affairs, often simultaneously, is reminiscent of such figures as Don Juan. People with this strategy, whether male or female, are in truth generally not great lovers: behavior of this kind would require the capacity to become emotionally involved with the other, even for a limited period of time, but it is this very involvement that frightens them. Their many affairs are a series of fleeting sexual encounters or friendships without great emotional involvement.

On several occasions, reconstructing the history of these people, I have discovered that the partner, who the patient has married later in life, had already been "chosen" ten or fifteen years earlier but the relationship had remained in a sort of limbo, even if the future spouse had never been completely lost from sight. This curious fact helps us to understand how people with this strategy are therefore frightened of commitment. For them, as for those with the opposite strategy, commitments are irrevocable. A close relationship therefore brings, for them, not just the risk of losing their personal autonomy and independence on which their self-esteem is crucially based. The development of a commitment is much more disturbing for the extreme difficulty in breaking it: once a significant relationship is established, it is difficult for them to emotionally escape from it. People with depressive disorders, for example, are certainly not afraid of becoming involved in a relationship, but the possibility of breaking it is part of their repertoire; it is one of their "permitted stories." For phobic people it is not like this.

The tendency not to break important relational ties fits with the phobic organization as a whole, not just to subjects with this strategy. This does not mean that such people never end friendships, emotional relationships, and even marriages. Some of my phobic patients had divorced and remarried. Almost all of them maintained some form of relationship with their previous partner, including those who did not have children with them. In some cases these links created difficulties and conflicts with the new partners; in others they did not. Therapeutic work with these people has taught me that a successful divorce does not necessarily end with a complete break. An occurrence of this type is difficult for subjects with phobic organization to endure. But to change the nature of the relationship is a "permitted story": the former partner will become, for example, a friend, a sort of family relation with whom there is no longer any emotional involvement nor any shared plans, but with whom some attachment remains.

In subjects with a strategy for emotional distancing, this tendency—which is common to the entire phobic organization—heightens the fear of being involved in a relationship because it creates the terror of falling into the grip of the other and no longer being able to escape from the entanglement created by the bond. This gives rise to a tendency to choose partners who are more committed and dependent upon the relationship than they are themselves. Such people are mainly individuals with claustrophobic symptoms that express, metaphorically, the terror of being trapped in a relationship that destroys them. The strategy described here is also a way of limiting this specific fear.

Patients of mine with a *strategy for limiting closeness* have been generally agoraphobic. They are positioned, also before the onset of symptoms, at the negatively-considered end of the semantic of freedom: they were defined, and defined themselves, more or less openly as dependent, afraid or weak. They had built and maintained very close emotional relationships that were capable of giving them an adequate sense of protection. Many of them had spent the whole of their lives in the place where they had been born, passing from one very intense, exclusive attachment with one of their parents to an equally close relationship with their partner. Though few had experienced breakups in relationships of vital importance, the fear of losing that link with significant people seems to have remained with them during the years leading up to the onset of symptoms because their individual functioning already seemed to depend upon those people. Equally characteristic was the tendency to control key figures, to keep the relationship under constant watch and suffer from physical and psychological, even temporary, detachments and separations. These people paid great attention to the relationship and its implications, and gave priority to the relationship and its requirements, even if they had a demanding work life.

Though they positioned themselves at the "dependence" and "attachment" ends even before the outbreak of the psychopathology, they also valued "freedom" and "independence": they were as they were because of some external constriction. Even before the onset of symptoms made this choice obligatory, their tendency to seek out protective relationships was attributed to specific causes inhibiting their "true" nature: they had poor health, they couldn't control emotions, they came from a confined upbringing. Precisely because of their lack of independence and autonomy, they already had low self-esteem prior to the development of the symptomatology: they were not what they ought to have been. The negative self-assessment did not usually relate to their personal affability and pleasantness but to the sphere of personal autonomy and related achievements. Their choice of friends was revealing in this respect. These people who had generally had a quiet life, away from situations that might trigger off powerful emotions, who had been born and brought up in the same place, who had not experienced crises or breakups in their career and emotional relationships, would often have friendships with someone towards whom they felt an unconditional admiration, who was their polar opposite. If they longed for "freedom" and "exploration," especially in their professional lives, their friend was a roaming business director who in one week would stop off in Paris, spend a few nights in Hong Kong and then set off again for Prague. If, on the other hand, they linked "freedom" and "exploration" with sexuality, this sort of "ideal self" was an individual who had had a series of frenetic relationships—in other words, someone not at all like them, who instead had spent a whole lifetime with the same partner. In the absence of friends to help them out, the same function was carried out through reading or cinema.

One of my first phobic patients was a woman who had recently developed agoraphobia. She was the typical 55-year-old, lower middle class, Italian housewife of thirty years ago, whose life was all housework, church, and family. Born and brought up in a small town, she married someone her own age when she was very young, they had two children and had lived together for twenty-five years without any major upsets. This woman who was so traditional used to turn her back on her children, her husband and her piles of ironing to avidly read stories from a series of women's romance novels. The plights and adventures of the heroines in these stories provided an irresistible fascination. Later I met many agoraphobic patients who remained glued to the television screen, watching soap series with the same hopeless passion with which Mia Farrow becomes transfixed by the big screen in *Purple Rose of Cairo.*

Hafner (1979) found that a large number of her agoraphobic female patients had abnormally jealous husbands and suggested that this syndrome, by thus limiting personal autonomy, might be a way of adapting to the pathologically jealous spouse. I, too, have found strong jealousy among the partners (whether husbands or wives) of my agoraphobic patients. But I tend to give a different interpretation to it. It seems to me that jealousy is an appropriate response to fantasies involving liberation and escape from the marriage held by subjects with a strategy for limiting closeness (and not just in those with a strategy for emotional detachment). Generally speaking these fantasies are not fulfilled but they remain present.[6] A more subtle and, in my view, no less plausible interpretation is that people with this strategy tend unknowingly, through non-verbal behavior indicating a wish to escape, to encourage the partner's jealousy and control because they fear losing control of their emotions if they are left free. The etymology of the term agoraphobia, which relates to the fear of being alone in public squares or open spaces with no kind of support, is a metaphor for the fear of personal freedom. What distinguishes the adaptive strategy for limiting closeness is the attempt to be anchored to protective relationships in order to reduce the risks to which they would be exposed if their desire for freedom got the better of them.

The two strategies I have described are more "ideal" than real. The reconstruction of the adaptation prior to the development of the symptomatology often provides a less polarized picture; on the other hand the symptomatology itself is often "mixed." Especially in agoraphobia, the symptoms that express the fear of subjects being left alone, helpless and at the mercy of their own freedom, alternate with those that express the fear of finding themselves in situations with no way out, from which it is difficult to distance themselves, to escape. Rightly, the *DSM* distanced themselves from the traditional definition, derived from the etymology of the term, which identifies agoraphobia with the fear of open spaces and with the symptoms associated with fainting, vertigo etc. They have in fact also included in this syndrome aspects that relate to claustrophobia, such as feelings of constriction and fear of places and situations from which it is difficult or embarrassing to escape. These include cinemas, bridges or journeys by bus, train, plane or car.

Both strategies I have described make it possible to overcome the characteristic dilemma of this organization: the reflexivity of the strange loop I have described in the previous paragraph is reduced. One strategy achieves this purpose by favoring the self to the detriment of the relationship: the subject maintains a positive self-image, is autonomous and capable of managing alone. The price is to forego relationships and the enjoyment of an intimacy which, though feared, is valued. In the other strategy, it is the relationship that is placed before the self: the subject maintains the protective relationships but for this very reason tends to have low self-esteem.

Separations and breakups tend to disorganize the phobic organization as a whole, as highlighted by many authors.[7] When the strategy for emotional distancing prevails, situations that can be interpreted as loss of independence and freedom also become critical. Falling in love, developing an emotional relationship and the birth of a child are examples of possible critical events. A career setback can also become a factor that can trigger symptoms, especially if the psychological or economic autonomy of the subject is compromised. They are mostly situations that lead to a loss of protection, placing in crisis those people based on the opposing strategy. For them, even a promotion or move to a type of professional activity requiring greater autonomy can be destabilizing because it takes energy away from key emotional relationships.

3.4 The Interpersonal Context in the Here and Now: A Positioning Balanced Precariously Between Two Subsystems

The critical events triggering the onset of symptoms acquire significance within the relational context in which they develop. So what are the characteristics in the relational context where disorders develop that make these events mentioned above become critical?

Family therapists in particular have tried to answer this question. Their explanations, formulated between the 1950s and the 1980s, have focused almost entirely on agoraphobia. Other types of phobic disorder have been neglected, and claustrophobia completely ignored. They do not investigate the relational history of people with phobic organization but focus on the here and now.

While they present many differences, all trace the psychopathology back to the marital relationship. Even systemic models ignore other family relationships in favor of that of the couple. As Byrne, Carr, and Clark (2004)[8] have emphasized, they almost entirely share the view that there is a complementary union between the agoraphobic patient and his/her partner. Both spouses, it is suggested, gain an advantage from complementary mutual positioning. The price is a marriage that becomes "compulsive," to use the definition of Fry (1962), one of the pioneers of treatment for agoraphobia: agoraphobic patients cannot do without their partner in order to face the world, while the "healthy" partner cannot escape from the other's need.

One phenomenon that had struck psychotherapists since the 1950s seemed frequent in agoraphobia: the "healthy" partner reacted negatively to, or undervalued, the improvements achieved in the other partner during therapy. In certain cases the curing of the agoraphobic partner provoked a breakdown in the marriage and more frequently led to an increase in marital conflict (Hafner, 1977; Hand & Lamontagne, 1976; Goostein & Swift, 1977). These clinical observations, which highlight the role of agoraphobic symptoms in reducing marital conflict, help to explain the exclusive attention placed on these models in the marital relationship.

During these years, agoraphobia was also thought to be a "woman's syndrome." Agoraphobic symptomatology frequently puts women into a gender dynamic consistent with the stereotype present in many cultures, which regards women as dependent upon a man who assumes a protective and controlling role towards her (Craske & Zoellner, 1995; Fodor, 1974; Hafner, 1984; Kleiner & Marshall, 1985; Shean, 1990; See also the review by Bekker, 1996).

Agoraphobic patients are viewed by these authors in only one way—as dependent, fragile, submissive, and lacking in self-esteem. The "healthy" partner is described in a variety of ways in the models put forward. They are described by some authors as pathologically jealous, or at least unwilling to allow their partner any autonomy, while others are said to have a personality which is so assertive and domineering that their partner is only able to achieve his or her needs through the symptoms. Only Holmes (1982) emphasizes the independence of the spouses of agoraphobics, but he interprets it as a counterphobic trait. These husbands, who according to their agoraphobic wives "are frightened of nothing," demonstrate, in accord to Holmes (1982), self-sufficiency because they are frightened of intimacy and their show of autonomy is said to conceal a hidden dependence on their wives.

No new hypotheses have emerged over the last twenty years on adult patients' intersubjective context. The objective of most recent studies has been to test theories put forward over earlier decades on the basis of clinical experience, using controlled research methods, broad samples of subjects, and reliable and repeatable measurements and tests. Something new has emerged. For example, the paradigm that made the "healthy" partner responsible for the genesis and continuation of the agoraphobic pathology has been challenged by some studies. There has been an exploration of the possibility that the complementary nature of the conjugal pathology is a result rather than a cause of the development of agoraphobia (Hoffart, 1997). This hypothesis has to be taken into account especially when therapists meet the couple after the psychopathology has already been established for years. It is therefore difficult to distinguish the responsibilities of each partner in creating the dynamics of the relationship.

The results of these studies can be easily summarized: none of the models and theories advanced has been either confirmed or disproved. Some of the studies gather information consistent with the theory being tested while others do not. Many, if not the majority of studies carried out, in order to empirically measure clinical concepts, end up using operational definitions of concepts that distance them—and by a long way—from those original definitions.[9] It is therefore difficult to assess what these studies confirm or disprove in the models and ideas advanced over previous decades. It seems to me, however, that one conclusion can be drawn. The claim by these etiopathogenetic models to explain the considerable variety of clinical cases classed under a single diagnostic label with a single conjugal pattern seems to have been invalidated. The fact that some studies confirm certain hypotheses wholly or in part, while others confirm the opposite, suggests that their results reflect dynamics that are ascertainable in clinical practice and relevant to many groups of patients, but not to all cases.

Irrespective of these results, the models put forward seem to be *imprecise*. The suggestion of a complementary pathology between agoraphobic patients and their partner can be extended to other psychopathological conditions and to more or less every married relationship where the symptoms first appearance prior to the meeting between the partners.

Focusing attention on the couple alone is, in my view, the principal limitation of these models. This approach is particularly inappropriate in an organization such as a phobia which favors vertical instead of horizontal relationships. Subjects with a phobic organization place their relationships with parents—and often with children—before the marital relationship, as do the Japanese (Beardsley & Smith, 2004). Vertical relationships are more secure than horizontal relationships. The perception of the human condition as being vulnerable, the world being construed as dangerous, and catastrophic beliefs (Beck, Emery, & Greenberg, 1985; Ellis, 1962; Stoler & McNally, 1991), which are so typical of agoraphobia (though not extraneous to claustrophobia) induce phobic subjects to maintain long-term protective links with parents and with their original family. When these are no longer capable of providing a secure basis, other systems of relationship will replace them. *It is most unlikely, however, that phobic subjects will commit themselves wholly to the marital relationship, as many people do.* The world is too dangerous to rely too heavily on one single relationship. Even an extra-marital relationship can save phobic people from feeling themselves at the mercy of one exclusive bond. An all-absorbing partner relationship is not only potentially suffocating but also intrinsically dangerous: if he or she walks off you are left high and dry.

The relational dynamics prior to and accompanying the onset of symptoms in adults are obviously not extraneous to the marital relationship. It may however happen, especially in younger adults, that the relationship with the partner only plays a marginal role. Generally speaking the relational situation leading to the onset of symptoms breaks the complementarity between the marital relationship and another system of relationships that are just as vital to that person as the partner. Breakups, threats of separation, the ending of a relationship, the birth of a child and all other events triggering off the onset of symptoms in adults, become critical because they alter the phobic subject's position within the semantic of freedom in precarious balance between at least two equally important systems of relationships. One of these relates to vertical relationships. And often, at least in my cases, *the onset of symptoms produces the pragmatic effect of enabling patients to maintain close relationships with both systems on which they depend, avoiding the threat that one excludes the other, or reduces it to any great extent.*

I will clarify this point by examining more carefully the intersubjective context that accompanies the onset of symptoms. The conjugal relationship bears undoubted similarities with the models already discussed. The patient is in a position of dependence and for this reason feels humiliated. For those with claustrophobia this position represents a complete turnaround, whereas for agoraphobics it is a step that worsens their already low self-esteem.

Partners can have two very different positionings that give rise to equally different relational scenarios and conflicts. They may be free, independent and easy going, as the partners of agoraphobics usually are. As well as being respected and admired, this type of partner enables the patient to feel free but does not provide protection and guidance. Insofar as the symptoms may reduce the patient's independence, this partner will never provide the guarantee of being there when needed. He or she is basically unreliable. On the other hand, the partner can be a protective person through the very fact of being autonomous, strong, and assertive: he or she is dependable and protective. A protective partner, however, ends up being limiting, a source of barely tolerable restrictions that lower self-esteem. Finally, it can happen—and fairly often does in the case of claustrophobics—that the choice of partner falls upon one who is weak, dependent, and insecure. Patients in this third scenario rule the marital relationship and acquire security by helping their partner. But if they lose stability they cannot rely on their partner.

In all cases, the marital relationship and its internal dynamic is complementary to another relationship or group of relationships which are equally fundamental, if not more important, for the phobic subject. The choice of an apparently uncommitted partner makes it possible and necessary for a person with phobic organization to maintain strong links with their original family, where at least one member continues to co-position him/herself with the patient in a protective position. In a country such as Italy, where links with the original family remain close throughout life, this is the most frequent situation. The protective position can, however, be assumed by a child, especially when the phobic subject is elderly, or by an employer, a close friend or even a permanent extra-marital partner. Even if these people do not personally take part in the family conversation, they become an integral part of it because they are essential in defining the mutual positioning within the family. If the partner is protective, what is left of the patient's self-esteem will be guaranteed by the relationship with the original family, but also by continuing a job that gives the patient an opportunity of establishing relationships offering autonomy, and by friendships and even extra-marital relationships that make it possible not to feel excessively dependent on the spouse. A weak partner therefore has all the more need to maintain protective relationships, even at a distance, which can be activated when the situation requires it. *The onset of symptoms in adults seems to result from changes that alter the balance between the two systems of relationship within which the subject, co-positioning him or herself, contains the reflexivity of the strange loop.*

When, for example, I met Ermia and Romeo, the explorer, his wife's panic attacks had caused Romeo to reduce the length of his journeys and to remain at least in telephone contact with Ermia during his absence. Ermia had already asked him to limit his explorations since the time of her mother's death but it had produced no effect, apart from arguments. The symptoms achieved their objective without useless conflict. It was an obvious fact. Nevertheless, it was equally true that for twenty years the marital relationship had continued happily despite Romeo's absences. Indeed, it could be argued that Romeo would have continued to take longer trips, making them more adventurous and risky precisely because for all those years Ermia had never imposed any limits on her husband. Because the marital relationship was virtual for much of the year, Ermia had been able to continue a sort of marriage with her mother. When her mother died, the protective positioning towards Ermia was taken on by the eldest daughter. It was in fact the daughter's decision to study for her doctorate in the United States, rather than Romeo's journeys, that was the critical event leading to the crisis in Ermia's mental balance in the here and now, and in her relationship with Romeo.

Elisa's partner, unlike Romeo, placed himself in a protective position from the very beginning. The critical event was the honeymoon. Let us examine closely the relational context in which this event acquires meaning.

Elisa was always frightened as an infant, very attached to her mother and "clinging." As an adolescent she became strong and independent enough to take over the role of her elder sister, Anna, who was powerful and overbearing like their father. At junior school it was she who defended Anna if her classmates attacked her, fighting back when the circumstances required it. At the age of eighteen this attempt at independence came to an end. Elisa spent a couple of months in hospital where she was diagnosed as having a heart defect. Upon her discharge she had to recognize that she was like her mother—as well as inheriting her heart problems (her mother had an irregular heart beat and other problems), she had her mother's character. She gave up sport and her assertive attitudes and returned under her mother's influence. A few years later she met her future husband and fell in love immediately. Matteo was strong, self-assured, and gave her security. Nevertheless, at the beginning he stalled:

I would have liked to have married immediately. He stalled for time in spite of him already working. He was perhaps playing for time because his mother was alone—her other two sons were already married. I don't know … When my father invited him to join his business, I pushed things along. I let him understand that I liked the idea. I forced him a bit …

In that moment Elisa felt she had rather trapped him. There were many reasons for anxiety. It would not have been easy working with his future father-in-law, with his terrible character. Matteo himself was also fairly uncompromising. He was affectionate and attentive, but did not like being questioned and felt humiliated. He wanted to be the person who decided, who gave protection and organized their life. Elisa became alarmed. For years she had suffered because her fragile, insecure mother had been unable to stand up to her husband's domineering behavior, even though she was very attached to him. Elisa had begun to criticize her for her submissive attitude towards her husband and her lack of self-respect. As her relationship with Matteo developed, Elisa gradually began to feel strange pains. The heart deformation, which had caused no further problems since her hospital treatment, began to play up with strange irregularity, followed soon afterwards by headaches and nausea. When she was unwell her fiancé was protective. He looked after her, occasionally told her off, but always kindly, and above all was prepared to change their arrangements and plans without any hard feelings.

The time came for the wedding and the honeymoon. Elisa suggested to Matteo that going to Greece was perhaps not a good idea, particularly because her mother was worried about her daughter going so far away. Matteo wasn't so concerned about his mother-in-law's worries, and the messages from his future wife were so subtle that he didn't entirely grasp what she was trying to say. Elise seemed happy when they departed for Greece, though a little anxious, but as soon as they boarded the ship she had a panic attack.

It was a really terrible attack. When I boarded the ship I began to feel ill. The worst moment was entering the cabin. It had no porthole. My mind went blank. I felt something uncontrollable inside me. In a fraction of a second I was on the stairs. I ran down like a shot. My husband was running after me but I wasn't going to stop. As soon as I was back on dry land I felt better for a moment, but I suddenly realized that Matteo was still on the ship and the attack returned. My husband, in fact, had realized that there was no way of holding me back and had gone to retrieve the car. I calmed down when he and the car finally arrived. But I needed quite some time before I was myself again."

Matteo didn't take it too badly. He changed their plans without entirely abandoning them. They went to Calabria and returned home a week earlier than
planned because Elisa had continued to feel ill.

At the moment of the panic attack the reflexivity of the strange loop reached
its highest point. For Elisa, going to Greece meant distancing herself from
her protective relationship with her mother and her family. Refusing to make
the journey was an attack on her own marriage and therefore on her own
autonomy and self-esteem. Her marriage with Matteo, having a home of her
own, and even the honeymoon itself were felt by the patient as an expression
of her autonomy, in that they acquired meaning in relation to her own family
and the close but suffocating link with her mother. The panic attack enabled
her to confirm her relationship of dependence on her mother and, at the same
time, took all responsibility away from her—something was happening that
went beyond her powers of control.

The patient elaborated the onset of her symptoms more or less in these
terms during the initial phase of therapy. Her version was sincere but partial.
She had already had strange feelings of illness many months before the honeymoon. Underlying her concern about losing the protective relationship with
her mother was the fear of jumping "from the frying pan into the fire." Elisa
was worried about becoming increasingly involved in a relationship in which
she risked being defenseless. Matteo was kind, affectionate, but determined.
He did not allow obstacles to get in his way. From being cheerful and lively, he
would become difficult if she upset him in the slightest.

The onset of symptoms at the beginning of the marriage made it possible to
reduce the reflexivity of the strange loop, not just because it made her original
family's protection indispensible. Because of the symptoms, Matteo also had
to limit his demands on her. The danger of ending up, like her, mother in a
relationship where she had to submit to her husband was intolerable for Elisa's
self-esteem. The symptoms also allowed her to keep her husband at bay, to
maintain her autonomy, without putting the relationship at risk by using the
word "no."

When Elisa and Matteo began therapy they had been married for twelve
years and were happy together. He was convinced that there had never been
any differences between them. They shared one single point of view—his
own—with which his wife was very happy. Looking more closely, however,
many choices had been made which were not what Matteo would have wished,
including the relationship with her parents and the question of a second child.
He had been clear at the beginning of the marriage: he had accepted to work
with his father-in-law but otherwise they had to be independent. Elisa had
also always known that Matteo wanted at least two children. After two years
of marriage the couple moved into the apartment adjoining her parents with
whom, from that time, they had always spent most holidays, including their
summer vacations. Ten years had gone by since the birth of the first child and

there was still no sign of a second. Matteo, fearing that his hopes of becoming a father for a second time were disappearing, had recently made more serious attempts to give substance to his desires. Elisa had had panic attacks of such intensity as to discourage him. She saw pregnancy as a long tunnel—for nine months there would have been no escape. Many other examples could be listed, because Elisa's symptoms regulated every aspect of her relationship with her husband and with her family. What is interesting to emphasize is that choices made by the couple had become compulsory as a result of Elisa's symptoms, and that her husband, in all sincerity, was convinced that his wife, as well as fervently desiring a second child, was suffering—more than him—as a result of the interference of her parents and could not wait to live a proper distance away from them.

As often happens when partners are in a protective position and therefore offer themselves as possible substitutes for vertical protective relationships, the onset of symptoms neutralizes the risk of the marital relationship distancing the subject with phobic organization too far from the protective bond of their original family, as in Elisa's case. Thanks to the symptoms, those such as Elisa are often able to maintain an equally close link with both systems of relationship, which are essential for their equilibrium, without entering into conflict with either of the two. They can also secretly control and direct the relationships upon which their now precarious equilibrium depends. Some self-esteem can therefore be restored. The "illness" does not leave them defenseless in the hands of either of the two systems.

3.5 The "Original" Intersubjective Context: What Phobic Patients Tell Systemic Therapists

The intersubjective context I have described does not shed any light on the origin of phobic organizations. It is limited to describing the conditions that upset relational strategies created in order to deal adaptively with the dilemma of phobic organizations. The major point of reference for models seeking to identify the relational origins of this psychopathology is Bowlby (1973), who traced phobic pathology to specific patterns of family interaction. His hypothesis is that phobic disorders are derived from patterns of anxious attachment developed in response to the same interactive models found in young children who refuse to go to school. According to Bowlby, school phobia is a precursor of agoraphobia. Bowlby identifies four different prototype situations that all have one common result: they produce such an insecure and anxious attachment by the child to the parents as to prevent the normal separation required by school attendance. Two of these situations are a direct consequence of the behavior of one of the parents who keeps the child at home. In one case, as a result of some tragic event involving the child during infancy, the parent fears that something bad might happen to the child. In the other, the parent suffers from chronic anxiety in relation to figures of attachment and needs the child's company. In the other two situations, the parents play an indirect role. In one of these, the child fears that something bad will happen to his or her mother (or father) while he or she is at school and therefore wants to stay at home or insists on remaining in the company of the mother (or father). In the other, as a result of repeated threats of abandonment or expulsion from the family, the child is frightened of leaving the home even for a short time: the home is not a "safe base" and therefore cannot be left.

The original formulation of this proposition was conjectural. Bowlby stated that he had developed it from the study of children's school phobias rather than from consolidated clinical experience with agoraphobic adults. It has been confirmed many times in subsequent years, and by various sources. Many studies of personal accounts by patients with phobic disorders have found that there is a significantly high frequency of separation anxiety (Biederman et al., 2005; Gittelman & Klein, 1984; Manicavasagar, Silove & Curtis, 1997; Manicavasagar et al., 2000; Manicavasagar, Wagner,& Hadzi-Pavlovic, 1999), as well as patterns of anxious attachment (De Ruiter & Van Ijzendoorn, 1992; Van Ijzendoorn & Bakermans-Kranenburg, 1996). The connection between anxious attachment in early childhood and anxiety disorders in adolescence has also been confirmed by longitudinal studies (Warren et al., 1997). Bowlby's model has also been confirmed by psychotherapists, especially cognitivists who treated a large number of cases (Guidano, 1987, 1991; Guidano & Liotti, 1983): phobic disorders are the "elected" disease of cognitivists. For example, according to Guidano, the phobic organization is based upon the main figure of attachment limiting (generally indirectly) the child's exploratory behavior. Guidano (1987) identifies two dysfunctional patterns of attachment at the origin of phobic organizations. In the first the normal exploratory interest of the child is impeded by the hyper-protective behavior of the main figure of reference.[10] In the second, the exploratory inhibition takes place through obstructive conduct by the parents.[11] The result of these patterns is, according to Bowlby (1973), the development of an anxious attachment in the child, fuelled by the fear that the main figure of attachment will disappear and a tendency to remain as close as possible.

Many researchers (Biederman et al., 1990; Van Brakel et al., 2006) Muris et al., 2001; Muris, Meesters, & Spinder, 2003; Muris et al., 1999; have also identified strategies in the parents of phobic subjects that limit the exploratory behavior of the child. The result is an etiopathogenetic model of the phobic organization entirely centered on the principal figure of attachment inhibiting the child's exploratory behavior. The phobic context would even seem to violate the child's biological needs for exploration, as some authors state.

This explanation conflicts with the assumptions upon which systemic psychotherapy is based. According to systemic and constructionist approaches, needs are socially defined and deprivations are always relative.[12] Their perception depends more upon social interaction and the criteria that this interaction establishes, rather than upon "objective" and absolute conditions. I think that reliance on biological, ahistorical, unchangeable limits for something like exploratory conduct, which displays such profound differences across various cultures, might cause misgivings even among those who are distant from constructionism. But let us leave aside these considerations that give rise to theoretical implications so general as to be unverifiable.

There are two reasons for concern about this model. First, it is not specific. As many studies have now demonstrated, *memorized experiences of anxious attachment are to be found not only in agoraphobia and other phobic disorders but also in other psychopathologies,* including post-traumatic stress, obsessive-compulsive and borderline disorders and depression.[13]

Second, these models *do not explain the need for freedom and independence that are characteristic of the phobic organization.* As I have already indicated, even those suffering from agoraphobia, though binding themselves firmly to a figure of attachment, retain in their mind a continuing desire to escape. Long before the development of the symptomatology, their tendency to form close relationships in order to guarantee the feeling of security and protection they require is seen by them as a demand which, if not pathological, at least limits their potential.

The inability to provide any explanation for this dynamic in the model put forward by Bowlby and other authors who identify the adult's inhibition of the child's exploratory needs as being at the origin of phobic organization, is even clearer in relation to subjects with an adaptive strategy for emotional distancing. These subjects, unlike those who adopt the opposing strategy, carry through their choice of independence. It is the development of symptoms that precludes this path and reveals latent conflicts in the pre-morbid period. People with this strategy usually regard relationships as being destructive, limiting their ability to function as individuals, even if having to reject their desires for deep emotional relationships in order to preserve their independence makes them feel uncomfortable.

The dyadic adult–child relationship described above does not explain this dynamic, which is so characteristic of phobic organizations. The etiopathogenetic hypotheses of Bowlby, and of therapists who have followed his model, explain it through the deep need for protection from a world that is seen as dangerous. But this need, which is certainly present in the phobic organization, is only one side of the coin. Bowlby's model ignores what is, according to my clinical experience, the specific nature of the phobic organizations, where the need for attachment is experienced in opposition to the equally deep desire for freedom and independence. In fact, Bowlby considers only agoraphobia and the aspects of this syndrome most related to the "attachment, need for protection" polarity: the fear of leaving the house, of being alone in the street, of moving away from the local neighborhood, etc. The presence of opposing

107

needs is fully recognized by Guidano and some other cognivists (Guidano, 1987, 1991; Guidano & Liotti, 1983; Lorenzini & Sassaroli, 1998; Sassaroli, Lorenzini, & Ruggiero, 2005; Villegas, 1995). Their etiopathogenetic model, however, like that of Bowlby, describes only the inhibition of exploratory behavior, which is present in the phobic organization but also in other pathological conditions. This inhibition, though a characteristic of phobic behavior, is not its prominent feature.

I believe that the model I am about to present is capable of explaining what most fully characterizes the phobic organization: the construal of attachment and exploration as mutually exclusive. This derives from my experience of systemic therapy with individual phobic adult patients and couples, and family therapy with adolescents and other young people. The adoption of a systemic approach has enabled me to place the dyadic adult–child relationship within the context of the network of relationships that these two people maintain with other significant figures. In the case of therapy with adults, this model is the result of subsequent reconstruction of events from which patients have already fully or partially distanced themselves. In family therapy phobic adolescents and other young people, the dynamic that I will describe was still present. It is a dynamic in which triadic interactions play a central role. The use of explanatory schemes that are at least triadic is a typical feature of systemic therapy. This practice is alien to Bowlby and cognitivist psychotherapists: the attachment theory, even though it has become more relational and two-directional than it was in its original formulation, adopts a dyadic explanatory model. It should be added that the psychotherapists we have referred to above rely exclusively on a practice of individual therapy.

The model I propose confirms that the child has a preferential relationship of attachment such as that described by Bowlby, Guidano and the other authors referred to. The point is that this adult—which I will identify for the sake of simplicity as the mother[14]—is involved in a particularly intense emotional relationship with a member of the family who is positioned in the "freedom, independence" pole of the critical semantics. This person is often the husband, sometimes another child, or even a parent. He is the member of the family with whom the mother has the strongest tie. Generally he is less involved in the relationship with the mother than the mother would wish. He is to some extent uncommitted, thereby producing feelings of insecurity and desires for reassurance in the mother. Though his/her autonomy and independence often gives little satisfaction and is sometimes the subject of heavy criticism and a motive for acute suffering, nevertheless it is often admired and, in some cases, envied by the mother and by other members of the family who also regard "freedom, independence" as important values.

As the child gradually becomes aware of his or her own situation in the terms I have described—even at varied and partial levels of understanding—he or she gradually construes his or her own desire for intense emotional ties and the need for freedom as being mutually exclusive. The relationship in which the child is involved with the mother entails a drastic reduction in exploratory behavior (independence, autonomy etc.), but the very forms of conduct that the mother discourages in the child are in fact characteristics of the figure who is emotionally more important for the mother. *Maintaining the relationship with the mother, for the child, therefore means receiving a negative self-definition, where the negativity of such definition is given by the fact that the mother values a member of the family whose conduct is opposite to what the child is encouraged to do.* It should be added that the child frequently finds him or herself playing a "consolatory" role for the mother. The figure to whom the mother is tied is not only independent and autonomous but is often someone who arouses feelings of insecurity and desires for reassurances within her. The close relationship that the child develops with the mother is an attempt to respond appropriately to these emotional states of hers.

This triadic relationship contains the ingredients that form the structure of a true strange reflexive loop, by virtue of which attachment and self-esteem become intransitive.

Three aspects of this configuration should be examined. These are:

a) the position of the mother;
b) the time factor;
c) the differences between the relational pattern generating the strategy of limiting closeness and that giving rise to the strategy for emotional distancing.

The hypothesis I put forward might suggest ambiguous conduct by the mother who encourages certain behavior in the child while she is emotionally involved with a partner (a husband, parent or other child) who interacts in an entirely opposite way. It should be emphasized that the conduct of the mother is not in any way intentional, nor does she demand that the child takes on this behavior. My clinical experience does not confirm what has emerged in several studies: that the mothers of phobic patients are lacking in warmth (Whaley, Pinto & Sigman, 1999), rejecting and controlling (Hudson & Rapee, 2001). Sometimes the mother of my patients were or had been controlling but the emotional exchanges with their children were very often intense and mutually gratifying. *What occurs, quite simply, is that the mother, being heavily involved in an emotional relationship with a partner who is independent and often apparently uncommitted, develops feelings of insecurity and a desire for reassurance. The child, who is organized in such a way as to adapt to the adult looking after him or her, senses this emotional state of the mother and develops forms of behavior that are complementary to it.*

The time factor in the intersubjective context at the origin of the phobic organization means we must consider the deep changes the child is experiencing through the normal processes of growing up and development as well as external events that are part of life (birth of a sibling, separation, death of a parent etc.). The position of each family member within the semantics of freedom is not determined just by relational dynamics but also by development processes that create constraints and possibilities. Furthermore, the relational pattern I have described is not external to, and independent of the child; it is not an "objective" characteristic of the context. Instead, it is a way through which the child senses the relational situation in which he or she is involved. For this reason it can exist only when the child begins to develop forms of awareness, even nascent. The dilemma involves aspects of self connected with self-esteem that play an important role from nursery age.

It can obviously happen right from birth that children find themselves involved with a mother who, having to deal with an uncommitted partner, has unsatisfied desires for contact and reassurance. This does not mean that infants find themselves in the intersubjective context giving rise to phobic disorders. What they are experiencing, *for the moment*, is simply a relationship with a mother who limits exploration.

Only from the age of four or five years can children develop the prerequisites for constructing a range of potentially phobic adaptive strategies. These strategies, which I have described in the form in which they appear in adulthood in Section 3.3, are the result of a process. At first, children—even if they begin to feel the situation in the way I have described—can give priority only to the relationship. Up to the age of seven or eight years, the relationship with the attachment figures has absolute priority. Children therefore position themselves in the "attachment, need for protection" pole, construing themselves in line with the needs of the main attachment figure. These children will therefore become very attached, sometimes clinging, not open to exploration and new experiences. However, since they will gradually become aware that the person emotionally more important to the mother behaves in a way that is opposite to their own behavior, they will develop low self-esteem.

Through childhood and adolescence, when problems of self-esteem acquire central importance and detachment from the adult becomes possible, the reflexivity between the self and relationship increases. The interactive situation consequently assumes the nature of a dilemma, and subjects deal with it by beginning to develop the strategies I have described. In reality there is no distinct sequence of events. The process does not actually happen in such a way that subjects first become aware (through personal experience) of the interactive situation in which they are involved and then develop appropriate strategies to deal with it. Instead, they elaborate a way of being that is an expression of the "entanglements" and communicational ambiguities of the strange loop they are experiencing, as well as strategies for dealing with such ambiguity and the connected difficulties.

110

Generally speaking, prior to adolescence and youth, the intransitivity between self and relationship does not reach those critical values that lead to the development of symptoms. However, it can sometimes happen that during nursery age and childhood the reflexivity between self and relationship reaches critical levels and the child develops symptomatic behavior.

The original intersubjective context giving rise to phobic disorders need not necessarily originate during nursery age or childhood. It can also arise in adolescence or youth. Specific events in the family, or outside, can induce adolescents or young people to perceive their positioning in terms of the critical pattern described.

I have come across the relational pattern described here in all phobic organizations, including those that are mainly agoraphobic or claustrophobic. The only difference I have noticed in the relational history of claustrophobic subjects, compared with agoraphobics, is an abrupt change of alliances in childhood: the child "passes" from the original figure of attachment to a member of the family positioned in the "freedom, independence" pole. Sometimes it is to the member of the family most admired by the mother, in respect of whom the child had played a consolatory role. The reversal is generally determined by a delusion triggered off by specific events, such as the birth of a child, a temporary abandonment or by repeated frustrations. Two aspects characterize this abrupt change of alliances. The child, from this moment:

a)   seeks to assume the characteristics of the recent ally, *without developing in this new relationship a deep emotional involvement* comparable with that developed with the original figure of attachment;

b)   drastically changes his or her relationship with the original figure of attachment: abandons "clinging" and "sheltered" attitudes in order to adopt independent and autonomous behavior. The contempt with which he or she treats a sibling (or whoever it is who, with their equally dependent behavior, fills the void left by him or her in relation to the mother) is an indicator of how the memory of the bond of dependence remains alive.

Even subjects with mainly agoraphobic symptoms make some attempt to position themselves in the positively-viewed semantic pole, but this happens later, during adolescence and youth, and never—at least in my cases—during childhood. These attempts, furthermore, do not sever the tie of dependence with the main figure of attachment: they weaken it. Nor does the child generally move over to the person positively considered by the principal figure; on the contrary, this person remains the object of repressed or explicit hostility. The alliances through which subjects seek to position themselves in the "freedom, independence" pole are with people who are less central to the emotional dynamics of the family. If this hypothesis is correct, the original intersubjective context, with its connected dilemmas and entanglements, is the same for agoraphobia and claustrophobia. Organizations that are mainly claustrophobic would therefore seem to be the result of a subsequent relational movement that modifies the position of subjects and their relational system, allowing them to find a different way of dealing with the ambiguities connected with the characteristic dilemma.

Before concluding this section I would like to emphasize once again that when (generally at the end of adolescence) the phobic organization is created—an organization which, as I have described, assumes various different forms, traceable to the two strategies described ("for emotional distancing" and "for limiting closeness")—a series of events *can* give rise to phobic symptomatology. *This may happen, but not necessarily so.* And it is only when this possibility arises that a true phobic organization is formed. This is the clinical material with which therapists come into contact during therapy, and is the result of the reflexive interaction between an organization that has generated the symptoms and the symptomatology displayed. Before the onset of symptoms, the organization of meaning in question deals *adaptively*, sometimes *creatively*, with the dilemma between self and the relationship characterizing it. It is therefore misleading to regard it as pathological. Instead, it gives rise to a range of adaptive strategies—in other words habitual practices—indicating a capacity for subjects to take part, along with other social partners, in the conversation, and to construct their own position in it. I have used the term "adaptive strategy" in order to emphasize that these are dynamic ways of functioning, capable of responding adequately to the tangled relational situation in which they are developed.

3.6 Two Clinical Examples

An Original Intersubjective Context Which Continues into the Here and Now

Emilio had a marked agoraphobic symptomatology when he began therapy at the age of twenty-four. His fear of going out alone and of open spaces (he came to therapy sessions accompanied by friends) alternated with feelings of constriction, suffocation, and fainting in circumstances where he had the idea of being trapped (in crowds, travelling by plane, etc.). To complete the picture he had violent somatic gastrointestinal attacks (nausea, vomiting) and frequent hypochondriac experiences of dying. Emilio described himself as homosexual. Though he was totally inhibited in his sex life, his manner was consistent with what he stated to be his sexual identity.

Three years earlier he had graduated with distinction at Milan Academy of Fine Arts and was due to move to Rome to become a set designer, but the development of his symptoms had made this, and other plans, impossible. Emilio remained in the small town where he had been born, completely dependent on his parents with whom he lived. Emilio's central conflict, typical of the phobic organization, was marked by his own particular symptomatology. Each time he felt the need for his mother (his key figure of reference) it was followed by violent attacks of vomiting and nausea. Every attempt to obtain autonomy—and with it self-esteem—was accompanied by panic attacks and hypochondriac experiences of dying.

The *pattern which connected the patient to the therapy* immediately revealed his conflict. The first contact with Emilio was through four sessions that ended when he announced that the therapy was unsuitable, followed by a paradoxical reframing. His initial request was confused—the possibility of therapy clashed with the patient's unrealistic hope of moving to Rome.

Emilio reappeared eight months later with a much more pressing and dramatic request for therapy. He described the efforts he had made after our sessions to be self-sufficient. They had ended miserably with a journey to England, which had been a way of testing out his capacity for independence. A few days after his arrival in London, staying with his sister, Emilio had a panic attack that was more intense and longer-lasting than any he had previously experienced. In the lulls between one attack and the other he implored his sister to force him to stay. "Tie me to the bed," he asked her repeatedly. In the end, due to the violence of the symptoms, Emilio had to admit defeat. He therefore left London. The return journey by train was hell. He vomited continually. He had reached rock bottom.

At that moment the strange loop was at its greatest. The idea of returning home was an unacceptable attack upon his self-esteem, but to remain in London had proven impossible. The symptoms were no longer able to reduce the reflexivity of the loop: all they could do was mark out its oscillations (Figure 3.4). It was at that moment that the "third possibility" appeared: therapy.

> "The idea of therapy was the only thing that managed to calm me down during that terrible journey."

The Original Intersubjective Context

Emilio was the eldest child. There was a five-year gap between him and his two twin sisters. Ann was independent and enterprising: when Emilio began therapy, she was studying and working in England. Elisa was timid and very attached to her father: She had finished her studies as a business secretary and had a job. The youngest child was a 10-year-old boy. Their mother was anxious and affectionate. She was the emotional point of reference in the family and had run a bar for many years. The father, powerful and authoritarian, controlled the family money, clashing frequently for this reason with his children, from whom he seemed to be somewhat detached. Only with Elisa was there a strong exchange of affection. With his wife he was "evasive" and had always been so. Even marrying him had not been easy for Emilio's mother. The engagement had lasted ten years. The relationship was important for both of them but each time the question of marriage arose, he avoided the issue. The bar should have crowned Emilio's mother's dream to keep her husband more closely tied to her. Over the years, however, he had ended up delegating the management of the bar to her for an increasing number of hours. For his part, he had been involved in other business activities with a sister, in organizing the town band in which he played the drum, and in his great passion, hunting. His role as husband was however confirmed at home quite blatantly by frequent and very noisy sexual relations—peculiar behavior for a traditional and conformist couple.

In this family, apart from the critical semantics, a "rejection of sexuality/ sexual power" polarity had an important history over three generations. It is not necessary to reconstruct it in detail here; it is sufficient to briefly describe the maternal family. The grandfather, a fiery, impulsive, and sexually exuberant man, was widowed at an early age, then seduced and married a novice nun ten years younger than him, with whom he had seven children. His passionate, ill-tempered arrogance, still well-remembered by his children, must have been intolerable for his wife who, at the age of forty, became "sick." No one ever understood what illness this woman of excellent constitution had: she was to die during Emilio's psychotherapy, at the age of 98, without ever having had hospital treatment. She took to her bed, however, for several months and from then onwards described herself as "sick." The effect, though, was clear to everyone: her husband was ousted from the bedroom. Afterwards, every time the sickness returned, the husband was kept away from the marriage bed. Despite this, at the age of 47, the former novice gave birth to their youngest

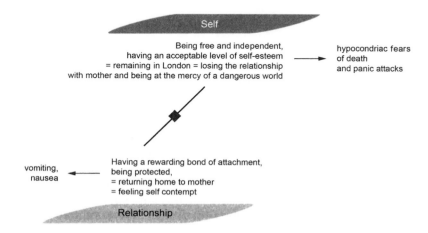

Figure 3.4 Emilio's symptoms mark out the oscillations of the strange loop

114

child, Emilio's mother. After this last pregnancy her religious devotion gradually increased and she became self-righteous and sanctimonious. The conflict between the grandparents must have been bitter: Its repercussions were still felt in Emilio's generation. Among the large number of cousins on his mother's side, homosexuality, whether declared or not, was widespread. Those who were heterosexual, even though they were older or the same age as Emilio, were neither married nor in fixed relationships. The second generation—that of Emilio's mother, aunts and uncles—was naturally also affected by the conflict. The eldest uncle married late in life, after being uncertain for a long time whether to dedicate his life to God or become an invalid (he had no job for several years due to what was loosely described as a "nervous breakdown"). The other uncle was tyrannical, domineering—the exact copy of his father whose thriving business he had continued—and a loner: None of his family had any dealings with him. All of the women, except for Emilio's mother—her father's favorite—had married men who were reserved and submissive, quite unlike the paternal model.

Emilio's position was constructed within these semantic dimensions. His mother, who was the main emotional support, had always inhibited autonomy and exploratory behavior, becoming cold, detached and sometimes very sad each time Emilio went away from her. These reactions persisted into the here and now, as became clear during therapy. One example: It was our twenty-ninth session and Emilio had succeeded, at least in part, in carrying out his plans. He had created the set design and costumes for a theatre production in a large nearby city, receiving praise in the local press and attractive financial offers for advertising and promotional projects. His mother, who had supported him, helping him to make the costumes, began to show a lack of interest during the event and even failed to turn up at a side-event linked to the production in which the costumes were featured. Emilio was deeply hurt by this behavior but did not attempt to re-establish contact with his mother. A few days later, she made an appointment with a neurologist who prescribed tranquilizers and for a week She was off work: She was depressed. Nothing like this had ever happened before.

The dyadic mother–child relationship, described by Bowlby and the other cognitivists referred to above, is not sufficient, however, to explain the dilemma and the patient's psychopathology. The point is that Emilio's mother was involved at the same time in an emotional bond of much greater intensity with an autonomous, independent, and "elusive" husband. This woman's absolute priority when it came to emotional investment was on her husband, who still had strong ties to his own extended family and especially to his sister, of whom his wife was extremely jealous. In the eyes of their son, with whom I reconstructed the family story, his mother found little gratification in her husband, except for sex, but he had nevertheless succeeded in tying his wife emotionally to him. In this relationship, Emilio's role had always been "consolatory." Throughout his childhood and adolescence, before his mother had the responsibility of running the bar, he had been her confidant and support. She complained to him about the absence of her husband who was always off hunting, or with the local band, or with members of his own family. It was with Emilio that she had furnished the home: even the furniture in his parent's bedroom had been chosen by mother and son. Emilio was involved in everything, even in bringing up the youngest child, to the extent of declaring, in one of the early sessions: "I am the one who has been a father to him." Despite this special position, Emilio had understood for many years that his mother's attentions were always on her husband. He had felt her anxiety when his father was off hunting, her resentment when he was delayed, and her joy when he finally arrived home. He had also always known how much his mother was sexually fulfilled by her husband. It was a wound that Emilio was never completely able to heal, connected to the crude way in which he related to his own sexuality and that of others.

It was only during late infancy, childhood, and adolescence that Emilio sensed and gradually became aware of his relational situation as I have described it here. And it was precisely his perception in these terms (at the level of "story experienced" and "story narrated") of the intersubjective context of which he was part, that gradually led him to construct an intransitivity between his desire for intense emotional bonds and his need for exploration and freedom.

A particularly dramatic moment in this process was the birth of his brother, when Emilio was fourteen. It was a heavy blow. The episode, which I described earlier,[15] gave rise to that change of allegiances that we generally find in all strategies of a phobic organization. Emilio did not ally himself to his father, towards whom he felt too strong a hostility, but to his paternal aunt. She was successful, independent, and wealthy (she had married a businessman) and was the pre-eminent member of the paternal family. Emilio's father worked with her in various business activities, incurring his wife's jealousy.

Emilio therefore attached himself to this aunt and began to visit her at home. She was a person with whom he could talk about art, whom he admired. At the same time he began to express contempt for his mother, criticizing her ignorance and her inability to understand art. His aunt looked after him, paid for lessons with a leading artist, bought him the materials he needed. In reality, the new bond did not replace the original one—it had the purpose, in fact, of involving his mother, making her jealous. Emilio still continued to depend on his mother. But now he was aggressive towards her. He attacked her, sometimes humiliated her and, above all, intensified her feelings of inferiority in relation to her sister-in-law, for whom Emilio felt out-and-out respect and admiration.

A Tragedy Giving Rise to an Intersubjective Context

We move now to an equally typical—indeed prototypical—case. Francesco, the patient, was an "expert" on the phobic condition. I mentioned him and his wife Elena in the first section of this chapter. He was 62 when I met him, and had experienced symptoms since the age of 17. He was treated several times by some of Italy's leading psychotherapist and at least one experience had been successful: He had been well for ten years.

This man combined exceptional intelligence with a particular affability and warmth in interpersonal relationships. He had been a top manager, had many different cultural interests and knew five languages. But for long periods of his life he had very low autonomy and needed to be accompanied even to a bookshop. Despite his language skills and his interest in places and people from cultures far and wide, Francesco often had to be content to remain an armchair traveller. Unbearable feelings of constriction prevented him from taking planes and trains. When, during a more optimistic stage in the therapy, he felt well enough to go with his wife into a bank vault, he had a very serious panic attack. Even being alone at home for more than an hour or two could cause him to panic. During our first meeting, Elena described how she usually had to avoid appointments or business trips that would keep her away from home for more than one night. The previous month she had even had to postpone a hair appointment because Francesco did not feel able to be left alone for a few hours.

The patient's psychopathology was placing a restriction upon his wife, and this was what led them to seek therapy as a couple. An equilibrium seemed to have been upset. Elena, now approaching the age of sixty, felt she could no longer cancel appointments for exhibitions where her work was being presented, or forego her passion for travel. She was a successful designer in Italy and abroad, and a particularly independent woman. She was tired of having to abandon her plans. She was no longer prepared to wait: She wanted to play a part in her own shows and to travel alone, as she had done in the past.

Elena was first seriously affected by her husband's disorders only six or seven years earlier. Francesco, as he repeated several times during therapy, had always admired Elena for her independence and curiosity. It was he who had organized the journeys on which he could not travel with her; he made her describe every stage of them; he was with her in spirit even though his problems prevented him from accompanying her physically. At most, he had sought—to use his words—to "limit" his wife's "excesses." Elena's version was rather different, but the couple had more or less succeeded (miraculously!) in finding a fragile, but generally satisfactory, compromise between their opposing needs, at least until a few years earlier. For the first twenty years of their marriage, Francesco's key protective figure was an aunt, who was a second mother to him. She was extremely attached to her nephew and had moved into the same apartment block as the young couple. The protective function had then passed to Francesco's brother and to his daughter. His aunt's death, his brother's move to another area, his own retirement and finally his daughter's falling in love and going to live with a man who, unlike previous boyfriends, left her little emotional space for her father, had all placed a strain on the couple. Their relationship worked well, so long as it was supported by protective relationships. These relationships had unfortunately ended and Francesco's symptoms deteriorated.

Now we will concentrate on the original intersubjective context within which Francesco's psychopathology began, giving therapy the task of finding a new equilibrium in which the couple might be able to find a possible co-position. It was a context embedded in a remote past but, due to repeated experiences in therapy, was still very much present in the patient's mind. The passages in inverted commas are taken from something that Francesco wrote about his own family story, which was discussed in therapy. Here, the intersubjective context typical of phobic disorders is mainly the result, as we shall see, of a tragedy.

The patient was born in the late 1920s. He was the first child who, as he described it, "had arrived to crown the union of a happy couple, bound together by strong emotional ties and true cultural interests."

His parents' marriage was certainly one of love. Each of them, as I have described earlier,[16] was independent. Both, as rarely happens, were positioned at the positively-viewed extreme of the critical polarity. Eleonora, his mother, was as far away as can possibly be imagined from the personality profile considered by the literature as typical of the mother of agoraphobic patients. Beautiful, intelligent, cultured and lively, she broke many hearts in her youth and received many offers of marriage, all of which she unhesitatingly rejected out of her love of independence. She had decided to dedicate her life to study and work. The daughter of landowners from a small town in Piedmont, she had shown exceptional intelligence from an early age.

It is difficult to say, after this space of time, from where Francesco's mother had got those extensive cultural interests that were to bring her into contact during the 1920s—first as a student of philosophy and then as a young academic—with Turin's cultural elite. Eleonora's academic success certainly brought her mother great joy. Her unconventional and courageous choice, to which she remained faithful to the age of twenty-six, probably had something to do with the game of favoritism to which the children were subjected. Her mother, unlike her father whose favorite was their son, defended the daughters to the hilt, and Eleonora was the apple of her eye. Her preference for this daughter was so fulsome and absolute that her mother, when she was dying and suffering from arteriosclerosis, recounted to her grandchildren, including the patient himself, how her Eleonora (who had unfortunately died several years earlier) had passed her school exams with such brilliance, going into great detail about the marks and the comments of her teachers. The combination of privilege, disparity, and favoritism must have been remarkable and, of course, stimulating. It led to conflict between brother and sisters, with jealousies, disagreements, and feuds that ended only with the death of the main players.

Eleonora, who had refused proposals from men of much higher social standing, yielded to a man two years younger. Amedeo was young and enterprising. On the birth of their first child—our patient—he was already the manager of a company and the family lived in a villa next to the factory. Eleonora, happy with her husband and the relationships within the family, seemed to have no regrets about the independent, intellectual life she had left behind and, three years after Francesco's birth, they had a second son.

The peace of this quiet middle-class life was shattered forever one morning in October 1930 when Amedeo was arrested. He was accused of involvement in a bomb attack against the Fascist regime in which two people had been killed. The patient was four years old at the time. A few months later, his father committed suicide in prison. Perhaps he wanted to save his honor, which had been damaged by the infamous accusation of responsibility in the death of two people, as the family legend suggested. Perhaps, more realistically, he was desperate. Among other things, the owners of the company had sacked him immediately. The patient was told nothing. He was to discover the truth thirteen years later:

> I soon realized, of course, that my father was dead. I was only four but I certainly wasn't stupid. The best demonstration of this fact is that, except perhaps in the first few days, I never asked what had happened to my father, who of course I loved dearly. In 1932, some time before I went to school, when I had to give my personal details, which at that time included paternity (in my case it meant having to write down that I was the son of "Amedeo deceased"), my mother told me that my father was dead, without of course telling me the circumstances, but talking vaguely about a bad heart. I remember the scene fairly clearly, the small desk at which my mother was sitting and other details. I don't recall exactly what was said but I know I remained impassive and my mother was surprised at my heartlessness. Even today, I find it totally incredible that for all that time my mother had failed to understand that I knew perfectly well what had happened (that my father was dead—not of course the exact circumstances) and that she continued even then not to tell me anything, finding it entirely natural that I, in turn, should ask her absolutely nothing. Of course, people sometimes spoke about how my father had said or done something or other. I listened, without commenting, or made some irrelevant comment or changed the subject.

Only when he was seventeen was his mother forced by circumstances to tell him the truth:

> It was the time of the Badoglio government. A decree was made—who knows on whose recommendation—which allowed my mother

and aunt to return to teaching. They had been dismissed shortly after 1930 because they were not worthy to teach the arts to Fascist youth. A short article appeared in a local newspaper describing those distant events of 1930, so I had to be told the truth. If Mussolini had held out a little longer, who knows whether today I might have known something more?

Let us allow the patient his entirely justified feeling of filial resentment. But that silence, that incapacity to understand, in a woman whose sensibility was just as sharp as her intelligence, gives us the sense of the situation. Let us try to understand what was going on inside her. Eleonora and her husband were a cultured, middle class, antifascist couple. When Amedeo was very young he joined the Republican Party. He was not a rebel. He did no more than continue a family tradition. His father was also a "free thinker," republican, antifascist and Freemason. He left the Freemasons when he realized that the incorruptible brotherhood was adapting all too well to the triumph of Fascism. Eleonora shared her husband's antifascism. Like him, she was not an activist. The blow was all the greater because neither of them had imagined the possibility of being persecuted. It should be added that this tragedy happened in 1930. The days of the Fascist action squads and the assassination of the socialist politician Giacomo Matteotti had by then been forgotten; the regime's imperial campaigns were still far ahead; Fascism had successfully molded Italian society and Mussolini was, as the Pope declared, the "Man of Providence." The political and psychological situation of the family and the patient has to be considered in this historical context. Eleonora had been sacked from teaching (along with her sister-in-law) and ostracised.

> The year after my father's death we had to leave the "villa" next to the factory and we moved to via X. It was not easy finding a new home. Many people found various excuses not to give accommodation to the widow of a subversive who had died in prison.

It was a bleak period for the young mother and her two children. Their shared disgrace induced her to tighten her links with her husband's family, where everyone dealt with the tragedy and their isolation by becoming even more resolute and intransigent than before. Eleonora did not remarry, and her life was increasingly dominated by her "tough, forbidding, wilful" mother-in-law and by her sisters-in-law, who never married and never managed to shake off the tragedy: one of them wrote a biography of her brother. The sisters and mother-in-law kept an eye on her, even intercepting her post, and exercised what amounted to an insidious influence even upon the patient and his brother.

It was in these circumstances that the relational pattern between mother, son, and father—who though dead was as present as ever—developed the characteristics that I consider to be typical of the original phobic intersubjective context. Eleonora had suffered a trauma; her world had suddenly been turned upside down; she was not anxious by nature, but became so. Her son had also been traumatized, both directly as well as through his mother. He was already very close to her, as often happens with the eldest child, and from that moment onwards he never left her for a moment. He was responding to his own need, but also to his mother's emotional encouragement.

As Francesco gradually grew up—in such a way, of course, that was consistent with his environment: needful of protection, dependent, frightened of many things—he became aware that the man to whom his mother was still bound had the characteristics of courage and independence that were opposite to his own. These characteristics, which his mother loved, were also extolled by his paternal family. To respond to his mother's needs, and to his own, thus meant receiving a negative image of himself, where the negative aspect did not relate to his likeability but to his lack of autonomy. Attempting to acquire a positive self-image meant comparing himself not with a real father—who, however free and independent he might have been, was still a human being with all his inevitable weaknesses—but with an idealized picture. Added to this, the mystery surrounding his father's death made him a terrifying figure. It is no surprise that the single hazy recollection that the patient had of him was something of a nightmare:

> It has long haunted me with its mysterious uncertainty and its vaguely threatening character. It is the memory mainly of a smell. The only visual element is the unclear picture of the staircase that led to my father's laboratory. It provided the background for an unpleasant smell which on several occasions I have associated with certain smells given off from garbage or produced from the burning of noxious substances. All of this linked in some way with a bluish-green color that I imagine to be poisonous. Highly significant, but of what I cannot say.

Throughout his childhood, Francesco was a sensitive child, firmly attached to his mother. She transmitted to him her passion for study, but he was timid and unable to assert himself among his friends. When he reached adolescence and his problems of identity became more pressing, the family atmosphere also changed. With the beginning of the World War II and the prospect of military defeat, the Fascist regime had lost credibility. The family no longer felt encircled, the outside world was no longer as maliciously dangerous in the eyes of the patient, who began to move towards the independence end of the polarity. He had friends and joined the antifascist "Giustizia e Libertà" organization. But at the age of eighteen the first symptoms appeared. The partisans asked him to do a small favor: to carry a letter. Francesco accepted but he was suddenly struck by an attack of panic. To refuse to do it would have meant completely losing face in the eyes of everyone, tantamount to cowardice, but to accept would have required him to overcome, in one single leap, a childhood and an adolescence lived out in the grip of fear. The panic attack removed the patient from the dilemma: the price he paid was the illness.

3.7 A Pathogenic Cultural Premise?

Is the dilemma of phobic organizations, which I have considered at great length, really the key trait of this organization of meaning?

The reader may, I think, have felt this doubt while reading the chapter. Many people, though not prone to phobia, feel that a commitment is a threat to their autonomy. In our culture, in fact, there is a certain degree of intransitivity between the continuance of relationships, the acknowledgement that the other person is necessary to us and the self-esteem we allow ourselves as autonomous and independent individuals.

In individuals with phobic disorders, the intransitivity and the reflexivity of this loop reach levels that are much higher than are to be found in other organizations of meaning. For a phobic position to be formed, there must be a family history which, for various reasons, makes the semantic of freedom central and schismogenetic. A specific relational pattern must also be created, as I have described.

It is, however, undeniable that phobic subjects do not convey just one particular family culture and one specific position within this culture. Phobic subjects take to the furthest extreme a premise that they find all around them in the world at large. It is the idea of freedom as an absolute and solitary independence *from* relationships. Bateson (1979) claimed that it is not so much power that corrupts, as the *idea* of power: "He who covets a mythical abstraction, must be always insatiable!" (p. 248). In other words, we can say that it is neither freedom nor its absence that lead phobic people into the blind alleyway of a full-blown pathology, but the *idea* of freedom as emancipation from the relationship and from its bonds.

But where does this idea of freedom come from?

It is an entirely modern concept. It is not to be found in the classical Greek world. Freedom as synonymous with absolute and solitary independence, declares Biral (1991, p. 15 et seq.)

> has nothing to do with that independence (*autarcheia*), which was the result of the good governance of all relationships in which man found himself and without which he cannot be regarded even as human, but as an animal or a god; an independence which did not certainly lead to being alone and rejecting all human contact, but which existed

within an association (in other words a political association) and, if achieved, bound him, according to proper established order, to his family, friends, fellow citizens.[17]

Aristotle wrote:

> By self-sufficient *(autarkes)* we do not mean that which is sufficient for a man by himself, for one who lives a solitary life, but also for parents, children, wives, and in general for his friends and fellow citizens, since man is born for citizenship *(politikon* or *anthropos)*.[18]

The concept of freedom as independence *from* relationships is, furthermore, a typically Western idea. It is, for example, alien to the Japanese tradition. Emotional dependence—*amae*—a central emotion in Japanese psychology, bears no negative connotation, as Doi (1971) has shown. It permeates interpersonal relationships and is expressed in many everyday forms of conduct and rituals. The word *jiyū*, the Japanese translation of the word freedom, is traditionally used to indicate freedom to behave as one wishes, even capriciously or oppressively, but always within the relationship. It never implies the possibility of breaking away or ignoring *amae*. Indeed, there is a freedom of expression precisely because each partner trusts in the benevolence of the other, with whom there is a bond of emotional dependence. At most, the partner's demands can be ignored. For this reason the word *jiyū* was often seen in negative terms, especially in the past, when Western influence was less widespread. Proverbs well express this cultural difference. In Japan there is no saying similar to "God helps those who help themselves";[19] there is, however, a very common proverb that means the opposite: "In travelling, a companion; in life, compassion."

For the Japanese, contact with the Western idea of freedom *from* relationships must have been a considerable shock. This, according to Doi, is the cause of that conflicting vision of freedom that is characteristic of contemporary Japanese literature. The way in which the Japanese today understand freedom and independence is nevertheless different to that of Westerners. This difference can be seen in even the simplest forms of courtesy. Doi gives some very amusing descriptions of his first contact with American culture. He found the practice of giving guests continual insignificant choices quite bewildering. It began with the aperitif: the host asks whether the guest prefers an alcoholic or non-alcoholic drink. Yes, an alcoholic drink is fine. Then he has to choose what kind of alcohol. The guest asks for a Martini; but how does he want it: with ice? Straight? With a slice of lemon? Fortunately, at the table, the guest can relax. But not for long: immediately after the meal he has to decide whether he wants coffee, tea, with sugar, with milk etc. But why do Westerners subject themselves and others to this tour de force? According to Doi, it is a ritual in which we are each reassured of our independence, and it is acknowledged by those with whom we have contact. Even a perfectly common expression of courtesy, such as "please help yourself," can be surprising for the Japanese. It is difficult for them to accept that such an expression can be regarded as a form of courtesy. Their sensibilities require that hosts should demonstrate sufficient empathy as to anticipate the desires of guests and serve them properly. To leave guests who are unfamiliar with the house to their own devices by saying "serve yourself" would be a serious breach of courtesy.

The idea of freedom that we find in phobic strategies is linked to a vision of the individual who is cut off from the group, in a separate world that is quite independent from the larger world around. From this point of view, society is "anything other than a collection of windowless monads" (Elias, 1939/2000, p. 480). In terms of self-awareness, this idea is like a feeling that the personal self, the true personal essence, is something "inside," separate from all other people and from things "outside." For this person—the *homo clausus*—the self is a cage or a niche: "Every other human being is likewise seen as a *homo clausus*; his core, his being, his true self appears likewise as something divided within him by an invisible wall from everything outside, including every other human being" (*ibid.*, p. 472).

But, Elias asks, how is this wall explained? "Is the body the vessel which holds the true self locked within it? Is the skin the frontier between 'inside' and 'outside'? What in the human individual is the container, and what the contained?" (*ibid.*, p. 472).

What it is important to emphasize is that the idea of freedom as independence from relationships is rooted in this conception that gives man an existence separate from nature and from the social world. Stolorow and Atwood (1992) consider it to be a pernicious and pervasive myth of contemporary Western culture, which has worked its way in to the basic ideas of psychoanalysis; they describe it as the "myth of the isolated mind." Many years earlier, Bateson (Bateson, 1972; Ruesch & Bateson, 1951) had contrasted this vision of the mind, the result of symmetrical pride (*hybris*), with the epistemology of the systems theory, according to which individuals and their mental processes only exist in connection with the context in which they are part.

The point is that this "curious aberration of thinking" has permeated not only psychoanalysis and many areas of psychology, but "takes on for a number of people in the course of the modern age the same immediate force of conviction that the movement of the sun around an earth situated at the center of the cosmos possessed in the Middle Ages" (Elias, 1939/2000, p. 481). It is now one of the basic ideas guiding our approach to everyday life; it is part of common sense.

What is the basic assumption that sustains it? Its earliest origins can be traced back to Christianity—in Paul, Augustine and above all Luther and the Protestant Reformation. It can also be traced back to ancient Greek writers. References such as these are too wide to be of decisive importance. According to Biral (1991), it is with Hobbes that this "dazzling" and "new" concept of freedom appears in modern philosophy, causing the freedom of the Ancients to retreat into a secluded corner. Hobbes forms his concept of freedom from an abstract, theoretical definition of human nature. In contrast to ancient philosophy, which tended to anchor knowledge to its practical purposes and to experience, Hobbes carries discussion on human nature to a purely speculative dimension. The author of *Leviathan* naturally presents this reversal as the passage from ignorance to science. In this context, "purged" of all practical concern, man is presented as a sum of powers:

> Man's nature is the sum of his natural faculties and powers, as the faculties of nutrition, motion, generation, sense, reason. For these powers we do unanimously call natural, and are contained in the definition of man, under these words, animal and rational.
> (Hobbes, 1640/2004, p. 4)

What is new about this idea of man? A great deal, according to Biral (1991).

In this definition, Hobbes removes from man all that is derived from history and relationships with other people. Human nature is pre-given: human passions, human intentions but also human action itself, are substantially the same at all times and in all places. People's position in time and space modifies their situation, but only in terms of external conditioning, not in constituent aspects of their nature: society is of coincidental relevance; it is an entirely external factor to the nature of human beings. This is one of the underlying assumptions from which neither a historical, nor a contextual conception of man took its form. Until fifty years ago, this alone had shaped psychology. From here is derived that idea, often found in psychological research, of environment as place, a scenario that can influence individual abilities, skills, development, but as a factor and an external stimulus.

Let us return to the concept of freedom. This conception of the human being enables Hobbes to define freedom as the absence of bonds:

> According to the proper, and generally received meaning of the word, a free man is he, that in those things, which by his strength and wit he is able to do, is not hindred to doe what he has a will to.
> (Hobbes, 1651/1968, pp. 261 et seq.)

Individual freedom is compared to that of a body that finds no external hindrances to its movement. For Hobbes there is no innate disposition to social relationship, there is no "deficiency" where people seek fulfillment from within. By nature, they are equal and self-sufficient. They do not need to mutually integrate.

Since the differences between people are irrelevant, necessary relationships do not exist. You can therefore form relationships with whomever you wish, and it is just as easy to get out of relationships when they become boring. The opportunities for encounters become greater and more varied, but these opportunities come to resemble more of a marketplace: each person is by nature extraneous to the other. Encounters are occasions for obtaining advantages or benefits. According to Hobbes,

> if they meet for traffic, it is plain every man regards not his fellow, but his business; if to discharge some office, a certain market-friendship is begotten, which hath more of jealousy in it than love, and whence factions sometimes may arise, but good never.
>
> (Hobbes, 1642/1998, p. 3)

But if nothing binds men by nature, "every bond appears to be an unnatural dependence, subordination, limitation and, therefore, a lack of freedom, whereas freedom means being outside, emancipated from any kind of relationship" (Biral, 1991, p. 16).[20]

Elias traces the origin of "self in its shell"—to which the concept of freedom from the relationship is connected—to Descartes, to Leibniz's "monads without windows," to the "Kantian subject of knowledge who from his aprioristic shell can never quite break through to the 'thing in itself'" (Elias 1939/2000, 253), and as far as existentialism and Max Weber. It is above all as the subject of gnoseological theory that, according to Elias, *homo clausus* becomes part of modern philosophy. In this role of *homo philosophicus*, individuals acquire knowledge about the "outside" world by their own powers alone. They do not need to learn from others. They open their eyes as if they were already adults.

The problem for modern philosophers of the "thinking self" is quite simply to establish whether the world and the concatenation of events, as they appear to man, are a characteristic of the facts observable "outside" or whether what appears to be outside is in fact a product of human perception and reason.

> "If we start with this image of man, from the *homo philosophicus* who was never a child and seemingly came into the world as an adult, there is no way out of the epistemological impasse. Thought steers helplessly back and forth between the Scylla of positivism and Charybdis of apriorism."
>
> (*ibid.*, 248)

But, according to Elias, this perspective that shapes modern philosophy and common sense itself, this feeling of personal separateness and the spatial metaphors that go with it, is only *a stage of reflexive self-awareness*. Let us follow him in this intriguing hypothesis. The history accompanying the passage from the geocentric to the heliocentric view is not just marked by a series of discoveries about the movement of the stars or in other scientific areas. This passage is also (and above all) the result of a growing capacity for people to mentally distance themselves. The geocentric view is an expression of man's spontaneous and non-reflexive concentration upon himself, which we still find today in every form of egocentric thought. The scientific method, with its search for objectivity, implies a distancing between man and the object he is studying, which is possible only if people have a high level of control over their personal affections. Elias's theory is that the birth of modern science has been made possible through concomitant transformations in the ways in which people live together and relate with each other, and consequent changes in the structures of personality, which go towards a greater control of personal feelings and emotions and an increased reflexivity. This process, however, is still not complete. And people, in immediate experience, feel the control of emotions as a "cage" that closes and excludes the world "outside." A process becomes reified.

The picture according to which individuals decide, act and exist entirely independently and "freely" from each other, and the idea of freedom *from* the relationship, would therefore be an expression of a stage in the process of civilization, and destined to be superseded. Individual personality, according to Elias, ought to evolve over the course of the centuries towards a complete interiorization of emotional impulses. New forms of self-awareness should emerge. Thanks to this process, humanity ought to be able to perceive itself as being part of a complex network of interdependencies formed by individuals who together create variable configurations through different social dances— namely countries, cities, groups, families.

If we accept Elias's view, the phobic subject, as well as expressing a particular family culture and a specific position within this micro-culture, carries to the furthest extremes the difficulty inherent in a specific stage of the civilization process. In this phase, individuals feel separated one from the other and transform this perception into a value through the idea of freedom *from* relationships.

4

BETWEEN GOOD AND EVIL: OBSESSIVE-COMPULSIVE DISORDERS

4.1 When Life Takes the Side of Evil

I suddenly snatched out my watch. It was twenty minutes since she went out. My guess was assuming the shape of a probability. But I decided to wait another quarter of an hour (...). Finally, I quietly opened the door, locked it with my key, and went to the shed. The door was closed, but not locked; I knew it could not be locked, yet I did not want to open it, but got up on tiptoe and began looking through the crack (...) I looked through that crack for a long time, it was dark inside, but not totally. At last I made out what I needed.

(Dostoevsky, 1873/1995, pp. 699–700)

Young Matrjoša had hanged herself, exactly as Stavrògin, the disturbing protagonist of *Demons*, had guessed. It was not difficult to predict. Having seduced her a few days earlier, Stavrògin had thrown her into the depths of desperation.

Why had Stavrògin remained an impassive witness—indeed, the secret orchestrator—of the tragedy? Was he frightened the child might talk? The reasons for Stavrògin's behavior lie elsewhere. Immediately after seducing her he had begun to hate her: "My chief hatred was at the remembrance of her smile. Contempt together with boundless revulsion would spring up in me for the way she had rushed into the corner after it all and covered herself with her hands" (p. 697).

But why did Stavrògin hate her? Had the child, without the slightest intention of doing so, unleashed a guilty passion within him? Not at all: Stavrògin had been visiting Matrjoša's house for some time and had not even been aware of that meek child with her ordinary looks. Why then seduce her? What is the meaning of the tragedy?

Dostoevsky has an answer to these questions: Stavrògin seduces young Matrjoša and leads her to suicide *through malice, deliberately wishing to commit evil*.

I have described this dramatic episode in *Demons* to introduce the reader to the family semantics in which obsessive-compulsive organizations develop.[1] In these families, as in *Demons*, at the center of the emotional dynamic is the

128

conflict between good and evil. The critical semantic polarity is "good/bad" to which are associated a series of meanings that contribute towards creating what I have called the "semantics of goodness," sets out in Figure 4.1. The importance assumed by this semantic ensures that the conversation in these families is organized preferably around episodes that bring into play the deliberate intention to do harm, selfishness, greed, guilty pleasure, but also goodness, purity, innocence, asceticism, as well as sacrifice and abstinence. As a result, members of these families will feel, and be seen as, good, pure, responsible or alternatively bad, selfish, immoral. They will meet people who will save them, improve them, or, on the contrary, who will initiate them into vice, lead them to behavior that will then make them feel guilty. They will marry people who are innocent, pure, capable of self-denial or, on the other hand, cruel egoists who will take advantage of them. Their children will be good, pure, chaste or alternatively will express their feelings without restraint, be aggressive in affirming themselves and their sexuality. Some of them will suffer from selfishness, and the malice of others or for the intrinsic badness of their own impulses. Others will be proud of their own purity and moral superiority. And some will feel gratified by the satisfaction of their own impulses.

There will be those, especially in families where this polarity dominates the conversation over several generations, who have so proven their particular self-denial as to seem ascetic, and those who have expressed their impulses with such selfishness as to be considered evil. An example of this is the great-grandmother of Giovanni, a patient with an obsessive-compulsive disorder who had a psychotic episode at the age of thirty.

The old people of the village still whispered there was something diabolical about the paternal side of Giovanni's family. His great-grandmother was the original cause of this gossip. In the 1890s she had left Italy for England with her husband and two sons, who were still small. The couple immediately found work in London and soon also had a baby girl. This third child wasn't yet a year old when Giovanni's great-grandmother left her husband and three children, and went off to America with another man. Having arrived in the New World, she left the man with whom she had been living and, with another man, made a fortune. Her husband returned from London to Italy with no intention of remarrying. He brought up the three children with the help of his sisters. After thirty years the great-grandmother, now elderly and in poor health, returned to Italy. She went back to live in the same village, a short distance away from her ex-husband, renewed contact with her children and demanded that they should respect and care for her. One of them, Giovanni's grandfather, refused. The others agreed, as she was wealthy. She ended her days more or less happily, "unpunished" as her great-grandson put it. Yet fate struck the daughter, who had the reputation of being a "witch": she was killed by a lover.

These distant events still had a direct influence over the patient. Giovanni was, for example, convinced that the serious illness his father had suffered

VALUES	
ABSTINENT GOODNESS	EVIL
CHASTITY	DEPRAVITY
SELF-DENIAL	SELF-ASSERTION
SAINTLINESS	WICKEDNESS
DEFINITIONS OF SELF / OTHERS / RELATIONSHIPS	
GOOD (ABSTINENT)	BAD
UPRIGHT	IMMORAL
STRICT	PERMISSIVE
INNOCENT	GUILTY
DEAD	ALIVE
WAYS OF RELATING	
ABSTAINING	CORRUPTING
SELF-SACRIFICING	TAKING ADVANTAGE
REDEEMING	DEPRAVING
CONDEMNING	ABSOLVING
EMOTIONS AND FEELINGS	
INNOCENCE	**GUILT**
DISGUST	PLEASURE

Figure 4.1 Semantics of goodness grid. The detailed grid is set out in Ugazio et al., 2009

shortly before his own psychotic crisis was divine punishment for an inheritance he had received from a direct descendant of the great-grandmother. And he was terrified by the idea that, being the only son, that "accursed" money would pass to him.

The conflict between good and evil that dominated the conversation in this family was the opposite of that expressed by St Augustine. Augustine encourages an optimistic view in the Western world: In the same way as darkness is just the absence of light, evil has no actual reality, it is just the privation of good.[2] He writes in *Confessions* (VII, *18*):

> ... .and the evil into whose origins I was inquiring is not a substance, for if it were a substance, it would be good. Either it would be an incorruptible substance, a great good indeed, or a corruptible substance, which could be corrupted only if it were good. Hence I saw and it was made clear to me that you made all things good.

But here, for the families we are concerned with, good is a privation of evil. The goodness we find in some of them is "abstinent," because it is no more than an absence of evil. Good people are *not* those who are helpful, friendly, polite, and generous towards others but those who renounce all expression of personal desire or defense of personal interests, who sacrifice themselves, who distance themselves from all "instinctual" urges. Bad people are those who express their own sexuality and their own aggressive impulses. In these families, as a result of dramatic incidents (such as persecution, rape, ill-treatment, deception or other evil behavior) in which some members have been either victims or perpetrators in the more or less recent past, sexuality and self-affirmation are generally expressed in a selfish manner. Events such as the episode in Dostoevsky's *Demons*, with which I began this chapter, occur rarely. A certain tragic pathos is nevertheless evident, since the critical polarity in these families is bound up with life and death, and life is to be found on the same side as evil, as indicated in Figure 4.1. *Vital expressions—sexuality, self-affirmation, investment in people and things—are where evil is played out whereas sacrifice, renouncement and asceticism are identified with good.*

It is no surprise that Freud introduced the theme of death several times in relation to obsessive-compulsive neurosis, even before the turning point of 1920. And obsessive-compulsive neurosis probably played a considerable role in inducing him to postulate the much-discussed death instinct. In his writings after 1920, he certainly expresses and maintains the conviction that hatred and sadism, as an expression of the death drive, play a crucial role in obsessive neurosis.

Due to the "abstinent"—or perhaps "subtractive"—nature of the goodness typically found in these families, "pure/impure" or "pure/corrupt" polarities are perhaps better than good or bad in expressing the central aspect of the semantics of sacrifice. But these polarities allude to sexuality, which is not always central to conversation in these families.

The emotions that form the basis of this semantic are *guilt/innocence* and *disgust/pleasure*. Precisely because sexuality and self-affirmation are linked with violence and other abusive behavior (at least in patients' perception), their expression generates a sense of guilt and disgust, whereas renunciation of impulsive urges, self-denial, is associated with purity and innocence.

Although the conflict between good and evil underlying the daily life of these families is far-removed from that of St Augustine or Thomas Aquinas,[3] the identification of sexuality, bodily phenomena and physical life with evil is present in Christianity, just as in other religions. Suffice it to recall the central role played by the contrast between pure and impure in the separation of Indian society into castes and, more generally, in Hindu ethics.[4] It is therefore no surprise that the culture of many families in which obsessive organizations develop is imbued with religious values, and some members actively participate in religious life. Other families subscribe to universalist principles such as socialism or communism, or to ideologies and movements that espouse the sacrifice of individual needs to idealistic precepts. Even in families with no religious values or ethical concern there is a "subtractive" concept of goodness. But it is not necessarily connected with sexual impulses. Sometimes it focuses on the evil of money, the desire to stand out, the affirmation of personal image, or business and money-making activities.

The fact that vital expressions—in particular sexuality and self-affirmation—are identified, obviously to a greater or lesser extent, with evil, does not mean that the impulsive urge is hardly present in these families. The desire and enjoyment in achieving it are, on the contrary, central in their emotional dynamic. Some psychotherapists have placed too much emphasis on the emotional coldness of obsessive contexts. Guidano (1987), for example, talks about a drastic reduction of the level of expansiveness and emotional warmth in the original family of these patients. Lorenzini and Sassaroli (1992, p. 81) suggest that "future obsessives have to deal with parents who are so cold and detached that it is impossible to achieve particular qualities in the relationship."[5]

As with phobic contexts, cognitivist authors highlight only one side of the coin. In the families with obsessive-compulsive disorders who have come to me for therapy, alongside positively regarded people who restrain their emotions, there are figures who experience extremely strong emotions, passions, and impulses. The point is that these impulses are guilty, selfish, sometimes perverse or malicious. The darker characters, those who maximize the negative polarities of the critical semantics, express guilty emotions; for this reason they are surrounded by disapproval, but exert a clear fascination on the family group. It is a sinister fascination, but nevertheless a fascination. All extreme characters have an attraction; in the case of these figures there is an additional reason: they are the life force. Their life is a "bad" one, but it is nevertheless stimulus that makes the plant grow, the urge which leads to copulation, the force which gives form to the crystal, and above all their "bad" life draws light from the sterility of the figures positioned at the opposite polarity.

The problem with these family contexts is therefore *not the lack of emotivity*, but if anything the overbearing, aggressive, at times perverse manner accompanying the emotions, where and when they are expressed. Sullivan (1956, p. 264) had this dynamic in mind when he stated that obsessive-compulsive patients "really know that their parents were not happy and that one of the parents, at least, was savagely cruel to them." Cruelty and violence are not generally expressed towards the future patient alone.

Salvatore, aged thirty-five, with a serious obsessive-compulsive disorder whose original intersubjective context I will describe in detail in Section 4.5, recalled during therapy witnessing several scenes of violence in which his father struck his mother, and also of his father hitting him and his four brothers. His father was unable to control his aggression any more than his sexuality—his habit of touching women's bottoms was so well known in the town where the family lived that he had been given an offensive nickname that alluded to his vice.

Such a pattern is to be found in the history of many patients: the "Instinctual" or "impulsive"[6] parent externalizes his or her own guilty urges—generally domineering, aggressive, sometimes sadistic behavior—towards the "abstinent" partner and, secondly, towards the future obsessive patient. I will return to this question below. First, however, I would like to reconstruct the drama of those people with an obsessive organization, as they experience it in their own subjective way.

4.2 The Origins of Doubt

Like phobic, obsessive organizations establish a strange loop that involves the levels of self and relationship. The loop, however, has a more complex structure than that for phobic organizations, and gives rise to a psychological situation that is generally more dramatic. As the reader will recall, the dilemma for people with phobic disorders can be expressed by the following question: should they be assured of a rewarding affectionate relationship (bringing with it protection and security) but through this feel suffocated and disparaged? Or should they break the ties, be free, but also alone, at the mercy of a dangerous world? When the reflexivity of the loop is greatest, phobic subjects fluctuate between two equally unacceptable prospects: to maintain the bonds of attachment, to be protected, means feeling suffocated by a humiliating dependence; but to achieve autonomy, and with it self-respect, means being overwhelmed by fear, since they are alone in a dangerous world. Of these two prospects, one prefers the relationship while the other gives priority to the self. In obsessive subjects, the fluctuation resulting from the strange reflexive loop is to the inner self: subjects, on entering into significant relationships, become prey to conflicting perceptions of themselves. *Erotic involvement, but also investment in people or projects aimed at self-affirmation, break the feeling of personal unity because they generate conflicting perceptions*, or, in other words, they create a split between one part which is "good," "right" and another which is "bad," "wrong." When the reflexivity is greatest, the subject fluctuates between completely dichotomous perceptions of self; *erotic involvement and self-affirmation become inconsistent with a unified perception of self (Figure 4.2)*.[7]

Psychoanalysis[8] and cognitive psychotherapy[9] have both emphasized, each using their own language, the presence in this organization of the significance of conflicting splits and perceptions of self. But why this presence of dichotomous self-images? For the moment I will leave aside the position of subjects in their family context; I will look at this in detail later on. Here, I will limit attention to the current situation, as experienced by those involved: what is it in the "here and now" that induces the patient to experience this split?

Cognitive therapists seem evasive in this respect. Answering these questions means entering an "instinctual" world that has long been the prerogative of psychoanalysis and is not congenial to the cognitivist tradition. Nor is systemic

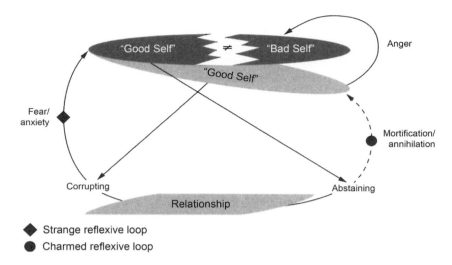

Figure 4.2 The strange reflexive loop of obsessive-compulsive organizations

psychotherapy familiar with the semantic world of obsessive organizations. This world is certainly more akin to and consistent with psychoanalysis. It is no surprise that Freud (1925/1959, p. 262) stated that "obsessive neurosis is unquestionably the most interesting and rewarding subject of analytic research" (1925/1959, p. 113). These considerations must not put us off: it is possible to enter semantic worlds that are closer to other approaches, even following stretches of road generally trodden by others, without compromising our own point of view.

Let us return to the dichotomous images that form the strange loop, trying to investigate their meaning. They derive from two equally unacceptable alternatives. The first is being involved in pleasurable relationships, being outgoing and assertive by entering into "instinctual" relationships with others. For subjects with an obsessive organization this alternative means "dirtying" themselves or others, infecting or being infected; it implies becoming bad, corrupt, disgusting, or even contemptible and, as a result, of exposing themselves to the risk of losing more significant relationships of attachment as well as being punished. This is why the taboo of contact is important in obsessive compulsive disorders. As Freud had previously pointed out, bodily contact symbolically expresses involvement of an erotic or aggressive nature; for this reason it becomes the central point of a system of prohibitions in obsessive organizations.[10]

The second alternative is also unacceptable for subjects with an obsessive organization. Respecting the taboo of contact, being pure, good, means being likeable, but requires withdrawal, renunciation of all pleasurable involvement with others, and consequently self-sacrifice. *Expressing sexuality and aggression, seeking personal achievement, involvement in rewarding relationships, means therefore being bad and unworthy of love; whereas being likeable, worthy of love, requires self-denial, personal sacrifice.* From here the continual oscillation between a self-image that is good, but sacrificial and ultimately mortifying, and one which is dynamic but intrinsically evil, which leads to disownment, rejection.

This dilemma confers a dramatic pathos on the strange reflexive loop because it brings life and death into play: being good, likeable, means taking a step back in life, dying (at least partially), but living involves becoming wicked, and therefore being exposed to the danger of rejection as well as becoming the target for reprisals and revenge.

In the face of such a radical alternative, *doubt*, the *search for certainty* and the resulting *decisional paralysis* which so often afflict those with an obsessive organization, become intelligent survival strategies.

Other members of the family, as we shall see later on, are able to deal with this inherent dilemma in the semantics of goodness by positioning themselves with those who are "abstinent" or those who are "impulsive." Those who are abstinent can be proud of their purity, they can feel disgust for those who indulge in pleasure, in the same way that those who are impulsive find pleasure and enjoyment in satisfying their urges or feel guilty about their conduct. They are able nevertheless to position themselves between those who are good or bad without being trapped in the dilemma: They take a step back in life or play a full part in it accepting the negative connotation resulting from any sense of guilt.

Two emotional states make it impossible for obsessive organizations to position themselves with one or other pole or to position themselves happily in a median position: one is *fear/anxiety*, the other *mortification/annihilation*.[11] Fear is generally experienced by persons with an obsessive organization when they take part in life, express their personal impulses and as a consequence feel "bad." More than actual fear, it is often anxiety. Fear is always fear of something specific, whereas anxiety does not relate to anything precise. Obsessive individuals, when involved in pleasurable relationships, feel unsafe, and it is often difficult to identify the source of their state of alert. Mortification, on the other hand, is experienced when there is renouncement: For these people being pure, proper, means being overwhelmed by feelings of mortification and nothingness which, in turn, generate anger and bitterness.

These two emotional states (fear/anxiety and mortification/annihilation) prevent subjects from positioning themselves at one or other pole and send them into a continual oscillation: when reflexivity reaches its peak, subjects literally bounce between two opposing self-images, because the one (the "bad self") generates fear and anger and has to be rapidly abandoned whereas the other (the "good self") creates annihilation and mortification and cannot be maintained.

Fear/anxiety and annihilation/mortification are not the exclusive prerogative of those with obsessive organizations. Fear, for example, is central to members of families generating a phobic organization, either for those who are victims of it, such as the agoraphobic patient, or for those who, through their courage, are capable of keeping it under control. What distinguishes obsessive organizations is the specific contexts in which these emotions are experienced. Moreover, individuals with an obsessive organization are the only people within their own family to experience these two emotional conditions systematically, in the contexts I have described. Members of the family who throw themselves into life, and as a result are seen and see themselves as bad, are not prey to fear and anxiety, feeling no more than a sense of guilt; in the same way, those who are good and pure are not afflicted by feelings of unbearable self-effacement and mortification as happens with those with obsessive organization.

But what are obsessives fearful of at the moment when they come into contact with people or things and perceive themselves as bad? The cases on which I rely, though conducted in a setting and with a clinical method different to psychoanalysis, confirm Freud's answer to these questions. The fear and anxiety of obsessives is based on very particular dangers—above all of losing the relationship with the main figures of attachment; but there is also the risk of punishment and reprisal in relation to personal physical and sexual integrity. This is punishment and reprisal that psychoanalysis has traced to the oedipal complex and related castration anxiety. The observations of cognitive therapists do not differ much from those of Freud. They also state that the fear and anxiety of obsessives is based on the fear of losing the preferred bond of attachment (Guidano, 1987, 1991). The area of convergence is still greater if we recall that in *Inhibitions, Symptom and Anxiety*, Freud (1925/1959) identifies castration anxiety as a form of separation anxiety.[12]

Feelings of mortification/annihilation, instead, derive from the repression of personal impulses and desires. For obsessives, unlike what happens to others in their family, abstaining from instinctual urges means self-annihilation. When the reflexivity of the strange loop is greatest, renunciation is experienced as an intolerable mortification, which generates anger and resentment. The dark, sad aspects accompanying this organization derive mainly from these feelings of mortification and annihilation. The obsessive appears as someone impoverished and empty. The impression of annihilation among obsessives is so strong that some psychoanalysts, such as Rado (1959), consider them constitutionally lacking in *joie de vivre*, enthusiasm, vitality: the "forces of id" are said to be marked by a congenital weakness. Nothing could be further from my observations: such mortification and annihilation, which are generally not hidden but on the contrary are apparent from the tone of voice, gaze, facial expressions and posture, give the measure of how much the renunciation of pleasure weighs upon people with this organization. Such an acute feeling of deprivation would not be present if the desire were not pressing, if the will for achievement were not overwhelming. Fear and mortification allow us to delve into the position of the obsessive subject within the crucial semantics. Even when the reflexivity of the loop is low and does not produce the critical oscillation between dichotomous perceptions of self ("good self"/"bad self"), subjects with an obsessive organization find themselves in that *median position* between the two extremes I described in Chapter 2. This is a peculiarity of this organization. Phobic subjects, as I have shown in the previous chapter, tend to construct their own identity by positioning themselves at the "freedom and independence" extreme of the critical semantics (strategy for limiting closeness), then the opposite "attachment, need for protection" extreme (strategy for emotional distancing). They oscillate between the two extremes only when the reflexivity of the loop is greatest. Nor do those with psychogenic eating and depressive disorders place themselves in a median position.

On the contrary, those with an obsessive organization place themselves neither at the "goodness, purity" pole, nor at the opposite extreme of "badness, depravity": they hold a median position. They generally place themselves in a position closer to the "goodness, purity, self-sacrifice" extreme, but always remaining mid-way and reducing the reflexivity of the loop through operations of compensation towards the two extremes. Fear/anxiety and mortification/annihilation are the emotions that accompany these movements. These emotions are systematically expressed by subjects with an obsessive organization, even when the reflexivity of the loop is low. Those placing themselves in the median position express themselves, and therefore live their lives, by moving first towards one extreme and then towards the other. Only in this way can they define themselves as partners and take part in the conversation.[13] For people with an obsessive organization, to move in the "purity, goodness" direction involves feeling annihilating mortification, producing anger and bitterness, whereas to move in the "badness, expression of personal impulses" direction brings the risk of a terrible punishment that becomes more distressing the more indefinite it is. These movements are generally limited and balanced, over a relatively short space of time, by conduct of an opposite kind. Subjects therefore generally manage to avoid feeling prey to an annihilating mortification (as would happen if they moved too far in the "purity, goodness" direction) or of seeing themselves, and being seen, as wicked, and feeling unworthy of love and so, rejected (as would happen if they moved too far in the "badness, expression of personal impulses, sensual pleasure" direction). Nonetheless, when the reflexivity of the loop becomes greatest, any oscillation towards one or other extreme, however balanced, becomes intolerable.

Every attempt at self-affirmation, at expressing personal impulses and desires, is accompanied by a feeling of personal corruption, disgust, fear, and anxiety. Every search for asceticism and purity is marked by feelings of annihilating mortification and anger, or is clouded by the doubt that the asceticism is a mask behind which are hidden foul intentions. Subjects thus enter the disaster area of the middle position. The processes of exteriorization that are obviously present in this position, even though partial, leave space for implogenetic processes[14]: subjects try even harder not to define themselves in relation to the extremes, following each movement towards one extreme with another of an opposite kind. The period of time of the oscillation thus becomes so short that they find themselves at the mercy of two completely dichotomous perceptions of themselves (Figure 4.3).

It is here that *doubt*, the search for *certainty* and consequent *decisional paralysis* take over. Subjects reject all expression of their own impulses, because they give them an unacceptable self image. Faced with the impossibility of finding an acceptable positioning either at the "abstinent" pole or at the "instinctual" pole, obsessives adopt a position of stubborn immobility, like a pendulum gradually reducing its swing until it comes to a halt. The primary function of doubt is to paralyze the subject, as Freud had perceptively shown when discussing the obsessive-compulsive case known as the "Rat Man":

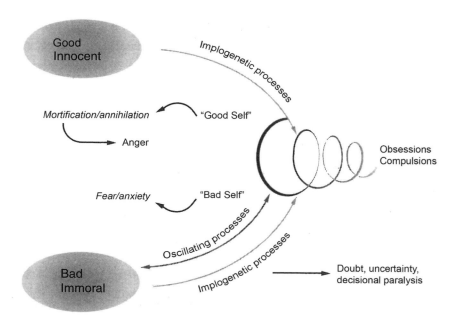

Figure 4.3 The strange reflexive loop inside the middle position

The creation of uncertainty is one of the methods employed by the neurosis for drawing the patient away from reality and isolating him from the world—which is among the objects of every psychoneurotic disorder. Again, it is only too obvious what efforts are made by the patients themselves in order to be able to avoid certainty and remain in doubt. Some of them, indeed, give a vivid expression to this tendency in a dislike of clocks and watches (for these at least make the time of day certain), and in the unconscious artifices which they employ in order to render these doubt-removing instruments innocuous. Our present patient had developed a peculiar talent for avoiding a knowledge of any facts which would have helped him in deciding his conflict. Thus he was in ignorance upon those matters relating to his lady which were the most relevant to the question of his marriage: He was ostensibly unable to say who had operated upon her and whether the operation had been unilateral or bilateral.

(Freud, 1909/1955, p. 232)

Freud is certainly right. Any therapist who has experience of obsessive patients knows that they frequently behave like the "Rat Man"—they are careful not to gather crucial information to resolve the doubts that beset them. This is also because obsessive patients are particularly suspicious of themselves. Who can guarantee that behind that non-aggressive, apparently well-intentioned search for success there is not some foul purpose? Who can convince them that even their sacrifice, their asceticism, does not conceal some ulterior personal gain, some secret vice? The profound feeling of mortification at the moment when subjects seem to accept the sacrifice, makes them feel, with emotional immediacy, that no one, not even they themselves, renounces life without some resistance. And is it right to forego their essential needs? Is pride in their own purity and moral superiority, disdain for those who are corrupt and evil, sufficient to make up for the sense of mortification and anger they experience? Thanks to these doubts, people with an obsessive organization make it more difficult for themselves to follow the path of vice or that of virtue, therefore limiting their fear/anxiety and mortification/annihilation. But it is the paralysis. The subject—by now the patient—risks implosion, which is the destruction of the middle position. And it's at this point of the process that the symptoms appear, which have by now become the only vital movements. Here I refer to their obsessions and compulsions. Obsessions generally express forbidden impulses (sexual thoughts and images, aggressive impulses), whereas compulsions are forms of repetitive behavior (hand washing, tidying etc.) aimed at calming the fear and anxiety that obsessions provoke. The distinction is often not so clear: compulsions can sometimes express guilty impulses (for example compulsive masturbation), whereas obsessions can be aimed at limiting anxiety.

With the development of symptoms, patients continue to do what they did before, namely balancing between two extremes. But the balancing now takes place egodystonically: It is no longer the patients who decide, but rather the symptoms that are imposed on them against their will. Compulsions and obsessions are permissible because they are egodystonic forms of behavior: patients are no longer responsible for them, even if they know they are produced by their own minds because they experience them as external events from which they cannot escape. In fact, thanks to the onset of the symptoms, the reflexivity of the loop is limited and the subject avoids impending punishment as well as total renouncement.

The strange reflexive loop also helps to explain their *ambivalence* and *lack of spontaneity*—two traits found in subjects with an obsessive organization, and no less characteristic than doubt and the search for certainty. Anxiety and mortification, the two emotional states found in the strange reflexive loop, encourage ambivalence. Each relationship that allows subjects to express their forbidden "instincts" gives rise to feelings of ambivalence, since it exposes them to terrible risks (punishment, rejection etc.). But also close relationships that lead them towards abstinence and self-sacrifice are marked by love and hatred: the mortification and annihilation that subjects experience in attempting to pursue the path of "abstinent" goodness produce hatred and anger towards those who are the source of these choices. The ambivalence, which accompanies all loving relationships, also explains why obsessives resort to *superstitious practices*. As Freud pointed out in the early 1900s, obsessives use these strategies to try to protect themselves from the guilt of desiring the death of their loved ones and from fate's revenge.

> Their thoughts (obsessive neurotics' thoughts) are unceasingly occupied with other people's length of life and possibility of death; their superstitious propensities have had no other content to begin with, and have perhaps no other source whatever. But these neurotics need the help of the possibility of death chiefly in order that it may act a solution of conflicts they have left unsolved. Their essential characteristic is that they are incapable of coming to a decision, especially in matters of love; they endeavor to postpone every decision, and in their doubt which person they shall decide for or what measures they shall take against a person, they are obliged to choose as their model the old German courts of justice, in which the suits were usually brought to an end, before judgment had been given, by the death of the parties to the dispute. Thus in every conflict which enters their lives they are on the look-out for the death of someone who is of importance to them, usually of someone they love—such as one of their parents, or a rival, or one of the objects of their love between which their inclinations are wavering.
>
> (*ibid*, p. 236)

140

The lack of naturalness and spontaneity, on the other hand, is due to the median position. This positioning requires of itself a greater control of personal behavior compared with that required by the positions at the extremes: Individuals in a median position, who are continually balancing themselves in relation to those positioned at the two extremes of the critical semantics, must be especially careful in their own behavior. If, on top of this, the dilemma faced by the obsessive raises questions of life and death, it is clear that the spontaneous expression of emotions is impossible. People with this organization express the absence of naturalness in their posture, in their cautious language, in their style of thought and in every other form of outward expression. This aspect is most noticeable in children, because it conflicts with our picture of infancy:

> The obsessive child is unhappy, unnatural, forced, and lacking of spontaneity. That is the critical issue: how to help the obsessive child to naturalness and spontaneity. It would be easier if we had a happy "pre-morbid state" into which we could reinstate him, but the obsessive child of ten years, for example, has often been markedly unhappy all of his life—he needs habilitation into happiness, not rehabilitation (…). For he is not at all the fantasized happy child of the primitivist. Instead, he is a miserable example of human misery—the misery of over-reflection to diminish his anxiety about himself.
>
> (Adams, 1973, p.4)

Adults with an obsessive organization also suffer from lack of spontaneity. This trait, together with the feeling of mortification, confers on people with this organization that gloomy, sad, unhappy aspect that I have already described.

4.3 Life: A Story Forbidden?

When therapists meet people with an obsessive organization, the reflexivity of the strange loop has already been reduced by the symptomatology.

A reconstruction of the type of life and personality prior to the onset of symptoms indicates a plurality of forms of individual functioning and lifestyle that can be seen as strategies aimed at dealing with the strange loop, reducing its reflexivity. Here too, as in the case of phobics, we are not dealing with anything that might be likened to a plan or program containing some kind of intentionality. What subjects experience is that certain stories are "permitted," in the sense of being easy to live, while others are dangerous, disturbing, and therefore "forbidden."

For those with an obsessive organization, life as such would seem, at first sight, to be a forbidden story. In reality the many and highly varied forms of individual functioning that precede the first appearance of symptoms are attempts to leave space for emotional commitment and personal achievement. For those with this organization, life is a story forbidden but also desperately desired.

Greatly simplifying, the range of strategies used by those with an obsessive-compulsive organization to reduce the reflexivity of the strange loop, prior to the first appearance of symptoms, can be categorized into two forms of individual functioning. I will call these two forms of functioning *strategy of purity* and *strategy of subjugated evil*. These have to be seen as extremes in a continuum of highly varied ways of individual functioning.

Through the *strategy of purity* subjects try to avoid the dichotomous perception of themselves, involving themselves in activities that are both "instinctually" neutral and prestigious. People with this strategy try strenuously to maintain a positive image of themselves which, in line with the critical semantics, is identified with their feeling and being regarded as good, pure, upright. The threat that brings out a dichotomous self-perception is kept at bay through a predominating (sometimes all-absorbing) involvement in areas which entail a *distancing from interaction* and which, at the same time, are *prestigious*, such as religion, science, law, politics, art, literature or philosophy. But intellectual work of any kind can become central because it encourages the development of interests and capacities that have no direct connection with aggression and sexuality.

Even if they are not entirely lacking in emotional warmth, capacity to empathize and tenderness, people using this strategy tend to show a limited range of emotions. Many psychoanalysts and cognitive therapists have insisted too much on obsessives being barren, unaffectionate, lacking in vitality. Unlike what happens to narcissistic personalities, people with this organization perceive intimacy as pleasurable and intensely desirable. Nevertheless emotional ties are felt to be dangerous because they lead subjects to see themselves as bad, unworthy. For this reason, people using this strategy control and limit the expression of emotional involvement, sometimes by devoting themselves entirely to intellectual activity, such as science, art, religion, politics etc. Even when the individual has stable sexual relations and has established a family, the priority is generally given to these "neutral" areas that are freer from fear and anxiety.

As often observed, subjects with an obsessive organization tend to belong to highly ethical worlds. Most of the "neutral" areas I have mentioned have an ethical value, and many of those with this strategy show a notable ethical concern. But ethical awareness is not a *sine qua non* of this strategy. Sometimes it is absent.

Angela, a 40-year-old primary school teacher in a small town in Piedmont, had never had any particularly strong ethical principles. From the onset of symptoms, five years before the beginning of therapy, she began consulting clairvoyants, priests, and fortune-tellers, placing them all on the same

level—collaborators who were more or less amenable and easily manipulated, through whom she could pursue her superstitious practices. Teaching,
to which she gave absolute priority, was not regarded as a vocation but as a
privilege. Though she had a husband and a daughter, she had never looked
after them. She dedicated herself entirely to her teaching, assiduously attending school bodies, accepting duties, and taking on responsibilities that went
beyond what was required of her. Teaching had been her whole world until
the moment when the seriousness of her symptoms forced her to stop work.
This apparently traditional woman, of modest social background, whose aspect
and culture was entirely in keeping with the reality of the small town where
she lived, had always behaved at home like a New York feminist. She had never
been interested in the home and always delegated domestic chores to her husband and parents-in-law. Even her daughter had been brought up by them.
Motherhood was a burden for her:

> Perhaps I was too young, or perhaps I am not cut out for it … when
> Sara was born I couldn't wait to get back to school, that is how I am,
> I like being out of the house. My mother-in-law adored the baby
> and I was happy for her to look after her … my husband also did an
> enormous amount for Sara.

Angela did not seem conscious of having given up all her most important
emotional commitments; instead, she was proud of her intellectual superiority. During the therapy she repeated several times, smiling with satisfaction:
"I am the brains, my husband is the brawn." And above all she was convinced
that, through her disinterest in all and everything, except for school, she had
enjoyed a position of absolute privilege.

During her childhood and adolescence, thanks to her academic ability, she
had enjoyed the pursuit of "advantage." Her mother was proud of her success
at school and released her from all duties and responsibilities on condition that
She applied herself to her studies. She sent her to a private school at fourteen
where she could study for her teaching diploma, spending the whole of her
salary on the fees. The experience was certainly not a happy one for Angela:
she was homesick and felt at a disadvantage with her classmates, who were all
from more privileged social backgrounds. But her mother, by relieving her of
domestic chores—chores not even her father could avoid—and then sending
her to a boarding school whose cost was out of proportion to the family's
meager income, had placed her in a position of superiority, which was the
cause, among other things, of bitter conflict with her father and her younger
sister.

As this example demonstrates, it is essential for this strategy that the
"instinctually" barren area on which subjects channel their energies is prestigious, whereas it is not essential for it to have any ethical nature. Through their

investment in science, art or other intellectual pursuit, they acquire a superior-ity. *The essential component of this strategy is the superiority itself: If not moral, then intellectual.*

People with this strategy are often proud and overweening, sometimes arro-gant and condescending. Their sense of superiority, based on the prestigious nature of the areas in which they invest, enables them to limit the ever-impend-ing feelings of mortification. Their desires for aggressive self-affirmation and their sexual impulses are strongly inhibited. The inhibition is expressed not only in the priority given to the areas I have defined as "neutral," but also in the way in which these people express themselves in such areas.

In reality the "neutrality" of such areas does not prevent them from satisfy-ing many forbidden impulses. Psychoanalysis has discovered mechanisms and provided examples in this respect that are so fitting that they have become commonplace. They bring to mind the magistrate who as guardian of the law can give vent to his cruel urges when dealing with the defendant, or the con-fessor who, in the name of God, can satisfy his morbid curiosity, and all forms of "black pedagogy"[15] through which scientists, professors and teachers, in carrying out their vocation, can express their personal sadism.

The satisfaction of impulses that this strategy allows is nevertheless *indirect*: the original desires are mortified, inhibited, along the way. It should be added that it is difficult for people with this strategy to achieve success, whether in art or science, or recognition as a political leader or religious authority. These people often remain as assistants, "eternal seconds" to outgoing personalities who can reach positions not open to them.

The choice of partner also frequently reflects this interactive pattern. Those with this strategy, needing to drastically limit their expression of aggression and sexuality, restrain their ever-impending feeling of annihilation and morti-fication by choosing partners who are ambitious, aggressive or sexually promis-cuous. Through their relationship with their partner they can thus experience vicariously what for them is forbidden, they can bask in their reflected light without exposing themselves to too many risks, and they can naturally fight against the negativity of their companion, re-educating, chastising him/her and so forth.

This pattern, which is often found in the married relationship but also in intellectual or professional partnerships, tends to encourage ambivalence. Since the person developing this strategy does not put his or her own skills and abilities to good use, the other is led to use them to their own advantage. It is often the subject who provides the necessary help and support to ensure the partner's success; nevertheless, when the companion receives recognition, the subject then harbors anger, resentment, envy, and bitterness. The rela-tional situation does not change if the forbidden sexual behavior is expressed by the partner, even though the sado-masochistic element of the relationship becomes more evident.

The "strategy of subjugated evil" is essentially "ethical." But, paradoxically, those who express it tend to externalize the bad aspects of themselves more, in comparison with the "strategy of purity." During the course of their lives, these people also give priority to "neutral" areas that provide a distancing from interaction, but these areas must have an ethical relevance. *What is essential for these people is to have a set of principles that enable them to "justly" divide the world into good and bad.* Having firm ethical principles that allow them to divide the world "justly" into those who are good and bad, subjects can express hatred, lust, sadism towards that part of the world which is identified as despicable, evil. In comparison with those whom I have described above, people who develop this strategy are less inhibited in relation to forbidden impulses, especially hatred, aggression, anger, resentment, and sadism. For this very reason they recognize and accept in themselves those elements that make them bad, unreliable or even malicious. The reflexivity of the loop is limited by submitting such impulses to an ethical consideration; the "bad self" is contextualized by the "good self"; the latter indicates to the former the persons and situations to whom they can "legitimately" express themselves.

The categorization on which this strategy is based is *external* and *rigid*. The person does not evaluate one by one whether a thing is good or bad, but relies on principles—codified ideas that are external and perceived as such—or on institutions (religion, political parties, etc.). Due to the reflexivity of the strange loop, subjects have no self-trust; to avoid uncertainty they must therefore rely on external principles and authorities. These principles are generally embodied in specific people who provide moral guidance; they are often substitutes for the original figure of attachment, and the patient is sometimes aware of this.

Salvatore,[16] when describing his faith in the Jehovah's Witnesses, had this to say:

> It is a strict religion, it is much, much stricter, more rigid, than yours [*referring to the therapist*]. Yours is a religion which allows you to do all sorts of things, provided you repent ... [*he laughs maliciously*]. It's rather like my mother, she was strict, she wanted honesty: Woe betide anyone who did wrong. My wife is also rigid ...

This strategy allows a greater expression of forbidden impulses, it therefore produces more outgoing personalities than the "strategy of purity." The behavior of heterosexual men towards their partners often falls into the well-known pattern of "saint/prostitute": they direct their guilty sexual impulses towards other women who are less respectable, at least in their estimation, obtaining pleasure from doing so, whereas they do not regard the woman they love and respect as sexually stimulating. What was, at least in the past, "the most prevalent form of degradation in erotic life"[17] (of the male) would seem pertinent (though certainly not exclusive) to this strategy.

A university professor, in his forties, who had long been an active left-wing militant, used to seduce attractive "bourgeois" female students with whom he freely gave vent to his sadistic urges. He was excited above all by hurting these young women with his sudden disinterest, or humiliating them by transferring his attentions to others. Though this conduct, in at least one case, had a dramatic consequence, the middle-class social condition of his victims freed him from any sense of guilt and fear, providing him with a sort of impunity. On the other hand, he remained on close and affectionate terms, though less sexually involved, with his wife with whom he shared cultural and political interests and who, like him, came from a modest social background.

People using this strategy can also exhibit aggressive, violent, bullying behavior, provided it is in the "right" direction.

The years of student protest in the 1960s were the happiest times in Francesco's life. His militancy had enabled him to exteriorize his considerable abilities, and to give vent to his aggressive self-assertion and willpower. On several occasions he had been violent and abusive. Everyone recognized his leadership, and he was respected and feared even by his political rivals. During that period, his aggression and self-assertion were placed at the service of a higher cause: Francesco was convinced he was acting in the interests of the proletariat. Later on, when he should have been acting in his own interests, having abandoned his activism and turned his back on the values in which he had believed, he came up against a series of "inexplicable" failures and frustrations that resulted in him going into psychotherapy. He first began a university career, but had to give it up: though he had the support of a leading academic, he decided to leave as he could not complete the research he had set out to do. He went to work for a publisher but couldn't make his mark—his initiatives and ideas were exploited by others and he was always left in a humiliating position on the sideline.

These two strategies—of purity and subjugating evil—tend to be brought into crisis by rather different kinds of events. In relation to the first strategy, these events relate to episodes that make it obligatory to express forbidden feelings.

Let us return to Angela, the primary school teacher who had never looked after her husband or daughter, let alone the housework. The onset of her symptoms coincided with her mother's admittance to a home for the elderly. The episode made her face up to her ambivalence towards her mother who, though old and in poor health, was still proud and authoritarian. She wanted Angela to let her come to live with her and care for her; the other daughter had to look after her husband, who suffered from recurrent depression. Besides, Angela had always been her mother's favorite and it was now her turn—and her duty—to pay her back for her many sacrifices. Angela well remembered the hardships, suffering, and sacrifices her mother had made to give her an education. She had once visited her at boarding school wearing no underwear: she had been so tired and busy that she had only realized she had forgotten to put it on when she was already on the train. But Angela didn't feel she could take her to live with her. One attempt at living together, after an emergency, had proved disastrous: her mother, already on the verge of senility, bullied everyone, including her son-in-law and granddaughter. One Sunday, while the three of them were off on a trip in the mountains, she had tried to commit suicide. Everyone felt guilty about having left her alone. But Angela's husband, who undertook the domestic chores with the occasional help of his own parents, refused to look after his mother-in-law as well; their daughter agreed, and rejected the idea of her grandmother coming to live with them. But it was Angela above all who didn't want to give in to her mother's demands. Her own feelings towards her had always been ambivalent. She had never tolerated her obstinacy, her parsimony, her authoritarianism, to which was now added her arrogance. But she felt duty-bound towards her. Agreeing to take her into her own home meant giving in to an intolerable demand, but putting her into an old people's home meant receiving a negative self-image. Angela did not choose between these two alternatives: she became ill.

In the case of the second strategy (the subjugation of evil), the critical events are all those situations that bring into crisis (directly or indirectly) the principles that allow subjects to divide the world into good and bad, and consequently to express their own bad impulses, subjugating them to the "good self." Often it is not the principles themselves that cause delusion or vacillation, but the people who embody them. The outcome, however, is the same: subjects lose the external point of view through which they had subjugated their "good self" and their "bad self," thus limiting the reflexivity of the strange loop.

Father Ruggero, after almost thirty years of relatively good health, at 59 had another crisis in which he was disturbed by erotic thoughts, anxiety, and insomnia. The first appearance of symptoms, when he was 30, led to hospitalization for over two months and a difficult period that continued for several years and ended only when he decided to scale down his ambitions and return to the small Tuscan village where he was born. From then on he lived with his parents and devoted himself to his parish. The whole village respected him for his remarkable intelligence; he was also liked by parishioners for his affability and sensitivity. From his intellectual and urbane past he retained a passion for poetry—a collection of his poems had been published—and for long periods travelling abroad. He went off once or twice a year to Third World countries, during which he had sexual encounters with local boys—sometimes the relations were purely erotic, at other times they were emotional, developing into love. His sexuality was exteriorized only during these journeys, and with boys from far-off places. He had never had sexual relations with anyone from his own town, even though his abstinence was hard for him: he was wracked by erotic desires. On his return from his travels, he would receive a cool welcome from his mother. She knew nothing about what Father Ruggero described as his "vice" but she seemed to have guessed something: she didn't like these journeys and since she couldn't stop him going she tried to reduce their length. The last crisis occurred just fifteen days after his return from a holiday in India. Nothing out of the ordinary had happened during the trip: Father Ruggero had met an Indian boy; he seemed to have fallen in love with him to some extent but had returned without too much regret, happy nevertheless to be back at his "secure base."

The patient was at first unable to explain the crisis: nothing particular seemed to have happened. But the crisis had been preceded by two crucial episodes. On his return from India his mother had not greeted him in her usual severe reproachful manner; on the contrary, she had welcomed him back. Authoritarian, strict, upright and religious, Father Ruggero's mother had always been his point of reference and his guarantee that the sexuality exploits would remain limited to particular contexts, in other words his trips abroad. When confronted with the unusual kindness of her welcome, Father Ruggero felt a powerful disorientation, as if his mother, now in her eighties, had relinquished her guiding role. A few days later, another episode increased his sense of bewilderment: his mother, who rarely expressed affection, approached him as he was reading, stroked his head and said: "You know, I won't live forever, sooner or later I'll have to go." Father Ruggero knew perfectly well that his mother was old, and this reference to her death disturbed him, but he was confused all the more by her meek submissive tone, by the realization that she was no longer an authoritative figure for him, and above all by her insecurity and fragility. Father Ruggero felt lost.

4.4 The Original Triangle

I will now widen the field of observation to the interpersonal context within which this organization of meaning is developed to try to give a more exhaustive answer to the following two questions:

1) Why are people with an obsessive organization unable to follow the path of asceticism? Why do they regard the renunciation of sexual and aggressive impulses as a terrible mortification?
2) What prevents them from being "bad," from devoting themselves to vice, from displaying hatred, aggression and guilty sexual behavior?

Though raised in earlier paragraphs, they have so far been answered only partially.

Experience of therapy with families of subjects with this organization shows that some members of the family choose the path of sacrifice, of renunciation, without being afflicted by the feelings of annihilation that make such a choice impracticable for obsessive subjects. Other members of the same family have guilty impulses without being threatened by intolerable levels of fear and anxiety. Why, then, are these two paths unavoidable and at the same time impossible for the subject with an obsessive organization?

Classic psychoanalysis, though it has made an essential contribution to the understanding of this organization, does not help us here since it resolves these questions within the intrapsychic dynamic. Instead it raises a question.

I am not inclined to accept that the oedipal complex has the universal importance that classic psychoanalysis ascribes to it, but nevertheless I have to agree that oedipal desires are often apparent in obsessives. This "empirical evidence" opens up this question: What characteristics of the pattern of family relationships in which obsessive organizations develop encourage oedipal desires? This is the third question I will attempt to answer.

Numerous post-Freudian psychoanalysts and psychodynamic therapists have connected the obsessive-compulsive disorder to intrafamily relationships. Whereas their single case descriptions are often deep and insightful, the hypotheses put forward regarding the family patterns involved in this disorder, are unconvincing. Some of them are so unspecific as to be of little use for our purposes (Salzman, 1966). Others, on the other hand, are specific. Rado (1959), for example, identifies as a characteristic feature in the interpersonal context of obsessive-compulsive neurosis the conflict between mother and son for independence and, connected to this conflict, the cycle between provocative anger and obedient fear. For Laughlin (1967) obsessive-compulsives', anger and rectitude area response to the mother's behavior, whose refusal to accept the child's negative feelings is seen as a key problem in the genesis of this organization. According to Adams (1973), the parents of obsessive children are deeply ambivalent towards their children and are disparaging and disapproving of their sexual and aggressive impulses. In addition, they develop educational practices based on a rigid observation of social rules out of proportion to their age. The result is a situation of this kind:

> Often, the children were outwardly copies of their parents. The boys were trained (often by the mother) to be overly correct, giving a result which their peers regarded as sissy or effeminate. The girls were joylessly prim and proper, and inflexible. The boys and girls seemed overly "straight," pseudo mature and often anxiously rigid and driven. Appearing older than their actual ages was the result of their being too socialized too soon. [...]. The little professors and eggheads were numerous among the obsessive children. [...] They were caricatures of straight-laced adults, hypercorrect on the outside, but deeply resentful and hateful below the surface.
>
> (Adams, p. 234)

The negative connotation given by parents to sexuality and aggression has been highlighted by some of the cognitive psychotherapists (Guidano, 1987, 1991; Guidano & Liotti, 1983; Lorenzini & Sassaroli, 1992). I quoted before as part of a more general pattern of devaluing emotional, expressive, and spontaneousbehavior in favor of pseudo-mature behavior.

The same psychotherapists have emphasized the ambivalence of the key attachment figures, giving rise to the "ambivalent-resistant" attachment, regarded as one of the most frequent patterns in the childhood of future obsessives. According to Guidano (1987, p.196), the crucial variable in the genesis of obsessive-compulsive organizations is the contradictory behavior of the key figure of attachment.

> The parental behaviour of at least one of the two parents (the other is usually a figure of lesser, *relatively marginal*,[18] emotional significance) is characterized by ambivalent and contrasting feelings towards the child. The basic aspect to be found in this ambivalence consists, more often than not, in a hostile and dismissive attitude, hidden and camouflaged by an external veneer of devotion and interest [...]The most simple and emblematic example is that of a parent who though totally committed and concerned about the child's moral and social education, never expresses affection with tenderness or other emotional signs. The simultaneity of these two contradictory aspects of parental behaviour seems to be an essential prerequisite for the development of an obsessive organization.
>
> (p. 172)

Whereas, according to Hoover and Insel (1984) and Lorenzini and Sassaroli (1992) the inability of parents to involve themselves in emotional exchanges, is the specific characteristic of the family in which obsessive organizations develop.

The picture provided by the psychodynamic psychotherapists and cognitivists above is not enough to explain the dilemma of obsessives, with their dramatic oscillation between fear/anxiety and mortification/annihilation. Moreover, as highlighted by Waters and Barrett (2000), the scarcity of contributions regarding the environmental factors in the development of obsessive disorders in the last twenty years has been disappointing. The role of the family in the development, maintenance, and treatment of this disorder has also been particularly neglected, despite the fact that two thirds of adult patients have reported the onset of obsessive symptoms during childhood (Rasmussen & Eisen, 1992). Genetic factors, though relevant, are not substantial enough to obscure environmental influences (Henin & Kendall, 1997).

My cases confirm many of the observations and hypotheses advanced above by psychodynamic and cognitivist colleagues, but limit their validity to the main figure of attachment. The psychotherapists cited generally refer to this figure. Although they speak of parents, in the plural, their analysis is in fact dyadic, because it does not distinguish the position of the two parents. I suggest, instead, that both parents are essential for understanding this organization; by limiting the field of observation to just the one parent towards whom the child has a preferential attachment, the context is not sufficiently wide to include the relational pattern necessary for explaining the aspects characterizing this organization. The other parent is certainly not marginal, as is presumed, for example, by Guidano.[19] He or she is certainly less important emotionally but, for the purposes of positioning the child within the critical semantics and of his/her identity, is as fundamental as the main figure of attachment.

My cases suggest a specific pattern of relationships characterizing obsessive organizations that are at least triadic, within which the obsessive patient's difficult position, and the dilemma characterizing it, take shape and acquire significance. It is a pattern that is the result of the patient's experience as it is reconstructed with a therapist using a model for gathering and analyzing information that takes account of a unit wider than the dyadic relationship. I will summarize it as follows:

1) Father and mother find themselves at two extremes of the critical semantics and the couple's relationship is characterized by complementary schismogenetic processes which often produce a fierce conflict.

In the cases I have examined, the conflict was often explicit, and the mother, in accordance with cultural stereotypes, was in the sacrificial position, while the father was identified as "bad."

Raffaella, a university biology researcher, highly intelligent, a virgin though over thirty, afflicted by obscene intrusive thoughts and images, described her parents as follows:

> My mother is a very intelligent woman, like me. She loves cinema. For several years she wrote a column about cinema in an arts magazine. She reads a lot. She devoted herself completely and selflessly to our cultural upbringing [hers and her sister's]. I don't know why she married my father. He is a shopkeeper, a vulgar man; he is arrogant in his physical appearance and behavior. Sometimes I feel sorry for him because for years he's been an outcast. He hates me and detests my mother as well. He hates my sister less, she is also less hostile to him. For as long as I can remember, my father and mother didn't sleep in the same bed. My mother is a beautiful woman, she has a natural elegance, even now, though she doesn't worry about her physical appearance or how she dresses. She is not interested in such things. She also told me she had never been interested in sex.

I have also found configurations where the mother was positioned at the negative polarity of the critical semantics. This was the case with Francesca, a brilliant university student who was unable to sit her exams at the end of her third year: she was paralyzed for more than two years by doubt and indecision. In her family it was her mother who was sensual and coarse. On the other hand, her father, an academic, was positioned at the "goodness, purity" polarity: he was a narcissistic personality, capable of involving himself emotionally only in idealized and non-sexual relationships. His daughter was aware of this:

> He made me understand that he always had a certain dislike, indeed disgust, for the body. He seemed to be repelled by my mother, by her body. Now she is ill, but I believe he rejected her even before. My mother forced him into sexual relations, she demanded it. I heard her with my own ears. Perhaps even now … I don't know. She is domineering. She was always like that, even before she was ill.

The original intersubjective context does not necessarily bring both parents into play, but can involve other members of the family, one of whom is the main figure of attachment. What is essential for constructing the semantic world of obsessive organizations is that subjects construct their own position in relation to two members of the family who position themselves at the opposite extremes of the critical semantics. Nevertheless, in the cases I have treated, save for a few exceptions, the protagonists in the critical intersubjective context (apart from the future obsessive) were the parents.

2) The main figure of attachment for subjects who will develop an obsessive-compulsive organization is generally placed at the "goodness, purity" extreme (the "abstinent" parent). This figure (who may be the mother or the father) with whom future obsessives develop an intense, often exclusive, attachment, in important contexts offers the child a *position of parity or superiority* compared with the other parent and other older members of the family. The generational barrier is thus broken.

The position of parity or superiority is assigned (by the attachment figure) to the future obsessives in various ways. However their interpretation of the opportunity is unambiguous: it is a sign of preference. *The main figure of attachment, by placing subjects in that position, seems to be giving them priority over his or her partner and/or other adult members of the family.* The reasons that subjects give for this are various: because they are more sensitive and good, or more considerate and helpful, or other reasons. In childhood, the preference is perceived by them in specific contexts: they feel that the adult concerned is better off with them than with his/her partner. Later, the preference is connected to qualities that make them superior to the partner as a person: they are more intelligent, more creative or even more mature than the partner of the attachment figure.

3) The child's position of superiority encourages him or her to challenge and compete with the other parent. The child—in certain circumstances, in important contexts and for certain roles—is declared by the main figure of attachment to be superior to the other parent. For this very reason, the child is induced to demand the same treatment, the same favors from the main figure of attachment as are allowed to the "impulsive" parent. The more the child is in a position of superiority, the more he or she claims equality with the "impulsive" parent, and with it the desire to adopt their behavior. It should be added that the impulsive parent generally gives a "malicious" interpretation of the subject's behavior: he or she interprets this child's search for proximity with the favorite parent as a sexual seduction and/or the child's demands as arrogant and selfish. These interpretations are in keeping with the critical semantics and the position within such semantics of the person making the interpretation: the impulsive parent, being perceived (and perceiving him or herself) as bad, can only provide malicious interpretations. This malevolence is also heightened by jealousy and irritation for the position of superiority that the partner accords to the child. These very aspects of his or her positioning all contribute towards *inducing the child to perceive sexual and/or aggressive impulses in him or herself.*

4) The drama begins as soon as the child attempts to express these impulses. The abstinent parent, who is the main figure of attachment, rejects the child because he or she sees in the child the hateful conduct of the partner: the same arrogance, the same selfishness, the same morbid interest in sex and so on. It is a bitter and violent rejection. The abstinent parent, who is prepared to accept the selfish or "bad" behavior of the impulsive partner, not least because he or she often feels an ambiguous admiration and attraction towards him/her, is certainly not prepared to accept similar behavior from the child. If the mother is prepared to put up with her husband's selfish vulgar sexual behavior in order to please him, she will nevertheless react with disgust as soon as the child, like all children, expresses affection using behavior that is sexual, or at least interpretable as such. If the stigmatized impulses are aggressive, every gesture of arrogance by the child to the mother will be responded to with hatred and scorn.

Rejection by the main figure of attachment deeply hurts the child for more than one reason:

a) *It is filled with a resentment that is out of proportionate to the gesture that gave rise to it.* For the child, it is therefore incomprehensible. The reason for the violence of the rejection does not lie in the relationship with the child, but in the relationship with the partner.

b) *It expresses disgust for the fact that the child is experiencing "guilty" impulses.* It is therefore not a rejection and prohibition of certain behavior by the child, but a *rejection of the child as a person.*

c) *It brings the child back, suddenly and incomprehensibly, to a lower position in the family hierarchy.*

As a result of this relational pattern, in order to maintain his or her position of privilege with the main figure of attachment, *the child has to disclaim, reject, those impulses which, by reason of his or her confrontation on equal terms with the other parent, increase and become inescapable.*

This pattern explains why the path of asceticism and that of expressing impulses are both unavoidable and, at the same time, impossible. The confrontation on equal terms with the impulsive parent and that parent's "malevolent" interpretation of the child's attachment to the favorite parent lead the child to recognize and experience guilty desires. The child cannot therefore position him or herself at the same polarity as the favorite parent and follow the path of abstinent goodness without experiencing intolerable feelings of mortification. Nevertheless the expression of impulses also generates unacceptable levels of anxiety in the future obsessive. Subjects quickly learn that, by expressing their own impulses, they risk reprisals from the impulsive parent and, above all, the rejection of the favorite parent: the main relationship of attachment deteriorates, and the child is in danger of falling from the position of privilege to a condition of being "infected," guilty.

When the favorite parent is of the opposite sex, the forbidden desires generally take on oedipal characteristics. However, *the triangular configuration that I have described is much more complex than the interpersonal relationship of an oedipal nature.* In the oedipal relationship the hierarchy between the generations is threatened by the child's sexual desires towards the parent of the opposite sex. On the contrary, in the triangular pattern described here, the oedipal desires dramatically threaten to re-establish the boundary between the generations through the initiative of the favorite parent, removing the child from the position of privilege that he or she enjoys.

Nor is the pattern I have described similar to Haley's *perverse triangle* (1967). Unlike the perverse triangle, the factor characterizing this pattern is not the exploitation of the child by one parent against the other. Since often serious conflict devastates the couple, it is possible and sometimes inevitable that parents will occasionally exploit the child; but the episodes in which the child ends up being a simple instrument in the marital conflict are infrequent in the relationship between the child and the main figure of attachment. Such relationship enjoys their own autonomy in comparison with the marital conflict, and have pleasurable aspects. The repeated dramatic and traumatic rejections that the child receives from the favorite parent are limited to the expression of sexual and/or aggressive impulses. These impulses are forbidden: the child is not only prevented from expressing them, but must not feel them. Other emotions, however, are allowed, and provide gratification.

I would suggest the literature most concerned with relational aspects has given an inappropriately dark description of the favorite adult's dyadic relationship with the child. The abstinent parent does not nourish hatred for the child as suggested by Adams (1973) and several other authors cited above.

He or she certainly rejects the child's sexual and aggressive impulses. It is a clear, explicit rejection. Even in those (few) cases where the favorite parent uses the child against the partner, the coalition is not denied, as happens in the perverse triangle. Nevertheless, the alliance with the favorite parent and the breakdown of the generational barrier, which continually fuels desires that must not be expressed, on pain of rejection, place the subject in a different though no less dramatic position to that of the perverse triangle.

One last question. In the past, phobic and obsessive-compulsive pathologies used to be classed together nosographically under the shared label of phobic-obsessive neuroses. Is this choice justified from a different point of view such as is put forward here? Is the triadic configuration I have described here similar to that of phobic organizations?

The differences between the two intersubjective contexts are greater than the similarities. The critical semantics are different. Furthermore the positions of the obsessive and the phobic in relation to the main figure of attachment have little in common. Phobic subjects know that this figure, though feeling affection towards them, places another member of the family before them. Future phobic patients enjoy no position of superiority. On the contrary, with their role of consolatory partner, they are in a position of total disadvantage compared with the person over whom the mother maintains the priority of the emotional commitment. In the triadic pattern connected with phobic organizations the boundary between the generations is rigidly maintained. Even when the two adults in the critical triangular pattern are the parents (as I have already indicated, this is not always the case), the oedipal desires are not central. The critical pattern, in fact, tends to reduce them, rather than encourage them, because it establishes an insuperable distance between the child and his or her "antagonist."

Despite these differences, the triadic patterns that accompany the development of phobic and obsessive organizations have one important similarity: they all stimulate the child's *ambivalence* towards the main figure of attachment even if the reasons for the ambivalence differ.

The anger that future phobic patients develop towards the adult with whom they have the preferential bond, and the feelings of guilt that afflict them as a consequence (the figure concerned is also much loved), derive from the frustrations and impotence that such children experience in their role of consolatory partner: the mother cannot be consoled. The child is unable to fill the emptiness and suffering produced by the uncommitted partner.

Future obsessive patients also experience the frustration of not being able to defend the favorite parent from the violence of the impulsive partner, but what unleashes their hatred and aggression towards the main figure of attachment is what they have to renounce in order to be approved and loved by this figure, and above all the crippling rejections to which they are subjected as soon as they express their own impulses. The anger, resentment, and even hatred are nevertheless always combined with love and affection. Ambivalence, for phobic patients as well as for obsessives, is therefore an expression of the subject's deep feelings towards the main figure of attachment. Both have developed feelings of affection towards the relevant adult during their childhood. The parent preferred by phobic subjects is often very affectionate and empathetic whereas, in the case of obsessives, he or she is less outgoing but capable of tenderness and kindness. Maternal or paternal love (unlike marital love) can be reconciled with abstinent goodness. Furthermore, this figure, by placing the child in a position of superiority compared with the partner, gives the child considerable gratification.

The intersubjective context I have encountered in my cases, though confirming the dramatic position of obsessive subjects and the ambivalence that marks their relationship with the main figure of attachment, make it possible to recognize the positive aspects present in this relationship, aspects that have often been ignored by the literature and which, indeed, I have frequently encountered even in serious cases of obsessive-compulsive disorder.

4.5 Will Therapy Make Me Feel Worse?

The consultation with Salvatore began with this question. It wasn't a joke; nor was the question prompted by a mistrust of psychotherapists, nor by any knowledge about the debate on the iatrogenic risks of psychotherapy. Salvatore, a factory worker in his forties and a Jehovah's Witness who had moved to northern Italy seven years earlier, knew little about the world of psychology and psychotherapy. The evidence before him was empirical: since he first came into contact with public health service psychiatrists and psychologists, two years earlier, his condition had deteriorated. The more he talked with them, the worse he became; the more understanding he received, the more his obsessions and compulsions increased and intensified.

He first sought psychiatric assistance for an ulterior motive: to persuade his wife, who had left him after two years of marriage, to return. By going for treatment he hoped to calm her feelings of resentment: he recognized that he was sick and wanted to get better. These were his wife's two conditions for repairing the breakdown in the marriage.

The care and attention he had been given was far more than he had expected: The psychiatrists and psychologists were skilled, efficient, and understanding. The involvement of the psychiatric service had also given him substantial secondary gains. His wife had returned, he had obtained an 80 percent invalidity status, and his working hours were reduced from eight to four. And thanks to the psychiatric center, a team of psychotherapists—ours—had been brought in: something that in his eyes was particularly prestigious. Yet, remembering his earlier experiences, Salvatore was concerned: the opportunity, instead of reassuring him, had heightened his fear and anxiety.

The care and kindness he had received from the doctors and psychologists over the past two years had produced such an obvious deterioration in his condition that even his wife, who had insisted on his seeking treatment, was now wondering whether it might be better for him to refuse his invalid's allowance and return to full-time work. His obsessions and compulsions were dramatically worse. He was so plagued by continual anxieties about hitting someone with his car, of causing accidents to work colleagues, of infection, of causing harm by leaving the gas on or the water running at home, that he was forced into compulsive rituals that left him exhausted. Over the past year he had been spending two or three hours each evening checking the gas, electricity, water pipes, doors, and windows. His hands, which he continually washed, were covered with sores. At work, he was under constant stress: he feared that colleagues would be hurt by the equipment he was operating, and was therefore continually checking it. He could no longer drive because he was constantly stopping to make sure he hadn't hit someone. These rituals had afflicted him before his first encounter with the psychiatric service. But they were now so intense that he had no time left even for his favorite pastime, painting.

The meeting with the psychologists and psychiatrists had caused an exponential increase in the role of what Salvatore called the "internal commander." He had to obey "him" like a soldier. He knew that this figure was a product of his mind, yet his subjective experience told him it was an external figure always ready to accuse him of willful misconduct. It was, for example, "he" who forced him to ensure he hadn't knocked anyone over with his car, or that he hadn't put the safety of his work colleagues at risk by leaving tools and equipment carelessly about. Salvatore, according to the "commander," always had evil intentions.

According to the "internal commander," he did not deserve the privileges the psychiatric center were giving him: Salvatore was a fraud. The worsening of his symptoms, his suffering, even the inhibition of his creativity (latterly he had spent less and less time painting), during his period of care under the psychiatric team, were a way of placating the "internal commander," giving him a negative self-image, a way of demonstrating to himself that he actually was ill, and of thus maintaining a positive and consistent self-image.

Tracing back his history, it emerged that what had happened with the psychologists and psychiatrists was part of a recurring pattern that Salvatore summed up in the motto: "When things get better, they get worse." In accordance with the dilemma that characterized his organization, when Salvatore felt better, when he became confident and self-assured, he became afflicted by fear and anxiety. During these periods he developed guilty desires. For example, three of four years before the beginning of therapy he had felt the desire to touch women's bottoms, as his father had done. For a brief period he had yielded to this vice:

During that time I was irresistibly attracted to the shape of women's bodies. Then I came closer to God, I became a Jehovah's Witness, and I stopped this behavior. If my brethren knew, they would expel me from the congregation. Even now that I'm better, I still think about it, but at that time I was unable to control myself. Then I was ill. If I wasn't a Jehovah's Witness I'd end up like my father, I'd be obsessed by sex. I also control myself for my mother. If I do things I shouldn't do, then I feel unclean before her and before God.

Even when Salvatore had found success, receiving prizes at painting competitions, he was gripped by anxiety and fear. When, on the contrary, he had behaved impeccably, or had lost out on pleasurable opportunities or achievements, he had feelings of demoralization and annihilation. Something like this had happened the last time he had been back to his home town: He had been beaten at an exhibition by his brother Ruggero, who knew one of the panel of judges. Salvatore felt dejected, and for many days was reduced to a state of apathy and depression from which not even his mother could rouse him.

The onset of symptoms, which in fact occurred several years before his referral to the psychiatric center, also reflects this pattern: when all seemed to be going well, the worst happened. I will reconstruct this dramatic episode after having described the intersubjective context at the origin of the strange loop.

The Original Intersubjective Context

The patient was the fifth of six boys. Concetta and Calogero, his parents, first knew each other from photographs, once a common practice among the poorest people of southern Italy. Both had lost their mothers as children. This experience was one of the few things they had in common. The two of them were at opposite poles when it came to the critical semantics and other relevant semantic polarities in the family ("strength/weakness," "impulsiveness/thoughtfulness," "laziness/zeal").

Calogero was highly-sexed—"hot-blooded," "too hot to handle" according to his son's definitions. He liked beautiful shapely women and was irresistibly attracted to them. Everyone in the local district knew about his habit of fondling women's bottoms, for which, as already mentioned, he had been given a crude nickname.[20] Even his wife, during more violent rows, called him by that offensive name. Not even the slaps he received from a woman in public did anything to temper his behavior.

He went to church services and touched the holy images, but he didn't hold back even there. If the opportunity arose he fondled. He had no qualms even during processions. As justification he used to say that even priests weren't saints ...

158

Calogero, almost to emphasize his status as leader of the pack (all his children were male) went to bed naked from the waist down: "When he got up in the morning he wandered about with his willy dangling free." None of the sons ever behaved with such lack of modesty: their mother wouldn't have allowed it.

Calogero showed no interest in his children's education, apart from when something went wrong. Then he got tough. When they were children he used to threaten them with an ashtray, though in fact he never hit them. He was impulsive and quick-tempered, but also generous. He bought ice cream for all the family when he could afford it, or bottles of good wine for friends and relations.

Concetta was kind, gentle, affectionate and concerned about her sons; if they were late home she would wait for them at the window, even when they had grown up. Though of mild character, she could be strict with them. In the face of difficulties she was very strong: a rock. Calogero, on the other hand, was basically weak: if he had a problem he would turn to his wife for support; he would sink into despair if he caught a cold; he was terrified of illness and death.

Concetta supported the whole family. She allowed herself no pleasure, never spent money on herself, and had no notion of enjoyment. She was frigid. Her feeling of revulsion for sexual intercourse was probably due to her shame at her husband's vice, or perhaps it had earlier origins: Immediately after her mother's death, her father's remarriage to an attractive young woman had been the main cause of her unhappiness as a child. Whatever the reasons might have been, Concetta openly declared her aversion to sexual intercourse on many occasions, and Calogero complained about her coldness.

The first fourteen years of family life were particularly hard. Seven of them (the youngest child hadn't yet been born) lived in a single room. Calogero was unemployed during this period, earning money here and there from casual work. Concetta worked continually as a domestic help, even during her many pregnancies, to feed the family. She was fortunate to be employed by a wealthy family who liked her: they allowed her to take the older children to the house and helped her out on several occasions. This family was particularly fond of the eldest son and he continued to remain on friendly terms with them. It was probably they who encouraged Concetta to send her sons to school: advice that she followed with determination. Their encouragement was well received: Concetta, though uneducated, was considerate and intelligent. She was interested not only in school results but also in their drawing, at which Peppino and Salvatore were particularly gifted, and developing their other talents.

Fifteen years after their marriage, Calogero found a job with the local authority. The family could finally move into a decent house. But the atmosphere didn't much improve. Calogero began an affair with a niece, on whom he showered gifts, thus whittling away part of his salary. Salvatore recalls in this respect an incident of violence:

I was fourteen at the time, we had moved to the new house. At a certain point my aunt and my father attacked my mother, who was pregnant at the time. That pregnancy ended badly: the child died at birth. It was a terrible blow for my mother, not least because it was a girl and my mother had all boys and really wanted a daughter. I don't say the cause of it was this argument ... there were others; but this one was particularly violent. I remember my mother crying, I was shouting. I think my mother had complained about the presents my father was giving to his niece. He was letting us die of hunger ... and was giving money to his niece. We weren't starving, but we were very poor. This woman was about ten years younger than him, she was pretty, had a nice body and a face like an actress, a bit like Sophia Loren. All she wanted was the money. [...] She had a nice house. My father always denied it, not least because she too was married, but there was an unhealthy relationship between them and I think they had sex together for several years. My father wasn't very close to the family at that time, he was more interested in this niece.

His parents' relationship later improved; in old age Calogero became increasingly dependent on his wife, and Concetta was bereft when he died.

Salvatore and the other sons had built their positions in the family around their parents' polar opposition in almost all of the family's semantic polarities. Three of them had chosen the path of goodness and purity. Two were closer to the "badness" polarity. Only Salvatore had developed an obsessive disorder. The other patient in the family, Rosario, the fourth son, had more serious problems than Salvatore: he was diagnosed as paranoid and by the age of twelve was taking anti-psychotic medication. He was the only one never to have left the family home and continued to live with his mother. None of the other brothers had any psychopathologies and were well adjusted.

The oldest sons, the only ones to have remained in Sicily, were positioned at opposite extremes of the critical semantics as well as most of the other polarities relevant to the family.

The first born, Edoardo, ten years older than Salvatore, had played the role of head of the family for many years: "He's my true father," Salvatore said on many occasions. On the advice of their mother, Edoardo looked after his brothers' problems. He was particularly intelligent and, since childhood, had been interested in telecommunications. As soon as he graduated, with the help of his mother's employers, he found a job with a large telephone company and soon became a manager. Honest, dedicated to his work, religious without being over-zealous, he had maintained a faultless relationship with his wife, a woman who was mean, ambitious and disinterested in sex, with whom he had two daughters. His authority in the family was such that his father, in his last years, talked to him as if he were a member of the government: "You make us scrimp and scrape, and now you've imposed this other tax on us," "You ought to think about increasing our pensions ..."

The second son, Ruggero, was at the opposite pole to Edoardo. Sexually highly active, of all the brothers he was least attached to their mother. Physically attractive—he was considered the most handsome—he had great success with women. His wife, with whom he had four children, was physically and sexually attractive. Due to the husband's infidelity, the marriage was fraught with violent rows, short separations, and passionate reconciliations. His wife always forgave him; at times she even seemed proud of his sexual conquests. He was the least honest of the family: He had a lowly job, which he supplemented with shady business dealings; he painted, without Salvatore and Peppino's talent; he had cheated them several times, keeping for himself the earnings from the sale of their pictures. He was cunning, arrogant, and dynamic.

The third son, Peppino, was the kindest, and most similar to their mother: "Pure and perfect" according to Salvatore's definition. A Jehovah's Witness, like the other brothers who had moved north, he was the most fervent. He had also been good-natured as a child. His was an ethos of sacrifice. Though exceptionally talented as an artist, he had foregone this passion to dedicate more time to his religion, work, and family.

Rosario, nicknamed "dickhead the slug," was regarded as the family's "identified patient." Lazy, aggressive and arrogant, as a child he attacked even the schoolmistresses, and as an adult struck his father. He was born with a crooked neck. Due to this physical defect, corrected by two surgical operations when he was an adolescent, he was mocked even by adults: Everyone called him "dickhead." He was now a fine-looking man, but as a child he had a comic appearance: very tall, lanky, as well as being crook-necked.

His mother felt sorry for him. Concetta was upset by the way he was mocked even by his father. Calogero found him unbearable. Before he died he admitted he had been violent to the boy and said he would have to ask God's forgiveness for the wrong he had done him. In his last years, Rosario certainly obtained his revenge: he treated his father like a slave and tried to hit him on several occasions. By handing over his bank messenger's salary to his mother, he felt entitled to be served and revered by his parents. Even as a child he was a bully and loved subjugating others. For many years Salvatore was his victim.

Rosario, like his father, was always obsessed with the fear of illness, especially cancer. Always suspicious, at the age of thirty he had an attack of delirium:

> All of a sudden, ten or eleven years ago, he started saying things that made absolutely no sense: he said he was being followed by the police, that they were searching for him. He said there was a woman who wanted him, and he accused a friend of plotting to take her

away from him. This friend came to our house saying he was worried about Rosario, that he needed treatment. Our mother started crying. He began sweating all over. The psychiatrists gave him Serenase: he looked like a dog, foaming at the mouth. He keeps saying, even now, that they had done him harm.

He never recovered after that; he absented himself from work for months on end, but only applied for an invalid's allowance when he heard that his brother had been given one.

Pasquale, the youngest, was five years younger than Salvatore and also very close to his mother, and also a Jehovah's Witness. Devoted to the family, good and honest, he was less self-sacrificing and pious than the third son.

Let us now consider the position of Salvatore, trying to understand why he had positioned himself in the median position since childhood.

Unlike Rosario, Salvatore did not have physical problems. He had been a fine and healthy baby: he weighed five kilos at birth and was breast-fed for two years—they called him the "chocolate chubby." Nor did he have to compete with the extraordinary intelligence of the eldest child, as did Ruggero, the second oldest. Edoardo was already ten when he was born. Though extremely close to his mother (like Peppino and Pasquale, if not closer), Salvatore had never really been able to share her choice of abstinent goodness. This path was not open to him for at least three reasons:

1) A little older than Salvatore, Rosario had a negative influence over him from several points of view: "He made me anxious. He used to say 'I had anxiety in my guts' and I felt it all over." Rosario stimulated his brother's sexuality at an early age. For a certain time he forced him to suck his penis, and Salvatore, in turn, compelled his younger friends in the area to do the same to him. Salvatore remembered that these sexual practices, begun with his brother and continued with his friends in the area, were a source of intense excitement and pleasure. Rosario, through his bullying, also induced Salvatore to feel and recognize a considerable amount of inner aggression, which he probably repressed so as not to lose his mother's favor: "He was violent by nature, when he attacked me, my head would start spinning, sometimes I became totally rigid, as if I was paralyzed: he'd get frightened when I went like that and would leave me alone for a while."

Their mother collapsed once while she was trying to separate the two boys, defending Salvatore. For Salvatore, this was traumatic: he thought his mother was dead and began to scream with panic.

The two of them, being close in age, always went to school and returned home together. Their mother, who was concerned about Rosario's complexes, encouraged this closeness. Salvatore, always being with his brother, ended up also being taunted: their classmates called them "dickhead" and the "ape," thus killing two birds with one stone. These events increased Salvatore's anger and shyness.

2) Their *father* had no less important a role in leading Salvatore to recognize in himself what he called his "bad nature." Calogero was aggressive towards all of his sons, apart from the oldest boy, whom he had respected from earliest childhood. He was more violent towards Salvatore than with his other sons, and at times more aggressive than with Rosario. He didn't like Salvatore's closeness to his mother: he was suspicious of this attachment:

> I was always in the kitchen with my mother, I liked her company, I preferred being with her than with my friends. Outside they made fun of Rosario and also of me; with her I was fine, I felt safe. I'm a good cook, even now. I learned how to cook from being with my mother. I helped her when I was a child, I cut the vegetables for her and she liked that. She used to tell me things, I think she was pleased to have my company [...] When my father arrived and found me in the kitchen, he got really angry as if I was doing who knows what. He used to shout out: "But you're always here. And what are you doing here?" And he'd say to my mother: "This one's never outside. Why's he always in here with you?" He used to yell at me: "Outside! Go and play with the others. Out!" He used to chase me out, and if I tried to resist he'd kick me, and he threatened me more than once with a knife.
>
> My father always had it in for me; he was always even more nasty to me than to Rosario. I don't know why. He tormented me; he seemed to hate me.

Salvatore's father wanted him to leave home as soon as he was an adult. He encouraged all his sons to move north in search of work, but with Salvatore he was insistent. The young man had no intention of leaving home but had to give in at the age of twenty-three when his brother, who had moved to Turin some years earlier, found a job for him.

3) One last aspect not to be ignored is *the extraordinary physical resemblance between Salvatore and his father*—he was his double. Salvatore had the same southern Italian features as his father: black hair, olive skin, the same protruding chin, which prompted Concetta sometimes to call her husband "pig face." This resemblance had probably encouraged both parents to interpret Salvatore's behavior as being influenced by his father's feelings and impulses. Such resemblance was certainly the cause of some of the mother's rebuffs and insults, which threw Salvatore into a state of bewilderment and dejection.

The overall effect of these factors was such that Salvatore could never see himself as completely good and pure. He never felt "pure." But he was also prevented from choosing the path of vice: he would have lost the love and the respect of his mother, which was more important to him than anything else. Even though Salvatore had many doubts about his mother's love for him, he nevertheless enjoyed a position of privilege in comparison with his brothers. He was, without doubt, the one to whom she was closest, except for Rosario, who certainly wasn't the one she loved most: Concetta had always felt compassion, rather than love or esteem, for that unfortunate son. Nor had the relationship between mother and eldest son ever been close. Concetta was proud of Edoardo and admired him, but it had never been a deeply emotional relationship. Conversation between Salvatore and his mother had always been easy, Concetta had always found him more interesting and reliable than her husband because he was more considerate, intelligent, and sensitive. From about the age of twelve, when Salvatore began to paint seriously, his mother's feelings towards him increased considerably. Even his father was proud of his son's artistic abilities, boasting about them to friends. For Calogero it was a narcissistic pleasure but his mother was genuinely enthusiastic when she saw Salvatore's pictures. When he began therapy she still had his first oil painting hanging over her bed: a seascape at dusk. Concetta had described the scene she would like him to depict and he had painted it.

Yet due to his demands and his "nature," Salvatore was often rebuffed by his mother, and thus risked passing from his position of privilege to that of being "tainted." He remembered many of these dramatic incidents. When he was four, for example, his mother surprised him while he was involved in an erotic game with a little girl. Concetta's reaction was violent. She grabbed him as if he were a wild animal, threw him with disgust into a tub of water in the courtyard and washed him. At that moment Salvatore felt he had lost the right to be human. Another time, when he was six, watching his mother breastfeeding his youngest brother, he too tried to suck her breast. His mother's reaction was brutal; it was on that occasion, for the first time, that she called him "pig face," an insult hitherto reserved for her husband. "Every now and then my mother comes out with these attacks that kill you, not least since you don't expect them from her."

But let us move on from these childhood incidents to consider the onset of symptoms. Being a relatively recent event that took place in the original family environment, it highlights the critical intersubjective context in greater detail.

The Onset of Symptoms

Salvatore remembered experiencing states of deep anxiety since childhood. The first real onset of symptoms was seven years before the beginning of therapy. Salvatore had moved to northern Italy a few months earlier. This was his second experience of living away from his home town. The first time, as I have already mentioned, was when he was twenty-three, when his father had forced him to leave. He continually accused him of not wanting to work, of being a good-for-nothing, though in fact he'd had several casual jobs. When the possibility of the work he had been promised as a public employee finally came to nothing, Salvatore had no other option but to go and live with Pasquale in Turin, where he found employment as an unskilled worker: his school diploma, for which his mother had made so many sacrifices, was worth nothing in Turin.[21]

The second experience of emigration, on the other hand, had been his own choice. He had been back in the South for several years. Seeing how her son was suffering in Turin, looking increasingly depressed and thin, Concetta had taken a firm stand against her husband and encouraged Salvatore to return to Sicily. Salvatore recovered as soon as he returned home and, by the time he had decided—independently this time—to move back north, he was infatuated with Iole. She was his great love—beautiful, prosperous, and attractive (unlike the person who would eventually become his wife, who was nice but had no sexual charm). Salvatore was emotionally and sexually committed to her, but was also prone to anxiety and fear because he felt guilty about this relationship. His mother did not like Iole, fearing she might be willing to have pre-marital relations with Salvatore, and intensified her sudden, unexpected "attacks" on her son during this period. One of these, during one of Pasquale's visits, was particularly hurtful:

> Pasquale complained about not having found a woman in Turin. My mother said: "Don't worry, if women want him [referring to Salvatore] who's as ugly as sin, then they'll want you as well." It was like being struck down, as if I'd lost everything … I felt completely crushed.

Salvatore realized that his relationship with his mother was deteriorating badly. At the same time he felt threatened by his father. Calogero loved Iole in rather more than a figurative sense. Each time Salvatore took his girlfriend home his father would dress himself up and anxiously await their arrival. He began insisting that Salvatore should invite her back more often and piled her with presents, just as he had done in the past with his niece. Concetta was irritated by her husband's attentions towards Iole, and they worried Salvatore.

When his brothers living in the North told him they could find work for him in a town near Turin, he had no hesitation. At that moment, the opportunity seemed providential: by moving back north he would be able to preserve his relationship with Iole without losing the relationship with his mother, and would have removed his girlfriend from the increasingly indiscrete advances of her future father-in-law. Iole joined him after a few months, thereby demonstrating that she really loved him. Salvatore was delighted, but found himself in an unexpected minefield: "I could no longer control myself, it was like doing 200 kilometers an hour with no steering wheel." His sexual desire had reached such levels that it was impossible for him to refrain from sexual intercourse. From Sicily, his mother was launching very clear messages of opposition to what appeared to her to be a pre-marital cohabitation. Salvatore was unable to contain his anxiety and fear. His sexual relations with his girlfriend, which were always incomplete (he could not totally disobey his mother, but nor could he comply with her demand for abstinence) brought him terrible pain. He ended up twice in hospital as a result of testicular complaints—first with inflamed testicles and then when first one testicle became enlarged and, immediately afterwards, the other. After two months living together, his girlfriend realized the seriousness of his problems and left him. Salvatore was distraught:

> For two years I was in a total darkness, I was depressed, apathetic, I passed from complete inertia to torments of jealousy. Even now I cannot bear the idea that Iole is living with another man. I know I shouldn't …

We will now consider a case where the intersubjective context in which an obsessive organization is formed arises at the present moment, rather than being reconstructed in therapy after the passage of many years, as had happened with Salvatore. It involves a young girl whose onset of obsessive symptoms had occurred three months before the beginning of therapy.

4.6 Will you Help me Get Rid of Bad Natascia?

I was amazed by this question which Natascia suddenly asked during the first session. Until three months before, this 11-year-old had been happy, sociable and more sensible than her peers. She had had no reason therefore for psychotherapy. I was the first person the family had consulted. No one had yet formulated a diagnosis for her nor even explained to the girl and her family that in obsessive-compulsive disorders patients feel a good and a bad part within themselves. It was she who described her inner split which she felt to be like a conflict between two Natascias: one who "doesn't want to talk to anyone, who just wants to study and nothing else" and the other who "wants to make herself pretty, wear makeup, jump on tables and dance."

Something else surprised me when I first met this family: The drama I had usually found in families where obsessive disorders develop seemed to be concentrated in Natascia alone. There was no doubt that this young girl was feeling disturbing emotions: her suffering had altered her features, her posture, even her voice. Her facial expression was somber, her hands clenched, her arms rigid inside a dark sweater on a hot summer's day; her cavernous voice seemed to come from beyond the grave. Even though her father had warned me on the phone about this peculiar vocal sound, I found it unsettling: it is difficult not to be affected by such a disturbance. Natascia gave me the physical sensation that a catastrophe was about to overwhelm her. It was a catastrophe that she recognized but could not hold back. Her bad part, which "doesn't care less about anything or anyone and wants to do only what she wants," which "is even happy if she hears her parents arguing," was about to get the better of her. Not even with what she called her "superstitions," to which she devoted hours, could she manage to control and render this bad part powerless. And Natascia was calling for help with the same urgency as someone shipwrecked about to be swept away by the current. More than a request, hers was an order—"help me get rid of bad Natascia!"—and a reproach: "Why are you asking me all these things? What have they got to do with the horrible things that keep jumping into my mind?" Natascia was disorientated at first by my efforts to put her symptoms into context. It wasn't difficult to understand why: she wanted me to carry her straightway into a safe port.

Her parents and Azzurra, her little sister aged seven, watched her with incredulity. They seemed to belong to another world. The father was a fine-looking man, a little overweight, with the warm, jovial expression of many southern Italians. The mother was charming and had a sweet face with regular features reminiscent of a fifteenth-century Florentine Madonna. Both were anxious to emphasize that they had never pushed their elder daughter hard with her education. It was she who had always been more diligent than necessary, it was she who had wanted to jump a year ahead at school. No one had ever stopped her going out with her friends. Indeed her mother, long before Natascia's problems began, had felt annoyed about the importance her daughter was placing on her schooling. What was more, in comparison to the seriousness of the elder child, she had never hidden her preference for the liveliness and sociability of her second daughter, who was always ready to go and play with one or other of her classmates and friends. That wasn't hard to believe. She certainly wasn't strict: when Azzurra, a real bundle of energy, began running around the consultation room in her colorful dress, she didn't bat an eyelid. Only the father made some affectionate attempt to control her. Unlike so many families in which obsessive disorders develop, who seem to have come straight out of the pages of Dostoevsky, there didn't seem to be any dramatic pathos, at least on a first impression.

Is the Battlefield Between Good and Bad Inside Natascia Only?

This was what I wondered when I met them. Where in this family were the "baddies," the "selfish ones," those who, to use the words of Natascia, "do what they want, without caring less about the others"? Who were the good ones, those who were self-sacrificing, who put the needs of others before their own? They were there, as we shall see, but their presence wasn't immediately apparent because the semantics of goodness had only begun to dominate the conversation in this family over the last five or six years. It hadn't therefore played a role in the formation of the personalities of Natascia's parents, not until the time of their first meeting.

Far more important, however, in the story of Natascia's parents, Louise and Andrea, and in their personalities, were the semantics of power and belonging. It was within the polarities of winning and losing, belonging and being excluded, already prominent in their families of origin, that their first meeting took place, which turned immediately into a passionate and all-embracing relationship.

Although they were very young, neither of the two had particular relationships within their own family of origin that had got in the way of their new union. Their families were separated, moreover, by a thousand kilometers and more. For reasons that I will explain in Chapter 6, Louise was unable to find any "co-positioning" with her parents. Despite being an only child, there was no place for her with them. So at the age of twenty she left Bruges, where her parents had immigrated when they were young, and moved to Italy, to her father's home town, almost as if she had wanted to regain something of him through her return to his roots. Unlike Louise, Andrea had a solid positioning in his family. He was the most respected of three siblings in his family, as well as in the community, where he had been much admired for his sporting prowess in his youth. But no one was upset when he left. His father had died many years earlier. His relationship with his siblings was not particularly close, partly due to their age differences. And his mother had too many other commitments to feel the loss of her third child: she was charismatic and generous, a pillar of the community and was closely attached to her two older children and her sisters, as well as having many friends.

Having lived in an "extended" family, which extended even into the local community, since the mother was ready to help anyone, whoever they were, while the father had kept himself to himself, Andrea was irresistibly attracted by the exclusive relationship that Louise offered him, to which he responded with unconditional love.

The happiness of the first three years of their marriage was also assured by Louise's capacity to adapt herself to Andrea, who was affectionate and kind, but also determined, persistent, and assertive. Having spent her childhood and adolescence with self-centered parents who were tragically needful of recognition and personal reassurance, Louise was easily compliant. This she did in a highly personal way: she never expressed her own point of view, always allowed space for others, and preferred to yield rather than going too far. Her submissiveness did not seem to be dictated by any recognition of the superiority of others but was a polite way of behaving, reflecting her marked refinement in manners and speech. As a result, the conversation between Louise and

Andrea did not have the tension and conflict experienced by all other young couples. They didn't even argue over the division of household chores. Louise did everything, even though she had a busy working life: She had left Milan to go and live with Andrea, and worked as a language assistant at the university in Verona, where Andrea had begun what would turn out to be a brilliant career in a merchant bank. Indeed, she would amaze her husband with delicious lunches and dinners and generous hospitality when his family and friends came to visit from the South.

Natascia's Intersubjective Context

When Natascia was born, the blissful period her parents had enjoyed during the first three years of their relationship had already ended eighteen months earlier, due to Louise's serious depression. It was a sudden and unexpected event. It coincided with the couple's first move, caused, like later ones, by Andrea's work. And it was Louise's depression itself, and the emotions it produced, that introduced the semantics of goodness into the family. But not at first: several years had to pass before it dominated the conversation.

Louise, who had always been happy, cheerful and full of energy, had suddenly fallen into depression shortly before their move to Amsterdam. No one connected her collapse with the imminent move, which was to end the university job she had so much enjoyed. Indeed, the cause of her collapse was blamed on the anxiety and tension built up over previous months when, out of the blue, she had had to replace a lecturer and take over a university course. Everyone agreed: this sudden and heavy responsibility for a 26-year-old had been too much. But in Amsterdam, despite having left the university job, her depression remained. Andrea, passionately in love with her, spent the nights comforting her in her despair, which seemed boundless. When, in a happier moment, she told him she'd like to have a child, Andrea had not a moment's hesitation in believing that motherhood would resolve his wife's problems. The decision seemed to have been a good one: Louise blossomed again during her pregnancy, regained her energy and good spirits, returning to work, this time as a translator, and to caring for Andrea. Unfortunately, the depression returned after Natascia's birth, and worse than before. Her depression would remain a feature of their life from then on: Louise could no longer work, except for short periods, even though there were moments when she was well, including the time of her second pregnancy, with Azzurra. Every time Louise seemed to recover, the couple started to plan again:

> "I'm so stupid," commented Andrea bitterly. "Every time Louise gets better, I forget everything, I fool myself, my enthusiasm returns, I want to do a thousand things, I'm now looking for a house to buy here in Milan ..."

That was no longer entirely true. The relationship between the couple over the last five or six years had deteriorated. There was good reason for this. When Louise was ill, she would shut herself up in her room and no one could go near her. It was her husband who had to do everything. It was he who had brought up their daughters, with the help of a nanny, who had been living with them for many years by then. It was he who had had to sort out the many problems arising from the four moves of house: after Amsterdam they had been to Berlin, Salerno and finally Milan, where they had been living for seven months.

Though Andrea was determined, he had felt powerless to deal with his wife's problems for some years: He was tired of having to look after everything, frustrated about not being able to enjoy the economic comfort he had achieved, and, above all, angry about Louise's increasingly provocative behavior when she was well. When his wife came out of her depression, she made no attempt now to re-establish her relationship with her daughters, nor to be involved in the organization of the house. Nor did she re-establish her intimacy and understanding with Andrea, as she had always done previously. On the contrary, all she thought about was herself and her own interests. She went off by herself, spending her time at museums, concerts, cinemas, exhibitions, theatres, and walking. Sometimes she didn't return until ten or eleven at night, giving no warning, and without being contactable, since she hated mobile phones. It was something that Andrea could sometimes excuse: "After months of being ill you can understand how she wants to make up for lost time ..."

But in reality he felt upset and angry. He tried to control himself, but recently there had been frequent episodes in which he had flown off the handle and been abusive to Louise. He couldn't accept his wife's complete abdication of responsibility and indifference towards the girls. During the session, while Andrea, with truly admirable patience, did his best first to console and calm Natascia, then to amuse and control Azzurra, Louise ignored them. Her refusal to show even the slightest maternal feeling left me and my colleagues somewhat astonished. One example is sufficient. While we were in discussion behind the one-way mirror, a colleague stopped us to watch what was happening: Natascia was agitated and making a noise, her father was trying to talk her out of one of her rituals, Azzurra was busy drawing a picture and Louise, seated by herself, took a large sandwich from her bag and ate it without offering it to her children or her husband. She then shut her eyes, visibly irritated by her eldest daughter's yelling, and her head nodded forward. Her husband, exhausted, powerless at Natascia's growing anxiety which he was unable to stem, turned to Louise for help. Finding her asleep (this, in fact, was a provocation—one of her toes was moving) he was at first dismayed. He then looked at Natascia, and for a moment the two of them laughed in bitter solidarity behind mummy's back. The complicity lasted only an instant, before being interrupted by Natascia's yelling, even louder than before. Andrea woke his wife, who told Natascia to stop it. Not a single word more!

It was quite clear that Andrea was unsure about his wife's fidelity. Louise didn't seem to have been unfaithful, but her husband had sometimes suspected so, not least because Louise had been sexually promiscuous for a short time before they first met. She was also attractive: thirteen years of depression and psychotropic drugs had diminished but not erased her charm.

Natascia had grown up in this atmosphere. She was the older of the two sisters, and therefore more involved in the family tragedy. She and her father had developed a close relationship: Both felt alone and had spent long periods abroad, without the support of friends and relatives. Natascia had never had a proper mother, Andrea had experienced the anguish, especially in the early years, of having a wife he adored who was absent, distant, suffering.

"During the bleakest periods of my wife's illness," said Andrea, "I received great support from Natascia. We would go out together, the two of us even took a couple of holidays together, as my wife wouldn't … couldn't come. We went to Hong Kong, just the two of us. Sometimes I'd take Natascia to visit my friends. I didn't want to go by myself and she was very happy to come. If there were children her age she'd play with them, otherwise she'd stay with us adults. I well remember when we were in Berlin she'd make coffee for me when I came back from work. She'd have been seven. And I told her about the things that were going on. I'd confide in her. Perhaps I was wrong but when I came home I was happy to see her and chat with her. Who else was there to talk to when my wife was ill?"

The generational boundaries had thus been broken, even though there was no eroticization between father and daughter. Natascia sought in every way to be a fitting conversational partner for her father and sought above all not to cause any problems for a man whom she saw as already overburdened with responsibilities. She was, of course, also proud of her prestigious positioning which made her so different from her classmates and placed her on a level that her younger sister could never attain.

As Natascia gradually grew she found herself more and more in the position of an adult. The relationship hierarchy with her mother had been turned upside down: In Salerno, Andrea's home town, where the family had lived for a couple of years before moving to Milan, it was Natascia who had looked after her mother. Her father, who worked in Rome and came home at weekends, often asked Natascia to stay close to Louise while he was away, to accompany her on her wanderings. In this way he kept an eye on his wife through his daughter, with whom he was in constant telephone contact. The inversion of roles between mother and daughter was therefore complete. Natascia was ten at the time.

But even though Natascia ended up assuming a hierarchical position over her mother and a relationship of parity with her father, she wasn't told that her mother was depressed, nor what depression was. Natascia therefore saw a father who never allowed himself a moment's leisure, was heavily committed to his work, always active, always busy. He was the first up in the morning, he helped the nanny get the girls ready, he sometimes took them to school, he watched over them doing their homework, he went to see their teachers, he took them to church on Sunday … Their mother, meanwhile, was in her room reading, not to be disturbed, or she had gone to the cinema, the theatre or a concert. In short, she did as she pleased, without a care for others or their needs. What could Natascia conclude from this behavior that she had to witness every day? That her mother was "bad" like the Natascia who was now about to get the upper hand, whereas her father was good, self-sacrificing, fair. When, in fact, I asked her who bad Natascia resembled, there was no delay in the answer: "my mum!" Was it Natascia alone who, being kept in the dark about her mother's clinical history, interpreted her family's situation in terms of the semantics of goodness? Certainly not. Her father, in the face of his wife's provocative behavior, wavered between two interpretations: "She is ill, in the grip of a depression which sometimes recedes but never goes away"/ "she is bad, selfish, despite appearances she is just like her parents." And most of his friends and relatives thought the same. Behind these interpretations were widely differing emotions: pain and feelings of impotence alternated with anger, demoralization, and also guilt because Louise was ill. Even Natascia herself knew something was wrong with her mother: no one had ever spelled it out, but she understood. She too therefore felt some guilt about her aggressiveness towards her mother.

Why the Onset of Symptoms Three Months Before?

We cannot attribute Natascia's onset of symptoms to the semantics of goodness, seeing that it had already entered the family conversation several years earlier. If anything, we have to ask why it was that Natascia could no longer remain at the goodness polarity where, like her father, she had been.

Nor can we ascribe the onset to a deterioration in the family's situation. The move to Milan, six months before our first meeting, had indeed marked the beginning of a new springtime for the family after their long winter in Salerno. Unlike what had happened on previous moves, not only had Louise not gone into depression on her arrival in Milan, but she was so full of energy that she considered returning to work. She had even stopped her provocative behavior. And Andrea had actually started making plans again—something he hadn't done for a long time. Their sexual relationship had also taken off again after years of abstinence. They were months of particular happiness and enthusiasm which had reversed a family situation that had been in danger of going badly wrong. In Salerno the family had risked falling apart even if, from a personal point of view, each of them had been better off. In Amsterdam and Berlin, even though they had been through far more difficult and dramatic moments, they had still remained as a family. The very fact of being alone as a family, with few outside contacts on which to rely, had cemented the relationship. When they arrived in Salerno, everyone was there to help. Andrea's sister and brother, his many friends, relations and neighbors were all ready to look after Natascia and Azzurra, who were continually invited to other children's houses. Louise also improved in health but had become particularly provocative: she went out for whole days, always kept her mobile phone switched off, and spent large sums of money on objects and clothes that she would get rid of within a few days. This was another reason why Andrea had asked Natascia to keep her mother company. Despite these onerous tasks, Natascia had shown no sign of any difficulty in Salerno.

It was on their arrival in Milan that the first indications of her problem appeared. Natascia wasn't happy at school: she wasn't learning, her marks were low, she didn't like the teachers whom she found unpleasant and demanding, she was friendly with only two classmates and complained about the others who seemed to look down on her because she was smaller than they were: Natascia was younger than her classmates because she had jumped one year ahead. She became strangely critical and demanding. Her father, somewhat surprised by this unusual behavior in such a level-headed young girl, put it down to her difficult age.

I had difficulty with her parents in reconstructing Natascia's behavior and attitude during the months prior to the onset of symptoms: her mother, as usual, seemed to have noticed nothing and her father admitted he had not been very attentive to his daughter during that period: he was too taken up with the newfound harmony in his relationship with Louise. Once again they could go out in the evening, they had been off for several weekends by themselves, and they had been trying to buy a house with the idea of settling in Milan, for a while at least, if not permanently … And yet it was immediately clear that the new family atmosphere after their arrival in Milan had changed Natascia's positioning in the family. There was no longer any need for good Natascia, who waited for her father to come back from the office and prepared his coffee, who phoned him to tell him what the situation was at home, thus enabling him to work on in peace and stay a little longer at the office: Her father was no longer alone and her mother was now doing a few things herself. Natascia could, in fact, have helped out with Azzurra, taking her to dance classes and going swimming with their nanny, as she had done in the past, but she had stopped doing them. There again, neither of the two conflicting Natascias was as "good" as Natascia had been in the past. Both were to some extent "selfish." One was obviously so because "she wants to have fun, with not a care for anything or anyone," whereas the other "wants to remain somewhere cool, dark, studying in silence, studying and nothing else," therefore abstemious, self-sacrificing, but for her own ends. When I asked her whether good Natascia was still prepared to be what her father called "the little housewife," the answer was a curt: "no, never again." Why this change? What had her father done to her? I had great difficulty reconstructing what had happened between them. Andrea was aware that Natascia had become distant. This could be seen even during the session, where he had demonstrated a truly remarkable patience with her, consoling and reassuring her, trying to calm her down, while she kept him at a distance, pushing him away. He described with amazement how she wouldn't let him touch her. She had rather more physical contact even with her mother. Over the previous few months she had certainly been hostile towards him: the romance had been shattered.

Natascia's terror at returning to Salerno for the forthcoming Easter holidays, as the family had planned for some time, was to provide us with an Ariadne's thread that would identify the critical episode that had triggered the onset of symptoms. Her father was the protagonist in the episode. Surprised at Natascia's unexpected difficulties in adapting to her school in Milan—she had adapted brilliantly even to the Dutch and German school systems where there had been a change of language—and irritated by her continual and unreasonable complaints, he had tried to resolve the problem. First of all he had suggested moving to a private school where she could have been helped during the afternoons with her homework. Natascia had categorically refused. On her next outburst of complaints, he wasted no further time. Andrea was never one to hold back, as was apparent with his five job postings that he hadn't turned down, despite his wife's depression. He therefore asked his sister in Salerno to take Natascia in to live with her: given that she wasn't happy in Milan, it seemed the best solution for her to go back to school in Salerno where she had got on well with her classmates and teachers. His sister, moreover, who had no children and had just separated from her husband, was delighted by the idea of having her niece as company. Natascia had overheard the telephone call and was horrified. For her it was an unwarranted and unjust rejection. The episode was so serious, in her view, that she said nothing to her father about it. After their arrival in Milan and her parent's reconciliation, she was already bitter about losing her high position in the family, and now found herself being abandoned and sent off to her aunt without even being consulted. How could her father behave like that? With her? The same father who had tolerated the intolerable from Louise! Natascia was well aware of just how deviant her mother's behavior had been. She had read this in her father's looks of consternation and his outbursts of anger, and in the expressions of surprise and indignation from her aunt and her classmates' mothers. For her part, all she had done was make the odd complaint, and she'd had a few bad marks at school, but also some sevens and eights, as she pointed out to us as we reconstructed the events leading up to the onset of symptoms. How could he do such a thing to her—she who had been his best friend and confidant? Natascia's anger towards her father, which she must already have been harboring with the loss of her central position on their arrival in Milan, must have exploded, finally pushing her away from the pole of goodness. Her parents' reconciliation had already unleashed her jealousy, envy and other "bad" feelings, which now became uncontrollable. On the other hand, it didn't seem possible for Natascia to adopt her mother's "selfish" behavior. Indeed, she was terrified by the idea of becoming like her. It would have meant losing her relationship with her father, which was the single most important tie. This tie, moreover, had given her a special role, elevating her in many respects to the rank of adult and placing her in a position of superiority over Louise, and naturally over Azzurra, whose status in the family was nothing like hers. It would also have meant identifying herself with a woman, her mother, with whom she had never developed a filial relationship, who she had always judged negatively and whose hostility she had always felt. For reasons that will become clearer to the reader when I deal with depression, Louise found the attachment between her husband and Natascia intolerable, even though it was she who had created a barrier between herself and Andrea, especially when she was depressed. It was the complicity between Andrea and Natascia that excluded and hurt her, inducing her to become defiant and to cut herself off.

A week after the critical episode, in fact, Natascia seemed to have given up her position forever as the "little housewife," the obliging altruist, and could no longer control her selfish impulses. She wanted to study, and nothing else, thereby placing herself at least on the side of rightness, correctness. She was frightened of not succeeding, of being swept away by her bad thoughts that made her behave like her mother. Her reactions at the moment when she was reminded of the critical episode were so intense that there could be no doubt about the impact it had had on her. It was only during the session that her father realized the importance of that episode. He recognized that he had been irritated about the problems shown by Natascia at the very time when Louise had finally recovered. Nevertheless he had never regarded his action as a rejection or, worse still, as an act of betrayal towards Natascia even though—with hindsight—he understood that his daughter might have seen it like that. Andrea had never placed his daughter in his wife's position; his love towards Natascia was intense but had never had anything to do with what he felt towards his wife. The two relationships, for him, were so different that he had difficulty imagining that Natascia could have made comparisons between his attitudes towards the respective difficulties of mother and daughter. That wasn't so for Natascia, nor for Louise. Even now, in the face of her daughter's symptoms, Louise seemed to react like a sister who was annoyed at seeing her taking over her position of "sick person," the only thing now that certainly belonged to her.

4.7 The Idea of Abstinent Goodness and Psychotherapy

At the root of obsessive organizations there is also an assumption present in our culture. It is the idea that good is the removal of evil. This idea is not limited to a small category of families, those who generate obsessive disorders. Nor is it the exclusive prerogative of certain religions. It is part of our culture, and even of certain branches of the psychological sciences. Freudian psychoanalysis certainly regards good as the absence of evil. Freud does not follow Augustine and Thomas Aquinas, for whom evil is the want of good. Freud's source of inspiration, for this as well as other important aspects of his thought, is Schopenhauer. In his major work, *The World as Will and Representation*, Schopenhauer (1819/1966) expresses the idea of abstinent goodness in the most radical way. In this work, which played such an important role in the construction of the Freudian edifice, it is possible to trace the cultural roots of obsessive-compulsive disorders.

According to Schopenhauer, the world is an insatiable will-to-live; it is the cruel, selfish, blind, and irresistible impetus that pervades and stirs the whole universe. Mankind is no more than a moment in this process:

> Man, as the most complete objectification of this will, is accordingly the most necessitous of all beings. He is concrete willing and needing through and through; he is a concretion of a thousand wants and needs.
>
> (Schopenhauer, 1819/1966, p. 312)

But need is pain, and its satisfaction frees us from want to bring us new suffering, or it plunges us into surfeit and boredom. As a result, life fluctuates between suffering and boredom. Need rules for six days, then pain; on the seventh, the Sabbath, boredom bursts forth. For this reason, no one is to be envied, whereas countless men are to be pitied, since they are condemned to live: unhappiness is the rule. Pain and tragedy are not only the essence of individual lives, but also of nations. History is the tragic repetition of the same events in different forms.

Schopenhauer regards sexual instinct and self-affirmation as intrinsically bad, in exactly the same way as families dominated by the semantics of goodness do. Will-to-live is self-affirmation to the detriment of others. The whole universe is moved by this primordial force, and every element forming the cosmos seeks to assert itself to the detriment of others. The relentless struggle, which is to be seen at every level, culminates in the human world with the crude conflict of egoism against egoism.

Egoism, for Schopenhauer, is the very form of will-of-live, which finds its greatest expression in man. And society is a brutal conflict of egoisms:

> In the consciousness that has reached the highest degree, that is, human consciousness, egoism, like knowledge, pain, and pleasure, must also have reached the highest degree, and the conflict of individuals conditioned by it must appear in the most terrible form. Indeed,

we see this everywhere before our eyes, in small things as in great. At one time we see it from its dreadful side in the lives of great tyrants and evildoers, and in world-devastating wars. On another occasion we see its ludicrous side, where it is the theme of comedy, and shows itself particularly in self-conceit and vanity. La Rochefoucauld understood this better than anyone else, and presented it in the abstract. We see it in the history of the world and in our own experience. But it appears most distinctly as soon as any mob is released from all law and order; we then see at once in the most distinct form the bellum omnium contra omnes which Hobbes admirably described in the first chapter of his De Cive. We see not only how everyone tries to snatch from another what he himself wants, but how one often even destroys another's whole happiness or life, in order to increase by an insignificant amount his own well-being.

(*ibid.*, p. 333)

Sexual instinct is the first, simplest and most direct manifestation of will-to-live. Genitals are the focus of the will-to-live.[22] Eros is therefore the prime principle, as many ancient poets and philosophers maintained. Schopenhauer agrees with them, but for him it is the prime principle of evil, because Eros is at the heart of egoism.

Having identified life with evil, Schopenhauer must necessarily identify good in a corresponding way as that which transcends or negates the will to live. For Schopenhauer, will-to-live, and therefore evil, can be overcome through art and asceticism. In the aesthetic experience, in fact, the individual detaches himself from the chains of will, distancing himself from all desires, all needs. Man is transformed into a clear eye of the world, renouncing will. Art liberates because it removes us from a world of impulses. It redeems for the same reasons that the neutral "instinctual" areas of obsessives reduce the strange loop—it distances from life, from involvement with others.

But the liberation offered by art can only be transitory, linked as it is to brief moments of aesthetic contemplation. In asceticism, on the other hand, will-to-live, the root of evil, is faced directly. By the word asceticism, Schopenhauer means:

This *deliberate* breaking of the will by refusing the agreeable and looking for the disagreeable, the voluntarily chosen way of life of penance and self-chastisement, for the constant mortification of the will.

(*ibid.*, p. 392)

Voluntas becomes *noluntas*: chastity that liberates man from the most primitive and fundamental fulfillment of the will-to-live. The renunciation of the impulse to generate, voluntary poverty, resignation, sacrifice and all forms of "mortification of the will" are instruments that, by appeasing the will to live, produce a deeper peace.

But the philosophy of Schopenhauer, though inspired by the Upanishads, as well as by Plato and Kant, ignores a principle of oriental wisdom: by fighting demons you give them power; the more you fight against the forces of darkness, the deeper and more threatening they become. For this reason the peace that man ought to obtain from asceticism ends up being short-lived in terms of satisfaction of desire. And "intentional denial of will" carries man into endless conflict, this time with *noluntas* rather than *voluntas*.

> However, we must not imagine that, after the denial of the will-to-live has once appeared through knowledge that has become a quieter of the will, such denial no longer wavers or falters, and that we can rest on it as on an inherited property. On the contrary, it must always be achieved afresh by constant struggle. For as the body is the will itself only in the form of objectivity, or as phenomenon in the world as representation, that whole will-to-live exists potentially so long as the body lives, and is always striving to reach actuality and to burn afresh with all its intensity. We therefore find in the lives of saintly persons that peace and bliss we have described, only as the blossom resulting from the constant overcoming of the will; and we see the constant struggle with the will-to-live as the soil from which it shoots up; for on earth no one can have lasting peace.
>
> (*ibid.*, p. 391)

The path of "abstinent" goodness is tremendously difficult. Nor can it be otherwise. By not considering good as having own substance, Schopenhauer ends up giving will-to-live the leading role: it holds center stage as both an impetus that stirs and moves the universe as well as an enemy to be fought.

By what is the path that takes us from the Augustinian conception that good is everything and evil is only the lack of goodness, to an opposite view, such as that of Schopenhauer, that good is the absence of evil?

Between Augustine and Thomas Aquinas, on the one hand, and Schopenhauer on the other, is the philosophy of the "thinking self," which introduces into the modern world view an "acontextual," solitary, self-sufficient being who is capable of acquiring knowledge of the world "outside himself" with his own forces alone. I am referring once again to Descartes, to Leibniz's "monads without doors or windows," and to Kant, for whom the subject of knowledge can never penetrate the "thing in itself."

The identification of life with evil and the idea of "abstinent" goodness are based on the same individualistic conception of man, on the same *homo clausus*, on the same "self in its shell" on which is based freedom as independence from relationships, as I have sought to demonstrate in the previous chapter.

In *Parerga and Paralipomena* Schopenhauer (1851/2007) compares man to a wild ferocious animal. Civilization has reduced him to a state of tame domesticity. But a little anarchy is all that is needed for man's true nature to reveal itself. Schopenhauer completely rejects the social nature of man. For him, man in his truest essence is a solitary, fierce "beast of prey," like the tiger or the cheetah who, as soon as he has "spied a weaker being nearby, pounces on him."

According to Schopenhauer, men are not made to have any need for their fellow humans; they have no lacunae or shortcomings that others can fill; there are no differences between them that make some indispensible to others. On the contrary, individuals are all basically identical microcosms. Will, according to Schopenhauer, is whole and indivisible in every aspect. It is to be found in innumerable individuals, always identical, always complete in itself. For this reason there is no complementarity between individuals, since complementarity can only develop between individuals who are different. On the contrary, each individual is a microcosm in continual conflict with other identical microcosms, and with the macrocosm:

> ... or this egoism has its continuance and being in that opposition of the microcosm and macrocosm, or in the fact that the objectification of the will has for its form the *principium individuationis*, and thus the will manifests itself in innumerable individuals in the same way, and moreover in each of these entirely and completely in both aspects (will and representation). Therefore, whereas each individual is immediately given to himself as the whole will and the entire representer, all others are given to him in the first instance only as his representations. Hence for him his own inner being and its preservation come before all others taken together. Everyone looks on his own death as the end of the world, whereas he hears about the death of his acquaintances as a matter of comparative indifference, unless he is in some way personally concerned in it.
>
> (*ibid.*, pp. 332–333)

Schopenhauer bases his ethics on compassion, a feeling that breaks down the differences between men. Justice and charity, like asceticism, in fact arise from compassion, which frees man from the illusion of feeling detached from others. But it is not a recognition that others are necessary, an awareness that there is no me without you or an admission that others are able to make up for what you lack. Not at all. On the contrary, man removes differences through pity because he understands that, though alone, detached from all others and self-sufficient, he shares with others the same fate of suffering and pain. Each person, by immersing himself in his own lonely solitary subjectivity, recognizes his identity in the ruthless primordial force that moves him, and the impetus that operates in others. This understanding enables man to regain a feeling of compassion for his fellow humans, who are otherwise worthy only of hatred and scorn. Sociability is therefore not a constituent part of man, but is the result of understanding and identifying with universal sorrow: The other person can avoid our hatred and scorn not because we need him to complete us, but because we find in him exactly the same tragedy that we discover in ourselves.

Nor, like Schopenhauer, does classic psychoanalysis recognize altruism, empathy and more general pro-social behavior that binds us to our fellows. This behavior and these feelings are traced back to sublimations, reactive formations, rationalizations, and other secondary re-elaborations that are socially useful but nevertheless distortions of the original, essentially selfish impulses. This is why Anna Freud, referring to obsessive disorders, stated, in perfect agreement with her father, that "no other mental phenomenon expresses with the same clarity the human dilemma of the ruthless and incessant battle between *innate* impulses and *acquired* moral obligations."[23]

The argument I have put forward in this chapter suggests that the dilemma of obsessive-compulsive individuals is a result of their particular positioning within a family semantics—that of goodness—which dominates the conversation in their families, but not in others. The semantic of goodness is also widespread in our culture and, like the semantic of freedom, I presented in the previous chapter, and the semantic of power, of which we will be talking in the next one, is an expression of individualism. The idea of abstinent goodness has also found its way into psychology, and above all psychoanalysis. It is perhaps the very presence of this idea at the basis of Freudian thought that explains what Esman (1989) has described as a paradox: Psychoanalysis, which has made an invaluable contribution in the *understanding* of obsessive-compulsive disorder, has achieved fairly disappointing results in its treatment, as many psychoanalysts including Brandchaft (2001) have recognized. It is a paradox that highlights the existence of a certain antagonism between "understanding" and "changing," something on which systemic psychotherapists have made interesting contributions and to which I will return in the last chapter.

5

THE SEMANTICS OF POWER: ANOREXIA, BULIMIA, AND OTHER EATING PROBLEMS

5.1 More or Less[1]

The family context in which anorexia and other psychogenic eating disorders develop introduces us to a completely different semantic world from that of phobic and obsessive organizations. The idea of freedom from relationships is alien to these families. Even the conflict between good and bad, with its cold light and its dark corners, is generally absent.[2] What dominates the conversation are the semantics of power (Figure 5.1), where some win and some lose, some are successful, some become central figures in the family and the community, and others give up.

VALUES	
SUCCESS	FAILURE
POWER	SUBMISSION
DETERMINATION	COMPLIANCE
DISPLAY	AUTHENTICITY
DEFINITIONS OF SELF / OTHERS / RELATIONSHIPS	
WINNER	LOSER
STRONG-WILLED	YIELDING
OVERBEARING	SUBMISSIVE
BOASTFUL	HUMBLE
GOOD LOOKING	UGLY
WAYS OF RELATING	
ADAPTING ⇄	RESISTING
WINNING	LOSING
FIGHTING	SURRENDERING
MAKING AN IMPRESSION	MAKING A POOR IMPRESSION
EMOTIONS AND FEELINGS	
BOASTING	**SHAME**
SELF-EFFICACY	INADEQUACY

Figure 5.1 The semantics of power. The detailed grid is set out in Ugazio et al., 2009

181

As well as the "winner/loser" polarity, these families have a second polarity—"strong-willed/yielding"—which is hierarchically dependent on the first, based on a relation of means to an end. These people are winners because they are willful, determined or efficient, or they are losers because they are passive, compliant or liable to give in to others. Affability, amenability, acceptance of the definition given by the other person to the relationship are construed within these families as passivity, faint-heartedness, ineptitude.

"Winner/loser," the first and most important semantic polarity in families with eating disorders, has a particular aspect that distinguishes it from the polarities we have looked at so far: its content is purely relational. People can only regard themselves as winners or losers in comparison to others.

In the first chapter I suggested that meaning is the joint action of two polar terms. In a group of people, if some are considered or consider themselves to be good, then others will be bad. When we are with people who are cheerful and happy there will be others in the same context who are sad or even gloomy, and vice versa. But in ordinary personal experience, at least in the West, personal characteristics are perceived as being relatively independent of interpersonal relationships. During the ongoing experience we can feel good, passive, intelligent, bad, generous without having to refer to others. Thinking about ourselves (when the process of "explaining" takes place) we can—either as naive psychologists, or as academics—reconnect what we feel as our way of relating to others. The winner/loser polarity cannot be perceived, even during the course of immediate experiencing in terms of an individual trait. It relates exclusively to the relationship. It is the result of a comparison.

Families in which eating disorders develop seem to confirm the hypothesis originally formulated by Festinger (1954) that people have an impulse to evaluate their personal opinions and abilities on the basis of those of others. Man, it is suggested, has a sort of instinct for social comparison. Festinger, in fact, uses this supposition to explain relationships within groups other than the family. Later on, Tajfel (1981), a charismatic figure in European social psychology, developed a theory on identities and intergroup relationships that focused on social comparison. Tajfel, too, was not concerned with family relationships—he was interested in those aspects of individual identity arising from membership of broad social groups such as race, nation or social class. In the families we are concerned with, comparison—using the criteria of success and rivalry which follow from it—guides internal relationships within the family group, as well as relationships with the extended family.

Among the reasons why these families give particular attention to the winner/loser polarity there is a history of social downfall and recovery or class differences between the original families from which the partners come. When, during a session with the family of Alessia, a bulimic aged twenty, I asked for information about her mother's family, there was an embarrassed silence followed by this intense dialogue:

MOTHER: My father died of cancer when I was three years old; I remember several months later I was taken to the cemetery. I couldn't drag myself away from his grave. A few years later his brother, whom I was very fond of, also died. With my mother there was never any attachment. I left home at the age of fourteen: I had no choice. It was a question of survival. Thanks to the help of a monsignor I went to boarding school and completed secretarial college. My mother died when she was thirty-six in an accident.

THERAPIST: They were years of great suffering for you …

MOTHER: Yes. Unless it is absolutely necessary, I would prefer not to say anymore. I never talk about it.

THERAPIST: *[to her husband]* Has your wife spoken to you about her family?

FATHER: No, I don't know much about it. I was twenty-one when I met my wife. When we decided to marry I spoke to the monsignor who was her guardian. He told me a few things. When I met her she had just finished at the orphanage. I never asked her much … I judge people by their actions, by what they do.

THERAPIST: Didn't you think your wife wanted to talk about what she'd been through, the problems she must have had to face during her childhood and adolescence?

FATHER: No, it seemed she did not want to talk about her family. I have always respected her silence. Her mother drank… That I do know, she told me… this was also the cause of the accident. She also had… how can I describe it? … a "busy" social life outside the home and was sometimes violent towards my wife.

THERAPIST: *[to the daughters]* Has your mother ever talked to you about it?

ADRIANA: No. Never.

ALESSIA: She did tell me something after I became ill, to let me understand, I think, that she has also suffered.

MOTHER: *[trying to hold back the tears]* I have fought all my life to avoid being the "poor little girl"… given my family circumstances… to do my best. That is why I always preferred not to talk about my childhood.

Her husband's prosperous family had welcomed Alessia's mother with love and humanity. Her mother-in-law, a very religious woman, had almost fostered her, but relations with the in-laws, who came from a very different social background, were the source of continual tension. Alessia's mother had succeeded in becoming part of her husband's family, but in doing so had had to sever her roots. Her background could not be talked about in the new family story; the social gap was insurmountable.

The parents of Viola, a 16-year-old anorexic, were both classics graduates from the same university, and both taught in secondary schools. Yet, to look at them, they were of two completely different kinds: The mother was cultured, refined and at home in the city, as were her parents and her brothers, with whom she shared an interest in music, cinema and theatre, whereas the father, the only member of his original family with a university degree, was coarse and provincial, despite the fact that he had been away from his place of origin for a quarter of a century. Twenty years together, the same profession and an almost identical income had done little to reduce or reconcile the couple's original social differences.

The parents of Costanza, an anorexic aged thirteen, really came from two entirely different social backgrounds. Her father's family were prominent members of the intelligentsia, while her mother, the second wife of her much older father, came from a poor, uneducated Sicilian family. When the two families met at funerals, weddings and other formal occasions, they were completely unable to communicate, and Costanza felt acute embarrassment and shame.

In other cases it is membership of family clans and family businesses—where love, business and economic prestige are closely connected—which has given central importance to a semantics that is so concerned about questions of status. A large number of family businesses feature in my cases. Generally the biological relationship and the considerable emotional investment involved in family ties, while not eliminating criteria of success, tend to relegate them to the background. But this is certainly not the case in these families, where social success is a contested but inevitable yardstick.

Since the polarity forming the basis of meanings in these families is purely relational, the relationship with others is seen, at all times and in all circumstances, as being central in defining the self. Everyone in these families is conscious about the judgment of others, about criteria for social achievement and about social appearances (Bruch, 1978; Guidano, 1987, 1991; Selvini Palazzoli, 1974; see also Koskina et al., 2011). This awareness of others and of their opinions generally means that members of these families tend to attribute the cause of their behavior to others, or consider their own behavior to be a response to that of others. This tendency is greatest in anorexia and bulimia. Bruch (1973, p. 254) stated that, in his experience, anorexics act "only *in response* to demands coming from other people in situations, and not as doing things because *they want to.*" And an ecological assessment study carried out by Steiger et al. (1999) suggests that bulimia is associated with particular sensitivity to negative interpersonal transactions even after recovery.

Perhaps because of this, family therapy, in all its forms, has become the preferred treatment for eating disorders. For adolescent and preadolescent anorexics, family therapy has proved to be so superiorly effective to other treatments (Dare et al., 2001; Eisler et al., 2000) that the NICE (National Institute for Health and Clinical Excellence, 2004) guidelines recommend its use.

The crucial "winner/loser" semantic polarity renders the central definition of the relationship between members of the family unit and their relative

conflicts central. The *conflict over the definition of the relationship is a continual issue in the conversation of these families*. The subject matter being argued
over—the "contents" of the conflict—is generally irrelevant: what is important
is supremacy (one-upmanship). According to Selvini Palazzoli (1974; Selvini
Palazzoli et al., 1978), interactions are dominated by symmetrical hubris.

In the past, systemic psychotherapy has placed great emphasis on problems of defining the relationship, thus creating a selective attention by therapists towards this level of communication. Since therapists' ideas contribute
towards creating the therapeutic relationship, in the 1980s I often found that
I was involved with families in battles for the definition of the relationship that
I myself contributed towards constructing. Obviously I was not aware of this.
Indeed, I was convinced that I was working in such a way that these conflicts
between me and them could sink into the background, in order to reach those
within the family. I became aware of the problem much later, when my attention moved to meanings and their construction during the session: to emotions, to the position of the patient and therapist—all arguments for which
the metaphor of power is not relevant. By some miracle the families stopped
involving me and my team in conflicts over defining the relationship. The
only exceptions were patients with eating disorders, and their families: They
continue, even now, to interpret my behavior, and that of my colleagues, in
terms of the problem of defining the relationship. Nor could it be different.
In that, members of these families construct reality through the semantics of
power, competitive conflict within the family, with the extended family, or
even with therapists or other figures, are the rule. Members of these families
are continually involved in schismogenetic processes, symmetrical escalations
and fierce rivalries. Some win and others yield; some are successful and others
are outclassed, defeated. *Some come off better and some come off worse*. No one
can avoid the confrontation and therefore no one can settle down into their
own position.

Precisely because the relationships are regulated by rivalry, *the definition of
the relationships between the members of the family is unstable and consequently
each member is uncertain about their identity*. A clear identity requires stability in the relationships between the various members of the family (Berger &
Luckmann, 1966); but this stability is lacking in the families we are concerned
with. In family contexts in which obsessive-compulsive disorders are developed,
even members who position themselves in the "nasty, bad" extreme accept
the resulting definition of themselves: They consider themselves to be selfish
or arrogant, or sexually unrestrained, and often display these characteristics
with sinister pleasure. Also members of families in which phobic organizations
develop, whether at one extreme or another, do not generally object to their
positioning. It is only the individual with a phobic organization who, for the
reasons described, has difficulty in finding a position in one or other extreme
of the critical semantic polarity. On the contrary, in families where eating

disorders develop, the person in the "losing" position does not accept defeat. The reason is simple: no one can accept that their identity is defined by defeat. For a person positioned in the "loser" polarity, to accept their position would be the same as admitting "I am my own undoing." For this reason, those who find themselves in this position, if they do not have a real possibility of undermining the winners, are at least able to redefine their defeat as a sacrifice. Along with those placed in the same pole and with the "winners" themselves (for reasons that we will see in a moment), they develop those sacrificial escalations so well described by Selvini Palazzoli (1974).

Precisely because the "losers" cannot accept their own defeat, the winners cannot stop working to preserve their own superiority. All of their energies will be channeled into maintaining and displaying the signs and symbols that make them superior. The path followed by the "winners," especially within the family, where it is particularly difficult for their superiority to be accepted, often involves presenting themselves and their superior behavior in terms of altruism. They work every day for the good of the family (not for their own success), they are active in the community, maintain social contacts and friendships in order to help the careers of other members of the family (not because they are flattered to be at the center of attention), they are efficient, well-organized, determined to compensate for those who are unfortunately unable to be the same, etc. Naturally, no one in the family believes in these good intentions, not even those who boast them: The "winners," precisely because they share the semantics of power with other members of the family, are the first to doubt themselves, to suspect that their altruism is an instrument for taking advantage of the others. For this reason their apparent good intentions often betray a false and manipulative tone.

The range of emotional states typically experienced by these families, which form the basis of the critical semantics, includes boasting, a feeling of personal effectiveness and skill, command, control and self-confidence against shame, humiliation, impotence or inadequacy. Jealously, envy and rivalry are naturally part of the daily emotional experience within these families.

Members of these families, like all human beings, each want to be different. But the process of externalizing individual characteristics is obstructed. Since every self-definition is felt in comparative terms and produces feelings of superiority or inferiority towards others, the differences are immediately understood, but feared, denied, rejected and often considered unjustified. *Differences do not in fact encourage cooperation. On the contrary, they serve to promote personal superiority or overbearing behavior against other members of the family, or they are an indication of personal failure or defeat.* For this reason, the relational dynamics in these families generally tend to discourage individual distinction. This aspect has been recognized by psychotherapists from different backgrounds. Minuchin, Rosman, and Baker (1978) have used the term "enmeshment" to describe this family dynamic that hinders the emergence of feelings of being "separate," favoring a poor distinction between self and others. Selvini Palazzoli (1974, p. 264) agreed that individual character is sacrificed in favor of uniformity: "The collective sense of the family is so pronounced that the individual is pushed into the background. There is a tendency to stick together like a brood of ducklings." According to Guidano (1987) this style of relationship can be summarized with the slogan: "It is through sharing the same views that we realize we love each other." This family dynamic, however we might wish to describe it, is the inevitable consequence of the particular semantic organization of these families, centered as it is on competitive conflict: When the competition reaches extreme levels, the individual differences lead to competitive escalations and therefore have to be stopped, or at least limited, because they represent a threat to the cohesion and the continuity of the group.

The centrality of the semantics of power also explains a typical characteristic of communication in these families: the extremely high level of rejection.

> Very rarely will one member bear out what another has said, particularly about how he defines himself in the relationship. Contradiction is common. This type of rejection, therefore, does not concern the general invitation to communicate, which is accepted and reciprocated, but the two levels of the message as such. In fact it is as though each member of the family reacted to the other's message in the following way "I reject the content of what you say, even though I acknowledge your right to say it. And I also reject your definition of yourself (and myself) in our relationship."
>
> (Selvini Palazzoli, 1974, p. 205)

Yet all of these families fear rejection as the worst form of invalidation and they yearn for acceptance above everything else. But, in a situation where differences are described in terms of superiority and inferiority, to confirm the definition offered by the other would mean exposing yourself to the risk of losing your own winning position or would be equivalent to admitting defeat.

The selective attention towards defining the relationship also makes it difficult to establish an effective leadership in the family (Minuchin & Barcai, 1969; Minuchin, Rosman & Baker, 1978). In many of these families there is a complete paralysis in decision-making: even the simplest decisions are impossible.

As a result of symmetrical escalations between Brunilde and Matteo, the parents of Alba, a 16-year-old anorexic, the house into which they had moved three years before had become uninhabitable. The bathroom was still unfinished: work had been suspended because Brunilde and Matteo couldn't agree on the choice of tiles. Nor could they reach any agreement or compromise on where to hang their pictures—paintings, prints and posters had been propped against the walls waiting to be hung. Brunilde and Matteo, she from Brunico,

187

on the Austrian border, he from Trani, in southern Italy, were poles apart on everything. He hated the horseradish she used for dressing salad, the jams she lovingly prepared and her favorite hobby of needlepoint embroidery. She hated oregano and chili pepper and Matteo's passion for the violin made her shudder: She claimed that certain chords set her teeth on edge. They agreed about nothing and continued to argue about everything. Alba, with her serious anorexia, ran her parents' life: She prepared their food according to her personal interpretation of their tastes and requirements, forced them to eat separately, decided what television programs they were to watch, stopped their visits to their respective original families and insisted that holidays could no longer be spent in the Brunico or Trani areas.

Cases such as Alba's are not uncommon. Anorexics, with their emaciation, often allow the family to find a leadership: The illness represents a greater power that can finally take control of the family.

Symmetrical escalations between parents are also present in families with other eating disorders. Sometimes these take the form of symmetrical schismogenesis between "winner" parents; in other cases the parents, both "losers" in relation to their relatives or the community, fuel the sacrificial escalation that I have just mentioned. Even when parents position themselves at opposite polarities—one is successful, active, full of initiative, sociable, while the other is unsuccessful, unable to face challenges, passive—the schismogenesis is never complementary but symmetrical. The superiority attributed to the "winner" partner by the community and/or extended family is generally not recognized by the "loser" partner, who regards it as unwarranted superiority. The successes of partners are not denied, but they have no value: A successful person has an important position in business, in politics, in the community because he or she has completely neglected the family, is cunning, has friends in high places or is a skilled manipulator, is only interested in success, has no values, no feelings, nor even any hobbies.

The partner in the losing position often tries to impose a moral order that undermines "success" and "power"—the central values of the semantics dominating the conversation in these families—putting them into the context of overbearing behavior or "display" and "conventionality." In fact, what the winners regard as personal skill is considered as overbearing behavior by all those who find themselves at the negative extreme of the critical—not just the partner—and they introduce "authentic" and "unconventional" values into the conversation that conflict with "success" and "power." But like success and power, the polar opposition of "authenticity-display" is lacking in content: "Superficiality" is all that the winners display, whereas "authenticity" is identified with what the winners reject.

The relational dynamic that I have outlined describes a crisis phase in the family, expressed, and at the same time exacerbated, by the development of an eating disorder in a member of the family. During the course of the treatment it is possible to reconstruct periods when the couple was able to limit internal rivalry, if only to deal with conflicts with the original families or with other relatives. Solidarity tends to appear at certain stages in the couple's relationship but is unlikely to be the dominant feature. The competitive conflict can be open or unstated. In my clinical experience the number of cases of couples in open conflict, such as Brunilde and Matteo, are as frequent as situations—similar to those described by many authors (Bruch, 1978; Selvini Palazzoli, 1974; Vandereycken, 2002)—where the conflict is hidden beneath a façade of apparent agreement. It is probable that this difference is the consequence of the growing social acceptance of marital conflict. Even families such as these, who are so concerned about social appearances, can now freely display their mutual disillusionment and intolerance.

5.2 The Dilemma and the Permitted Stories

The position of those with an organization typical of eating disorders also assumes the characteristics of a dilemma or strange reflexive loop in relation to the critical semantic polarities, which involves the levels of the self and the relationship. The dilemma, however, does not contemplate, even in hypothetical terms, the possibility of independence from the relationship, as happens in phobic organizations. Nor does it leave open the possibility, as occurs in obsessive-compulsive organizations, of substitute investments in areas outside the relationship, such as art, religion or literature. For this reason, subjects with this organization, however determined, intelligent and motivated towards success, are less likely to be among those who provide significant contributions towards science and the arts. A commitment in this field requires the ability to be detached, if only temporarily, from the "here and now" of the relationship. That is not the case with dancing, acting or singing where artists remain under the eye of their teachers or the audience, and the organization typical of eating disorders excels in these fields. They do not have that possibility of disconnecting from the relationship necessary to novelists, painters, and scientists. For individuals with eating disorders, *the ongoing relationship in the here and now is the context through which individuals give meaning to their internal states and define the boundaries of self, and not vice versa (see Figure 5.2).* In order to exist it is necessary to be in a relationship.

Generally speaking, in the West, the self—in other words, the stories that each individual has in order to give meaning and unity to their inner biography—provides the context for forming and regulating relationships with relevant people. The personal inner biography provides the controlling point of view that determines, more or less unwittingly, choices regarding personal closeness, distance, changes of allegiance or perhaps the termination of relationships with relevant people. For this reason the disillusionment and frustration arising from the failure of important interpersonal relationships (even

189

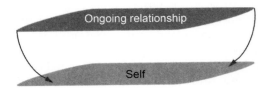

Figure 5.2 Levels in eating disorders: The ongoing relationship defines individual internal states and the boundaries of the self

with the main attachment figures), though generating pain and anger, or even confusion and disorientation, do not generally produce the sense of emptiness and personal ineffectiveness that we find when the semantics of power dominates the conversation.

In fact, even in the West, the tendency for the self to contextualize the relationship does not always arise. Among women, for example, even today, for cultural reasons that are so well known that it is unnecessary to describe them, interpersonal relationships often act as the context for self. In children (irrespective of age) the relationship also tends to contextualize the self. It is no surprise that most eating disorders affect women and begin during adolescence. Anorexics and bulimics are generally young and, in 90 percent of cases, are women. Obesity is more evenly distributed between the sexes (Keski-Rahkonen, Raevouri, & Hoek, 2008; Striegel-Moore, Franko, & Ach, 2006).

My experience, which encourages the involvement of the family in the therapy process for anorexia and bulimia, has led me to conclude that the relationship contextualizes the self in all members of the group, not just those suffering from eating disorders. The semantic organization of these families, which is so dependent on such a purely relational polarity as winner/loser, the fierce struggles to gain the upper hand, and the consequent instability in the definition of relationships, means that everybody's identity is insecure and therefore in need of constant support from others. For this reason (unlike families with other diseases) the onset of symptoms in patients with eating disorders is generally preceded by an uneasiness experienced by all members of the family. The question of age and prevalence among women would therefore only emphasize the tendency of the self (shared with other members of the family) to contextualize the relationship. Anorexics, bulimics and those suffering from obesity certainly experience a feeling of devastating emptiness when faced with the loss of supportive relationships. They also demonstrate a characteristic sensitivity to criticism. Disapproval, even by people of little importance, triggers off a perception of self that is then so intolerable as to produce a sense of total disorientation (Bara & Stoppa Beretta, 1996; Guidano, 1987. See also Steiger et al., 1999).

Giovanna, a bulimic aged thirty-five, was in a state of disorientation for days after some criticism from a friend she had lost contact with for years and had recently met again. The cause of so much suffering was a phrase such as: "Sometimes you put people in difficulty," said in reply to a friendly expression of regret by the patient about an appointment that the newly re-found friend had failed to keep. From the patient's account, the comment seemed to be an inappropriate reaction by the friend to justify her improper behavior. Giovanna agreed with the therapists that this was the most plausible interpretation, but the episode had caused her to vomit throughout the whole night, and it took her a week to recover. Her feeling of dejection was so intense that her partner had become jealous: he got it into his head that there was (or had been) a love affair between the two women: only in this context did Giovanna's reaction seem understandable. His suspicions were entirely unfounded: It had been a rather superficial friendship without any sexual implications.

Monica, a bulimic aged eighteen, felt totally inadequate every time she met a cousin a few years older.

> I feel terrible when I meet her... She always finds something wrong in me. For example she says: "Look, your hem's unstitched". Or "Haven't you noticed? You have a button missing", or "You look pale, are you OK?" She always makes you feel bad. She used to write me letters full of criticism. Even if she says nothing, her look of disapproval makes me feel terrible. Yesterday after seeing her I returned home and went to bed: I could do nothing else, I felt useless.

Those suffering from obesity also present similar emotional states in the face of criticism, especially from significant family members and friends. Flavia, a lawyer aged forty, described an episode in which her mother had made a dismissive comment about her:

> At that moment I wanted to disappear; for me it was more than a criticism. I was that disgusting thing, that kind of shabby tramp, that mass of flab that my mother made me feel I was, and I just wanted to vanish. It has always been like that: When my mother looks at me it's as if I were looking at myself through her eyes. It's a horrible feeling.

Paolo, aged thirty-five and seriously obese, described how he had managed to graduate in architecture with excellent marks thanks to his friendship with someone his own age who was on another course. Sharing a room with this friend enabled him to enjoy a period that was happy as well as productive. In three years he was able to catch up on the time lost during the previous two years, taking all the exams he needed to get his degree. This account was given by the patient in order to explain to the therapists that he felt ill, unable to work and incapable of doing anything during those weekends when his partner left him to look after her daughter from a previous relationship. Paolo felt an emptiness when she was away that he was only able to fill with gigantic blow-out feasts. Being diabetic, he was well aware that these binges were putting his life at risk, but the sense of disorientation was such as to give him no other choice.

These examples show the intensity with which the relationship contextualizes the self in subjects with eating disorders. When we meet them in our clinical practice, it is impossible to understand the dilemma they face without understanding the fundamental importance that the views and opinions of other people have on them.

The dilemma we are considering involves the particular way in which these persons relate to others: "adapting/resisting." The critical semantics, and the consequent selective attention to the problem of defining the relationship, induce members of these families to construct relationships as forms of adaptation to the other person and their demands, or as forms of opposition. The other ways of relating, set out in Figure 5.2, are also typical of the semantics of power and therefore well-practiced by people with eating disorders as well as by other members of their family. "Adapting/resisting" is, however, especially critical for those whose positioning depends mainly on adult members of the group, such as adolescents and young people, who represent the large majority of anorexic and bulimic patients. Those who wish to maintain their supposed or real superiority, or to improve their position, have to adapt to those who hold a winning position in the family group or in the community; those in a losing position, who see no possibility of improving their situation, challenge the winners by seeking to undermine their superiority.

The dilemma, which assumes the characteristics of a strange reflexive loop,[3] occurs when both "adapting" and "resisting" become incompatible with maintaining an established perception of the self. For subjects experiencing the dilemma, conforming with the other's expectations means being passive, a loser, and feeling violated and therefore overwhelmed. To resist means regaining a sense of personal effectiveness, but involves being rejected and implies losing the other's confirmation and with it the sense of their own individuality (see Figure 5.3)

The more the reflexivity of the loop increases, the more conforming to the expectations of attachment figures is felt to be a submission, a defeat, a surrender to their overwhelming power, and therefore a violation of personal integrity. But resisting, becoming involved in a symmetrical escalation with the main attachment figures, means losing that clearly defined perception of the self that only the confirmation and acceptance of the other person is able to assure.[4]

When the reflexivity of the loop is at its maximum, individuals waver between "adapting" and "resisting" without finding a validation of self. Adapting means

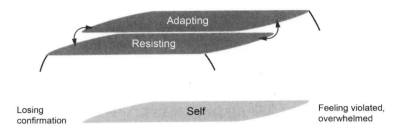

Figure 5.3 The strange reflexive loop of eating disorders

being overwhelmed and humiliated, but resisting means losing the confirmation of attachment figures who are essential for preserving integrity of self. This very difficult moment overlaps generally with the onset of symptoms. Though their causes remain partly unclear, their effects are all too apparent. The reflexivity of the loop is restrained, thanks to the symptoms. Through refusing to eat and vomiting, anorexics, as well as bulimics, place themselves in opposition to the attachment figures, at the same time intensifying their relationship with them. Food becomes an area of conflict, a battleground, where patients refuse to do as they are told. The vexed question about the extent to which symptoms go beyond the conscious control of anorexics and bulimics is therefore not so important. Irrespective of their intentions and their symbolic meaning, vomiting and refusing to eat represent a challenge to the parents because this is the meaning attributed by the families in which the eating disorders occur. Parents generally feel that they are also being publically challenged, blamed and humiliated by anorexia and obesity. For many years, family therapists, especially those involved with eating disorders, have emphasized that families should be involved as a resource in the treatment. Some of them, who are not satisfied with this self-evident truth, go on to say that the participation of the family does not imply that they play any role in the etiology of the eating disorders (Dare & Eisler, 1997; Lock et al., 2001). These therapists seem to extend to family therapy what Cerletti said about electric shock treatment, which he had just begun to investigate: it works but we don't know why. In actual fact, many things are known. A large amount has been written about the interactive characteristics and patterns of families where eating disorders develop, which also provide the background for this chapter. Among family psychotherapists, eating disorders have been the "elected" psychopathology, playing a role similar to that of hysteria and obsessive-compulsive neurosis in psychoanalysis. The ideas and theories put forward have not been verified, nor can they ever be, since in almost all sciences explicative mechanisms generally can only be falsified. Such caution among eminent colleagues is not unjustified: it avoids adding to the difficulty faced by parents who already feel under attack. The child's disorder, by reason of the semantics of power, is experienced by the parents as a personal defeat and often as a public humiliation. But rarely do parents, especially those of anorexics, refuse to be involved. On the contrary, they resume their full role of nursing the patient: how can they not feel responsible for guiding, counseling and making decisions for a child who cannot eat? Due to their dramatic condition, anorexics, above all, return to playing the role of the child and the couple to that of parents, even if the girl (the patient in more than 90 percent of cases is female) has reached a stage in life (generally adolescence or youth) where the relationship with the parents should be more equal and less close, allowing more space for building new relationships.

The dilemma I have described can be developed adaptively. This is what happens in the pre-morbid state, as I have seen in cases where the onset of symptoms occurs in adulthood, or working with people with no symptoms who have a personal organization in which the dilemma typical of eating disorders plays a central role, whose request for therapy arises from existential problems. Their way of life reveals the presence of various styles of adaption that can be summarized in the two ways described below. These styles generally make it possible for individuals to adapt quite normally, often quite satisfactorily.

The style of adaption that I have come across in women who have become anorexic or anorexic-bulimic in adulthood takes the form of a total, often conventional, acceptance of the values of their family and social group. These women, who are strong-willed, determined and hard-working, behave, at home and at work, in the way that respected members of the group expect and encourage them to act, and they pursue objectives that are always approved by the significant figures in the environment in which they belong.[5] The tendency to depend upon the approval of others means that they are unlikely to be involved in long-term projects where the result is uncertain and remote. What is more, since their surroundings tend not to offer them much in the way of confirmation, they are perfectionists: by performing their task perfectly they hope to receive approval (Fairburn et al., 1999; Halmi et al., 2000; Lilenfeldet al., 2006; Wonderlich et al., 2005). Approval is sought especially from people in higher positions in the hierarchy. Emotional and sexual involvement is generally feared—to allow it would mean being at the mercy of another person, letting go, losing self-control, and being exposed to the risk of losing.[6] These women, therefore, are unlikely to reach orgasm. Nevertheless, since their identity in all respects—and therefore also their sexual identity—depends upon another person, they generally feel the need for a stable partner as a matter of priority, and the partner, once chosen, becomes the center of their attention even if they develop a low level of intimacy (Vandereyckey, 2002). Bulimics also seem to depend particularly on the opinions of their companion and upon their approval (Schembri & Evans, 2008).

I have often found the opposite way of relating in cases of obesity, also prior to the onset of the problem. These individuals are unconventional, generally friendly, but hypercritical of anyone who is socially committed and they tend to unmask those in a higher position. They tend to be antagonistic towards people of higher status and to develop that kind of equality enjoyed by the "opponent." The warning of the Gospel: "why do you look at the speck of sawdust in your brother's eye, with never a thought to the great plank in your own" suits them perfectly. With generally low self-esteem, they seem to maintain what remains of their positive identity by bringing down other people and exposing their supposed positive and superior attitude.

These subjects do not refer to difficulties in reaching orgasm. For them there is sometimes a greater fear of an intimate, deep and equal sexual relationship because there is a risk of bringing out that negativity fuelled by their "co-positioning" at the negative extreme of the critical semantics. For this reason they often choose people who need them and their help, rather than true partners.

The most important sexual relationship for Flavia, the obese 40-year-old lawyer I referred to earlier, was with a man several years younger, from a very modest background. When Flavia met him in his youth, he had no plans to become a lawyer, nor even of going to university. Flavia elevated him socially and culturally; she fostered new interests in him; she convinced him he had a talent for the law, helped him stage by stage through his degree and then employed him as her assistant. Their sexual relationship did not last long but they lived together for more than ten years. His relationship with Flavia, which never became equal, probably made him feel inferior, and in fact he broke off the relationship with her to marry a secretary in the same office, who was neither young nor attractive, nor clever, but submissive. Flavia, who by this time was seriously obese, then had a lesbian relationship with a young woman of no financial means or education, who she helped to transform into a competent interior designer; later she lived for a short while with a client whom she had helped to be released from prison. Both relationships came to an end when her help was no longer needed.

From what I have been able to reconstruct through my experience as a therapist, these ways of adapting are often the continuation of conduct and attitudes that emerged in adolescence. I will describe them below.

5.3 Adolescence: A Critical Period

For most anorexics and bulimics, as well as those with obesity problems, infancy does not appear to be a theatre for tensions and conflicts that can be interpreted as precursors of the subsequent psychopathology, as is frequently the case with obsessive and phobic patients. The dilemma I have described emerges during adolescence or, at the earliest, in pre-adolescence.[7]

As I have already emphasized, the conflicts in defining relationships, while painful even before the onset of symptoms, create an insecurity of identity. All relational positions become unstable and precarious: the "winners" feel, and in fact are, under threat, while the "losers," who regard their inferiority to be unjustified, seek to redefine or reverse their position. Children who are involved in a conversation of this type will be more vulnerable than adults: Their sense of self will be particularly insecure and in need of approval from other people. Selective attention in defining relationships will also induce children, in particular, to restrict the range of possible ways of "co-positioning" themselves with others to those characteristics of the semantics of power set out in Figure 5.1. Children, unlike adults, do not have previous experience of other emotional conversations of such importance.

Nevertheless, so long as they remain children, they will not feel the dilemma I have described. They will, of course, take up a position among the winners or the losers, or a position midway in relation to the critical semantics, but their positioning does not appear to be problematic.

If they are active, determined, strong-willed, if they identify with the values of success in their group—as happens with future anorexics and bulimics—they will try to excel at school and in sport, they will be self-disciplined and strive not to disappoint their parents. Their tendency to compete will be limited to their siblings and their own age group. There will therefore be no lack of approval and support from their favorite parent, and from the other adult members of their family, all the more since a child, however attractive and clever, is unlikely to be regarded by adults as a threat.

If they are closer to the "losers," as generally happens with those with future obesity problems, they will be children who perform poorly at school, lack discipline and tend not to obey their parents or teachers. They may be high-spirited and rebellious or absent-minded, sometimes lazy or submissive. They will also be children who love playing and will be on good terms with members of their own age group. As they do not compete with their friends or fellow pupils, they are unlikely to be isolated, as frequently happens with future anorexics. They will sometimes be leaders. They may be criticized for their lack of discipline and erratic approach to study, especially by the more active and determined members of their family, but there will be no lack of approval from adults less concerned about their school results, or lack of friends from those in their own age group.

With pre-adolescence and adolescence the balance is upset. Those who position themselves at the winning pole, including future anorexics and bulimics, in order to maintain their position, inevitably find that they have to compete with the same people whose approval they continue to need. A rivalry therefore begins, which is generally covert, with parents who are playing at more than one table. Being used to competing with those their own age, and encouraged by their parents to beat their friends in order to demonstrate their superiority, as they grow older they inevitably find themselves in confrontation with their parents and other adults in the family. The area of contention might be physical beauty, sporting ability, intelligence, wit, elegance, culinary skills etc. The subject matter is irrelevant when the semantics of power dominates. What counts is who has the upper hand. Obviously, it is not just the children who compete with the adults; the adults also see their children as threats. Being accustomed to offering themselves as models for their children, they feel displaced by the importance their children give to their teachers, sports trainers, friends' parents, as well as their admirers. They become irritated by behavior, ideas and interests different to their own, which the adolescent develops through new independent contacts, and brings into the family.

Parents also control where adolescents go in order to protect them—especially their daughters, though they also limit the freedom of their sons. These adolescents are annoyed by controls and limits, not least because they consider them unnecessary, having always proved themselves to be responsible and reliable. What makes such controls particularly hateful is that they regard them as humiliating. The selective attention to the definition of the relationship does not enable them to interpret their parents' restrictions as forms of protection—that may be excessive and pointless, but intended to safeguard them from harm. In their eyes, their parent's control is an expression of their desire to command, an attempt to ignore their capabilities, in order to keep them in a state of subjection. The complementary relationship with adults—even with key attachment figures, winners, formerly in positions of unquestionable authority and models to emulate—are now seen in terms of inferiority/superiority. To accept a complementary relationship with them, continuing to place them in the position of someone who guides, counsels, commands, is seen as passivity and subjection, and therefore leads to a certain degree of intransitivity with the maintenance of a positive self-image. On the other hand, opposition would mean losing the confirmation that the insecurity of their personal identity makes indispensible.

Adolescence is also a difficult period for those who "co-position" themselves among the losers, as happens with those with future problems of obesity. This stage of life, however, is not so critical as it is for those who position themselves at the positive pole of the family semantics.

These adolescents also regard the controls and limits imposed by adults to be a sort of abuse of power. But the conflict with adults—especially those in a position of authority—is not so unsettling for them precisely because by confronting these figures they establish their own identity, as they had already begun to do during their infancy. During adolescence, the clash with adults who are active, determined and successful, from being indirect and generally unwilling, becomes clear, transforming itself into open rebellion. These adolescents often display provocative behavior at home and sometimes play a negative leading role among fellow pupils and peers. Since they are in danger of being the object of rejection by those in a winning position, the preferred way of "co-positioning" themselves, which during adolescence is through opposition, can become intransitive with the self, as happens for future anorexics. In a situation where rejection tends to be frequent, to actively encourage it with provocative conduct exposes these adolescents to the danger of finding themselves with a self-perception that is so negative as to be unacceptable. This risk is mitigated by two aspects of their positioning. They are not a threat: they have no ambition to obtain a place among the winners, nor do they generally excel in the qualities admired by members of these families. They intensify their conflict with adults in a winning position but do not lose their links with key figures of attachment who are generally positioned at the losers side of the critical semantics.

To summarize, the dilemma that I have suggested as being a characteristic of eating disorders does not seem to emerge in infancy. It appears in adolescence or pre-adolescence. When the semantics of power prevails, and conflict for definition of the relationship becomes the central argument in the family conversation, adolescence—with its normal developmental tasks and its inevitable changes in the parent/child relationship—is such as to fuel the conflicts between self and relationships that are typical of the strange loop described. These conflicts, experienced above all by adolescents who position themselves at the two extremes of the crucial polarities, become devastating for those, such as anorexics and bulimics, who place themselves at the positive pole of the semantics of power. The conflict in the definition of the relationship with winners threatens to deprive them of the anchor giving stability to their identity. It induces them to adopt opposing forms of behavior that place their position in the family and in the community at risk and are contrary to the values of success and power that they continue to pursue. *These reasons help towards explaining why anorexia and bulimia are more frequent during adolescence than obesity.*

5.4 The Intersubjective Context in the Here and Now: An Instigation and a Double Disillusionment

The picture outlined so far is not sufficient to explain how tensions and conflicts develop into a full-blown eating disorder.

Subjects with organizations typical of eating disorders are generally able to adapt themselves to the dilemma I have described where they can rely upon a figure of attachment who provides a context for defining the boundaries of their self. I will call this preferred attachment a "confirmative bond." Adolescence and the dilemma described do not involve the subjects (whether at the losing or winning end of the critical semantics) in severing their involvement with their attachment figures. They cause only an increased tension between these figures, especially for future anorexics and bulimics. Cases where symptoms first develop relatively late (in the late twenties or adulthood) indicate that maintaining just one "confirmative bond" provides these subjects with the security needed to deal adaptively, and even creatively, with that dilemma between the self and relationship that usually develops in adolescence.

Therefore, *so long as the relational situation makes it possible to maintain at least one "confirmative bond," the reflexivity of the strange loop is kept within such limits as to avoid the onset of an eating disorder.*

It is only at a certain point in the family story that the reflexivity of the loop assumes such proportions as to produce an actual psychopathology in young people or adults.

The relational situation in which therapy generally begins, and the reconstruction, made with the family, of the events accompanying the onset of symptoms, sees the patient at the center of what we might call an instigation process whose outcome is a double disillusionment: both the figure who is the target of the instigation, as well as the person who through his or her criticism has induced patients to distance themselves from this figure, become objects of disillusionment. Patients find themselves alone, without links capable of providing sufficient confirmations to validate the self.

Before examining more closely the interactive process leading to the onset of symptoms, it should be made clear *that the "confirmative figure" for anorexics and bulimics at their ideal weight is generally in the winning polarity: like them, he or she is active, capable of initiative, strong-willed.* For anorexics, this figure is generally the mother or another member of the family who takes the caring role. For bulimics, particularly those of ideal weight, this "confirmative" position is more frequently taken by the father, or by another member of the family who does not carry out a caring function. *The adult who provides a "confirmative bond" to those with future obesity is, however, in a losing position.* This figure often does not have a caring role but provides the emotional support and alliance necessary to face the risks to which they are exposed as a result of their position of "opposers."

The interactive process that leads these people to full-blown psychopathologies can, for purposes of clarity, be broken down into five phases.

1. The target of the "instigation" is generally a parent in the "winning" position, therefore active and determined. For anorexics and bulimics of ideal weight the target is the "confirmative bond." The future patient is set against this parent by someone in a losing position. Generally this person is a grandparent, uncle, aunt or an older sibling. Sometimes, as in the example described in Section 5.5, this role may be taken by a person outside the family who is trusted by the "confirmative" parent.

2. During the course of the "instigation," the future patient becomes a "valued interlocutor" of special importance for the "instigator" and often also for other losers. At first this new position has a "confirmative" value not just for those positioned in the negative polarity of the critical semantic dimension, but also for those positioned among the "winners." The former find themselves at the center of an interest and attention they were not accustomed to, while the latter, especially if they are adolescents, are

flattered by the new position given to them as the chosen conversational partner: the "instigator," even when he or she is a loser, is always an adult or older sibling. His or her friendship therefore gratifies adolescents or makes them willing to accept (partially or wholly) his or her arguments and criticisms and attacks against the winning parent. During this stage, future patients receive confirmations from both sides.

3. The "instigator" is generally not one of the parents. The future patients' criticisms and subsequent attacks upon the winning parent are, however, generally supported, indirectly and sometimes only occasionally, by the other parent. In the process, this parent therefore plays a role in supporting the instigation.

4. The "instigation" finds fertile ground because the parent who is the target provides confirmation of the criticisms made through his or her intolerance towards the child's attacks, or with overbearing attitudes, or simply by being irritated by the child's attempt to redefine the relationship in more equal terms. Various reasons and types of behavior may, in the eyes of the future patients, justify the negative view that is being developed about the parent under criticism. The outcome, however, is the same: the future patients become disillusioned, distance themselves from the winning parent and place themselves in active opposition. This happens to those who were particularly close to this person (anorexics and bulimics at ideal weight) as well as those who were more detached (those with obesity).

5. The subjects, who by this stage of the process are patients, are disillusioned by the new alliance and by other losers. Here also, there may be different reasons: patients become aware of the ill-will of the "instigator," or discover that they have been manipulated against the parent who has been criticized, or other reasons. Here too the outcome is the same: Patients distance themselves from the new allies and are now alone, having become disillusioned by both sides. At this point the reflexivity of the strange loop is at its greatest. The instigation has made it impractical to adapt to the winners in their own group, but active opposition to these people is no longer a means of positively defining the confines of the self: In the eyes of the patients, the losers are as disqualified as the winners. The patients, from the initial situation where they received confirmations from members of both sides, are precipitated into a situation in which their experience can no longer be reliably validated by any relationship.

I have found these stages in the main eating disorders. But those involved, and the importance of each phase, varies according to the type of disorder.

In the case of anorexia, phase 4 is central, where the patient is disillusioned by the winning parent. The fact that the instigator and the opposing side also cause disillusionment (phase 5) is emotionally less devastating: the disillusionment towards the new allies is limited to closing off a possibility, making it impractical to pursue a scenario that they had sighted during the interactive process leading up to the onset of symptoms. The disillusionment towards the winning parent is terrible: that parent, who is generally the mother for anorexics, has been not only an example, a model on which the daughter had shaped her own personality and organized her ideas, but also a continual point of reference that has accompanied her throughout her daily life, providing care and guidance. Emaciation alludes to the central importance for anorexics of the relationship with the mother: they set themselves against her, they refuse her food, but at the same time, through their incapacity to eat, they invite her to assume a caring role towards them. Despite being disillusioned, they continue to remain anchored to the behavior and values of the winners. Like their mother, they are active, determined and strong-willed. If anything, their spectral thinness and their terror of getting fat is comparable to a parody of the winner. The social imperative, which imposes the ideal of thinness upon everyone, is hyper-respected by anorexics in a sort of *reductio ad absurdum* because, irrespective of their motives, they demonstrate the sad abyss into which control, determination and self-will can lead.

For bulimics, the disillusionment towards the "supportive" parent, who is usually the father (or another successful figure who does not take a caring role), as well as the subsequent disillusionment towards instigators, often have an equally strong emotional impact. Distancing themselves from the father, they often become closer to the mother or to other figures who have taken a caring role during infancy, who are in the losing position. As with anorexics, the onset of symptoms takes them back to the original position. Their symptoms express a more limited difficulty: They refuse food but do not generally place their lives at risk. Attempting to maintain their body in an eternal adolescence, bulimics of ideal weight refuse to be identified with their mother: They will not neglect themselves like their mother, they will not give in to pressure, they will not allow themselves to become passive, but will fight hard against their own weakness and submissiveness.

For those with obesity problems, the most disturbing phase in the interactive process I have described is the last (phase 5) because they lose their "confirmative" bond. Patients have never really trusted the successful parent, or they stopped doing so long ago. Those with obesity, despite the disillusionment, do not reject the values of the main figure of attachment: They continue to be unconventional and rebellious. Yet the symptoms suggest disillusionment. Obesity is a surrender to the winners. With their fatness, they recognize they are on the wrong side: Passivity, giving in to impulse and lack of self-control are destructive. Their obesity is the tangible confirmation of the failure, which leads to pliancy, affability and indulgence in relation to their own impulses as well as to other people. Obesity is also a defense: By placing a thick blanket of fat between themselves and others, they rule out a normal love life, thereby protecting themselves from strong emotional involvements that could still lead to further disappointment.

The ways in which the disillusionment towards the favorite "confirmative" adult occurs is different in anorexia and bulimia, compared with obesity. My cases confirm Guidano's observations (1987, 1991): anorexics and bulimics put their favorite parent to the test and check out (or try to check out) the criticisms made, explicitly or indirectly, by the instigators. *Both actively provoke disillusionment, resorting to behavior that induces the parent being criticized to come out into the open or go looking for proof.* Conversely, those suffering from obesity do not provoke disillusionment from new allies and even less so from the favorite "confirmative" adult. *The unreliability of such a figure and the consequent disillusionments, in the eyes of the subject, are construed as external destructive events.* They do not have, nor in their view could they have, any control over such events.

The hypothesis put forward here confirms the importance given by some therapists (Bara & Stoppa Beretta, 1996; Guidano, 1987, 1991) to disillusionment in eating disorders and also the differences in this respect presented by anorexia and bulimia in comparison with obesity. But unlike these authors, and in agreement with Selvini Palazzoli and colleagues (Selvini Palazzoli et al., 1989; Selvini Palazzoli & Viaro, 1988), I suggest that the disillusionment is part of an instigation process in which subjects find themselves at the center.[8]

Families with organizations of meaning typical of eating disorders are an exceptionally fertile breeding-ground for developing instigative dynamics, and at the same time are particularly vulnerable to such dynamics. In a semantic world marked out by the winning/losing polarity—where relationships in the family unit as well as the extended family are governed by competitive rivalry, in which a constant theme of conversation is the definition of the relationship, in which some succeed and others submit, some are successful and others are outclassed and defeated—*instigation appears as an inevitable but also a disastrous move.* These families do not equip their members to deal with one of the most frequent results of the instigative dynamic: the loss of "confirmative" bonds. In a context where the main semantic dimension is purely relational and where the prevalence of rejection and conflict in defining relationships make it difficult to draw a clear distinction between the self and the others, it is particularly unsettling to discover that a person in whom subjects place their trust, and on whom they have modeled themselves, is unreliable.

5.5 A Family Story Over Three Generations

Having described the interpersonal context *in vitro* at the time when symptoms first appear, I will now move on to examine the situation *in vivo*. Two daughters of the family we are about to examine had different eating disorders: one was obese and the other anorexic. The case is therefore an example of how, within the same family and within the same critical semantics, different positionings can be constructed and linked with different eating disorders.

The Daughters' Reserve

During the first two consultations—which is generally how the therapy begins—the team and I were surprised by one apparently marginal aspect of the Santucci family: the total absence of boyfriends or other young male friends in the family entourage, even though the family had four attractive girls aged between fourteen and twenty-two. In actual fact, Mara and Sabina,[9] the second and third in order of age, had lost much of their charm: Mara had grown fat over three years and Sabina, who seemed to have done very well in overcoming her anorexia, which had begun two years earlier, had had a relapse: in three months she had lost twelve kilos. Lucia, the eldest, though not presenting any psychopathology, spoiled her physical appearance by dressing in a severe, masculine style. Only Sonia, the youngest, maintained her femininity intact: The well-developed curves of her body, her perfect facial features and her sweet and sorrowful expression, made her seem older than her fourteen years. Sonia was the only daughter, they told us, to have shown an interest in boys since primary school: She had always had a "boyfriend," usually a school friend whom she lost with much grief as a result of the continual family moves and immediately, though reluctantly, replaced with another. The other three sisters had no male friends:

> "We get along very well together," says Lucia, "perhaps that's why we don't feel the need to be with others. And we are also independent. "Boys don't interest us," Mara added more directly, ending with a wry smile, "we can do perfectly well without them."

This behavior of the daughters contrasted with the openness of their parents. Zita and Attilio, both extrovert, physically attractive and certainly not asexual, would have been happy for their daughters to have had a normal social life. They had always allowed them the greatest freedom: The older girls (Lucia and Mara) had even lived on their own for a year. Nor did the concern about Sabina seem to be the cause of such reserve. Everyone was concerned about Sabina's sudden relapse and angry silence, but no one was particularly upset.

The older three girls' disinterest in males was to prove valuable in reconstructing the interpersonal context accompanying the onset of Mara and Sabina's symptoms. But first we will say a little more about the Santucci family.

A difficult transition

At the time when the family began therapy, it was going through a particularly delicate transition: The Santucci's were returning to Italy for good after twenty years of living in various foreign countries. Attilio was still working as a manager in the Persian Gulf branch of a large Italian company, but had already arranged to return to Italy. They had always planned to return but it was proving particularly difficult.

The eldest daughter Lucia's start at university, three years earlier, marked the beginning of the difficult transition with which we are concerned. The Santucci family's return to Milan and their attempt to settle in the metropolis was disastrous from the start. Attilio found it difficult to work in the Milan office and his salary was not enough for the family's usual lifestyle and for the cost of living in the city, which was higher than they expected. Zita was tied to a small house in the suburbs, without servants. For transport, she was forced to rely on her daughters and husband: in the Middle East she hadn't needed to learn how to drive. Conflict broke out between the parents: The father, who was generally diplomatic, cheerful and not prone to being aggressive, became highly irritable towards his wife. It was during this period that Mara became fat.

Given that the situation had become intolerable, Attilio was happy to accept the offer of a two-year contract in Kuwait. The two older girls decided to remain in Milan, even though attendance on the degree courses they had chosen was not compulsory, while Zita went with her husband and the two younger girls to Kuwait. This separation was a bad experience for all of them, especially Zita. The splitting up of the family was against her values and principles as she had always placed the unity of the family above all.

As soon as Sabina arrived in Kuwait she became sad, stopped eating, and quickly developed serious anorexia. The pediatrician, a friend of both parents, suggested that the family should be reunited. Attilio explained the family situation to his company and was able to end his contract. They all returned to Milan. Even though the family tensions quickly returned to the same level as on their previous return, Sabina's health improved and within a few months she was well again.

A little under a year before the start of psychotherapy, their father accepted a contract to work in Saudi Arabia. Sabina was completely well again and the contract this time had a promise of the position of area manager, something he had always hoped for but had never before achieved. This time Zita made no opposition: The two older daughters had shown they could manage and she agreed to accompany her husband, along with Sabina and Sonia. Their stay abroad was due to last for a year or two and the position on offer, as area manager, was too attractive to be passed over. Moreover, the alternative proposed by the company was the manager of a branch in Tuscany, a few kilometers from their home town, which both Attilio and Zita, for reasons we did not at first understand, did not like.

It was Sabina who upset the arrangement: She announced unexpectedly that she would not be accompanying her parents. In Saudi Arabia she would have had to attend a secondary school where the emphasis was on science, whereas she wanted to go to art school in Milan, which was more in line with her interests. Her parents failed to persuade her. In the past, Zita and Attilio had always been uncompromising when their daughters had objected to their various moves from one country to another. This time, the specter of anorexia made them more cautious and they gave in. Sabina enrolled at the art school and her mother remained in Milan with her and the two oldest sisters, while their father moved to Saudi Arabia with the youngest child, Sonia.

Therapy began in this situation of a divided family. It was a difficult situation for everyone, and Zita in particular did not like it:

> "The pact I made with my husband," Zita said with resentment, "has not been maintained: I made my choices at that time, I left my family with whom I was very close, all my relations remember how I cried when it was time to leave. I left my job, which was a very good job—at that time I earned more than my husband. But now, even though I've worked myself into the ground, I'm dependent on everyone: I can't drive, I'm always having to ask for a lift from the older girls. I've been an idiot, I've ruined myself for my family; I find this life ridiculous: The wife in one place and the husband in another doesn't work. It's too much of a sacrifice, even if it's only for a year or two."

Sabina seemed at first to benefit from the "sacrifice": She enjoyed art school, made friends with her classmates and went out. But once again, after a couple of months, she was unresponsive, unhappy, moody. In three months she lost twelve kilograms.

This was more or less the story leading up to the onset of Mara and Sabina's symptoms, as initially described by the family. It gave rise to many questions. Why did Attilio refuse the proposal to run a small branch office a few kilometers from their home town, even before he was offered the prospect of moving abroad to become area manager? Why did Zita, who was so attached to her extended family, reject that proposal which would have enabled her to keep the family together and to rejoin her own original family? And why was Sonia, a girl of only fourteen, now with her father in Saudi Arabia? His work responsibilities certainly did not allow him to look after his daughter. Sonia remained very much alone, something that everyone chose to ignore.

The answers to these and other questions gradually emerged as the therapy continued and the family history became clearer.

The Couple's Relationship in the Context of Three Generations of Family History

Zita and Attilio first met when they were children: Their relationship began during their early years at secondary school. Their two families came from very different backgrounds, but the semantics of power dominated both conversations.

Attilio's mother, who was strong-willed and hard, bossed her good-natured husband. While his father was kind and sensitive, she seemed cold, little interested in affection, always willing to sacrifice them on the altar of success. In order to achieve her ambitions for Attilio, she had no hesitation in sending her only son to boarding school once he had reached junior school age. Attilio was his mother's absolute priority investment. She and her husband had made great financial sacrifices in order to use the profits from various properties to benefit their son. She had always supported his moves abroad, provided they brought financial and professional rewards; she had even encouraged him when it meant travelling thousands of miles away.

Relationships in Zita's family were warm and close, but there was a similar sensitivity towards questions of status. The question of who had more than whom, of who was better than whom, of the fierce competition and rivalry, were matters that constantly clouded the conversation in her mother's family for at least three generations. The first generation, Zita's grandparents, established a small empire: They owned a company and a large amount of property. All of the property passed to the three sons—at the time of the therapy, their heirs lived in magnificent apartments in the center of Florence. The five daughters, including Zita's mother, through submissiveness, complacency and ignorance, allowed the males to take everything. They voluntarily relinquished the whole inheritance, even the real estate, in favor of their brothers. The two youngest girls—Rosa and Alma (Zita's mother)—expressed certain doubts. Even though they were less submissive than their elder sisters and less in thrall to the patriarchal culture, they were too young for their voices to be heard when the decision was made. Rosa succeeded in marrying a landowner while Alma, against the wishes of her family, married a man of no means whom she loved, and soon found herself in serious difficulty. During World War III, she and her husband lost their business and, after the war, they found themselves jobless with four children. They were saved by Rosa. She invited them to go and work in the artisan business she and her husband had just set up. The agreement created a large family: the two couples and their children (nine in all) lived together for twenty-five years. The company agreement by which Zita's parents became part of the small business, as well as the policy for jointly managing the family expenses, referred to a parity that never existed. Rosa held the purse strings, owned the company property and the large house where they lived, and benefitted from the income from her husband's land. In short, Alma, her husband and their children, despite the idea of equality that reigned among the family group, were always in the situation of the poor relations. Alma's four children, especially during their adolescence and youth, suffered for the inevitable comparisons made with their five cousins, who always had more. Alma was continually humiliated because of her husband. The clan never forgave her for marrying him, and Aunt Rosa herself always complained about the indolence of Alma's husband. Later on he began to drink too much and became distant and unresponsive. Alma reacted to these humiliations by working harder than ever: she would often get up at two or three in the morning, carrying the same work as the men, as well as looking after the children and the home. Her hard work and kindness were recognized by everyone. Alma was active, strong-willed, but obedient to Rosa, who was the real "head" of the clan. The small age difference between the nine cousins made the competition, confrontation, jealousy and rivalry particularly harsh. The conflict between the brothers was no less acute than that between the cousins.

So long as the clan was led by Rosa the ill-feeling never degenerated into open warfare. But on her death it exploded violently. The company was taken over by one of Rosa's sons, Lorenzo, who ousted his uncle and aunt. After working there all their lives, Zita's parents received no compensation at all. Lorenzo later fell out with his brothers and sisters, who tried to have him removed from the company. At the time of the therapy, the main dispute was between Rosa's three sons, who were fighting a legal battle, but the cousins and their children were also inevitably involved in the conflict.

This context of symmetrical schismogenesis also marked out the life of Zita as much as those of her siblings. The competitions and rivalries between the two families had a positive effect on Zita's siblings as well: They developed a mutual solidarity. Zita, for example, was made by her eldest sister to study. She worked diligently, making sacrifices and obtaining a good diploma and an excellent job. When she married, she soon realized the danger of ending up in the same position as her mother. Attilio was bright, attractive and had a natural charm that made the clan like him, but it was immediately apparent that he did not have much fighting spirit or determination. The first two daughters were born in the first three years of the marriage, but Attilio could not find a decent job; His wife's salary was larger than his.

Attilio's mother was favorable at first to the marriage, but when she realized that Zita and her family were the clan's "poor relations" she became aggressive, so that Attilio demonstrated a preference towards his wife's family rather than his own parents. His mother's scenes of jealousy became more frequent. But what most upset Zita was Attilio's unfaithfulness. He had already occasionally betrayed her during their engagement, but after their wedding his betrayals reoccurred. Zita was wounded by her husband's infidelity, but also frightened that his behavior might become public knowledge.

The chance for him to work for a large company overseas enabled the couple to overcome many difficulties. They acquired a respectable social status (the sacrifice in moving far from home was compensated by a handsome salary and the prospect that Attilio might obtain a management post, despite having no degree); they distanced themselves from their families and the family squabbles, and could ensure that any unfaithfulness by Attilio would not leak out.

Their Daughters' Lives Abroad and Position as Go-Between

By placing several thousand miles between them and their extended families, Attilio and Zita reduced the conflict but did not eliminate it. Zita continually urged her husband to work harder for promotion. Attilio worked, but was not ambitious in his career: Instead of company rivalry, he preferred to play tennis and socialize with friends. He was irritated by his wife's goading and fought back through betrayal, which placed his wife in difficulty. His unfaithfulness (from his point of view) was a means of holding his wife's willfulness at bay. It was his weapon in the power struggle with Zita, a struggle that had begun during their schooldays. He had admired and also felt intimidated by Zita's diligence. He had been upset when she accused him of not studying. But he could get his own back through jealousy: all he had to do was look at another girl and Zita immediately felt insecure.

Attilio always admitted his affairs to his wife: "Ten minutes of questioning is enough and I cave in: I tell her everything." They were generally one-off encounters, sometimes affairs lasting a little longer. Attilio never expressed any wish to leave his wife; he continued to say he loved her; he always promised to be faithful but didn't keep his word for long. Zita was never able to come to terms with this. Attilio had always used jealousy as a weapon—even against his mother. When he was a child he curried favor with certain aunts and, during his engagement and their early years of marriage, with his wife's family. His mother, who was generally cool and composed, reacted with angry scenes of jealousy. He was never able to face up directly to his mother, nor even to Zita, who had none of the arid hardness of her mother-in-law though, like here, she was active, strong-willed and persistent in her demands for social better-ment. But Attilio, unlike his father and his father-in-law, was not meek and submissive: He at least fought against his wife, and achieved some success. With the hope of a management post and the specter of unfaithfulness, he had persuaded Zita, for example, to leave her extended family with whom she was very close, and to move abroad.

The distance from Italy had not meant a separation from their families of origin and from the wife's clan. As the years passed, contact became more fre-quent. Zita never left her husband, not even during her pregnancies: The last two daughters were born in Asia. But their daughters, as they gradually grew up, spent increasingly longer periods of time in Italy, with their grandparents, aunts, and cousins. The older daughters, in particular, became the point of contact between the couple and their extended families, and were increasingly involved in the family disputes.

The context in which each daughter defined their personal position was therefore influenced not only by the conflict between Attilio and Zita but also by the symmetrical escalations of the families of origin. Lucia, like her mother, was determined, good at school, honest, and assertive. She was also obedient to her mother, to whom she was close. Only recently had she distanced herself from her. Until a few years earlier she had always defended her and since she was a child she had never left her. Zita also felt very close to this daughter. Mara, on the other hand, had until recently allied herself with her father and had supported all losers in the clan. She had been good at school but was undisciplined and lazy; at home she had always rebelled against her mother. All of the family agreed that Mara had great ability but not much perseverance and determination.

Sabina was the most stubborn, honest, and outspoken member of the family. She was more secure and decisive than her mother. The family felt she had some of the authoritarian manner of her paternal grandmother but, like her mother, she was also sensitive and aware of the feelings of her sisters, parents and even those of her grandparents, aunts, uncles, and cousins.

Sonia, the youngest, had been rather overshadowed by her sisters. Her sad expression reflected her position in the family. Like her father, she hated conflict and, like him, was diplomatic and always careful not to hurt the others. Rather than getting involved in exhausting battles, she preferred to yield and withdraw; she was submissive and at times apathetic.

The Critical Episode and the Onset of Mara's Symptoms

Four years before the start of therapy, two friends became part of the family life. They made an important contribution in destabilizing the adaptive strategies of Mara and then indirectly, shortly afterwards, of Sabina.

Until that time the daughters were unaware of their father's unfaithfulness. They saw their parents' conflict as being between the determination, hard work and ambition of their mother and the casualness of their father, who preferred to enjoy life rather than slaving away for success. The older daughters were growing up, Lucia had already begun to distance herself from her mother, annoyed by the priority she gave to her husband. Sabina was taking her place at the center of her mother's attentions. Mara argued with her mother: Like her father, instead of Zita's determination and hard work, she enjoyed herself; she was pretty and, unlike Lucia, had several boyfriends during that period. Sonia, the youngest, was still isolated from the rest of the family. Her father preferred Mara, with whom he played tennis, and her mother could not stand her laziness. She did not fight for a better position in the family but found consolation instead in her many friends and the boyfriend of that moment.

It was then that Attilio and Zita became friendly with Franco and Monica, who were a little younger and had no children. Franco was Attilio's work colleague and Monica, his wife, had been Lucia's teacher the year before. Attilio and Zita became very attached to their new friends, as they had done previously with other couples, and as often happens with Europeans working abroad. The new aspect was the friendship created between Monica and the two older daughters. For Lucia and Mara, Monica became a sort of older sister, but also an opposite to their mother. The two girls were fascinated by this young, exuberant, sporting, independent and carefree woman. Together they played tennis, went swimming, to the gym and to parties held by the European community. Outside working hours, they were joined by Attilio, who also enjoyed sport.

Mara and, to some extent, also Lucia saw Monica as a model to contrast with their mother. The two girls confided in Monica, told her about their boyfriends and the family disagreements. Monica criticized Zita, even at times in her presence, accusing her of being traditionalist, subtly domineering, lacking in independence from her husband, oppressive towards her daughters, incapable of treating them as equals, now that they were growing up, and too attached to her extended family. Attilio supported these criticisms, more by his eloquent facial expression than in words. The older girls distanced themselves from their mother, who became more attached to Sabina. Monica involved the girls in her problems, talked to them about her marital disappointments, but also about her casual way of dealing with them. She told them she was having a very exciting extra-marital relationship; a few months later she added that she had fallen madly in love with this man and intended to leave her husband in order to live with him. Finally, in Milan, where the Santucci family and their friends had by that time moved, she revealed to Lucia and Mara that the man with whom she was having the affair was their father. It was a heavy blow for both of them, but especially for Mara who, within a few months, put on fifteen to twenty kilos. During the previous two years the relationship with her father, to whom she had always been close, had become particularly intense. So her sense of disillusionment was deep.

The Secret, its Disclosure and the Instigation

The two sisters decided to say nothing to their mother. The secret, which they kept for a year, cemented their relationship, which became exclusive. They stopped seeing Monica; they distanced themselves from their father and impotently watched his outbursts of anger, which displayed an unusual lack of tolerance towards Zita. She, who up to this time had not suspected Monica because her husband had never previously dared to bring his lovers to the house, became aware of his betrayal through the behavior of her daughters towards their erstwhile friends, who continued to come to the house, though less often than when they had been abroad. Zita, busy in dealing with the difficulties of their return, failed at first to notice that the two older daughters had broken off their friendship with Monica, that they looked for any excuse to disappear when Franco and Monica were invited to the house, and had distanced themselves from their father. When she became aware of this behavior and questioned them, they told her everything. This time, Attilio, through his irresponsibility and lack of self-control, had destroyed the family. This was how Zita saw his betrayal. It was not an adventure like the others. This time he had fallen in love. Worse still, their children had been involved, and for some time. Zita was devastated. There were dramatic scenes with her husband, but in the end she forgave him. In order to bring an end to the impossible family situation (on top of the difficulties of returning to Milan, there were Zita's scenes and his daughters' accusing looks) Attilio decided to accept the offer of work in the Middle East and Zita agreed to go with him. The move was the best guarantee that the relationship with Monica, now living in Milan with her husband, would not continue.

Lucia and Mara were adamant they would not leave Milan. They were convinced at first that their mother would remain with them. The eldest daughter thought that Zita should get a divorce. If that option was impracticable, then she should at least punish their father by leaving him alone in Kuwait. Mara agreed. Their father should be taught a lesson. When they realized that Zita had decided to go with her husband, leaving them alone in Milan, they felt a deep disillusionment. It was then that they began to set their sister against their mother. Sabina did not "officially" know about the betrayal but in fact knew perfectly well, having overheard what was going on. Only Sonia, who during the worst period of parental conflict had been staying with relatives, was entirely ignorant of what had happened. Sabina realized the seriousness of the situation. The two older daughters did not tell her openly what had happened but they became closer to her and opened her eyes to what their mother was doing.

Above all, Lucia put her on her guard, perhaps through annoyance that Sabina had stolen her position as their mother's favorite or perhaps to protect her from future disillusionment. At first by hints, then more openly, they warned her not to become too attached to their mother, with words such as: "All she cares about is her husband … She leaves us alone in Italy so she can be with him, a man who doesn't even respect her … She stays with a husband, whom she'd be better off without, so as not to lose face with her family and friends." Mara also backed up her older sister on several occasions by supporting her advice and warnings. This was a heavy blow for Sabina, who had seen her mother as a symbol of perfection and family devotion. Being strong-willed and determined, like her mother and many other women of the extended family, she sought to test out her sisters' accusations. When she arrived in Kuwait, she became sad and stopped eating. Faced with her daughter's anorexia, Zita took action, forcing her husband to end his contract and return to Italy. This behavior rehabilitated the mother in her daughter's eyes. Sabina returned to health, but her doubts about her mother's love remained. Her mother, when faced with Sabina's anorexia, returned to Italy, but with her husband. When it became clear that Zita had decided to follow her husband to Saudi Arabia, leaving the two older girls once again in Milan, Sabina put her to the test once more. The situation at school gave her the opportunity.

She would have to begin secondary school that year: If she went with her parents to Saudi Arabia it would mean abandoning her plans to go to art school. Sabina placed her mother in a difficult situation: she refused to go with her and decided to remain with her older sisters in Milan, where she could go to art school. Sabina won the battle: her mother stayed with her and her older sisters in Milan. But, as she was soon to discover, it was a Pyrrhic victory. Zita was devastated by her husband's absence, her jealousy was heightened by his distance, she suffered insomnia, anxiously awaited his telephone calls, never left the house, refusing to go with her daughters to the cinema or to eat out. Above all, Zita became intolerant and hostile towards her daughters, including Sabina. This behavior was clear confirmation to Sabina of what her sisters had suggested: all that Zita cared about was her husband. It was at this point that she relapsed into anorexia. Sabina was alone. She was disillusioned by her mother and, before that, by her sisters, who had been jealous and antagonistic towards her when her mother had decided not to follow her husband entirely for Sabina's sake.

5.6 The Idea of Equality as a Breaking Down of Differences

Eating disorders offer a particularly valuable way of considering the relationship between psychopathology and society. Such disorders were rare prior to World War II, yet they spread so fast between the 1970s and 1990s as to become one of the disorders of greatest interest to the mass media. Such a rapid spread over a relatively short space of time makes it clear that there is a connection between social conditions and mental illnesses that biological psychiatry prefers to ignore.

A considerable amount of epidemiological research in Europe, especially in northern Europe, as well as in the United States and Australia,[10] has now documented the spread of these disorders. It has been estimated that anorexia, bulimia, and "binge eating disorder" (BED) are to be found among 2 to 10 percent of women in the West during the course of their lives. Many studies, however, underestimate the extent of the phenomenon—they are based on those patients who seek health service treatment and exclude the less serious cases, which are the majority. In addition, they use self-reporting methods and/or interviews with patients who tend to underplay their pathology because it is egosyntonic (anorexia) or a cause of shame (bulimia and BED). It is therefore reasonable to suppose that a higher estimate is closer to reality. This means that 10 percent of women suffer from anorexia, bulimia or BED at some time in their lives. Added to this, obesity has reached around 33 percent in the United States, and in Europe it ranges between 8–9 percent in Italy, Switzerland and Norway and 23 percent in the United Kingdom. About 25 percent of the European population will therefore suffer from eating disorders during their lives, and 43 percent of Americans.

Epidemiological research shows a clear trend over time. Obesity has continued to increase over the last decade (Zachrisson et al., 2008). In Western countries, anorexia and bulimia, on the other hand, have stabilized after reaching their height in the 1970s/80s and 1980s/90s respectively (Hoek & Van Hoeken, 2003; Hoek, 2006; Currin et al., 2005). The incidence of anorexia among adolescents, however, continues to rise (Van Son et al., 2006; Kieski-Rahkonen et al., 2008). Both anorexia and bulimia also continue to be young women's pathologies, with a ratio between the two sexes of less than 1 to 9. Anorexia and bulimia are most commonly found between the ages of 12 and 25. These pathologies are also primarily urban, and typical of the West, even if they may no longer be unique to Western societies (Nasser, Kazman, & Gordon, 2001). Their spread seems to include all social levels. Anorexia, which at first seemed to be found mostly in the middle and upper-middle classes (Bruch, 1973; 1978; Selvini Palazzoli, 1974), today affects the whole population.

The clear prevalence of anorexia among women, and the sudden spread of these psychopathologies among young women during a specific historical period, makes them comparable with hysteria. Like it, they seem to be connected to critical aspects of the position of women in Western society.

Psychotherapists involved in eating disorders are therefore enticed out of their own field of research, beyond the limits of their own discipline. Like all mental disorders whose diffusion assumes significant proportions during particular periods of time, anorexia and bulimia, as well as obesity, seem to indicate a conflict taking place in Western culture. But what specific conflict is expressed by the alarming spread of eating disorders? During the course of this section I will attempt to provide a possible answer to this question.

Building on Bateson's essay, The Cybernetics of "Self": A theory of Alcoholism, Selvini Palazzoli put forward the hypothesis in 1978 that the anorexic expresses one of the "epistemological errors" characteristic of Western civilizations: "The idea that there is a Self capable of transcending the systems of relationship of which it forms a part, and hence of being in unilateral control of the system" (p. 232).

This is the idea of power and control:

> If we were to take a snapshot during the very first therapeutic session, we should see an anguished expression on the parents' faces, the patient sitting apart from the rest, straight as a statue, pallid and detached, her face showing utter indifference to the others' distress. Her behavior is a clear message, not least to the therapist: "If you think you can get me to break my fast, you'll have to think again. Just look at me. I am nothing but skin and bones and I might easily die. And if death is a price I have to pay for my power, than I shall willingly pay it."
>
> (*ibid.*, pp. 232–233)

And he added:

> She is prey to a most disastrous Cartesian dichotomy: *she believes that her mind transcends her body* and that it grants her unlimited power over her own behavior and that of others. The result is a reification of self and the mistaken belief that the patient is engaged in a victorious battle on two fronts, namely against: 1) her body, and 2) the family system.
>
> (ibid., p. 233)

The hypothesis that the idea of power and control traps the patient and her family in the anorexia-bulimia spiral has been suggested various times by the literature. This is still an acceptable view. Likewise, it has to be acknowledged that this pathology is typical of a society where food is available in abundance. In developing countries, where food is scarce, anorexia and bulimia are more or less absent. In pre-industrial and pre-modern societies, where no particular emphasis is placed upon infancy and parenting, a psychopathology that casts doubt on the role of parents is unthinkable. The refusal of food (and symbolically of the parent) becomes an act with a meaning only in societies where the child assumes a central role and adults acquire value through their role as parents.

All of these considerations, acceptable though they are, and now at least partially documented by epidemiological studies,[11] do not answer certain fundamental questions posed by eating disorders. Why did pathologies that so dramatically expressed the idea of power and control become so widespread between the 1970s and 1990s? Why did they become a stable presence during subsequent years? What changes taking place between the 1970s and 1990s help to explain the spread of eating disorders and their quite stable presence after then? And why should a psychopathology involving mainly women manifest the idea of power and control in such an extreme manner?

The conflicts at the root of anorexia, bulimia, and other food disorders are not, in my view, a result of resistance to change which is gradually destined to be overcome as the values of the patriarchal culture lose ground, as Selvini Palazzoli (1974) suggested. The transition from a rural-patriarchal to an urban culture relates to the 1950s, when eating disorders were making their first appearance. The phenomenon reached alarming dimensions later on when the urban culture and its values were more solidly rooted. It was from the 1970s that eating disorders began to spread, when women went out to work and progress was being made in sexual equality, bringing about forms of family "co-positioning" quite different from traditional ones. The conflicts and underlying rifts in these psychopathologies therefore relate to *internal* aspects of that culture which, during the 1960s and 1970s, began to irreversibly modify the shape of family relationships at all social levels. The spread of anorexia and bulimia reached its peak between the 1970s and the 1990s: these were the years that saw radical changes within family relationships. The movements and campaigns at the end of the 1960s had brought no change to the economic or political world but had revolutionized interpersonal relationships. Not only were relations redefined between men and women in all social classes, but also those between adult and child, between teacher and pupil, between doctor and patient. Even people's relations with their pets had changed. They had all become less hierarchical.

Anorexia and other eating disorders develop in contexts where the hierarchy and differences are regarded as unjustified. Differences are seen in these families as the result of an unjust and arbitrary power; but above all, the differences that regulate the relationships between men and women are considered as oppressive.

And in these contexts they are in fact unjustified. This is the origin of the rejection of gender expectation, which is a characteristic of eating disorders highlighted, for example, by Gordon (1990):

> Through her shape, the anorexic makes a powerful statement of rejection of gender expectation. In effect, "I have sharp contours. I am not soft; I do not merge with you. I have nothing to give you". Some are quite explicit about the relationship of thinness to the rejection of femininity, like one patient who said "I want to stay slender because I look more like a man. I push myself to do as much as any man can do".

> (p. 68)

Sexual identity, the basic difference, is denied both by anorexics, as well as by those suffering from obesity, when their pathology becomes serious: A skeleton does not have sexual identity, nor does a formless mass of fat. The bulimic, in trying to maintain her body in eternal adolescence, does not deny but limits sexual differentiation.

In families where eating disorders develop, there is extreme difficulty in settling differences. Every difference is interpreted in terms of superiority/inferiority, which is not based on shared values, and is therefore regarded as harsh and unjust. For this reason the families in which food pathologies develop become the scene of intense power conflicts. When the differences are seen as unjustified, there is no alternative but the battle for power, meaning "everyone against everyone."

The difficulty in resolving differences is not limited to families where eating disorders develop. It is a characteristic problem in modern Western cultures built on the rejection of the concept of hierarchy. In all relational contexts, from the family to social and political institutions, the resolution of differences becomes a complex alchemy. Eating disorders seem to carry to the extreme those conflicts and tensions connected with establishing the idea of equality as a breaking down of differences. The spread of eating disorders since the 1970s coincides with the establishment of an egalitarian ideology in daily life. Egalitarian ideology had never, by itself, had such an effect upon the daily conduct at all social levels as it has had from the end of the 1960s up to now. And it is women who have increasingly felt the ambiguities and contradictions underlying the concept of equality.

Equality is almost a taboo in Western cultures because of the fundamental role it plays and the acceptance surrounding it. It is, indeed, perhaps the last taboo in a culture reluctant to treat any idea as sacred. Its opposite, the concept of hierarchy, also remains largely unquestioned for similar reasons: the aversion, irritation and antipathy that we all feel towards it tends to prevent any critical analysis.

Few authors, starting off from non-reactionary stances, have dared to question the concept of equality and to go right to the heart of the contradictions and difficulties that are inherent in it. These include Dumont (1970, 1986) and Biral (1991), who are both, not surprisingly, involved on two fronts—anthropological and political—where the problem of differences is as central as it is for psychotherapy.

For both of these authors the idea of equality represents a challenge to human society because it destroys the whole way in which man had thought of himself for centuries. Everything, in relation to which man was positioned as one element, becomes an indistinct mass. To use a metaphor from Dumont (1970), the sack holding the balls breaks open and the balls are scattered in all directions. Or, to paraphrase Tocqueville, the Great Chain of Being, which stretched up from the peasant to the king and to God, is broken and every link becomes separate. But why is the idea of equality so devastating?

What induces people to share and lead them to form societies or associations, are solely and entirely their particular differences; there can be no association without inequality.

But if people are equal?

> Association becomes a suffocating unnatural prison, because everyone is made self-sufficient by nature and only if they are free, if they can freely use their powers, their energies, their reason, will they be happy. If people are equal, and therefore indifferent, they will never find anything that they share, and no community or communication can be formed between them. A society built upon equality will not be an association. Furthermore, society itself is not based on nature and is destined always to remain external to people as an overlapping and additional "order," because each person is entirely unrelated, has no need to be a part of it, and seeks unconditional independence and unconditional freedom (Biral, 1991, p. 19).[12]

Equality is an aspect of individualism thatI have considered several times in the previous chapters. It has been a crucial factor—along with the idea of freedom from relationships and from their restrictions—in the creation of *homo clausus*, as he has been fittingly called by Elias (1939/2000). Dumont (1986) described this independent and self-sufficient creature of individualism as a *moral individual*, to be kept quite distinct from the *empirical individual*, an example of the human species in the flesh, present in all societies.

The ancient Greek world, where this moral individual was unknown, had no notion of the idea of equality and was conscious of differences. Aristotle declared: "A state is not made up only of so many men, but of different kinds of men; for similars do not constitute a state."[13]

All traditional societies have generally been indifferent to equality, as they have been to freedom. Equality is a prerogative of the Christian West. It is perhaps the main value that distinguishes Christianity from the other great religions, as well as its astonishing novelty.

The relationships between Christian subjectivity and individualism are in truth complex. Christianity, in its origins, introduces an ideal equality that pertains to the "individual in relation to God." Christian equality has an other-worldly quality. It is a point that Dumont (1986) emphasizes forcefully; we shall see the reasons shortly. When St. Paul declares: "There is neither Jew nor Greek, there is neither bond nor free, there is neither male nor female: for ye are all one in Christ Jesus"[14] or when Lactantius asserts: "In [God's] sight no one is a slave, no one a master; for if all have the same father, by an equal right we are all his children[15]," they are not referring to this world, where there are Jews and Greeks, men and women, as well as social distinctions. On the contrary, they are thinking about the world to which Christians are destined. It is these very distinctions and inequalities of this world that indicate the abyss separating the promised world from the real social world in which the Christian is a pilgrim. The wholly idealistic and other-worldly nature of Christian egalitarianism enables Dumont to establish a link between Christians, as they originally appear, and the figure of the Indian renouncer.

Indian society, through the caste system, imposed on everyone a strict interdependence with binding relationships. But the practice of renouncing the world gave anybody choosing this path the fullest independence. Since the religious innovations in India were generally the work of renouncers, such people were never completely outside society. Nevertheless, the man in search of the ultimate truth abandoned, not society itself, but everyday social life and its obligations to dedicate himself to his personal development and destiny.

For Dumont (1986) even the individual living in Christ is also an "other-worldly individual," like the renouncer. The first Christians lived in expectation of the imminent return of the Messiah, who would have founded the kingdom of God. For them the promised life had a concreteness that is now difficult for us to imagine. Subsequently, when earthly existence became far more important for Christians, the concept of equality remained a religious fact, extraneous to the practice of social relationships and their effect upon them. This is clearly demonstrated by Thomas Aquinas's hierarchical concept of totality and order, expressed in short by the formula: "Order consists principally in inequality (or diversity: *Disparitate*)."

Such a formula is out of tune with our modern sensibilities. Medieval Christian thought was far from presuming that full humanity was present in every man and that all men were therefore equal. When reference was made to the "individual in the world," holistic categories were used that were not so different from ancient thought. There was a complete contrast between the life promised to mankind and the life that human beings actually led. The promised life, according to Christian thinking, is still the true life. For this reason believers are strangers in this world. They do not reject the world, however, nor did they do so in the past, because life on earth is a present obstacle and a condition for salvation. And in their earthly life Christians have long thought and behaved according to a holistic approach. Not unlike people in traditional societies, they felt part of an all-embracing society and hierarchy.

It is surprising to note, observed Dumont (1970), how recent and late has been the development of the idea of equality and its implications. This development, though slow, has however—once again according to Dumont—a specific direction: equality, from an inner and other-worldly quality, as an attribute of man as son of God and destined towards communion with him, gradually becomes a feature of the "individual in the world."

The Lutheran and Calvinist Reformation was a fundamental step in this process. But it was the French Revolution that marked the watershed: *Equality, from being an attribute of the "other-worldly individual," became political equality.*

> The Revolution was to attempt to put natural law into effect as positive law. One can see with Babeuf and the Conspiracy of Equals how the demands of equality swept away the limitations that the *Philosophers* found in the nature of man. These demands not only put equality before liberty but were even ready to hold liberty cheap in order to bring about an egalitarian Utopia.
>
> (Dumont, 1970, p. 13)

The dualism inherent in early Christianity was destroyed. It was a dualism that contained an indomitable tension between the "individual in relation to God" and earthly life, and accepted the world as it was, including all its social distinctions, while undervaluing it. In modern societies, established in the wake of the French Revolution, equality is transformed from an attribute of man as son of God and destined to communion with him, into a question of fact. The transformation of an "unworldly" attribute into a guiding principle of social life inevitably produces devastating conflicts. Equality, created for a world

218

radically different from our own (the world to come), and so dazzling that it had obscured our own world for centuries, is now in the position of guiding it.

Dumont's account, which I have summarized here, cannot be interpreted rigidly. The process, as Dumont himself points out, is neither straightforward nor simple. Suffice it to recall that Augustine, while considering man to be a social creature and while not rejecting the concept of hierarchy, gives a surprisingly "modern" interpretation of the evangelic message, as emerges from this passage: "[God] has not willed the rational creature made in his own image to have domination over any but irrational creatures, not man over man, but man over beasts. Hence the first just men were set up shepherds of flocks rather than as kings of men (Augustine, 413–427/2003, XIX, 15)."

There is no possible doubt: Augustine is referring to man in this world and not to "other-wordly individuals."

Though Dumont's theory should be interpreted with all necessary caution, it helps to explain why the concept of equality gained ground slowly, even after the French Revolution. And, above all, it shows us one disturbing aspect of equality: its capacity to damage the social fabric. By introducing an unworldly element into the modern "worldly being" who emerges from the French Revolution, the idea of equality becomes subversive in terms of the organization of social relationships. In this respect, many aspects of life remain marginal to the process, above all the family, where the most basic differences are encountered—between man and woman, old and young, healthy and sick. Equality made its mark only after World War II, first among the upper classes and subsequently in the population as a whole, as a principle governing all dealings in everyday life, including personal relationships.

This is not the appropriate place to discuss the origins and development of such a basic and inalienable concept of modern societies. While examining the idea of equality, in an attempt to understand how eating disorders started and developed, I could hardly avoid considering myself, as a person, and above all as a woman. And there is no place for me in a world where the idea of equality is silenced. Dumont himself (1986) emphasizes that every apparent attempt to reject the idea of equality has led only to duplicity and barbaric dominion: The Christian West cannot disregard equality, because it is its cornerstone. There are, however, two tremendous risks to equality, when it is placed in opposition to its polar opposite—hierarchy—and tries to destroy it. The first is the frightening importance the metaphor of power acquires. Once men consider themselves as equal, without differences and shortcomings that lead them to achieve mutual completion, the relationship with the other person will inevitably be perceived through the metaphor of power:

> Everyone tends towards supremacy and to use others as means; everyone simultaneously seeks dominion, caught in a situation of general mistrust and competition, precisely because they are equal. They

necessarily fall into this web which weakens, as well as perpetuating the same passion for power because they are indifferent to each other, or rather they have nothing in them which demands a fixed, constant and habitual relationship with the other, since their nature does not admit and does not accept any difference.

(Biral, 1991, p. 14)[16]

The failure to recognize man's social nature, and the profound differences arising from involvement in different cultural groups, also creates a terrible emptiness between individuals and their fellow human beings. Having eradicated the differences derived from the many forms of community between people, there is a danger that only the biological differences will remain. The emptiness created between individual and species takes us into the second risk produced by the concept of equality when it attempts to eliminate hierarchy, its polar opposite: values are reduced to simple human preferences, which are entirely arbitrary. Giving importance to an idea, giving it value, means placing it in a hierarchy. It is perhaps for this reason that the very word "values," generally used in the plural, sounds unappealing and obsolete. "Being comparative in essence, it seems doomed to emptiness: a matter of value is not a matter of fact" (Dumont, 1986, p. 237). Behind the feeling of emptiness that values prompt, there is the entirely modern distinction between facts and values. The concept of hierarchy is supplanted by "facts"—for modern society the most important dimension of existence—facts being the realm of science. Values are relegated to a weaker, secondary, marginal position. But people do not only think, they also act; they cannot therefore ignore the ideas that guide their actions. If values are silenced, action becomes anchored to that "conflict of everyone for themselves" which is so worryingly widespread at the level of common awareness, "a sort of commonplace of cultural deficiency," with its bleak tendency towards skepticism, disillusionment, and cynicism.

But let us return to the eating disorders that have prompted these more general considerations. I opened this section by suggesting that "winner/loser"—the polarity at the center of the semantics of power—is different to other semantic polarities. In comparison with these, the winner/loser polarity is semantically poor. Its content is purely relational; it is the result of comparison and exists only through comparison. The observations I have raised also enable us to consider another aspect of this polarity's specific nature: its lack of reference to any value. The independence/attachment polarities, relevant in situations where phobic organizations develop, and good/bad, which are typical of families in which obsessive-compulsive organizations develop, refer respectively to the idea of freedom and abstinent goodness. These ideas, precisely because they guide action, are also values. These values can be discussed, as I have demonstrated. Nevertheless, they organize behavior in a moral

220

universe. The winner/loser and what I call the semantics of power, on the other hand, disregard values: The "good," to use an old word, is identified with superiority in its own right, and with willpower, which coincides with the determination to achieve pre-eminence, largely irrespective of contents.

It is no surprise, then, that eating disorders have increased over the last forty years as values have gradually been relegated to second place. For reasons connected to their particular history, families in which eating disorders develop have been more entangled in a process that has involved each and all of us. Let us look at the Santucci case once again. The whole family knew about the women in the first generation who, though their inheritance was guaranteed to them by law, left it all to the men in order to strengthen the family name. When they were old and sick and in need of support, the two sisters who had fought hardest to convince the others to renounce their inheritance realized that their own way of thinking no longer existed: their brothers no longer had time or money for them. It was Alma, the family's Cinderella, my patients' grandmother, who looked after them. Given what happened later, the conduct of these women, rather than being generous, was rash or even irresponsible. Even the girls' grandparents, who had placed unity and the family good above the protection of their own interests, were in the end fired from the family business without any compensation, or even a word of thanks. Finally, Zita, the girls' mother, who had always placed the family first, who had always done her best for all of them, had been living, during the period in which two of her daughters developed eating disorders, under the constant threat of abandonment from her husband. This, at least, is how the daughters saw it, without going too far away from the "facts". If this is the reality, then kindness, generosity and devotion break down into gullibility or foolishness. What counts, instead, is to try not to be outclassed or defeated.

But it is precisely this breakdown of values, an expression of individualism, giving central importance to the winner/loser polarity and to the semantics of power, which binds members of the family within the same chain. Each person, having to define him or herself within purely relational and comparative semantics, is imprisoned by the judgment of the others. The definition of their own self is dependent *at all times* and *in all circumstances*, upon a confirmation that the other person cannot give, on penalty of defeat. This leads to the conflict in defining the relationship characterizing the family contexts in which the eating disorders I have considered at such length develop. I would add only that this is an expression of the ambiguities arising from the concept of equality. When understood in terms of identity or removal of differences, equality is reversed into its opposite: everyone is condemned to the most frustrating and restrictive coexistence. The links in the chain—to return to Tocqueville's metaphor—are no longer separated; they are once again joined together, but it is difficult for the chain to form any pattern because everybody strives to be equal and consequently have difficulty finding their proper place.

We can therefore conclude by noting that the spread of eating disorders reveals some of the difficulties inherent in the idea of equality, such as the breakdown of differences, and forces us to think about what Dumont calls the "unforeseen core issue" for modern societies: the concept of hierarchy. It is an issue that systemic psychology and psychotherapy, despite focusing their interests on the co-positioning of differences, has often neglected.

6

DEPRESSION: DENIED
BELONGING

6.1 What Serotonin Doesn't Explain

Depression raises many questions. Why, for example, is it cyclical? It is well known that this psychopathology tends to resolve itself on its own and reoccur after a period of full or partial remission, when it becomes chronic. Drugs, at best, accelerate a remission that occurs in the natural course of the illness.[1] If we exclude dysthymia (to which the hypotheses developed in this chapter do not apply[2]), the other forms are characterized by an *on-off* pattern. Depression is either there or it isn't. Patients often describe entering or emerging from the "illness" as sudden, sometimes unexpected events. This is the peculiarity of depression. When other psychopathologies become chronic, they tend to remain over time without much variation. If a psychic disorder is not rapidly overcome, irrespective of its aetiology, it reorganizes the interpersonal relationships around it, creating new positionings, roles and relational configurations that inevitably contribute towards stabilizing it (Sluzki, 1981). As family therapists are well aware, attempts by families to find a solution often increase the problem (Watzlawick, Weakland, & Fisch, 1974) and the self same ability of a nucleus to deal with the difficulties of one member generally becomes an obstacle to change when the problem persists. Depression, however, with its cyclical nature, does not seem to follow this rule.

The link between depression and the arts raises another puzzling question. Why are people prone to depression, typically with particularly low self-esteem, able to produce important works that include some of the greatest masterpieces? It is well known that many of the greatest artists have experienced periods of depression during their lives. The phenomenon has a much wider implication than the connection between the arts and depression might seem to suggest. The history of the world does not abound with geniuses, and artists are likewise few in number. Yet there are many people prone to depression who display an uncommon capacity to create important works in business, sciences and the professions as well. But how can people with a three-fold negative vision—of themselves, of the world and of the future—according to

223

Beck's (1967) well-known definition, find the necessary resources to make notable achievements—works of art included? This is another enigma we need to try to unravel.

If the lack of serotonin was indeed the cause of depression, as biological psychiatry and the pharmaceutical industry have been proclaiming for years, there would be no answer to these, or other questions I will be considering below. The available research, in fact, does not demonstrate at all that a deficiency of serotonin has a causal effect on depression. There is a deep gulf between what has been advertised and what the scientific literature has managed to prove (Lacasse & Leo, 2005).

Since 2000, there has been great dispute about the idea that depression is a brain disease, comparable with asthma or diabetes; about its apparent astonishing growth in the West; and about the effectiveness of Selective Serotonin Reuptake Inhibitors (SSRIs) (Greenberg, 2010; Healy, 2004; Horwitz & Wakefield, 2007; Kirsch, 2010; Lane, 2007).

The evidence currently available shows that about 25 percent of depressed patients have low levels of serotonin or norepinephrine (Horwitz & Wakefield, 2007; Valenstein, 1998). If the hypothesis of serotonin deficiency were correct in aetiopathological terms, it would therefore explain only a limited number of cases. But it is not correct, at least aetiopathologically. The low levels of serotonin found in these patients may in fact be the consequence rather than the cause of depression. *There is no empirical evidence to show that chemical imbalance is the cause of depression.* Indeed, we know that exactly the opposite happens in non-human primates, as was demonstrated in laboratory tests carried out in the 1980s by the psychiatrist Michael McGuire and his colleagues (McGuire, Raleigh, & Johnson, 1983; Raleigh et al., 1984) on the vervet and other monkeys whose social life is characterized by close and stable hierarchical relationships with a dominant male in each group. These studies showed that the levels of serotonin, and of other neurochemicals connected with depression, vary according to changes in the social status of the monkeys. When the researchers removed the dominant males from their respective groups, their levels of serotonin, which were twice those of the other males in the group, rapidly decreased, along with their levels of activity, and the monkeys began to refuse food. In short, in the view of the human observers, they seemed "depressed." On the other hand, the serotonin levels of those monkeys who had gained a higher status after the removal of the dominant males increased, reaching the levels of the dominant males who had been removed. These results have been repeated more recently with female monkeys (Shively, Laber-Laird, & Anton, 1997) and in natural settings (Berman, Rasmussen, & Suomi, 1994). Among baboons out of captivity in East Africa, the neuroendocrinologist Robert Sapolsky also found that the position of chronic subordination produces high quantities of stress hormones, similar to those found in depressed people. But when the position of baboons in the hierarchy changed, their stress hormones were reduced (Sapolsky, 1989). It also emerged that there are behavioral and neurochemical advantages in positions of high rank only if the dominant hierarchies are stable. When the hierarchy is unstable, and therefore the dominant positions are precarious, the high-ranking primates also produce quantities of stress hormones similar to their followers (Sapolsky, 2005).

Likewise, the theory that depression is a genetically-transmitted illness has not been confirmed by empirical evidence. On the basis of what has emerged from longitudinal research on twins conducted mainly in the last century, most experts agree that the genetic component in depression is around 30–40 percent (Coyne, 1982; Gilbert, 1982). The extraordinary developments in genetics enabled researchers to map specific genes and to examine links with the development of depression (Caspi et al., 2003[3]). Yet the results so far produced by this research indicate that genetics plays a limited role in the development of depression: at most it may be a risk or protection factor (see, for example, Bentall, 2009; Horwitz & Wakefield, 2007).

Of greater significance have been the results relating to the effectiveness of Prozac and other SSRIs and their side effects, which have emerged from double blind clinical tests. These results are disturbing. Though presented as miraculous, such drugs have had effects that are identical to, or little better than the placebo. A meta-analysis carried out by Kirsch and colleagues (Kirsch et al., 2008; Kirsch et al., 2002) on research presented by the pharmaceutical companies to the Federal Drug Administration found no difference between SSRIs and the placebo for moderate or light depressions and a minimal difference for more serious depressions. Other meta-analyses found no difference whatsoever between placebo and SSRIs for all levels of gravity (Kahn et al, 2002) or for moderate or light depression (Fournier et al., 2010). Moreover, the SSRIs produced no better results than the placebo effect in what were the most reliable tests, namely those with an "active placebo."[4]

The most worrying data concerns the side effects of SSRIs: These antidepressants increase the already high risk of suicide. This was proved for children, adolescents, and young people (Hammad, Laughren, & Racoosin, 2006), so much so that the Federal Drug Administration recently concluded that "when compared to placebos, SSRIs double the risk of suicidal thoughts and behavior in depressed patients up to the age of 24" (Kirsch, 2010, p. 151). An increase in suicide risk also among depressed adult subjects has been revealed (Fergusson et al., 2005; Healy, 2004; Stone & Jones, 2006), but these results are controversial. Furthermore, it has also emerged that these drugs can cause impotence and other sexual disorders (Clayton et al., 2002), as well as numerous other side effects (Kirsch, 2010).

Also the disturbing increase in depression, investigated by sociologists, psychologists, philosophers and indeed economists, is questionable. There has been an increase not in the number of depressed patients but in the *diagnosis and in the pharmacological treatment* of this disorder, since the criteria for diagnosis have changed.

The *DSM*, from its third edition in 1980, introduced criteria that were so indiscriminate and far-removed from the context of diagnosing "major depression" that this category includes just as many individuals normally saddened by negative events as it does patients affected by clinical depression. Two and a half thousand years of Western clinical tradition were swept away by the third and later editions of the *DSM*. Even the traditional psychiatric distinction is ignored between "endogenous" depression—caused, by definition, by internal processes in the absence of external negative events—and "reactive" depressions triggered by loss and other negative social events.

> In attempting to characterize the kinds of symptoms suffered in depressive disorders without reference to the context in which the symptoms occur, contemporary psychiatry has also inadvertently characterized intense normal suffering as disease.
>
> (Horwitz & Wakefield, 2007, pp. 9–10)

A depressive mood, loss of interest in usual activities, insomnia, loss of appetite and inability to concentrate can occur for a fortnight following the discovery of a partner's betrayal, an illness that places our life or that of someone close to us at risk, a business failure, a missed promotion and many other negative events. So long as they are appropriate to the circumstances, such kinds of behavior are not symptoms but normal reactions.

The difference between serious unipolar depression and what used to be called manic-depressive psychosis has disappeared to a large extent through the creation of two subtypes of bipolar disorder, the second of which (bipolar II disorder) has ended up including unipolar depressions. It is unnecessary, in fact, for patients to display manic behavior in order to be diagnosed with bipolar II disorder. It is enough for them to be in an irritable mood for four days, together with a decreased need for sleep and higher level of activity and talkativeness to satisfy the criteria for a "hypomanic episode," and therefore to be eligible to be diagnosed as a "bipolar" patient. As a result, people who would once have been regarded as having ordinary life problems have become patients to be treated pharmacologically, and depressed patients are now in danger of becoming chronically ill (affected by bipolar disorder) and of being kept under medication for the rest of their lives.

We in the West are not facing an implosion into depression. Serious forms of unipolar and bipolar depression remain infrequent. It is the criteria for diagnosis that have changed: Sadness has been transformed into a mental disorder and clinical depression has become a successor to manic-depressive psychosis. Horwitz and Wakefield (2007) observe ironically:

There is no evidence that pharmaceutical companies had a role in developing *DSM-III* diagnostic criteria. Yet, serendipitously, the new diagnostic model was ideally suited to promoting the pharmaceutical treatment of the conditions it delineated. (…). The diagnosis of Major Depression, which used common symptoms such as sadness, lack of energy or sleeplessness as indicators, was particularly well suited for expanding the market for psychotropic drugs because it inevitably encompassed many patients who formerly might have been thought to be suffering from problems of living.

(p. 182)

This is what happened: the use of antidepressants among adults in the United States tripled between 1988 and 2000. The increase was particularly high among children, adolescents and the elderly: For them the percentage increase in prescriptions for antidepressants rose during the 1990s by between 200 percent and 300 percent (Crystal et al., 2003; Thomas et al., 2006).

Clinical psychologists and psychotherapists are being encouraged to focus their attention on depression because of the disappointing results for SSRIs, as well as the debate that has developed over the last decade and the increasing number of studies on the positive effects of psychotherapy for all forms of depression.[5]

More than twenty years of unchallenged rule by biological psychiatry over this disorder has left us a difficult legacy: There are no shared diagnostic criteria or even diagnostic categories to enable us to distinguish depression from sadness. The main reason for the success of the *DSM* is its ability to offer criteria that allow for uniform and comparable clinical diagnoses, an essential prerequisite for the development of knowledge in this area. Yet this is certainly not the case with depression. The general label of "major depression" is now given to people saddened by loss and other negative events as well as to patients of very different kinds. It is no surprise that the results of one study are often contradicted by others, since the most likely problem is that they relate to different clinical conditions. Even psychiatrists who follow a biological approach are beginning to realize that the lack of clear results from their own studies on depression is probably due to a lack of uniformity of subject samples (Nierenberg et al., 2011).

In the absence of shared guiding criteria, I must therefore be clear, as far as possible, about the clinical situation to which the theories I am putting forward relate.

The cases, on which the hypotheses here are based, are treatments specifically requested because of the patient's depression either as the only problem or together with others. They were serious cases which, in addition to the depressive condition, exhibited anhedonia, suicidal ideas and/or attempts and persistent insomnia, generally morning insomnia, the symptoms that best distinguished depression from sadness (Lewinsohn et al., 2003; Santor & Coyne, 2001).[6] None of the cases considered presented other psychopathologies at the same time, nor were they classifiable with other psychopathological organizations.

The generalizations I am putting forward in this chapter can be extended to what some cognitive psychotherapists (Arciero & Bondolfi, 2009; Bara, 1996; Guidano, 1987, 1991; Neimeyer & Raskin, 2000; Villegas, 2000, 2004) describe as depressive organizations, where the personal meaning is characterized by events that are actively construed in terms of loss, and where anger and despair play a decisive role. In terms of neurosis, we find them in clinical practice in cases of unipolar depression, in their psychotic slide into manic-depressive psychosis. While reconstructing the pre-morbid history of patients who later become depressed, or who come to us with existential problems, we also encounter these organizations as forms of normal individual functioning.

Depression, as a symptom, is found throughout all organizations previously presented. Anorexics are unlikely to suffer from it, but many obese people do. Phobics can also display depressive disorders, especially agoraphobics whose self-esteem is structurally low since they suffer through their dependence. Depression is particularly frequent among obsessives. These patients often ask for therapy for depression more than for their obsessions or compulsions, which they sometimes manage to control. The main reason that brings people with narcissistic disorders into therapy is depression. In this chapter we will not be considering these forms of depression. The semantics that I describe below, and the positioning assumed by patients and those most important to them within this semantic, therefore relate to only one type of depression, that of unipolar depressive organizations, and help towards identifying these organizations more clearly.

6.2 A Conversation in Which Some Belong and Some are Excluded

The conversation in families where one of its members has a depressive organization gives prominence to what I have called "semantics of belonging." The grid set out in Figure 6.1 summarizes its central meanings. The two main polarities are inclusion/exclusion, honor/disgrace. They are fuelled by joy/cheerfulness and anger/despair, the emotions typifying these semantics. The most important thing for members of these families is to be included as part of the family, as well as being part of the wider community. The reason is that within the same family group there are also those who are excluded, marginalized or rejected. Expulsion from the group, or not belonging to a family, is seen by such people as an irreparable disgrace, whereas the greatest good is to be well-established and respected within the groups to which they belong, including family and community. Yet it is often in the name of dignity that permanent rifts occur. Honor in these families is therefore a value just as fundamental as belonging.

VALUES		
BELONGING		EXCLUSION
HONOUR	⟶	DISGRACE
CHOSEN		REJECTED
GLORY	⟶	DOWNFALL
DEFINITIONS OF SELF / OTHERS / RELATIONSHIPS		
IN THE GROUP		OUT OF THE GROUP
HONOURABLE	⟶	UNWORTHY
ELECTED		OUTCAST
GRATEFUL		ANGRY
ENERGETIC	⟶	RUN DOWN
WAYS OF RELATING		
INCLUDING		OSTRACIZING/OSTRACIZED
HONOURING		USURPING/USURPED
OVERWHELMED BY GOOD FORTUNE		DEFRAUDING/DEFRAUDED
VENERATING	⟶	DESTROYING
EMOTIONS AND FEELINGS		
JOY		**ANGER**
CHEERFULNESS		DESPAIR

⟶ It can also be part of the negative pole

Figure 6.1 Semantics of belonging grid. The detailed grid is set out in Ugazio et al., 2009

Breakups with parents, with relatives, and with the community are frequent in these family groups. Sometimes they are irreparable, at other times they are healed, but nevertheless they have a profound effect on the destiny of certain members of the family. Piecing together the history of these families, I have often come across people who have been dispossessed, defrauded or disowned, as often happens with illegitimate births or children abandoned by their parents. There are often members of the family who end up in a mental hospital, prison or other institution because they are considered, rightly or wrongly, unworthy to be a part of the community in which they should belong.

The paternal grandfather of Arianna (a 40-year-old sculptress with recurrent depressive crises) was disowned by his mother when, at the age of fifty, he married an Argentine girl from the lowest social background. His relationship with his prosperous family was already minimal. He was an anarchist and had fled to Argentina when accused of involvement in a terrorist attack. His marriage was regarded by the family as an intolerable affront: the girl was a foreigner, uneducated, poor, and moreover the daughter of the woman with whom he had previously been living in Argentina. Arianna's grandfather was a fine-looking, well-educated man, and when he returned to Italy with his new family he managed nevertheless to reintegrate, thanks also to a considerable inheritance from his father. His children also integrated well in the city where they lived. But Arianna's grandmother was totally marginalized. Having been cut off from her own roots, she failed to integrate in Italy and was an outcast even among her own children. Her contact with the world was her husband. When he died, her grief was inconsolable. Arianna, who, according to everyone in the family, bore a striking physical resemblance to her grandmother, knew her through her mother's stories—her father never spoke about his mother.

> She lived segregated, cut off from everyone. My aunts felt not the slightest concern for her. They had married into prosperous families. [...] They regarded their foreign, poor, ignorant mother as a disgrace. When my mother went to live in the villa, my grandmother never left the two upper-floor rooms where she lived with the assistance of a carer. She came downstairs only once a week, at 11.00 every Thursday morning, and let out desperate cries of grief for at least half an hour: That was the time and day of the week when her husband's funeral had taken place.

It was only after two years living there that Arianna's mother managed to establish a minimum of communication with her mother-in-law:

> At a certain point my grandmother began coming downstairs and making short visits to the kitchen, probably attracted by the smell of cooking [...]. My mother immediately tried to talk to her, but she ran away, until one day she accepted a plate of risotto. From then on she established some sort of relationship with my mother [...] My mother found it reassuring to have some contact, though limited, as she felt terrified by this figure [...] My mother was frightened by this woman, in the same way as she is frightened by me.

These stories must have affected Arianna. There were, in fact, clear similarities between her grandmother's ritual laments and the patient's recurrent depressions over a period of twenty years, which coincided with the anniversaries of the suicides of her father and brother.

Josè's history began with an abandonment. He was two when his parents died in a car accident and he was brought up by his uncle Miguel who had owned a business jointly with Josè's father. As soon as they reached adulthood, Josè's two older brothers, who had been brought up by other relatives, began legal proceedings against Miguel, accusing him of having cheated the orphans out of part of their inheritance. When he reached majority, Josè did not feel he could involve himself in a legal action against his stepfather. This caused conflict with his biological brothers. He refused his stepfather's proposal of legal adoption and at the age of twenty left Brazil for Italy. When I met him, after a serious episode of depression, he was thirty-two, divorced and his current relationship was in crisis. But his feelings towards all of his relatives remained strong: It seemed as though he had only just left Brazil.

The histories of depressives do not necessarily contain tragedies. But there is invariably a conflict between those who are at the center of their own world and those who are alone and isolated.

> In the last six years I've lived in five cities, three European countries and 21 houses.

This is how Francesca introduced herself: she was a company executive, 30 years old, who I met during her first serious depression. But was it really her globetrotting that had sent her into depression? It was difficult to accept this explanation, seeing that Francesca herself attributed the breakdown of all relationships—including her latest—to her forceful character more than to her difficulty in reconciling work commitments with her personal life. Her emotional solitude (caused certainly in part by her unconditional agreement to travel for her work) placed her in a position similar to that of her father. Alone, without family, without friends, without support, he had created a good professional standing in the town to which he had moved at the age of seventeen when his mother had left him to join her husband, who had emigrated to the United States many years earlier. But he had never felt truly integrated. Francesca's mother, on the other hand, was a focal point of this town. The owner of a flourishing beauty parlor, where several members of her family worked, she was lively, kind, full of energy, she organized lunches and social events for friends and relations and had a smile for everyone. "I could never go out shopping with my mother when I was a child," the patient complained. "Everyone greeted her, they chatted and she always had something to say to everyone." Not even when her eldest son became a drug addict did Francesca's mother give priority to her family: "Her world is her beauty parlor, her brothers and sisters, her friends and only then us."

In families where depression develops there are often people who are lively and joyful like Francesca's mother. Sometimes they are positive characters like Mrs Ramsey, Virginia Woolf's portrayal of her mother in *To the Lighthouse*. But even when they are difficult personalities who cause suffering in other members of the family, they are generally the focal point around which a family or a social world revolves.

A gentleman, a couple of generations older than me—that was my first impression on meeting Rodolfo, a seriously depressed, drug-resistant patient who had received hospital treatment on several occasions. I was astonished to realize we were both the same age, neither of us yet fifty. Later I realized that behind his manner of the early twentieth-century gentleman lay his tragedy. Rodolfo was living in the world of his father—and it was a world that had always rejected him.

Rodolfo's father was charming, with a magnetic personality, and had held political appointments until the age of seventy, playing a leading role in civic life. He was present at all events, was sociable and witty, regularly attending fashionable parties where he scored success with women. Everyone in the town greeted him, everyone admired him for his invariably kindly nature. No one had ever seen him at public events with his wife. She was more a servant than a companion. She adored her husband who seemed to belong to another class of being. She devoted herself to looking after the sumptuous wardrobe of clothes he wore in a world in which she played no part, almost as if it were enough for her to know her husband held center-stage thanks to her services. Mother and son were excluded from such society. They were alone even at New Year. Rodolfo's mother kept silent, but the stress as they waited for his father's return was considerable. He sometimes arrived in time to toast the New Year but generally appeared a few hours after midnight. Rodolfo could not forget his father's complaints if the meal was not ready as soon as he arrived, nor the slap he gave his wife on a couple of occasions when she dared to reproach him for his repeated unfaithfulness. Outside the home the man was charming. Everyone admired his elegance, gentlemanly manner, and good humor. Even the directors of the consultancy company who were dealing with Rodolfo's business failure were struck by this old man who had no hesitation in assuming responsibility for the collapse to ensure his son did not end up "in a cardboard box in front of a church," to use one of Rodolfo's recurring expressions. This was also a reason why the patient was convinced that he and his mother were tainted, to be kept as far from polite society as possible. "It would have been better if the other had been born," his father had told him when he had reached adolescence. He was referring to the first child who had died at birth and was buried in the cemetery for unborn children that father and son had visited at least once a year for twenty years. And Rodolfo, convinced that he had inherited neither his father's fine appearance nor his personality, thought of himself as a source of humiliation for his father by reason of his inherent inadequacy.

The central position enjoyed by Rodolfo's father, as is generally the case with well-loved members of the family, is not the result of work and effort, at least not in the eyes of the patient; these individuals are naturally likeable and worthy of respect—they seem almost to have been elected by a divine grace that has showered them with many gifts. This destiny is quite different from that of the depressed patients who, if they achieve anything, do so with such effort that they end up putting their health at risk.

The personalities and family events in my case studies naturally vary. When the semantics of belonging has a long history in a family, extending back over several generations, those who are black sheep, or have been disowned, defrauded or forgotten co-position themselves with individuals who are respected, or worthy of being remembered for their actions, or have simply been included by divine grace among the elect. Illegitimate births, desertions, abandonments are matched with fortunate events such as inheritances, fairytale weddings, professional honors, dazzling careers. Life for some seems to have been harsh, while for others it has been particularly kind. Some members of the family are adored and admired while others are ignored or become the object of aggression and violence. At other times, especially when the semantics of belonging has only recently acquired central importance in the family, events are less typical but generate anger/despair or, alternatively, joy/cheerfulness, and are interpreted in terms of exclusion/inclusion.

6.3 The Dilemma and the Adaptive Function of Depression

The prevalence of the semantics of belonging in family conversation was a recurrent presence in my case studies. As I have found with other organizations, it is the positioning assumed by the patient in the dominant semantics that makes a decisive contribution towards the development of a depressive organization. It is a positioning that causes patients to experience the following dilemma[7]: *Belonging means being unworthy of consideration and respect, but being excluded or isolated means relinquishing the status of human being. Two essential aspects of existence—belonging and personal dignity—are in danger of cancelling each other out.*

In this section I will examine the dilemma by focusing attention on those who experience it and their emotions, as well as on the typical situations that trigger it off.

As I have shown in Figure 6.2, the dilemma is marked by joy/gratitude and anger/despair. Belonging generates joy and gratitude, at least at first. People

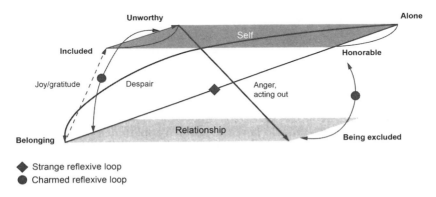

Figure 6.2 The strange reflexive loop of depressive organizations and the emotions that distinguish it

with a depressive organization are aware of these positive emotions, even if they experience them only for short periods. Capable of intense emotional involvements—for them, falling in love is a "permitted story"—they can feel joy for the fulfillment and sharing offered by love or deep friendship. The beginning of a new intimate relationship, for example, generally ends a clinical depression. Pregnancy can have the same effect: for the expectant mother there are finally two of them. A 44-year-old patient of mine, who had had twelve years of serious recurring depressions, felt splendid during her pregnancies:

> "It's crazy," said her husband repeatedly, "during both pregnancies Lorenza was exactly the woman I had known in the early years of our marriage: lively, vivacious, full of energy. During both of them she stopped taking medication and she was still absolutely fine. During the first pregnancy she even returned to work. Everyone had advised us against a second child. [...] But considering the wonderful experience of the first pregnancy I thought a second child might have helped her, all the more so because Lorenza really wanted it. When we discovered that the second child was a girl, we were overjoyed ... She really wanted a girl. What a pity that after the birth of Elisa she had perhaps the worst depression of all."

Various studies on teenage pregnancies confirm this clinical observation: Girls prone to depression were those who had been most positive about their unexpected pregnancy. Unfortunately the beneficial effect was short-lived: it was they, in fact, who most frequently suffered post-partum depression (Wagner et al., 1998).

By belonging, people with a depressive organization find themselves at last in the position they had always desired, of someone who is included, who is recognized as a member of a group. But they soon end up feeling unworthy, precisely because of their longed-for position of belonging. Joy is converted into anger and resentment, which risks degenerating into episodes of verbal or physical violence capable of threatening and destroying the very interpersonal relationships that guarantee their inclusion. The price paid for maintaining the position of belonging is extremely high: their own sense of honor.

When the dilemma reaches its height, the subject oscillates between two equally unacceptable alternatives: continuing to maintain the relationship means being contemptible, while ending it means leaving human society. Generally speaking, aggressive behavior, often described by patients as acting out, provokes a crisis or breakdown in the relationship but lowers the reflexivity of the loop. Patients are in danger of losing what they have, but the reflexivity of the loop is reduced because they have at least saved their sense of honor. Unfortunately, as soon as their anger dies down, they are overcome by despair about what they have lost, and their consequent solitude.

For the depressive, solitude is a punishment, a stigma. Unlike those affected by narcissistic disorders, who are more vulnerable to attacks on their overblown self-image than to the emotional vacuum in which they find themselves, depressives suffer terribly from their emotional isolation. Even when they are self-sufficient, they are not proud of their ability to manage alone. Being self-sufficient is not an achievement, as it is for those with phobic organizations: it is, if anything, a sad necessity. Yet at the time when subjects feel despair, clinical depression does not develop so long as they are able to re-establish relationships capable of giving them a feeling of inclusion, or to find other ways of feeling they belong.

Various contexts of belonging can trigger off the dilemma—the family of origin, the nuclear family, extended family relationships, the workplace, friendships. When the dilemma involves the partner, emotions become intense. The notion that the relationship with the partner is capable of producing the most destructive feelings is particularly true among depressive organizations.

Certain situations that fuel the dilemma are recurrent. One example is jealousy. Patients, in this case, are convinced they have been betrayed, or are not loved. In certain cases the partner really is incapable of fidelity: patients seem to have made the classic "wrong choice" in their companion. More often the suspicion of infidelity is unjustified or patients have obviously contributed towards their partner's infidelity by their own behavior. These betrayals, whether real or imaginary, produce the same result: subjects feel rejected or abandoned and regard the continuation of the relationship as a source of disgrace.

Money can also trigger off the dilemma. If patients are rich they generally feel exploited; if they are poor they think they have been robbed. They are, for example, convinced their partner continues to live with them for financial gain. My depressed patients are often generous. Being convinced they are unlikeable, or aware of the destructive nature of their attacks, they lavish their partner or other members of the family with money or services so as not to lose them. But this in itself makes them feel unworthy: one particularly wealthy patient of mine described himself as a "beggar for love." Others tyrannize their families for the same reasons.

Matteo's case is a typical example. He was a lawyer suffering from manic-depressive psychosis who tormented his whole family over money. When I met him and his wife with their five children, all were so poorly dressed that my team and I decided (without the family asking) to allow them more favorable terms. We were soon to discover that the patient came from a wealthy family. He was also a tireless worker, as often happens with depressives, passionate about his profession, and competent. Despite his mental instability, he was professionally respected. Money was his weapon. Convinced that he was tolerated only for the financial security he could provide, he made his wife and children live in poverty, save for exceptional acts of generosity. He had nevertheless paid a considerable sum into the bank accounts of his wife and each of his children. What a pity that money could not be touched. No one had ever dared to draw on it. And yet they all needed it. Whenever conflict with his wife became particularly bad, he suspended all distributions of money to the family. His wife had even pawned some jewelry of modest value inherited from her mother in order to meet some essential expenses. Even then she was careful not to draw on her own bank account or to pawn the magnificent Bulgari jewelry her husband had given her during happier periods in their relationship.

Among those patients who feel they have been cheated, the most frequent culprits are the family of origin who have denied them what, in their view, they were entitled to have. Ex-spouses, business colleagues or partners are also often accused of having swindled them. Other personal resources, such as professional and scientific skills or friendships, can of course produce similar feelings.

A range of situations may fuel the dilemma but patients have generally played a vital part in creating and continuing them with aggressive and provocative behavior. Some studies have shown that these individuals more often contribute *actively* (though not *intentionally*) than other people in bringing about the negative events that afflict them, since they lack relational problem-solving skills (Pettit & Joiner, 2006).

The presence of a powerful active emotion, such as anger, in subjects with depressive organizations helps to explain why it is unlikely they will show obvious signs of sadness or dejection in the pre-morbid period, or during remission in chronic depression. We generally find this type of attitude, corresponding to the idea of a person inclined to depression in the popular sense, in patients with an obsessive organization at the stage when they renounce their personal impulses. Here, however, we are concerned with people who are generally active, energetic and have many interests. Sometimes they are dynamic, lively, provocative, capable of dominating discussion, bold and aggressive, even though they may often feel like Søren Kierkegaard (1834–1835; 1978) in this passage from his diary:

> I have just now come from a gathering where I was the life of the party; witticisms flowed out of my mouth; everybody laughed, admired me–but I left, yes, the dash ought to be as long as the radii of the earth's orbit ... and wanted to shoot myself.

> (p. 69)

Naturally, when depression erupts, despair does not emerge at particular moments, as in the passage I have quoted, but takes over the entire scene. All enjoyment, activity, interests have gone; the depressive, having now become a patient, feels such despair that it is impossible even to get out of bed.

The onset generally appears after breakups, separations from a partner or the failure of business ventures. Sometimes the depressive response is imme-

236

diate, but often it occurs later, when the anger has died down and despair is not enough to re-establish the relationship lost because the partner does not intend to make any new commitment or because subjects themselves are not induced by despair to change their conduct. The sense of personal dignity does not allow reconciliation.

In the depressive's relational world, anger and aggressive behavior provoke conflict, breakups and separation in significant relationships. The pragmatic effect of depression in my cases is to make patients renew contact with other people as a means of escaping from isolation. Since these contacts were required by a condition regarded as "illness," the dignity of the patients could be preserved. The price paid, of course, was the prolonging of a terrible suffering.

Some studies (Pettit & Joiner, 2006) have documented the fact that full-blown depression interrupts a cycle of destructive interpersonal behavior. These studies support the theory, first advanced by Bateson (1971) in relation to alcoholism, that the symptoms of depression have a self-curing function. Depression therefore has an adaptive value. It forces the patient, in fact, to bring an end to negative interpersonal behavior. The prerequisites for re-establishing the significant relationships, and therefore for recovery, are thus put into position.

The authors of these studies assign quite different functions to depressive symptoms. For Hammen (1999), they are "breaking mechanisms," actual mechanisms for breaking off conflict. For Gardner and Price (1999) they are an expression of an "involuntary subordinate strategy." Patients, according to them, at the moment they enter the full-blown depression, send "no threat" signals to their partners, rivals, and superiors. These signals discourage aggression against them that had previously been encouraged through their aggressive and provocative behavior. Depression—once again according to Price and Gardner—functions as a sort of "alarm signal" that indicates to patients themselves the need to change course and invites others to do the same.

Leaving aside the notably different functions that these researchers attribute to the symptoms of depression, they all suggest that full-blown depression at least inhibits destructive interpersonal behavior and often starts off relational repair mechanisms. Unfortunately the corrective mechanism tends not to last long. The remission of symptoms, at least in chronic depression, in fact reopens a new cycle of negative interpersonal behavior that causes a relapse.

The hypothesis that depression aids the re-establishment of interpersonal relationships torn apart by conflict, explains why this disorder is cyclical. The patient, having regained stability, can once again start creating conflictual situations that can easily degenerate until they produce conflicts and destruction that clear the way for a new depressive episode. It is a hypothesis that helps us to understand why the natural course of depression allows it to be overcome. If the adaptive function of depression is to re-establish links with others, once its purpose has been achieved, the depression must necessarily come to an end.

These factors move our attention from the symptoms of depression to the behavior leading up to its development. Why do people with depression behave in such a way that they require adaptive mechanisms as dramatic as depression? Why are they so prone to conflict? If the underlying dilemma is as I have outlined, why do they involve themselves in situations where maintaining the relationship undermines their own personal dignity?

In attempting to answer these questions we have to examine the intersubjective conversational context within which the depression develops. That, of course, is not an "outside," external and independent context, but it is constructed by the patient together with the other significant members of his/her family.

6.4 The Intersubjective Context in the Here and Now

My depressed adult patients, though different from one another in terms of gender, age, professional status, and personality, often find themselves in a similar relational situation at the beginning of therapy: *emotionally distant from their family of origin, with whom they have broken all contact, they are either involved in a seriously conflictual relationship with their partner or have recently ended a relationship.* In both cases the relationship with the partner has had such a central position in their emotional life that it is often difficult during therapeutic conversation for them to focus on other relationships. Even though their lives have centered around work, money, power or creativity, what they yearn most is a loving relationship that is deep and all-embracing, within which they are recognized as a person worthy of love. They have found such a relationship hard to create and impossible to maintain, and even though it has fallen short of meeting their expectations, it has generally been the central focus of their emotional life, despite its conflicts.

This picture from my cases is consistent with what emerges from many studies: there is a significant connection between marital conflict and depression (Beach, 2001; Benazon & Coyne, 2000; Coyne, Thompson, & Palmer, 2002; Davila, 2001). As we saw in the previous section, the interpersonal conflicts that precede the onset of symptoms, and which the onset of depression brings to an end, generally relate to patients' relationships with their partner. It is, of course, an unacceptable simplification to presume that the conflict in the relationship is the cause of the depression or vice versa. It is an association that raises more questions than it resolves. Why are individuals prone to depression so prone to marital conflict? And why are they also so vulnerable? Many researchers have in fact been interested in identifying the variables involved in this association (Caughlin & Huston, 2002; Davila & Bradbury, 2001; Heene, Buysse, & Van Oost, 2005, 2007; Scott & Cordova, 2002). Given the importance of this conflict, it is well worth looking more closely at the relationship with the partner.

Contrary to what might be imagined in an organization where the perception of solitude is so significant, only two of my patients seemed to have chosen a life of true emotional solitude, without a stable partner—a choice that is more frequent in narcissistic disorders. All others had long-term relationships. If they were single at the beginning of therapy, they had recently been involved in a devastating emotional breakup. My clinical experience confirms that depressives are, as Linares and Campo (2000) have suggested, "among the few psychiatric patients who establish systematic and significant long-term relationships. Certainly, together with bipolar patients, they are the ones who most frequently succeed in doing so among those with serious mental disorders"[8] (p. 26).

The partner can be very highly valued. Patients, at least in the initial stage of their relationship, will have adored, idealized, loved their partner, looking to receive the same, and devoting their time, attention, and resources to the relationship.

Andrea's[9] wife's recurring depressions, her provocative behavior, including her refusal to look after their two children or the house, even during her remissions, had transformed his life over the past twelve years into a nightmare. And yet he could not forget the first happy years of their marriage. He had been captivated not only by Louise's angelic face but also by her gaiety, her emotional commitment, and her devotion to him. Despite professional demands, Louise cooked delicious meals for him, left love-letters for him under his pillow and in his jacket pockets and worked to win the affection of his friends and family, including his mother who adored her. Andrea had never felt so much the focus of another's attention; he had never felt so much loved and so much a man.

Chiara and Carlo had slept every night in each other's arms for the first three years of their life together. Carlo was a bipolar patient, age thirty-five, whose interpersonal context prior to the onset of symptoms I will describe later. Chiara, who was six years older, with several past relationships behind her, had never experienced such a full relationship. No one had ever been so devoted to her. No one had ever placed her so completely at the center of their world as Carlo had done. The union had been so happy that she had managed to obtain a qualification, change job and become more attractive. It was thanks to Carlo that she had changed, even physically.

When the partner is, or has been, idealized, it is easier for the relationship to become tense, sometimes violent. Some of my patients have begun therapy precisely to control their aggression towards their partner.

> I began slapping my husband, I destroyed his office, tore up his papers and whatever I could lay my hands on. And I'm terrified at the idea of losing him.

Viviana had resumed therapy with these words. She was a cardiologist, aged forty-four, who had begun therapy five years earlier after a serious episode of depression. Her meeting with Valerio, which took place at the end of the first course of therapy, had filled the patient with joy—she feared she was condemned by then to a life of solitude. Valerio was a colleague who was successful, physically attractive, and likeable. Their meeting was as positive as it was unexpected. Having overcome the devastating pain she had felt on being left by a fellow student with whom she had lived while specializing in cardiology, Viviana had spent fifteen years in an emotional wilderness. All of her energies had been channeled into her profession, and in looking after a nephew who had been abandoned by his mother. Her world of relationships had gradually become a desert. She had few friends. Her original family lived a thousand kilometers away and her contact with them, after her father's death, was infrequent. With Valerio she had found a new lease of life; with him she had developed an exclusive, intense relationship and had devoted all her energies to him, even reducing her work commitments. Annoyed by Valerio's lack of involvement in looking for what should have been their new home, which she interpreted as indicating a lack of affection towards her, she became extremely jealous of her husband's group of female colleagues. She was convinced there was a mutual attraction between him and one of them and could no longer control her anger: She was seized by an uncontrollable fury whenever her husband returned home late or this colleague telephoned.

Partners are just as frequently regarded as being inadequate by nature. Such patients, at least in their own opinion, have made the wrong choice from the very beginning. Their partners are beneath them; patients seem to have chosen them so as to avoid remaining alone. Preserving the relationship contributes towards making them feel unworthy, and excluding them from what they feel to be their rightful destiny.

Rodolfo did not want children because he felt his wife was incapable of being a mother: "She is not a woman who can have children, she doesn't have the refinement, the necessary education. [...] I really can't see her with a child."

A former girlfriend who appeared repeatedly in his accounts could have been the mother of his children: "She had such fine ways ... She wasn't particularly beautiful, but she was courteous, refined ..."

I was amazed when I met his wife: She was a charming, elegant lady. Rodolfo didn't see her in that way. He was convinced his wife had married him for convenience, and that he for his part had been enticed into the marriage through sexual dependency. He could not forget the cultural and human drabness of her upbringing even though she had clearly freed herself from these roots.

Relationships with these partners are generally less conflictual since possessiveness and jealousy are less pronounced. Although their partners are subjected to disparagement and criticism, rarely do my patients ever think of leaving them. The obstacle is often gratitude (the partner has been faithful to them, has saved them from despair) or lack of self-esteem: "In the end I don't think I'm worthy of much better." Sometimes these patients identify with the hopelessly inadequate partner, vehemently defending him or her. But they are nevertheless convinced that preserving the relationship will increase their marginalization, although they can push the blame onto their partner for an exclusion they would have suffered anyway.

Among my patients who have established their own family or a long-term relationship, two recurring relational configurations arise in the period prior to the onset of symptoms. We can understand the significance of these configurations if we examine the couple's conflict in the wider interpersonal context. Although people prone to depression focus their attentions on their partner, the couple still lives within a wider relational context.

These configurations are not applicable to young adults whose symptoms first appear when they are still living with their parents, even though such symptoms are also generally preceded by the breakup of a romantic involvement.

The first configuration *sees the patient in a position of exclusion while the partner is at the center of all relationships.* This configuration, which is more frequent when the companion is respected, is the outcome of an often long conversational process to which patients contribute with the expectation of a total relationship with the partner (Linares & Campo, 2000; Loriedo & Jedlowski, 2010) and consequent jealousy and possessiveness.

The desire for an all-embracing long-term relationship and intolerance towards anyone who intervenes in the relationship place these future depressives in a marginal position with regard to all family relationships other than that of the couple. Children, relatives, and friends are seen as threats. Their children feel them to be distant or openly hostile and develop a close attachment with the other parent, who is generally more amenable. Their friends ally themselves more to the partner who is generally more open to outside contact. The partner's family remains distant and maintains individual contact with him or her, rather than with the couple. Disappointment as to their partner's incapacity to respond to their needs, as well as the marginal position in which they actually find themselves in the family, generally makes those with a depressive organization aggressive and provocative towards their partner and only indirectly towards their children. Conflict with their children can be intense, but the prime target is still their partner. When the relationship becomes strained, generally through their aggressive behavior, they find themselves completely alone. *Their relational world is empty because their contact with other people was through their partner.* It is also for this reason that people with this organization—though capable of breaking up relationships—are reluctant to bring the relationship to an end and they accept a situation that fuels their anger and their feeling of shame. They feel marginalized, outcast or rejected by those they support, or ignored or tolerated by a partner who has often obtained his or her position of security and centrality thanks to their exclusive attentions, to their adoration, especially in the early period of the relationship. Yet despite their seething anger, they are generally reluctant to leave their partner.

241

Ferdinando, a 50-year-old advertising executive, was totally excluded by his family just before the development of his depression. A few years earlier he had achieved his ambition: to buy a large house that could be his home as well as his office, and finally to work with his wife. She had been opposed to her husband's plan for some time: She was head of public relations for a large company and was happy doing a job that gave her stimulating social contact, opportunities for travel, and an excellent salary. In the end, overtaken by enthusiasm for the new house, she had given in to the pressure from her husband but soon bitterly regretted it. She couldn't bear her loss of independence, nor having to deal with her husband's mood swings, and took advantage of every occasion to get out of the house. Ferdinando, disillusioned by his wife's behavior, became increasingly aggressive. As a result, his wife and children avoided him as much as they could, even arriving late for meals, eating as quickly as they could and leaving as soon as they had finished. He complained:

> I have to call them, shout for them to come for lunch or dinner. Ornella is worst of all. She's the last to arrive. Then as soon as they've gobbled it all down, they rush off like cockroaches when you switch on the light.

In the second configuration *future depressives are not only in the position of someone who is an outcast from their own family, but a witness at the same time to the inclusion of their partner into their own family, an inclusion which (as we shall see below) they themselves have never been able to enjoy.* Generally the partner has not intentionally sought to win over the patient's family, nevertheless patients feel their partner has robbed them of their own family:

Carlo was amazed when his parents invited him to take part in buying what we were, during the therapy, to describe as the "cage in the woods": an attractive small country villa surrounded by extensive gardens. As we discovered during the course of the therapy, Carlo had always felt alone. Though an only child, he had never felt accepted by his parents, Angelo and Angela. They were an ill-matched but close couple. She was a graphic designer, intellectually curious, politically committed and a feminist; he was a timid bank executive, without any talent or ambition, least of all intellectual. She repeatedly claimed to have *decided* to love her husband, whom she had known from childhood, implying that she had never felt any real interest in such an insignificant man. But she never went anywhere without him, and he followed her wherever she went: to political meetings, exhibitions, the theater. Carlo showed a chilly response to the invitation to share the house, but perhaps he was pleased he could finally share something with his parents. Chiara was enthusiastic about the project: the house was pretty and the financial conditions offered by her parents-in-law were advantageous: they paid all the expenses and the young couple were left only to pay off a small mortgage. Chiara had never received anything from her own parents, who were separated and in poor financial circumstances, and she felt grateful to her parents-in-law for their kindness and generosity.

As soon as the two couples moved into the house, the relationship between Chiara and her mother-in-law became very close. Carlo had never had such an intimate relationship with his mother, not even as a child. The two women seemed to understand each other well. Their alliance did not seem to upset Angelo's position as companion, who often joined them in good-natured criticism of Carlo, describing him as the "young master" who had been supported by parents who were always ready to lavish him with money and support. A sort of "adult" alliance developed between Carlo's parents and Chiara (who was six years older than Carlo and had had a difficult earlier life) in which Carlo was marginalized, what's more, placed moreover in the position of spoiled child. Carlo had certainly not even found himself in this situation as a boy: His childhood memories were of waiting at home for his parents who were always out; of distance from his father who never seemed to have any space for him; of afternoons spent playing alone in the yard; of the company of a deaf grandmother with whom it was impossible to communicate.

Carlo had begun to show signs of intolerance towards the situation at least a year before his depression: He no longer slept in Chiara's arms; he was sexually unresponsive; during meals with his parents he went off to work at his computer; he took long cycle rides alone. Most of all, it was the birth of Remo that made Carlo feel unwanted. The baby was underweight, not much larger than his hand. He was actively and emotionally involved at first. But he soon felt extraneous even to him. His mother, on the other hand, who had always warned them she would not look after their children, and had never been particularly interested in him, became morbidly attached to her grandchild. Born underweight and with an anomaly—he had no corpus callosum—this child had won over his grandmother, who had always felt a sympathy for those, like her husband, who were unfortunate in some way. This was the relational situation that had brought about the onset of Carlo's depression: Suddenly, as happens in serious depression, there was an eruption of despair:

> I was in the garden, trying to fix a step that had come loose. I went
> to fetch my tools and all of sudden I felt an excruciating pain—it was
> as if the weight of all the despair in the world had fallen on top of me
> and had sapped away my whole energy.

These two configurations, as well as the serious conflict between the couple that generally precedes the onset of depressive symptoms, can be better understood when interpreted in the light of the breakup between subjects with depressive organization and their family of origin which I have regularly encountered in my cases. Some of my patients had not broken off their association with their family, but their contact was in most cases rather formal. Others were in the position of black sheep since they had behaved in ways that their original family considered unacceptable.

Arianna,[10] for example, claimed she had been rejected and kept at a distance by her family, which had become traditionalist and sanctimonious after her eldest brother and her father had committed suicide. Her mother and brothers did not approve of her lifestyle in any way: Her decision to become a sculptor, though it had brought her recognition and financial gain, bound her to a bohemian world. Her refusal to have children became apparent when she admitted having an abortion, and they found her radical ideas as well as her emotional life disturbing. Everyone criticized her incomprehensible decision to leave a dependable and wealthy husband and to go and live with a journalist who they found arrogant, and was an avowed atheist. These choices reflected the unconventionality of her father, whose suicide her mother and brothers couldn't forgive.

Others seemed to have become self-marginalized. All of them, including those who had left their family of origin years earlier, felt an anger and resentment towards their parents and siblings, often masked by indifference. Sometimes they were unaware of the reasons for such violently negative feelings and this increased their negative evaluation of themselves.

Antonio had suffered morning insomnia for at least ten years before becoming seriously depressed. Unable to remain in bed, he walked the city streets waiting for the first bar to open where he could have breakfast and read the newspaper:

> My eye always wandered down to the deaths column. I was looking for the announcement of my father's death. I don't know why. The idea was absurd. I would have known if he were dead. Yet every morning I read the deaths column hoping to find my father's name there. He had never done me any harm, so why did I want to see him dead? And why, yesterday while he was on the balcony, did I have the idea of pushing him over? […] It was something more than an idea—I had half a mind to do it. Tell me: is there a difference between me and those people you read about in the papers who have killed their wife, their parents? I can't see any.

Patients' emotional distance from their family of origin, irrespective of the stories they had created, helps to explain the conflict with the partner. An affectional vacuum is in fact created that fuels expectations and demands for a total relationship with the partner. It induces patients, who have already experienced the pain of loss, not to end the relationship too quickly, even though breaking up relationships is, for them, a "permitted story." They fear abandonment: If the relationship does not work there is no longer a family of origin to welcome and support them. Moreover, the partner of many of my patients represents the only interpersonal relationship in which they were emotionally involved.

In short, the conflict with the family of origin means that patients with a depressive organization become excessively involved and committed in the relationship with their partner and this damages their ability to negotiate the rules of the relationship with the partner who, however, often has solid relations with his or her own parents and siblings. There is also the possibility (arising in the second configuration) of the partner, in the event of contact with the patient's family, developing a closer link with them than patients themselves have ever been able to achieve with their own family.

This closer examination of the context preceding the onset of symptoms enables us to move on several steps. It becomes clear, for example, why people prone to depression preserve a relationship for as long as possible, even though it gives them a feeling of shame. It also explains why these patients tend to expect a total relationship with the partner. But why have they never undergone such an extreme breakup with their original family? To answer this question, let us now examine the original intersubjective context as it is reconstructed by patients during the therapeutic process. This context has a direct role in the here and now when symptoms first appear in young adults who have not yet managed to develop a long-term emotional relationship.

6.5 Reconstructing the Original Triangle in Therapy

Since the 1990s, with the shift towards a predominantly biological approach, there has been a drastic decrease in research and clinical models concerning the intersubjective context of depressives. There was, however, a rise in the investigation of relational problems that affect children when one or both parents suffer from depression (Focht-Birkerts & Beardslee, 1996, 2000; Hamilton, Jones, & Hammen, 1993; Herring & Kaslow, 2002; Whiffen, Kerr, & Kalloss-Lilly, 2005). In any case, there is substantial agreement among clinicians and researchers that the relational experience of individuals with serious depression is marked by a failure in primary relationships.

The inability to establish a close relationship with at least one of the parents during childhood, adolescence, and early adulthood was regarded by Bowlby (1980) and also by some cognitivists (Bara, 1996; Guidano, 1987, 1991) as the root of the severe depression. This is consistent with a study by Brown, Harris, and Copeland (1977), from which it emerged that loss of, or separation from, the mother before the age of eleven increased the risk of depression in adulthood. Later research by Brown and others made it possible to clarify that the crucial variable was not so much the loss of the mother as the quality of subsequent care. The loss of the mother is therefore a factor that tends towards depression as it increases the risk of abandonment and abuse. Brown and his colleagues (Bifulco, Brown, & Harris, 1994; Brown, 2002) in fact discovered that the experiences of abandonment and abuse before the age of seventeen duplicated the risk of depression in adulthood.

Few of my patients had lost their mother during childhood, but many of them seem never to have succeeded in developing stable affectional bonds with anyone in their family. Others were unsuccessful in maintaining them during their development. The view that avoidant attachment patterns are the cause of chronic depression (Bowlby, 1980) is certainly plausible. It is, however, unspecific. Avoidant forms of attachment are to be found in other psychopathologies (Dozier et al., 2008). This aetiopathogenic view does not distinguish depressive organizations from pathological narcissism and other disorders. It does not explain why, for example, in depressed patients, despite the absence of stable affectional relationships in childhood, there is no trace of the emotional petrifaction and absence of empathy that characterizes pathological narcissism. And above all, Bowlby's hypothesis fails to cast light on why depressives have an ability to develop emotional relationships. This ability is unknown among narcissistic personality disorders and greater among these patients than in any other serious psychopathology (Linares & Campo, 2000).

During therapy, the reconstruction of the network of relationships among which my patients have positioned themselves as they grew up has highlighted a complex intersubjective context characterized by three components. This reconstruction, of course, makes no claim to objectivity. It describes, on the contrary, the way in which my patients, alone or with their families, reconstruct their relational history with a systemic therapist who, using at least a triadic heuristic, helps patients to link their personal emotions with what is happening in the interpersonal relationships in which they are involved.

1) The family context of the future patient generally consists of a couple who allow no space for vertical parent–child relationships. Future patients have therefore not been able to develop moments of intimacy with their parents during childhood and adolescence. In the family dynamic in which depressive organizations develop, not only is there no triangular relationship with the child—the future patient—but the child him/herself feels substantially ignored, as suggested by Linares and Campo (2000).

The parents can be a cohesive and well-functioning couple. In this case their boundaries are too rigid to allow space for the child who cannot find a positioning of any importance between the parents. Often the couple is not united in any way. Here, one frustrating partner—frequently a narcissistic personality—totally monopolizes the attention of the other who often adores him/her. The frustrated parent could, in theory, have a lot of emotional space for the child, given the emotional void left by the frustrating partner, who is the object of one-way adoration, but unfortunately he/she does not have such space. The difficulties in the relationship between the parents absorb all the frustrated parent's emotions, or their residual relational capacity is directed towards the other children. The result is that potential patients find no place for themselves with either parent. The parents of my patients were so varied that it was impossible to categorize them, though they shared two aspects: the emotional dynamic of the family was centered around the parents' own relationship—and the child who would become depressed was excluded from it.

2) The exclusion by a couple that focuses the family's emotional dynamic upon itself, and their lack of substantial concern for their parental roles, produce jealousy, envy and a rivalry in the child towards one or both parents. These feelings, generally experienced violently by my patients, are not in their view justified because the parents do not behave in a hostile or persecutory manner towards them, if anything they are aggressive towards the partner. The potential depressive is therefore forced by these emotions to develop a negative self-perception. Aggression, hatred and bitterness towards one or both parents, being in their eyes unjustified, give them a self-image of someone unworthy of love.

3) In this relational situation, an opportunity arises during childhood, adolescence or early adulthood for the future depressive to take a place among the "elect." It finally seems possible for him/her to establish a potentially exclusive and satisfying relationship with one of the parents or with another important member of the family. The future patient would, of course, be very happy to pass from the position of exclusion to one of being received and accepted. But the response of the adult with whom the future patient had sought inclusion is one of indignant refusal. The child's relational offer is rejected: the child is trying to usurp a position that is not his/her own. Sometimes the child is unable even to offer him/herself to the parent in the favored position because the other parent, with whom the child spends more time, blocks the relational move by condemning it as unworthy. In some cases it is the child who does not pursue the possibility of inclusion among the elect as he/she is convinced such a move would bring shame to one of the parents.

In all the situations mentioned above, future depressives find themselves in a relational position that produces a negative self-image: *Maintaining a position of exclusion, in fact, means experiencing feelings of rivalry, envy and jealousy towards a couple who is incapable of offering opportunities for emotional sharing. Attempting to move their positioning to among those who are loved, honored, accepted would nevertheless mean being unworthy, despicable.*

The death of a parent offers a particular opportunity for creating a relational situation with the ingredients I have described, as can be seen in this case.

Paola, who was 6 years old when her mother died of pulmonary cancer, felt no pain or sadness at her mother's death. When she began psychotherapy at the age of fifty she still had a clear recollection of the serious, grieving manner she had adopted during the funeral: The tragedy had suddenly placed her center-stage, the focus of everyone's concern and respect, and she played her part to the full. Unlike the older son, who was close to his mother, Paola had never managed to develop a bond with her: shortly after her birth, her mother, Beatrice, was taken ill and had delegated the care of the newborn child to her sisters-in-law. Paola's few memories of her mother indicated her hostility towards her: she remembered her as being possessive, impulsive and self-centered. Beatrice was twelve years younger than her husband, who adored her. Her death devastated him to such an extent that, according to Paola and her family, he developed tuberculosis in his grief for the loss of his wife. During his year in a sanatorium he certainly seemed more interested in joining his dead wife than in worrying about his young children and starting a new life. This was not the case for Paola, who had felt excluded for years, on the margins of a family where the mother was at the center of all her husband's attention. On her death Paola saw the possibility of finally gaining a position next to her father. The suffering that everyone saw in her position as orphan made them compare her with her mother and made her worthy of her father's attentions. Paola, like all children, was also more interested in the future: after her mother's death, she wanted to look ahead. Her mother now buried, when her father returned home eighteen months later, Paola sought to console him by offering herself as a substitute partner. Many episodes during her childhood were aimed towards this end: She even went as far as pretending to be ill to attract her father's attention. His response was always the same: an indignant refusal which signified: "How dare you think of substituting your mother!" Paola did not resemble her mother, except in her beautifully delicate hands. When, as an adolescent, she showed them to her father saying: "Look, they're just like my mother's," the reply she received was: "No, you must be joking, they're not like hers in the slightest"—as blunt as it was indignant.

The case I describe in detail below has the characteristics I have indicated as typical of those contexts not involving death. This is the most frequent situation among my patients.

6.6 "Crazy Alcoholic Whore"

This is how her ex-husband and parents-in-law regarded her. And Giulia introduced herself to me at the first meeting with their words, because it was better to be a "crazy alcoholic whore" than a "pathetic wretch."

This thirty-something had as many resources as she did psychological problems. Exuberant, highly intelligent, with a wild seductive charm, Giulia had been through two periods of in-patient treatment and as many suicide attempts, had been diagnosed as having bipolar disorder and also faced a lawsuit from her husband to prevent her having custody of their seven-year-old son, their only child. The risk of losing custody of Alberto was great. As well as the diagnosis of bipolar disorder and two attempted suicides, she was refusing to take medication, a decision that her ex-husband's lawyers were contesting.

I was taking more than forty drugs a day! Lithium in crazy quantities. They even tried to inject me five or six times a day! They must
have thought I was a guinea pig, I don't know [...] After eight days
I asked to be discharged and they let me out. Fortunately my father
supported me, otherwise who knows how long I'd have been there.
Straight away I replaced the forty pills with homeopathic cures. After
two months I stopped everything. What could I do? They thought I
should have been going about carrying a suitcase of drugs. They had
to be joking. I lifted up the toilet lid and flushed them away, all of
them, knowing I would have my highs and lows ... but I got rid
of all of them. Now I've been accused of failing to follow the therapy
of Prof. X ... that if I'd done so I'd have been cured. Bullshit! I'd have
been a vegetable! Since then I haven't taken a single pill. I can't even
stand the sight of them.

Above all, there were the repeated separations from her son, Alberto, who had
been left with his grandfather and his partner. The first occasion, after the acute
depressive phase and subsequent hospitalization, three years earlier, was an actual
abandonment. After a period in a community at the end of her treatment, Giulia
went to India, where she stayed for three months without making any contact.

Giulia was not an alcoholic, though she had abused alcohol at certain times
in her life, especially beer. Nor had she ever been sexually promiscuous, but
during her short-lived marriage there was no lack of extra-marital relationships
and after the separation, five years before the beginning of therapy, she seemed
unable to find a lasting relationship. When I met her she had been living with
a 21-year-old Latin American for a year, a union that had further exacerbated
relations with her ex-husband and his family.

Realizing she had many problems, Giulia had begun various therapies, abandoning all of them after a few sessions. I do not think we would have continued seeing each other for two years, as we did, if it had not been that Giulia was
in danger of losing Alberto whom she loved. Alberto was also very attached to
her, and to his maternal grandfather. This was why her lawyers had sent her to
me: they were well aware of the difficulties Giulia had in looking after Alberto
but feared that allowing custody to the father, who lived with his partner thousands of kilometers away, could be disastrous for the child as well as for Giulia.
And they were uncertain what position to take, all the more since Alberto had
learning difficulties. Would he be able to deal with another setback?

Let us examine the interpersonal context in which Giulia lived until she was
19 years old. It is also the context to which the onset of symptoms relates,
which I will consider later. The serious episode that led to her full-blown
depression three years before the beginning of therapy was entirely bound up
with relationships within her own family of origin, even though it had taken
place after the breakdown of an emotional relationship.

The Original Intersubjective Context

It was hard for women to have a respectable positioning in the Albertini family. In Giulia's family, where the paternal branch had a clearly dominant role, the men had a destiny. Some were the elect, kissed by fortune, showered by wealth, like her paternal grandfather and her uncle. Others were rebels, persecuted, cast out, but able to survive if they were fortunate. The black sheep could always pick themselves up again, as had happened to Giulia's father. The women, instead, remained a part of the group only so long as they enjoyed the benevolence of their men and followed the rules. This was the case with her father's partner, Beatrice, and her paternal aunt. If they lost favor, or came into conflict with the men, they were ignored, abandoned and cast aside, as happened to Giulia's mother and her paternal grandmother. This was how Giulia presented her extended family with whom she lived until she was nineteen, becoming a black sheep in her attempt to find an identity, even if it was a negative one, though it was an identity all the same, for which she was nevertheless rejected. In her family, as she told me straight way, if the black sheep were women, they had no rights at all:

PT: I have the character of my father and my grandfather.

TH: In what ways are you alike?

PT: We are hot-headed, tough. But I'm a woman, unfortunately … If I were a man it would be different … My grandma, out of her five grandchildren, would prefer me deep down since I'm a black sheep like her son. In a certain sense her husband was also a black sheep. She always preferred my father to my uncle. But unfortunately I'm a woman and for her I'm worth less than nothing.

TH: But what did you do to become a black sheep?

PT: That's how it is. Then I broke all the traditions, I did what even the men are not allowed to do. I was the first in my family to seek a divorce. I'm the only one who doesn't care what people think. I've been given a really hard time. I know what they think. I know even without them saying a thing, without ever seeing them, because we're of the same blood …

During Giulia's childhood and adolescence, the Albertini family lived in two villas enclosed by a large garden: Her grandfather lived in one villa with one son's family while her grandmother lived in the other with the other son's family. Giulia's grandparents had in fact been separated for years. Her grandfather was the "elect": courted, revered, feared by everyone. Though uneducated, he had built up a company producing electrical materials that were exported throughout the world, and had become one of the region's most important industrialists. He was considered a genius. His granddaughter's descriptions of him were reminiscent of Beckett's novel *Watt*. As with Mr Knott, it was impossible to try to understand this reclusive, unfathomable man, in relation to whom the family were in the position of Watt, servants incapable of finding any sense in their master's behavior.

PT: He was the king. It was his manner ... Even now, if you ask my grandfather's friends (some of them are still alive) they'll say: "When your grandfather spoke, the whole of Italy fell silent."

TH: Why did "the whole of Italy fall silent"? Was he authoritarian, were they frightened of him?

PT: I don't know. I haven't the faintest idea. I live with my grandfather but I don't see him; I'm the favorite granddaughter but I never see him. He doesn't eat with us in the kitchen, he eats in the sitting room, served on silver plates.

TH: Ah, you eat in the kitchen with the servants and he's alone in the sitting room?

PT: Yes, we used to eat in the kitchen. It was a lovely kitchen, large ... the maid sometimes used to eat with us, sometimes not. Then there was nanny who was like a mother to me. I still go and visit her—there's no formality between us.

TH: And him?

PT: He was served by the maid and by my grandmother's step-sister. This step-sister of my grandmother prepared the food and made sure he had everything he wanted. She was an excellent cook, completely at his service.

TH: Why did he eat alone?

PT: I don't know. That's how he liked it. Never the same food for lunch and evening, when he was at home of course, because often he was away.

TH: And when your father arrived on Saturday evening?

PT: He ate in the kitchen with us.

TH: And at Christmas?

PT: I never spent Christmas with my grandfather.

TH: That seems strange ...

PT: [laughs] ... but for me it was normal. No one ever dared to say a word about my grandfather. I was very fortunate, I lived in an enormous villa, and it was clear to me even then that the situation I was in was all due to my grandfather.

TH: He was almost a god?

PT: He was more than that. He *was* a god. He was a genius. Just think ... he left school at fourteen and yet he spoke perfect French. I don't know where and how he learnt it.

TH: It must have been very hard for your mother to live in that house.

PT: Yes, and now she says: "God, how I suffered with that man. I couldn't do a thing. I was always worried when he was about because you couldn't make a noise or shout ..." There had to be absolute silence when he was around, we couldn't breathe.

TH: A torment …

PT: Yes. For her it was torture, but I only realized that afterwards. For me he was "the big boss.".. he's the big boss even now because I still see him as I did when I was a young girl. Perhaps I'm still grateful to him because they say he preferred me to the other four grandchildren. It's hard to believe.

For decades, Giulia's grandmother was completely excluded from her husband's life. Her mother had died when she was young, and she was turned out of the house when she became pregnant with Giulia's father. Her marriage to the patriarch took place only after the birth of their second child and after she had contracted a syphilitic infection transmitted by her husband, which made her lame. She helped her husband make his fortune, assisting him in the early stages of his rise before being forgotten, but not abandoned: "[My grandfather] made sure she lacked nothing: She had given him two sons" and she retained a sort of canine devotion towards him. Everyone knew he had a mistress with whom he travelled, but no one knew, or dared to ask, who this woman was.

This story provides the background to the stormy marriage between Giulia's parents, Veronica and Giacomo. Added to the couple's own problems was Giacomo's conflict with his father. Giacomo and his younger brother worked with the patriarch, whose favorite was the brother. The brother was deferent towards his father, lively, fun-loving, likeable: "Kissed by fortune, he always lived a life of luxury, doing very little." Giacomo could not bear his father's authority and when Giulia was not yet three he moved to Milan where he founded his own company, independent but affiliated with his father's. "If I cannot be king here, I'll be a prince in Milan," he had said, or at least that is how the family story went. His wife and children were left in the villa where, at first, he returned for a couple of evenings during the week, but later only at weekends—he never missed a single weekend until Giulia was nineteen. The marriage was already in difficulty by the time of his move to Milan: "I never saw my parents sleep together in the same bed and I always saw my mother alone and desperate when he left."

When Giulia was conceived, Beatrice, the woman who was to become her father's companion, was already on the scene. They were to marry thirty-five years later, when Giulia's therapy was coming to an end, but their meeting and courtship caused an immediate and irreparable break between Giulia's parents. This at least was the patient's version:

All my spite, my anger against my mother is for this whole thing. I told her: "You're an idiot, what were you doing conceiving me! I don't care a damn if you're religious, if you believe in marriage or if you believe in God. What were you doing conceiving me when you knew my Dad had already been with another woman for two years; are you crazy? Allow him at least to conceive me with the other woman, give me the chance to be born ... at least I'd have had ... I'll say nothing, you're a mother and that's fine—but at least I'd have another mother and my father. Why do you have to make me suffer before I'm even born?" [...] Because then it was my father who wanted the second child, not my mother. But it's madness all the same. If my ex-husband had said to me: "I want another child from you", I'd have said: "No, my dear, no, forget it, if anything I'll have one with my current partner."

Although her father wanted her, Giulia was convinced she had been an obstacle in his relationship with Beatrice, and that this was the reason why, for many years, he had concealed her existence from his companion. Moreover, her mother gave up her job as a teacher when she was born, becoming completely absorbed within the Kafkaesque family situation.

Her parents' matrimonial situation must have been more complex than it later seemed to Giulia. Although her father gradually reduced the length of his stays, he was to spend every weekend with his official family for more than twenty-five years, even after the patriarch had died. Furthermore, twenty years were to pass before the relationship between Giulia's father and his companion was brought into the open and the children informed, and it was thirty years before he applied for separation and divorce.

It was certainly a devastating blow for Giulia's mother. Betrayed, confined within her husband's estate, Veronica was to experience serious psychological difficulties, passing from one "nervous breakdown" to another after the death of her father-in-law who had guaranteed her status of official wife. It was a difficulty that remained. When the therapy began, Veronica was still living in the villa with her aged mother-in-law, living a life between impotent anger, railing against her husband, and psychotropic drugs.

PT: My mother now comes out with these stories: "I'm not going to give him a divorce." She comes out with these stories, after thirty, forty years [...] It's incredible. I don't know how she can fail to understand the effect these things have on me and my brother ... It's terrible, really terrible.

It is hardly necessary to point out that Giacomo and Veronica had no positive space to give to Giulia and her brother during their childhood and adolescence. Giacomo was too busy making good his own position. Having abandoned his father's company, he had to succeed in his own business so as to overcome his family's rejection. For a long time the competitive battle with his father and brother and his double emotional life gave him neither the time nor the energy to worry about his children. For her part, Veronica's suffering was ever greater and she found herself incapable of looking after the children. Having stopped teaching, being relegated to the claustrophobic world of the two villas, constantly comparing her life with the happiness of her brother-in-law's family, she ended up becoming completely absorbed by her marital misfortunes. She was the daughter of a respectable middle-class city family, clever at school, her parents' favorite, admired by her brother: unlike Giulia's paternal grandmother she was psychologically unprepared to deal with such a frustrating and humiliating situation. And no one helped her, while there was still a chance to get out of the claustrophobic world that was destroying her—neither her parents, who stepped away, disorientated by the vast difference between the financial circumstances of the two families, nor her brother, who was devoted to her but went no further than offering love and understanding, without encouraging her to take any firm decisions.

Giulia and her brother Edoardo, who was four years older, both inevitably suffered. They hardly saw their father. Every day they watched the pain and solitude of their mother, and their more fortunate cousins whose parents were happily married and enjoying life. Of the two, Giulia was the one who was truly alone. Edoardo was their grandmother's favorite grandson and had a close relationship with his mother, even though the roles were reversed: it was Edoardo who looked after his mother, rather than the other way round. It was he who sought to remain close to her and acted as her confidant. What was more, on reaching adolescence, his father began to take an interest in him, offering him a job in his company and introducing him to his mistress during a vacation. When the patriarch died, Edoardo's father sought at least to involve his son in his life.

Giulia was ignored and excluded from all these family relationships: she was younger, and a woman. Being born a girl in that family meant being rejected by the only adult capable of showing any care, the paternal grandmother, whose bias towards the men of the family was just as strong when it came to the younger generation. She was forever thankful for having given birth to two boys. She had no interest in girls: "Give me ten boys to look after, not a girl," she said.

Incest between Giulia and her brother developed in this context of solitude. Giulia, aged eleven when it began, was excluded by her grandmother, her mother was concerned only about her broken marriage, her father's invitations were made only to her brother. She no longer enjoyed the benevolence of her grandfather, who had recently died. In her usual provocative manner, Giulia was to describe it as "the best sexual relationship in my life." In reality it was something that weighed on her. Heavily. When her symptoms first appeared, it is no surprise that she threw it in her parents' faces, as we shall see. The incest lasted two years. Their mother, who knew about it, did nothing. Giulia, moreover, claimed to have been the prime mover. This seems unlikely, given that her brother was four years older. But she certainly played an active role in the affair, whose motivations were quite understandable: Giulia was able to break out of her exclusion and solitude through the incestuous relationship. The price she paid was the construction of an intransitivity between belonging and dignity. *She found that being excluded was intolerable but the only possible way of being included—incest—rendered her unworthy.*

From her experience of incest, Giulia also began to position herself as a black sheep in the family, in opposition to her mother, whose honesty and purity had not saved her from her fate of lone expectation. The incest was to play a major part in modeling Giulia's personality, characterizing it as a depressive organization, but this did not lead her to psychopathology. Once the incestuous relationship was over, her adolescence and early adulthood were a positive period. She was finally able to leave the confines of the Albertini estate: other contacts, outside the family, were finally possible. Giulia was extrovert, attractive, the first to be invited to parties and the first to accept: "I was cheerful, energetic. I certainly had plenty of admirers and friends."

At nineteen, her father offered her a job in the company. She was overjoyed: "My father was my idol." Giacomo was his mother's favorite, the man whose wife, Veronica, was desperately trying to win him back. And he was also the black sheep who had succeeded: his company was now prospering. But Giulia's happiness was not to last: a month after joining her father's company, he introduced her to Beatrice. Having been kept in the dark about her father's double life, and having been hostile towards her mother, she began to reconsider Veronica's behavior in the light of this betrayal and to see her as a woman destroyed by her husband. This process wasn't going on just in Giulia's mind. Veronica involved her daughter in the torments of her married life. Devastated by her husband's decision to reveal his relationship with Beatrice to his daughter, which he regarded as the final step towards legal separation and divorce, Veronica told her everything. Giulia was deeply shaken. *In the light of her mother's revelations, the idea of belonging to her father's world, of finally taking a place in the Albertini family, meant destroying her mother.* And though Giulia yearned to be part of her father's world, she could not taint herself with what she saw as a crime. She took her mother's side. Her brother had already managed to find a means of retaining contact with his father without betraying his mother: he worked with Giacomo but did not spend any other time with him since he did not accept Beatrice. Giulia was unable to consider such an option, and preferred exclusion to shame. The break between father and daughter was sealed when he slapped her across the face in response to her accusations of disgraceful behavior. Only with the onset of symptoms was there any attempt at reconciliation.

Giulia's exclusion was a heavy blow for her, all the more since her brother worked in the company and her mother was giving her no financial or emotional support. It began a period of instability marked by travel abroad and short-lived relationships. Two suicide attempts suggest that Giulia was already clinically depressed. Her encounter with her future husband brought this troubled phase of the patient's life to an end. The marriage seemed to offer an opportunity for a new start: Her husband was the son of an illustrious family, less wealthy than her own but educated and with better social connections. But the marriage was short-lived: it was brought to an end after a few years of excessive quantities of beer and mutual betrayal. Her husband was reluctant to agree to the divorce: He wanted to retain control over their son but was happy that she didn't follow him abroad. She therefore remained alone in Milan, in the apartment owned by her parents-in-law, who lived in the same building. When her new companion moved into the apartment with her, her relations with her parents-in-law deteriorated. She also felt angry when her father gave her brother a luxurious apartment as a gift, while she herself was still in such difficult circumstances. But she was also furious with her mother, who gave her no help in looking after her young child. When her companion left, her already precarious state of mind became worse.

The Onset of Symptoms

Her entry into the full-blown pathology was played out entirely within her family of origin. Giulia felt she could no longer manage, was wracked by insomnia, highly anxious and agitated. She thought her whole life from the age of eleven onwards had been completely wrong, a sham. She rang Veronica: "Mum, I need you!" Her mother replied, as she had always done: "My child, I'm more poorly than you, I can't help." Giulia felt lost: "And who'll look after me?" She realized she couldn't stay alone; she was no longer able to take responsibility for Alberto:

> I felt a howl which rose from my toenails up to the ends of my hair. I wanted to go up a mountain, on top of the world, and yell out. Let me cry out like a child, I need to cry out, I need to! My body needs to cry out, physically. But I can't. What would my four-year-old child see … a mother in tears? No, I can't go crazy in front of my child; my feelings of guilt prevent me. It brings back pictures of my mother screaming in front of me because my father had gone. I can't do the same thing to my child.

Giulia decided to arrange for both of her parents to visit her home in the presence of a psychotherapist. When they both arrived she began shouting, unburdening herself: "I'm going to say everything, because I'm no longer interested in pushing all the blame on my mother." She realized that her father knew nothing about the incest, or about her two attempted suicides. "I went into the kitchen at a certain point, and from there I heard him say to my mother: 'But how could you have kept this from me?'" The things that Giulia threw

256

in her parents' faces were true, but she was agitated, she could not control her emotions. It was clear she could not look after a four-year-old child. Her mother, as usual, avoided the issue. "For the first time my father enters my life and says: 'I'll take your child'."

The psychotherapist pointed out to her parents that they could not leave Giulia alone in this state. Giulia agreed. "No one wants me. Who do I go to? Not even my mother will take me. Alright, then I'll say it. Put me in hospital!"

Hospital, for Giulia, meant regaining her father, but losing her mother: "For me it opens one world, but closes another. I find my father, lose my mother." Mother and daughter didn't speak to each other for two years, not even by telephone. Giulia could not forgive her mother for failing to let her return home at that dramatic moment. And she was grateful to her father and his companion for looking after Alberto. She was well aware how difficult it was for a man of 65 and a woman of 60 (someone who had never had children, and who for many years hadn't even known about Giulia's existence) to take responsibility for a child of four years. They had only met Alberto twice when they took him to live with them. Giulia was also grateful to her father for visiting her every day during her stay in hospital and helping her to be discharged as soon as she had regained some self-control. *But she made no attempt to find a place within the Albertini family.* She left for India. This was to be the most dramatic three months of her life. It almost ended badly. In the end her will to live prevailed. She returned. She was happy that an extraordinary understanding had developed between grandfather and grandson. *Finally at least her son had found a positioning among the elect.* She liked Beatrice and admitted she thought of her as a second mother: "She was my father's woman, she shared everything with him, they still love each other." So she was pleased that Beatrice had carried out a maternal role towards her child. She left Alberto with them for another year. But she remained on the sideline; she did not want to be included among the Albertini family, even though her father once again offered her a job with his company. She could only involve her father when she had been really ill, when she was in no condition to look after her child and needed a psychotherapist beside her to confirm she was sick.

Giulia wouldn't have found it difficult to work in her father's company: She was educated, knew four languages and had good communication skills. And it was what she most desired. But she could not do it: to work in his company would have meant being unworthy because it would have been a final blow for her mother. Seeking a divorce made her feel guilty towards her mother, convinced as she was that her father had done the same thing only after she had broken the taboo that had existed in the family for three generations. This, of course, was not true. Times had simply changed. Divorce in Italy was now legal and the number of divorces and step families was increasing there as in every other developed country. But statistics and rational arguments would not mitigate that mixture of anger, despair and impotence that Giulia had always felt in the face of her mother's anguish, and that formed an insurmountable obstacle to her belonging to the Albertini world. When she began therapy, Giulia was highly antagonistic towards her mother. But a telephone call was all it took to send her to pieces. This is her account of what happened, just after the beginning of the therapy, when her mother telephoned to ask forgiveness for having unloaded her despair onto her:

> I couldn't sleep last night. For me it was something ... I'm completely confused. My mother telephoned and said: "Forgive me for the wrong I've done you." My reaction, what was it? "No, you don't have to ask my forgiveness. Please Mum, you don't have to say these things to me." I felt awkward, I felt really ill. I've been waiting for these words for 33 years and now I'm in pieces. She said this yesterday afternoon at two thirty, and since then I haven't been able to eat or sleep. I don't know what's happening to me. Three years ago I had finished with her, for me she was dead ...

It wasn't so much her attachment to her mother that had made Giulia so fragile. Throughout her life she had never managed to establish a firm relationship with her. What bound them was Veronica's suffering, along with the aggression she had always felt towards her, an aggression she had in the end always felt to be unjustified. Veronica had never behaved harshly towards her daughter. Quite simply she had always been too unhappy to look after her. This was also why Giulia could only move closer to the Albertini family when she was depressed. In her own words: "The most beautiful relationship I had with my father was when I was ill." But not even her depression allowed her to feel a sense of belonging to that world. Giulia seemed content, however, to have found a place in that world where her son could belong.

6.7 Resources in Depressive Organizations

Depression, and the specific kind of depression I have considered in this chapter, has undoubted links with the melancholy of the Ancients, treated by Hippocrates and Galen, and studied by Aristotle, Galen, Avicenna, John Cassian and many others. Nor is it very different from the melancholy of the Renaissance period, the subject of essays by Marsilio Ficino, Timothy Bright and Robert Burton, and masterfully painted by Durer.[11] It certainly doesn't seem a pathology limited to the West alone. It seems to have spread everywhere, but its frequency varies much from country to country, as is shown by the accurate trans-cultural studies by Brown and his colleagues (Brown, 2002). Mammals who live in a group—monkeys of course, but also others including the opossum—also seem to display "depressive" behavioral patterns, especially where there is a loss of status. It therefore seems reasonable to suppose that "depressive" behavior is part of the evolutionary history of mammals and has, as I have already mentioned, an adaptive significance.

Implicit in depression there is therefore no cultural premise typical of the West today. Hobbes, Descartes, Leibnitz's monads with no doors or windows, or Schopenhauer's *noluntas* are in no way responsible. On the contrary, underlying this psychopathology there seems to be an essentially pre-modern premise that individuals are inextricably bound to a group of relationships, generally those with their own family of origin. People with a depressive organization construe their own exclusion from the group (real or supposed) as a disgrace, an irreparable injury that harms their personal dignity, like the disruption of a natural order that destroys their personal future once and for all. This is also why the depression I have considered in this chapter, which has little to do with sadness or simple low spirits, is not widespread, as indeed it was not in antiquity.

It is therefore interesting at this point to discuss an issue that I think is much ignored—the resources of depressive organizations. All organizations have specific resources connected to the semantics and positioning of the patient. The semantics of power, for example, gives those for whom it is relevant the capacity to "co-position" themselves in work situations; these people are able to understand the dynamics of power that characterize large and small organizations and to behave accordingly. Anorexics, bulimics and those who position themselves in the positively valued pole in this semantics also possess an extraordinary will and determination, as well as a motivation for success, which are the necessary pre-requisites for personal achievement in almost all fields.

At first sight, nothing seems less resourceful than depression. In reality, the semantics of belonging and the position experienced by the individual with depressive organization during childhood or adolescence offers, as it does for the other semantics we have looked at, certain important resources which may be used during the course of therapy. We find them by reconstructing both the way these patients function and their life stories. Certain possibilities are also to be found within the limitations in this organization.

The exclusion experienced in the family of origin often allows those with a depressive organization to live their adolescence and early adulthood with fewer problems than during childhood. In less pathological situations, access to worlds outside the family provides them with that possibility for belonging that had been denied them in their family of origin. To grow up, and to grow up fast, is often what these people yearn. Having no close ties nor triangulations, the release from the family of origin that is necessary in adolescence or early adulthood (at least to a certain extent) is for them a "permitted story" and often very exciting. Leaving home, which is generally a difficult moment, for example, for phobic organizations, poses no problems for depressive organizations.

This opportunity of involving themselves in contexts outside the family can, of course, prove dangerous. Such individuals can, for example, end up depending emotionally on their circle of friends to the point of indulging in self-destructive actions in order to belong, or they can form too early and harmful intimate relationships. There are, of course, many risks but the affectional vacuum that subjects with this organization have left behind gives them a strong incentive to build new conversational situations.

Above all, what young people with this organization want is to create an exclusive intimate relationship. Even in the later stages of life, including old age, the central objective of these people is sharing and intimacy with their partner. Having no important links with their own family of origin, people with this organization generally soon enter intimate, often all-absorbing, relationships. The experience of living in contexts where the intimacy of the couple was so central—sometimes sought only by one of the partners, as in Giulia's family, but nevertheless of key importance—provides even those who are excluded from it with emotional registers. Perhaps the very experience of having been excluded makes the relationship even more desirable.

Romantic fusional love, as it is understood today, where each is the center of the other person's universe, is certainly a feeling typical of depressive organizations. The future depressive's expectations for a total relationship, as well as the difficult relational history with the family of origin, expose such relationships to the risk of disaster. The result is often conflict with the partner. Nonetheless, the interest individuals prone to depression have in the relationship, and their capacity for fusion and intimacy, provide valuable resources. First of all for themselves. Even patients who are seriously ill—as I have already emphasized in agreement with Linares and Campo (2000)—are frequently able to construct and maintain the relationship as a couple. But also in therapy: while the family of origin will probably be unwilling to involve themselves in the therapy process and to renegotiate a different positioning with the depressed patient, the partner is usually a fundamental resource in the therapy process because of his/her emotional tie to the patient. I am often astonished at the willingness by partners who have been the subject of a patient's violence, insults and provocations, to forget the past and try once again to reconstruct the relationship. The fusional capacity of people with depressive organizations is a powerful attraction for the partner. Apparently hopeless situations between couples can take an unexpectedly positive turn during the course of therapy, and far more frequently than happens with other psychopathologies. This is also thanks to the initiative taken by the depressed patient who, though often responsible for destructive behavior within the relationship, on seeing the emotional commitment of the partner, resolves to repair and rebuild a relationship that often becomes one of renewed passion.

CONCLUSION:
THERAPEUTIC PERSPECTIVES

7

FAMILY SEMANTICS AND THE THERAPEUTIC RELATIONSHIP

7.1 And What Position Does the Therapist Take?

The reader may already have wondered this and might, I imagine, already have an answer. It is clear, in fact, that the therapist and the experience of therapy itself end up being positioned in the dominant semantics in the family conversation. It is impossible also in individual treatment for therapists not to position themselves in the semantics within which patients have learnt to place themselves in their families. If it is true that the patient's conversation with the family is organized around very different meanings, fuelled by specific emotions, as I have suggested in this book, then the therapist will also find herself taking a position, often unknowingly, in the dominant semantics when interacting with the client. This is confirmed by the results of a study we have carried out on the transcripts of the first two sessions with sixty patients (Ugazio et al., 2011). *We do not, therefore, have a single way of building up the therapeutic relationship, but have as many different ways as the number of semantics.* The therapeutic relationship is constructed distinctively by each semantic of freedom, of goodness, of power and of belonging. There are as many differences in the therapeutic alliance, the rifts created within it, the dysfunctional circuits, as the number of semantics that prevail. What I suggest is not just that patients with the four psychopathologies considered in this book construe the relationship in a particular way. Patients with psychopathologies other than the ones I have considered here, or with existential problems, if they belong to conversational contexts dominated by one of the four semantics I have described, will also construe the therapeutic relationship in a way more or less similar to other patients typified by these semantics. *The crucial variable that shapes the therapeutic relationship is not so much the psychopathology but the dominant semantics in the patient's conversational contexts.* Let us consider, by way of example, the very different positions in which therapists end up when the semantics of freedom or power are dominant.

Therapy: Exploration and Protection

When the semantics of freedom dominates, as generally happens in conversation with phobic patients and their families, but also in other clinical situations, therapists, especially at the beginning of treatment, will find themselves positioned in the "freedom" pole. Like it or not, they will end up in the position of someone, for example, who encourages the patient to break away from oppressive ties and widen their horizons. For this very reason they will have to deal with patients' fear of therapy. Phobic patients, like other members of their families who are positioned in the "attachment, need for protection" pole, are frightened of therapy above all because it is a new experience. This is an aspect that makes it disturbing, yet attractive, especially in the eyes of phobic patients who would like to conquer their fears and learn how to move in unfamiliar surroundings. The specter of dependence on therapists, the fear of being influenced by them, the concern about being encouraged to venture out into a world in which they might be defenseless, make individual therapy a particularly frightening and, intriguing experience.

As a result of these worries, patients' requests for an individual therapy generally take the form of a *cautious exploration*, often followed by a swift distancing. Patients return after several months. I think it is no coincidence that many of my patients were uncertain about their future at the time they asked for therapy. Some were considering going abroad for study or work, while others were about to move to another city or, because of a change in their job or work responsibilities, did not know whether they would be able to take time off for the sessions. These were all situations that limited involvement to one consultation until the patient had a clearer idea about what the future held in store. The therapeutic aims have to be limited: time constraints allow no space for doing any more. This is what happened with Emilio, who I described in detail in Chapter 3.[1] As you may remember, the first contact took the form of a consultation of four sessions: a therapy couldn't be started as he intended to move to Rome. His plans were unrealistic, given the seriousness of his symptomatology, but their pragmatic effect was clear: to delay the beginning of the therapy, which in fact began a few months later.

Equally significant from this point of view was the way in which Alessandro's therapy began. His onset of symptoms, which I described in the opening pages of this book,[2] coincided, as often happens in young phobics, with a failed attempt to move away from his family.

At the age of seventeen, Alessandro got rid of his watch as well as many rules and routines, including church on Sunday with his parents, and family meals. The process of emancipation suddenly took off when he started university in Milan, and moved into an apartment there. Alessandro freed himself completely from timetables and family restrictions, asserting his independence above all through travel. Suitcases became the dominant theme in his life. Alessandro never refused an invitation. He organized trips around Italy and abroad, or travelled alone where his fancy took him, ready to change plans if another more exciting opportunity arose. This itinerant life reached its culmination during an Erasmus scholarship in London. Independence was transformed there into vagrancy. London became a base for aimless wanderings around various parts of Europe:

> I roamed about, hitching lifts, going here, going there, a thousand kilometers ... two thousand. For me it was enough just to see new places and people. Maybe I didn't eat for two days, and now and then I went without sleep. I stayed one month with one girl, a fortnight with another, I met lots of people. And he added, I felt really independent, I was independent but directionless ... I was just drifting.

The onset of symptoms, in Amsterdam while he was smoking a joint, led to his return home. At first Alessandro tried to resist, and remained in London where he was involved in his first meaningful relationship: this time he had fallen in love. The symptoms however were enormous: if he went out by himself he had frightening panic attacks, anxiety crises, disorientation, and cold sweats, added to which were shifts in perception: "While I was walking, I was in London, I looked up: the houses were all crooked. I looked at them and said to myself "No, they're straight!" But they still look crooked to me ..."

When he was no longer able to go out alone, even for a few steps, he returned to his parents in Italy. Back home, after a few weeks of relative calm, as soon as he tried to leave the house, the panic attacks returned. As his stay with his family continued he also began to experience vomiting, suicidal thoughts, and depression. Several times he ended up in hospital. It was the local psychiatrists who referred him to me. For reasons I understood only during the course of the therapy, Alessandro was convinced he had an illness far more serious than a phobic disorder. Feelings of depersonalization had led him to think he was suffering from a serious psychosis, and he was petrified.

Given the dramatic nature of his account and his symptoms, I was amazed when, while questioning him about his expectations, I realized Alessandro was very uncertain about the idea of beginning psychotherapy:

> Seeing that you ask, I'll be honest: I'm frightened of a prolonged course of therapy. I waited before contacting you, though I've had your phone number several months. Starting something which you don't know when it will finish, it's frightening. The idea that among so many commitments ... university, things to do ... there's also a person, stuck there, who you have to go to on that particular day, at that time ... it worries me. [...] I just can't say: "Tomorrow I'll see you at three o'clock." I'll say it, then maybe at three I'll be there ... If it's something important, like coming here, I'll write the appointment on

the calendar, make reminder notes. But it's something I don't much like, I am not used to it... my days aren't planned out.

Alessandro was also frightened about dependence on therapy:

> I'm also frightened about tying myself down too much to this relationship. My ex-girlfriend in London wasn't able to decide anything without her psychotherapist, yet she was tough.

Even more worrying for Alessandro was the fear of being changed, altered. It's a fear we find in many who are used to positioning themselves in contexts where the semantics of freedom prevails. Having been sheltered too long by protective ties, they often feel they are not fully developed, and therefore liable to be altered by contact with people who for them become essential. This fear emerged little by little. Firstly with a reassessment of his "illness," which completely astonished me, seeing that he had presented his symptoms as totally debilitating and the last three years as an inferno:

> This period of crisis has also given me things ... (...) Even my symptoms ... I don't know whether I really want to get rid of them completely, they are a part of me (...). No, I don't expect to overcome them. Nor do I want to (...) I have also learned many things ... I have learned to understand myself better. I have understood my mother better, I have learned things about her which have brought us closer. Yes, the way I am now. ... no, I'm not too badly off... (...) there have also been positive things.

Alessandro finally went as far as saying: "I don't want to change. Basically, I like being as I am, the idea of becoming different frightens me."

Rather than resolving his problems, Alessandro wanted to find ways, through therapy, of keeping them under control:

> What bothers me is not so much the crises, but not understanding them, not knowing how to manage them, feeling helpless, in the grip of panic (...) Once I have reached an understanding of how to deal with things, then I could look after myself ... I could stop and say: "Hold on a minute, now I'll try psychoanalyzing myself."

Alessandro was asking for a consultation, not therapy. His aim was to learn how to deal with his symptoms, not to free himself from them:

> What I haven't got are the instruments that'd let me understand how these things get inside me and then bring out this physical sickness in

me. I have to learn not to be taken over by fear. And to do this I have to rely on a person, on you, and try to be as clear and honest as possible.

Alessandro would have clearly liked to "trust" me, but he was terrified because he had placed me in the "freedom and independence" pole. He expected to be helped to free himself from the ties he considered to be binding, but for that very reason he was frightened of therapy. All that was left was for me to agree a few sessions of consultation with the aim of putting the patient into a position to control his symptoms. It would then be for Alessandro to decide whether to continue the experience. The removal of escape routes for a person who had grown up in a context where the semantics of freedom prevails increases the likelihood of dropping out. The therapeutic alliance can only be established when the patient is sure of being able to go in and out of therapy without it compromising the relationship with the therapist. For patients in whom the semantics of freedom is dominant, therapy can only begin, as Bowlby (1988) pointed out, when the therapist provides a "secure base" from which they can move closer or further away with a certain liberty.

Even where patients feel they can exercise at least partial control over the therapeutic setting, this does not in itself place the therapist at the more reassuring "protection, safety" pole. Psychotherapy is seen by society as an experience that promotes freedom of personal expression and liberates sexuality from oppressive taboos. Likewise, patients who are seeking to distance themselves from oppressive protective bonds, or to overcome overwhelming limits, have the same expectations. This means that the therapist is almost always placed for a long period at the freedom-independence pole. This positioning is not without its dangers. The difficult situation in which I found myself with Emilio clearly shows the risks of this position. At each session during the first stage of therapy, this young man reported improvements in his symptomatology without there being any significant changes in his life. My impression, and that of my team, was that he tended to exaggerate them. I also felt I was being treated with the deference paid to someone who is seen as dangerous—with whom one wants to maintain a relationship, but from a safe distance. His account of the death of his cat, with which he began the fifteenth session, left my colleagues and me in no further doubt. Emilio was frightened of me.

> "I never let the cat go out," he said pathetically. "I talked to a friend of mine about the cat and the parallel me-cat/ me-my mother. My friend persuaded me to let it go out. Twenty-four hours later it was gone: it had been run over by a car. I knew it… When I let it out, I'd said goodbye as if I wouldn't see it again. I felt that by letting it out as it wanted—it was on heat—I was exposing it to risks. Now I blame myself. I was wrong in the timing and the way I did it. I was rash and hasty."

Emilio seemed to be saying to me: "Dear Doctor, if I choose freedom as you would like it, this is how it all ends: on the roadside, stone dead like my cat. Freedom is alright, but go gently!"

The patient had persuaded me to follow his emancipative projects. I too expected him to leave his parents' home and move to Rome to carry out his artistic plans. I too had supported the idea, typical among patients who have grown up in conversational contexts where the semantics of freedom was prevalent, that self-fulfillment and self-esteem had to involve a release from protective relationships. And as a result, in this young man's relational context, I found myself in a similar position to that of Emilio's aunt during his adolescence: I was placed in contrast with his mother, who symbolized Emilio's need for protection. If I hadn't distanced myself from the "freedom, independence" pole in which the patient had put me, thereby releasing the therapeutic relationship from the "cage" of expectations that held the problem rather than resolving it, the therapy was in danger of having the same function that his art school had had: of allowing Emilio to project his emancipative projects into a distant future, making the state of deadlock in which he lived more acceptable.

The therapist's positioning in the "protection" pole, which generally occurs during the later stages of the therapy process, enables us to understand that the patient is not wrong in fearing the experience of therapy. Once therapists have become a dependable point of reference, their expectations become difficult for the patient to avoid—the patient cannot afford to lose the therapist's guidance.

This is what happened at the end of Antonella's therapy. There was an entirely unexpected reoccurrence, albeit mild, of the symptom of depersonalization in this young woman. It wasn't just her problem about bringing the therapy to an end, but something else. Antonella was convinced I expected her to have a child, and that the psychotherapy had to end when she decided to become a mother. For this reason, during the final sessions, she had told me about friends who had just had children, about women who were pregnant, about relatives who had asked her when she would decide to have a child. These stories certainly didn't reflect her own wishes. Antonella, for complex reasons, had no intention of having a child, and especially at that time in her life when she had accepted a job that frequently took her abroad. She had also found a partner who didn't seem interested in having children. The problem was me. And I didn't realize it. When I finally understood what was going on between us, and when we spoke about it, the patient relaxed. The therapy could end because the patient was sure she could rely on me even if she didn't give birth to a child, either then or ever.

The examples I have given relate to individual therapy, not just because they are more straightforward. Coming from conversational contexts in which the semantics of freedom are prevalent, though terrified by the experience of therapy, these patients are unlikely to agree to bringing their families into therapy, especially in the earlier stages. Involving their own families or their partners in an experience over which they can exercise no control is more dangerous for them than risking it alone. For better or worse, if they are alone they can always bring the experience to an end without compromising the relationships on which they feel they depend so much. Only after they have come to know the therapist can they share the experience of therapy with their partners or families.

When patients are very young, or their condition is serious, the therapy includes the whole family from the beginning, but the responsibility for start- ing off the experience is taken by other family members. If that person is a free and independent member of the family, the therapist is once again in the position described above: feared by the patient and by the other apprehensive family members.

All the positions occupied by the therapist in the semantics of freedom dur- ing the course of treatment may worry the patient, who feels completely adrift or trapped in the cage of the therapist's expectations. Dysfunctional circuits may be created in which, for example, the more the therapist encourages the patient's independence, the more the patient clings to protective relation- ships. Nevertheless, in the semantics of freedom, the therapist's position of help is recognized: whatever the risks may be, the therapist is there to help the patient. Building a therapeutic alliance is therefore usually possible and often relatively easy.

The Therapist: Opponent and Ally

When the semantics of power dominates the conversation, the therapist is rarely regarded as someone trying, alongside patients and their families, to find a way out. Rarely do members of these families see the therapist as someone working alongside them to transform limitations into resources, to encourage new ways of interpreting their history in order to help towards the resolution of their devastating conflicts. It is not a question of suspicion. The problem is that they interpret the asymmetry in the patient–therapist relationship through the metaphor of power. *The therapeutic relationship is therefore regarded as humiliating.* This is a pattern that begins with the first contact.

Even arranging the day and hour of the appointment can be difficult. "Is next Tuesday at 6pm alright for you?" "No, no, that's too late. I leave the office at 4 … I'd have to hang around for two hours…" "How about Wednes- day at 4.30? "No, Wednesday's no good." "Friday?" "That's rather difficult because we go away for the weekend … but it's you who decides the time, is it?" Conversations like this are fairly frequent. If the therapist asks first about the availability of the patient and the family, unless by some luck there's a free space at the time and on the day proposed by the patient, there are likely to be

269

comments such as: "Ah ... they told me you were very busy. We're the ones who have to fit in, I see, indeed we ought to be grateful you'll take us at all ..."

The therapeutic setting can even be regarded as a sort of "abuse of power," as is well illustrated by the way in which this patient who had been anorexic for almost forty years agreed to the presence of a colleague and a video-recorder behind the one-way mirror:

> Of course, I accept whatever you want, just to get out of this dead end, I'll even stand outside in the square! No, perhaps not the square, I'm rather shy, it's always rather painful being on show ... that's how it is.

It was obvious, in the patient's view, that the therapist was exploiting her situation to humiliate her, creating embarrassment and shame. And the patient had to accept this until she had achieved what she wanted.

Irritation over the asymmetry of the therapeutic relationship clearly emerges from the account of previous therapeutic experiences:

> The therapist never, I mean never, allowed me to ask questions. And then she told me to take notes about what I was eating, when I was sick and even what I vomited. [...] Between me and her, the relationship was never easy, there was never much of a feeling between us. In fact she didn't like me at all. Once she told me: "You're the kind of patient I never wanted to cross paths with!" I might not be an easy person, I've been anorexic all my life, I'm difficult to deal with, I know, but I have my reasons [...] Six months ago I said enough! I stopped therapy, I couldn't take any more of her little exercises!

Obese patients often joke with the prospective therapist about their past therapeutic experiences. Stories come out that are warnings to the candidate therapist. They are often ironic, sometimes amusing, like the descriptions given by this patient:

TH: You've had quite a number of therapies over the past eight years, haven't you?
PT: Yes, yes. I've had the lot, absolutely everything. From water rebirthing therapy to belly dancing. I met a girl who said: why don't you try it? I went to this therapist, told him my story. "Everything," he said, "depends on how you're born!" He got me to tell him how I met my boyfriends and then said, "certainly, with a start like that it could never have worked!" In short, he managed to convince me. I began the therapy. He said he was pleased with the way the rebirthing was going; it was hard work but

I gave it all I'd got. The point is I didn't lose a single pound. I thought perhaps it wasn't working because I don't like water. So I moved on to chair therapy.

TH: Chair therapy?

PT: Yes, yes. The therapist worked with chairs. She wasn't interested in anything to do with my birth. The therapy wasn't such hard work because at least I was sitting down, even though I had to keep changing chairs. With this therapy you didn't just sit there talking quietly like we are now. She moved chairs around, she made them talk. Pointing to a chair she would say: "This is your mother. Now tell her everything you never had the courage to tell her! Be honest! Don't be afraid!" Then she moved the chair closer and asked me: "How do you feel about her being close to you?" How was I supposed to feel? It was a chair! Close up or far away, for me it was just the same. Another time she made me sit where my mother had been and then I'd become my mother who answered me … It wasn't very easy! I've done amateur dramatics but playing the role of my mother, it wasn't very easy [...] The therapist had the idea I had to free my emotions. It seemed a good idea, she was also very committed. She said some interesting things about my mother, my sister, all things that seemed true … but what use was it if I still put on weight?

TH: You didn't lose any weight with this therapy either?

PT: No, I lost absolutely nothing. The only thing that got lighter was my wallet … I thought perhaps it wasn't working because I had no imagination: for me a chair was a chair. So I changed therapist, this time I went to a man, he was famous, even wrote books … With him it started badly: I arrived, and he put me on the scales. It's something I hate. I'll weigh myself if I have to. What's the point of putting me on the scales? To embarrass me? According to him I didn't know how to express what I felt in words. That's true. My ex-boyfriend left me for that very reason—he asked me what I thought of him, if I loved him, if I was happy and it made me angry: what's the point of talking about us, we're fine, we go out together, make love … I don't know what we need to tell each other … In short, this therapist was right and for that reason I agreed to start talking with a fluffy monkey.

TH: A monkey?

PT: Yes, a monkey. I suppose it's a way of therapy, you'll know all about it. He gave me a fluffy white toy to hold and I had to tell him what I felt …

TH: And did you have any success with this fluffy white monkey?

PT: No. Worse. I even put on weight. The fluffy monkey made me hungry. I was so angry about it that I walked on coals. Yes, don't look at me like that: on burning coals! These people, I don't know, perhaps they weren't psychotherapists, but they were just as convincing. They said: if you're able to walk on burning coals it's because you have great motivation, you've got willpower. And then you can achieve whatever you want. They talked me into it: and I walked on their burning coals.

TH: Did it hurt?

PT: No, not too much. One foot got a bit scorched ... I put some cream on it. And when I went back to tell them I hadn't lost even a pound, they told me I didn't really want to lose weight. I had the willpower and I simply wasn't using it. But I already knew this: I want and I don't want to lose weight. That's the problem for everyone who goes on a diet.

TH: And the belly dancing?

PT: This was a course. One of the therapists persuaded me to do it. She said: if you manage to belly dance then you'll be cured because either you come to terms with your body, you accept yourself as you are, or you lose weight. I did the course, I even called my parents to come and see the final performance. It was a pretty awful experience, I was ashamed at showing my tummy, but nothing else had changed.

Even if the therapist avoids behavior that might be interpreted as over the top, *developing a therapeutic alliance with these patients is an arduous task*. When the conversation is dominated by the semantics of power, the therapist's attempts to resolve the problem are generally seen as ploys to gain a position of superiority in the therapeutic relationship. Such attempts therefore encourage either direct opposition—patients refuse to do what the therapist asks, engaging in open warfare—or they encourage indirect opposition—patients show they are doing what the therapist is suggesting, but it's not working: the problem hasn't been altered one little bit. This is often what happens with eating disorders, but also with certain forms of male impotence or withdrawals from interaction that the *DSM* classifies as social phobias. When competitive dynamics are at play, as generally happens when the semantics of power prevails, sexual intercourse can become more paralyzing than a university exam, but even normal day-to-day relationships lead to confrontations that are best avoided.

Psychoanalysis was the first to chart these difficulties. "These women patients," wrote Freud in relation to anorexics, "are inaccessible to psychoanalysis, they reject us with their polite coldness." Bruch (1973) and Selvini Palazzoli (1974), several decades later, confirmed the difficulty that classic psychoanalytical treatment encountered with these patients. They realized in fact that interpretative practices were regarded by patients with eating disorders as "threatening intrusions."

Not just psychoanalysis, but all individual therapeutic approaches, especially if centered on the subjectivity of the patient, encountered numerous difficulties when the semantics of power were dominant. As a result of the prevalence in the family conversation of a purely relational polarity such as winner–loser, and the competitive dynamics, the interest of this patient is aimed selectively

272

at those others with whom they are in continual confrontation, to whom they either set themselves in opposition or adapt, who seek to dominate, win, overcome, or imitate. Their feelings, their abilities and individual resources, their inner world, are neglected both by they themselves as well as by other members of the family. By focusing attention on their subjectivity, the psychoanalyst, but also other psychotherapists who follow an intra-psychic approach, aggravate that feeling of powerlessness against which those with psychogenic eating disorders fight strenuously. Direct confrontation with personal subjectivity makes these patients feel like losers, because it takes them into a world they cannot master.

Does this mean, then, that therapists can only co-position themselves as "antagonists" with such persons? Family therapy—which is the preferred treatment for eating disorders and the one which has been shown to produce the best results for anorexia and bulimia among adolescents and young people (Carr, 2009; Dare et al., 2001; Eisler, 2005; Eisler et al., 2000; NICE, 2004)—has certainly elaborated a series of meta-complementary strategies (Haley, 1963) during the course of its history to neutralize the symmetry between patient and therapist or to exploit the antagonistic position of the therapist for therapeutic purposes. Many of the paradoxical interventions of which Selvini Palazzoli were masters, used challenge as a therapeutic instrument. Minuchin and colleagues (Minuchin et al., 1978; Minuchin & Barcai, 1969), Andolfi and many other family therapists have also used techniques that revolve around challenge. Provocation and challenge are delicate instruments, however, used in the past by same family therapists only when other possibilities seemed impractical.

Where the semantics of power are dominant, in addition to the position of antagonist, the therapist has the more promising position of ally. *The patient, to win over an ally, is prepared temporarily to accept a relationship that is disagreeable because it is asymmetrical.* I think a large part of the success that family therapy has had with anorexia, bulimia and other disorders developing within the semantics of power, is derived from the possibility that the family setting allows for the therapist to take the position of ally from the earliest contact. Those who make the first telephone contact feel they are on the losing side and are therefore often ready even during the telephone conversation to offer their personal alliance to the therapist. So it sometimes happens, after ten minutes of conversation, that the mother of an anorexic says: "If you tell me to stop work, I'll do it, *but you have to tell me ...*" Straightway you are told that the family is coming into therapy because the person telephoning believes in the effect of family therapy whereas the partner would have preferred to send their daughter to a clinic where she would be dosed up with psychotropic drugs, or would have continued to wait for some kind of miracle while the patient carried on wasting away. This, unfortunately, is an alliance that is very different from the kind the therapist wants, since *it is an alliance against someone else.*

Family therapy is often the only treatment acceptable to the patient who has grown up in the semantics of power, precisely because it places responsibility for the problem on the whole family. Involving everyone is seen by the patient, in line with the semantics of these families, as a recognition that the parents and other members of the family are at least equally responsible for the problem. It is no surprise that if the therapist leaves the children at home in order to work on the parents alone, the patient and her siblings are jubilant: here at last is the proof of who's to blame! Even when the sessions involve everybody, the parents regard the therapist as an adult competitor depriving them of their authority, abusing their role as parental guides and offering herself as an alternative model. Such a situation above all irritates the parent in the winning position. The other, who has never had, or has lost, a position of leadership towards their children, often sees something to be gained from the therapy: at least they can see their partner cut down to size.

The children are also ready to interpret the therapeutic relationship in this way, especially the patient, who often assumes an active role in this dynamic, pitting the therapist against the parents. It is no surprise that many of my anorexic and bulimic patients enroll for courses in psychology during the therapy, or tell their parents they intend to do so. Such a choice is particularly irritating for parents who would very much like to be seen as a model for their children. Follow-up sessions show that the experience of therapy has not encouraged the development of a new vocation: when therapy ends, these young people move on to other study courses or, if they haven't yet begun to study psychology, they change their mind.

The therapist, of course, strives to transform the alliance "against" into an alliance "for." If the semantics of power continue to dominate the conversation, even in therapy, and other semantics do not relativize their importance, the treatment will be necessarily brief. Selvini Palazzoli (1974) recommended that treatment for the families of anorexics should be limited to a maximum of twenty sessions. Brevity is, in any event, a characteristic of family treatments, but when the semantics of power is dominant the choice becomes obligatory. As soon as patients abandon their symptoms, the parents generally stop the therapy, often delighted that an experience they regard as arduous has come to an end. When, at the end of the therapy and during the follow up, I ask everyone, as is my practice, how they have found the therapeutic experience, the parents above all state they have felt themselves "vivisectioned," that they have emerged from the sessions "upset," "reeling," "emptied," "turned inside out." Families with other semantics do not, of course, describe anything of the kind. This dynamic, though certainly frustrating for us therapists, is also a formidable resource. Parents, in order to bring an end to the therapy and regain their lost leadership, are often able to make remarkable changes and thus, whether they like it or not, become invaluable co-therapists. I have been amazed by the extraordinary speed, especially when the problem is not particularly serious, with which the family develops creative solutions and carries out changes capable of overcoming the impasse.

The therapist, of course, has one or more prevailing semantics that contribute towards the creation of the therapeutic relationship. However, in my view, it is the semantics of patience that tend to prevail in the therapeutic conversation, above all at the beginning. The study I have mentioned (Ugazio et al., 2011) in fact shows that therapists, at least in the first interviews (the only ones studied), draw on, expand and re-elaborate semantic polarities proposed by the patient, introducing very few of their own semantic polarities. Such a result is consistent with how therapists are trained. Whatever model they belong to, they are, by and large, trained to help patients express their own meanings and to explain them.

7.2 As Many Different Therapies as There are Semantics?

I don't know whether all semantics require their own special path of therapy. But the four semantics illustrated in this book (which don't of course cover all possible semantics) certainly offer quite differing constraints and possibilities for therapy because they shape the therapeutic relationship in particular ways. Certain therapy stories that are possible in one type of semantics—in the sense of being productive, easy to implement, boding well for change—are forbidden in another, in the sense that they are difficult to develop, incapable of making best use of personal resources, destined to encourage dropping out or dysfunctional circuits.

It could be said that we already have different therapies for the four semantics with which we are concerned here. Although the main clinical approaches are, in theory, concerned with all forms of psychic disorder, in practice, each of them has focused during its history on certain psychopathologies, and as a consequence only on certain semantics. Let us limit ourselves to the psychopathologies considered here. Phobic disorders have been the concern, above all, of cognitivists. It was thanks to my contact with them that I began receiving patients with phobic disorders. In a review by Compton, back in 1992, on psychoanalytical contributions to the phobic condition, he observed that very few of the many articles on this widespread clinical condition came from psychoanalysis. It had been first behaviorism and then cognitivism that had focused special attention on investigating phobias. This tendency has continued over the last twenty years: Almost all of psychotherapeutic contributions on phobias is of cognitive or behavioral origin. But despite the lack of recent contributions on obsessive-compulsive neuroses, it is hard not to recognize the contribution that Freudian psychoanalysis, in particular, has given to the understanding of this condition. Even those, like me, who follow other clinical approaches, have to agree with Esman (1989) that psychoanalysis has sketched out a very convincing picture of the conflictual battle that torments the obsessive-compulsive patient:

The ambivalence, the desperate need for control, the struggles against what the patient experiences as forbidden wishes [...] the propensity for magical thinking, the confusion between thought and action—all of these are live and experience-near data which few sensitive observers could question.

(p. 330)

Likewise I think it has to be recognized that:

It was Freud who brought the obsessive-compulsive syndrome out of the fog of nineteenth-century mysticism into the light of human experience. His constructions and those of his followers have made it possible for the observer to empathize with the torments of the obsessional, to lend content to his irresolute doubting, and to place his ritualization and rumination in the developmental and interpersonal context. They have enabled clinicians, researchers, and in many cases patients themselves to make sense of a baffling and often crippling disorder.

(*ibid*, p. 329)

Obsessive-compulsive neurosis and hysteria are both a product of psychoanalysis, and have both played a crucial role in the construction of the psychoanalytical edifice.

Eating psychopathologies, on the other hand, are the chosen psychopathologies of family psychotherapy. The main authorities in the international field are family therapists, such as Mara Selvini Palazzoli and Salvador Minuchin, or those who have given special attention to family dynamics, such as Hilde Bruch. A characteristic feature of these psychopathologies is that they have been proven to be particularly unsuited to be treated and understood within rigidly intrapsychic approaches. It is significant, when dealing with these psychopathologies, that two of the pioneers in the field of eating disorders—Mara Selvini Palazzoli and Hilde Bruch—have developed models for interpretation and intervention that were "anomalous" compared with the prevailing intrapsychic approach at the time they began considering the question. For Selvini Palazzoli, anorexia played a crucial role in leading her to that complete change of direction that led her away from psychoanalysis to family therapy. No less interesting is the career of Bruch. She was still a pediatrician when she began to deal with child obesity. Her article Obesity in Childhood: The Family Frame of Obese Children (Bruch & Touraine, 1940) caused a stir, being one of the first to find a link between psychiatric disorder and the family context. This attention to the dynamics of the family, developed at first through the study of obesity, led her not only to move away from pediatrics to concentrate on problems traditionally dealt with by psychiatry, but also to decide to train at the Baltimore Washington Institute whose members included Fromm-Reichmann, Sullivan and Hill, in other words, some of the American psychoanalysts most interested in interpersonal relationships.

It is perhaps unnecessary to add that depression has been the chosen pathology of biological psychiatry over the past twenty years. The hypothesis that depression was an illness of the brain had been accepted, as we have seen, more or less without dispute during the 1990s. Only with the beginning of the new millennium have criticisms of the biological approach become progressively more cogent and well-documented. Clinical development follows from experience: therapists investigate, propose hypotheses, develop theories and models on the psychopathologies they treat. It is therefore legitimate to suppose that patients play a not insubstantial role in guiding the interests of their clinicians towards one psychopathology or towards another. In other words, the patient's choice of therapist is based not only on personal characteristics (sex, race, age group) but also on a particular model. But what leads patients to choose one model rather than another?

As I gradually studied the semantics that characterize the various psychopathologies, I was struck by the link between each and the psychotherapeutic approach that focused on its study and treatments. This link seems to suggest that *patients choose those psychotherapeutic models that are consistent with their own semantics.* I realized this for the first time over twenty years ago when I examined a request for therapy that seemed unusual, made by Alberto, a 35-year-old doctor, who was single at the time.

Alberto did not have a full-blown phobic psychopathology. His fear of lifts and his difficulty when flying had never interfered with his normal daily life, nor had they generated the "fear of fear," which is so typical of phobic disorders. His was the adaptive strategy of "emotional distancing" described in Chapter 3. Alberto had preferred his career over his emotional life. He had devoted himself unstintingly to his studies and then to his profession. Family relationships had remained marginal in his emotional life. Likewise, there was no deep commitment in his emotional relationships: Albert had notched up a large number of short-term relationships that were ended by him or by each of his partners when it came to the point of discussing a long-term future. Decisions over emotional commitments had always been postponed.

Though he described his emotional situation in negative terms, this strategy had seemed to work until the year before. Alberto had always managed to have an emotional support to turn to and, thanks to his personal qualities of tact and politeness, he had no great difficulty in getting out of a relationship or in coming to terms with being left. His crisis was brought about, first of all, by reaching his thirties, and then by several critical events leading to bouts of anxiety and depression. In order to overcome this period of crisis Alberto asked me for an "individual systemic therapy." I was struck by such precision: twenty years ago, when this therapy was carried out with Alberto, such a form of treatment was not well known, even in specialist circles.[3] I was therefore flattered and surprised. In a politely seductive way, Alberto told me he was fascinated by this type of therapy and explained that he had been told about it by the friend who had referred him. That person was certainly not responsible for Alberto's enthusiasm, being an academic who was not familiar with psychotherapy. I tried to understand why this man, who presented problems of an existential nature and moved in circles where analysis at that time was a regular part of the training curriculum (in much the same way as a Ph.D. or an American Masters degree), had not preferred psychoanalysis. Alberto admitted that almost all of his friends had had one or more experiences of analysis. But his case, he thought, was less suited to psychoanalysis. A therapy focusing on relationships was, he thought, more appropriate.

When I investigated further, I realized that Alberto had no interest at all in systemic psychotherapy. He was not without intellectual curiosity but hadn't read a single book on family therapy. I tried to understand whether he identified his crisis with events in his family past. Not at all. As became apparent during therapy, Alberto rejected the idea that what was happening to him had anything to do with his family history, which he (wrongly) considered to be of no interest at all.

The real reason for his choice emerged very slowly: He didn't have the slightest intention of allowing himself to become involved in an intense, demanding relationship that was hard to control, as he imagined the relationship between patient and analyst would be. He was terrified by the idea of ending up trapped in a relationship that involved frequent sessions and intense emotional exchanges and that, moreover, was "interminable." Systemic therapy was therefore in keeping (in the patient's view, obviously not mine!) with that tendency towards short non-committal relationships that he now considered to be one of the main causes of his crisis.

I was later to meet other phobic patients who kept well clear of psychoanalysis. People with phobic disorders distance themselves from psychoanalytical sessions and their rules because of their fear of emotions, their tendency to regard emotional bonds as forms of humiliating dependence, and their desperate need to control their emotional states. Cognitive behavioral psychotherapy, with its focus on symptoms, seems to be reassuring for those with a phobic organization. Systemic psychotherapy can also represent, for this organization, a safe base for exploration. Being short therapies, they are certainly preferred to psychoanalysis. But the option of family or couple therapy is not easy to combine with their desperate need to control interpersonal relationships. The reason, I think, why a large number of my cases involve phobic patients is because I conduct individual treatments as well. Only at a later stage, as I have already said, when phobic patients feel they can trust the therapist, are they prepared to involve their partner or their entire family in the treatment.

Much later, studying obsessive-compulsive disorders, I realized that the contribution provided by psychoanalysis to the understanding of this psychopathology, of which psychoanalysis is rightly proud, is also the result of its close links with the semantics of the obsessive organization. As I tried to show in Chapter 4, classic psychoanalysis shares that idea of good as an absence of evil that plays a decisive role in the construction of the obsessive's dilemma. The idea of "abstinent" goodness, in the same way that it is not the exclusive prerogative of subjects with an obsessive organization, is not the exclusive prerogative of psychoanalysis either. It belongs to our own culture and to others. In our culture, however, it is not ubiquitous. In Judeo Christian-based civilizations, along with this dialectic between good and evil, there is also the opposite (certainly more optimistic) conception of Augustinian origin, by which good alone has its own intrinsic reality: evil is none other than the absence of good. But Freud, as we have just seen, does not follow Augustine and Thomas Aquinas. His source of inspiration, for this as well as other important strands of his thought, is Schopenhauer, whose greatest work *The World as Will and Representation*, traces the cultural roots of the obsessive neurosis. Classic psychoanalysis, precisely because it is based on the idea of "abstinent" goodness, considered the world of impulses as egoistic and saw in the dilemma afflicting the obsessive subject the repetition, in an extreme and dramatized form, of the eternal conflict between innate impulses (egoistic and antisocial) and the moral obligations acquired.

A similar link is present between eating psychopathologies and systemic relational therapies. I found it difficult to grasp these similarities. It is hard to "put into perspective" the model to which one belongs. But I think it has to be honestly recognized that the great attention given to the defining of the relationship, a characteristic of the conversation of these families resulting from the centrality of the semantics of power, has also been a characterizing feature of systemic psychotherapies. At least in their founding phase, when the pragmatic approach prevailed, there was selective attention to this dimension thanks especially to Haley, the most brilliant of Batesons's pupils but also the one most dominated by the semantics of power. The fact that systemic therapies then abandoned the idea of power and control, and that the pragmatic approach would betray Bateson's ideas on this aspect, is another story.[4]

I have emphasized the role of the pharmaceutical industry in promoting the idea—based very much on supposition—that depression is an illness of the brain, caused by biochemical imbalance. But it cannot be ignored that many depressed patients themselves were, unfortunately, the first to subscribe enthusiastically to this notion. Nor should this be a surprise. As Linares and Campo (2000) point out, "the character of depressives makes them ideal patients for biological psychiatry" (p. 15):

> To begin with, they usually have an "awareness of illness," that rare self-critical introspection which psychiatrists look for in vain in most other

patients. Some are pessimists, without doubt, but serious and control-led, while others may be likeable because they are so anxious to please that they become the focal point at parties and social events. Their good manners and caution do not allow them to disobey medical instructions to the point where they feel almost sorry to contradict the therapist with a relapse. They do relapse—that is true—but they never challenge the doctors; on the contrary it is they who feel in the wrong.

(ibid)

What, after all, is more consistent with the semantics of belonging than being set apart (not through any personal fault) by a chronic illness from which there is no escape, deprived of good health forever, condemned for life to taking medicines because something inside these people makes them biologi-cally unfit for living? What, at the same time, could be better for reconciling patients with their partner and with relatives tyrannized by their rages and their extremes, than such a clear definition of organic illness?

The sharing between the patient's semantics and that of his/her therapist's psychotherapeutic approach certainly makes it easier to develop the therapeutic relationship, without which therapy is impossible. Nevertheless, this commu-nality can represent an obstacle to therapeutic change. Systemic psychothera-pies have suggested—in my view rightly—that change is crucially connected to the capacity to construct new meanings with patients and their family. A therapist who reaches the maximum level of empathy would become the patient: the two points of view would become fused. This is a theoretical hypothesis: the therapist could share the patient's semantics but could never (like a family member) be in exactly the same positioning. Nevertheless, sharing the same semantics can be limiting for the therapist. By suggest-ing that the therapeutic relationship is constructed in a different way for each semantics and therefore requires particular therapeutic strategies, I do intend to suggest that the therapist must continue to take a position within the same semantics of the patient throughout the whole course of the thera-peutic process. On the contrary, *once the therapeutic alliance is constructed, the therapist must seek to give relevance to other semantics, thereby relativizing the critical one.*

The concept of family semantic polarities, which forms the basis of the psy-chopathological model I have presented, sees the organizations of meaning as open systems susceptible to modification. In all families, there are several salient semantics. Schismogenetic processes tend to reduce, but not to elimi-nate, the variety of semantics around which the conversation is organized. The story of each person is therefore defined by their position in relation to sev-eral semantic polarities. Although a single semantics can assume considerable centrality in the family conversation, and plays a central role in defining the position of each member, it does not exhaust the conversational possibilities available to each individual. His or her position always offers access to stories different from those generated by the critical semantics.

The model I have presented for each psychopathology, for the very fact that it refers to *one single* semantics, provides only a partial, simplified, and incomplete picture of the actual person in the flesh. It describes and explains those aspects of the semantic organization of the family and the patient that are present in all those who share the same psychopathology. These shared aspects constitute the *conditio sine qua non* for the development of each of the four disorders examined, but they certainly are not enough for a proper description of the specific individual. Even for diagnostic purposes classification it is often necessary to define the position of patients, and of those around them, within several semantics. But it is above all in relation to the process of change that we must remember that individuals have constructed their own story according to several semantics and for this very reason they have a much wider range of ways for organizing the experience than those generated by the critical semantics.

The therapist has, indeed, to impede a process by which the relevance of the critical semantics is amplified by the onset of symptoms. Think for example of, psychopathology. Panic attacks to which the patient becomes prey, the fear of fear, the need for a reliable person who takes on the accompanying role, are all situations that amplify the tendency for the family to organize the conversation around the semantics of freedom. This selective attention tends to obscure collateral strategies, connected to other semantics present in the patient's intersubjective context.

Therapy generally contributes towards this process of amplification of the critical family semantics. Patients and/or their families often choose a treatment that is in keeping with the critical semantics. But even when this does not happen, the therapy amplifies the critical semantics if only because it must necessarily examine the particularly acute conflicts that are produced within this semantics and the relative positionings. It is an inevitable process, which the therapist cannot *at first* avoid. But there are stages during the course of the therapy when the therapist must ignore the critical semantics and the position of the patient and other members of the family within it, so as to allow space for other emotions and semantics.

Until such time as other stories can be told, the therapist must put all psychopathological knowledge aside. If the therapeutic experience is not to be limited to prompting adjustments in the patient's position within one semantic organization that is not substantially modified, the therapeutic conversation must, at a certain point, give salience to semantics other than the critical one. I think, therefore, with regard to the psychopathological model I have presented in this book, as well as the other models of mental disorders, that the therapist must maintain a wise irreverence.

NOTES

1 THE CONSTRUCTION OF PSYCHOPATHOLOGICAL DISORDERS IN INTERSUBJECTIVE CONTEXTS

1 The reader can find answers to these questions in Sections 4.6 (Natascia), 5.5 (Sabina) and 6.6 (Giulia). I deal briefly with Alessandro in Section 7.1.
2 The ethological investigations that have brought these results are mentioned and discussed in Section 6.1.
3 I deal more fully with these studies in Chapter 6.
4 See Chapter 6.
5 We both agree that meanings are created and maintained in interaction. But Procter's concept maintains a Kellian emphasis on individual construal as a way of anticipating events. His "family constructs system" is "a dance of mutual anticipations" (1981, p. 355).
6 MacIntyre, one of the most important contemporary philosophers to have supported a social conception of self, emphasizes how positions such as that of Goffman, for whom the self is a simple representation of roles, end up reaching conclusions similar to those of Sartre and other radical individualists:

> Thus at a deep level a certain agreement underlies Sartre's and Goffman's surface disagreements; and they agree in nothing more than in this, that both see the self as entirely set over against the social world. For Goffman, for whom the social world is everything, the self is therefore nothing at all, it occupies no social space. For Sartre, whatever social space it occupies it does so only accidentally, and therefore he too sees the self as in no way an actuality.
>
> (MacIntyre, 1981, p. 32)

7 Castiglioni et al, 2013; Veronese, Romaioli, & Castiglioni, 2012.
8 This premise is also shunned by some psychoanalysts, who reject or doubt Freudian meta-psychology. Lichtenberg (1989), for example, outlines personality structures as variegated ab origine according to the order given to the five motivational systems that he considers fundamental (physical regulation of physiological needs, attachment-affiliation, exploration-assertiveness, adversity, sexuality). The psychology of self, as Kohut (1977) presents it in numerous steps, seems to be a complementary development in comparison with the classical (drive) psychoanalytical model, necessary for an understanding of narcissistic pathologies and more generally of disorders of the self. Two development paths would therefore seem to exist: that of neurotic disorders, for the understanding and treatment of which the drive model is sufficient, and that of disorders of the self that require categories of intervention and indeterminate analysis provided by the psychology of the self.

9 See Dozier, Stovall-McClough, & Albus, 2008, pp. 718–44; Lyons-Ruth & Jacobvitz, 2008, pp. 666–697.
10 Translation by R. Dixon.
11 Translation by R. Dixon.

2 FAMILY SEMANTIC POLARITIES

1 It was Haley (1963) who first emphasized the impossibility of not defining the relationship, but also the inherent instability of this process. Symptoms, according to Haley, were a "tactic" to escape from this rule in human relationships and to avoid the commitment which each definition of the relationship implies, however temporary and revocable that may be.
2 The very term "inter-subjectivity" is misleading. It appears to refer to individuals who have developed autonomously and must *then* organize themselves together. I have put it in inverted commas in order to stress that I am using this term in a meaning different from the one used in modern and often also in contemporary philosophical debate, and specifically as a community of interconnected identities.
3 See also: Winter, 1994; Winter & Viney, 2005.
4 One of the eleven corollaries with which Kelly summarized the main assumptions of his theory—the corollary of dichotomy—holds that an individual's cognitive system consists of a finite number of dichotomous constructs.
5 Wundt and James, two of the founding fathers of psychology, have for example used the concept. Wundt used it in his proposal for a theory of emotions according to which emotions vary along three polar dimensions (pleasure/displeasure, tension/relaxation, enthusiasm/depression). James used it when he identified two types of thinkers: rigid or flexible.
6 See in particular Jung, 1921/1970, 1955–1956/1970.
7 The treatise *On Breaths*. The theory that a cure would be effective if it counterbalances opposites is to be found frequently throughout the whole of the Hippocratic Corpus. For a more detailed study of this argument, see Lloyd (1966 and 1991).
8 "I might compare him to a person who began by maintaining generally that mind is the cause of the actions of Socrates, but who, when he endeavoured to explain the causes of my several actions in detail, went on to show that I sit here because my body is made up of bones and muscles; and the bones, as he would say, are hard and have ligaments which divide them [...]; and as the bones are lifted at their joints by the contraction or relaxation of the muscles, I am able to bend my limbs, and this is why I am sitting here in a curved posture: That is what he would say, and he would have a similar explanation of my talking to you, which he would attribute to sound, and air, and hearing, and he would assign ten thousand other causes of the same sort, forgetting to mention the true cause, which is that the Athenians have thought fit to condemn me, and accordingly I have thought it better and more right to remain here and undergo my sentence; for I am inclined to think that these muscles and bones of mine would have gone off to Megara or Boeotia—by the dog of Egypt they would, if they had been guided only by their own idea of what was best, and if I had not chosen as the better and nobler part, instead of playing truant and running away, to undergo any punishment which the State inflicts." (*Phaedo*, 99 c-a)
9 Plato, *Phaedo*, 97 d, p. 158.
10 In the *Metaphysics* and in the *Organon*, Aristotle distinguishes as follows between the four categories of oppositions:

a) Opposing *correlatives*. These include opposing terms in which each of the two is what it is in relation to the other. For example: double and half, but also previous/subsequent, senior/junior, mother/child.

b) *Contraries.* These are extremes of a kind, such as black/white or good/bad. Aristotle distinguishes between the contraries that allow intermediates and those that do not. Yellow, green, grey, and all other colours are intermediates with regard to black/white, while the opposition between equal/unequal allows no intermediates.

c) Terms of *privation* and *possession.* These are used in connection with a single thing if it is natural that there is a positive opposite; for instance, sign and blindness in connection with the eyes.

d) *Contradictories* and *affirmations* and *negations.* These are opposites without an intermediate term, of the type "A/not A"; they can be represented either by things or by affirmations. In some contradictions it is the attribute of universality that is affirmed and denied (for example: "all men are white"/"not all men are white"), in others, a universal affirmation is opposed to a particular negation for example: "all men are just"/"some men are just"). It was with reference to this class that Aristotle formulated the principle of excluded middle. The analysis of the different types of opposing affirmations allowed him to formulate the principle of non-contradiction: "It is impossible that the same thing belong and not belong to the same thing at the same time and in the same respect." (Aristotle, *Metaphysics*, IV, 3, 1005b).

11 The concept of the double bind appeared in 1956 (Bateson et al.) and was popular in the 1960s and 70s. The distinctive features of double bind relationships can be summarized as follows:

1) "Two or more persons are involved in an intense relationship that has a higher degree of physical and/or psychological survival value for one, several, or all of them (…).

2) In such a context, a message is given which is so structured that (a) it asserts something, (b) it asserts something about its own assertion and (c) these two assertions are mutually exclusive. (…)

3) Finally, the recipient of the message is prevented from stepping outside the frame set by this message, either meta-communicating (commenting) about it or by withdrawing" (Watzlawick et al., 1967, p. 212).

The Double Bind was initially presented as a theory to explain schizophrenia and introduces the idea that mental illness is the result of radical and systematic confusion and ambiguity in communication processes. The mental balance of the subject comes under threat when he finds himself in a situation where the relationships in which he is involved continually elude him and every attempt to understand them takes him back to the initial situation of undecidability In other words, if the structure of significant relationships assumes the form of a double bind, the person concerned no longer has a stable point of view through which to judge events and to direct his actions. An action is always one episode in a possible story. Each of us is able to express ourselves in a meaningful way only if we are able first of all to answer the question: "What story am I part of?" According to Bateson et al. (1956), anybody who finds himself in a double bind situation is unable to answer this question.

12 In the *Critique of Pure Reason*, Kant states that "all *a priori* division of concepts must be by dichotomy" (Kant, 1787/1929, p. 116).

13 In the closing pages of *The Measurement of Meaning*, Osgood, Suci, and Tannenbaum (1957) ask: "But what about the use of bipolar scales defined by

verbal opposites? We have been following a more or less implicit assumption that thinking in terms of opposites is 'natural' to the human species; data presently being collected on Indians in the Southwest seem to support this assumption, and the ethno-linguists we have talked to—after due consideration and checking with their own experiences—usually agree that semantic opposition is common to most, if not all, language systems" (p. 327). Needham, one of the most respected figures in contemporary anthropology, also states (1987) that the duality of meaning and semantic contrasts that we find in all languages express a law or, at least, a tendency in human cognition: Human beings seem inclined to think in terms of opposition.

14 Part of Blake's quotation, see opening of this chapter (Blake, 1790–1793/2008).

15 See, for example, the section dedicated to triadic processes in issue no. 47(4) *Family Process*, pp. 445–499.

16 The concept of "apparent transmitter/receiver" was formulated by Ricci (1986). Considering the communications exchanged between two people as a private matter involving only them can be, as Ricci (1986) warned, a dangerous oversimplification, even if no other conversational partner is physically present at the moment of the exchange. This would be exactly the same as accepting the hypothesis of a perfect independence between separate dyads (mother–son, father–daughter, brother–sister, etc.), thereby ignoring the complex relationships between the various components on the one hand (father–mother–son, for example, or mother–children), and between the components and the whole on the other (father–family, daughter–family, etc.). For this reason, Ricci considered the two protagonists in a communicative exchange as the "apparent transmitter/receiver" and suggested this reformulation of the first axiom (*"one cannot* not *communicate"*) of the *Pragmatics of Human Communication* (Watzlawick et al., 1967, p. 219): "One cannot not play the ongoing N-person game" (Ricci, 1986, p. 162). The players temporarily not present are also part of it.

17 Later, his encounter with cybernetics would provide Bateson (Bateson, 1938/1958; Ruesch & Bateson, 1951), through the concept of feedback, with a scientific basis for the two-way nature of behavior that the concepts of complementarity and symmetry and schismogenesis imply.

18 The italics are in the text. See Bateson (1949).

19 I use the term "polarization" to refer to the extremities of behavior and attitudes.

20 Translation from Italian by R. Dixon.

21 The extraordinary spread of Bowlby's attachment theory psychology has resulted in the expressions "bonds of attachment" or simply "attachment" being used frequently as synonyms for emotional relations. And it is in this broader sense that I use the term here and in other parts of the text.

22 The fact that Bowlby suggested "working models" of attachment figures and of the self implies neither the acceptance of the issue of meaning (at least in the strong sense in which I understand it) nor a questioning of the universality of the model of secure attachment. By introducing into his theory the concept of "working models" of attachment figures and of self, Bowlby limited himself to reformulating the concept of internalization of experience, borrowing a term of cognitive origin. Bowlby himself (1973, p. 261) says: "Although the concepts of working models and forecasts derived from working models may be unfamiliar, the formulation adopted is no more than a way of describing, in terms compatible with systems theory, ideas traditionally described in such terms as 'introjection of an object' (good or bad) and 'self-image.'" And also: "What in traditional theory is termed a 'good object' can be reformulated within this framework as a working model of an attachment figure who is conceived as accessible, trustworthy, and ready to help when called upon.

Similarly, what in traditional theory is called a 'bad object' can be reformulated as a working model of an attachment figure to whom are attributed such characteristics as uncertain accessibility, unwillingness to respond helpfully, or perhaps the likelihood of responding hostilely. In an analogous way an individual is thought to construct a working model of himself towards whom others will respond in certain predictable ways. The concept of a working model of the self comprehends data at present conceived in terms of self-image, self-esteem, etc." (Bowlby, 1979, p. 140). In substance, Bowlby believes that working models are the set of expectations that the subject, on the basis of his childhood experiences, has constructed around the *behavior* of the attachment figure toward him—in terms of accessibility and willingness to provide help and comfort—and his own capacity to love and obtain love and attention from this figure and theirs.

While the hypothesis I am putting forward here envisages that the attachment behavior develops from the very beginning, in accordance with the various meanings of the semantic polarities in the family, Bowlby suggests that *for the child, what is a prime importance is the experience of attachment with the mother, developed in accordance with universal patterns of meaning. Only later do the working models (the expectations) gradually acquire an increasingly important role,* as can be seen from the following passage: "The theory proposed can be formulated in two steps: from the early months onwards and throughout life the actual presence or absence of an attachment figure is a major variable that determines whether a person is or is not alarmed by any potentially alarming situation: from about the same age, and again onwards throughout life, a second major variable is a person's confidence, that an attachment figure not actually present will none the less be available, namely accessible and responsive, should he for any reason desire this. *The younger the individual the more influential is the first variable, actual presence or absence; up to about the third birthday it is the dominant variable. After the third birthday forecasts of availability or unavailability become of increasing importance, and after puberty are likely in their turn to become the dominant variable*" (Bowlby, 1973, p. 260; the italics are mine).

23 See Wood, Bruner, & Ross (1976).
24 See Doise & Mugny (1984); Doise, Mugny, & Perèz (1998); Mugny & Carugati (1987).
25 Doise et al. have shown that imitation is not responsible for the cognitive advances observed. Two children, both equally unskilled in relation to the notion to which the experiment relates, can in fact acquire the skill during the interaction. On the other hand, too broad a disparity in performance can lead to a situation of acquiescence on the part of the less able person toward the more able partner, such as to hinder progress: the "incompetent" child accepts the solution of the partner, but later, during the post-test examination, shows that he has not acquired any new understanding.
26 Kahneman (2011), Kruegar (2012) and Fiske (2004).
27 In accordance with Cronen et al. (1982), here I have considered the episodes as pieces of conversation to which a single meaning is given by the participants, observers or other narrative voices. For the other three levels, in this paragraph and in the following chapters, I have also used a narrative definition: relationship, self or personal life script are likened to "stories experienced" or "told." The "stories experienced" revolve around unspoken cognitive processes (the emotions), whereas the "stories told" (often very different from those "experienced") relate to explicit processes. What differentiates the three levels is the thematic content of the stories. Relationship and cultural patterns feed stories which, in the one case, have as their argument the interpersonal relationships experienced directly; in the other, the

stories have as their subject a "we" in which the individual is part insofar as being a participant in the community. The stories that feed the self, meant here as personal biography, have instead as their subject the *position* of the individual in the various narratives in which he or she is a part, narratives that relate to personal life and that of others. Each of us is a part of the story of other people in the same way as they form part of our story, the narrative of the life of whoever forms part of a series of interconnected narratives. The self in this respect is a narrative form, and its very unity coincides with the availability of narratives within the personal repertoire that link together the various stories (MacIntyre, 1981).

27 See note 24.

28 The example is freely reported. One of the distinctions introduced—that between "story experienced" and "story told"—is not present in the original version.

29 At that moment only an impulsive action was possible, similar to that of an *acting out*. Instetten in fact no longer had a viewpoint from which to evaluate the events: his self was divided ("social self"/"individual self").

3 SEMANTICS OF FREEDOM AND PHOBIC DISORDERS

1 See, for example, Shilkert, 2002; Whaley, Pinto, & Sigman, 1999; Wood et al., 2003. See also the review by Bögels & Brechman-Toussaint, 2006.

2 It is defined as derealization (feelings of unreality) or depersonalization (being detached from oneself).

3 See Section 3.6.

4 The changes of positioning throughout life will be examined in Section 3.5.

5 With patients alone in the case of individual systemic therapy or with the partner or whole family where therapy includes the family or the couple.

6 For example, Wolpe (1976) indicated the presence in agoraphobic patients of deep dissatisfaction with their marriage, with frequent fantasies of separation that then evoke the fear of solitude, and has suggested that the intensification of a desire to be liberated from the marriage bond is one of the most common conditions unleashing the first appearance of symptoms.

7 See, for example, Bowlby, 1973; Franklin & Andrews, 1989; Guidano, 1987, 1991; Leibowitz & Klein, 1982.

8 Briefly describing these models, the authors state: "In PDA a circular homeostatic pattern develops in which the dependent role of the person with PDA is complemented by their partner's caretaking role. These complementary roles entail benefits for both partners. The apparently healthy partner is permitted to avoid addressing anxiety-provoking personal issues such as low self-esteem or fear of psychological and sexual intimacy. The person with PDA is protected from having to face the challenge of individuation" (Byrne et al., 2004, p. 107).

9 See also the review by Marcaurelle, Bélanger, & Marchand, 2003.

10 "The parent portraying the world as a threatening and dangerous place, while at the same time impressing upon the child that he/she is weak and particularly vulnerable to these perils. While such parental behaviour is usually an expression of the parent's intolerance of the child's normal separation initiatives, they invariably justify the restrictions imposed on the child's freedom as not depending on their own wishes. For example, even in the frequent case of phobic-prone parents who actively keep the child back with them because of their fear of being alone, it is never explicitly stated that they prefer to have their children nearby for their own pleasure or company. On the contrary, reasons given by parents for limiting autonomy always concern an alleged weakness of the child of either a physical nature (e.g. "you are

frail") or of an emotional nature (e.g. "you don't know how to control yourself in front of other people"). In fact, it is the parents' overprotecting attitude that makes the child not only perceive such weakness as real, but also accept it and take it for granted" (Guidano, 1987, p. 140).

11 "The parents are not apt to be perceived by the child as a safe base, and this makes him/her feel insecure when outside the home. In other words, children refrain from autonomously exploring the environment for fear of losing their parents if they get too far from them" (*ibid*, p. 141).

12 The "relative deprivation" concept refers to the experience of being deprived of something to which you think you are entitled. It is a long running story in sociology and social psychology. See Olson, Herman, & Zanna, 1986 and Walker & Smith, 2001.

13 See Dozier et al., 2008, pp. 666–697.

14 The child can also have a preferential relationship of attachment with the father or another member of the family.

15 See above, Section 3.2.

16 See Section 3.1.

17 Translation by R. Dixon.

18 See *Nicomachean Ethics*, I, 7, 1097b,

19 In Aeschylus we find "God loves to help him who strives to help himself" (Fragments, 395); it was a common English proverb by the late sixteenth century.

20 Translation by R. Dixon.

4 BETWEEN GOOD AND EVIL: OBSESSIVE-COMPULSIVE DISORDERS

1 The relevant area for the considerations set out here is contained in the psychopathological categories classified by the *DSM-IV* as "obsessive-compulsive disorder" (300.3 axis I) and "obsessive-compulsive personality disorder" (301.4 axis II).

2 Augustine takes the concept of evil as "non-being" from Plotinus.

3 Thomas Aquinas states in *Summa theologiae*: "Now, we have said above that good is everything appetible; and thus, since every nature desires its own being and its own perfection, it must be said also that the being and the perfection of any nature is good. Hence it cannot be that evil signifies being, or any form or nature. Therefore it must be that by the name of evil is signified the absence of good (p. 456)" (I, q. 48, a.I).

4 Louis Renou, a Sanskrit master, wrote that the notion of impurity "forms the basis, at least in theory, of the caste system." The conflict between pure and impure is what establishes the distinction between Brahmins and untouchables and, more generally, "underlies the hierarchy, which is the superiority of the pure to the impure, underlies separation because the pure and the impure must be kept separate, and underlies the division of labour because pure and impure occupations must likewise be kept separate" (Dumont, 1970, p. 43).

5 Translation by R. Dixon.

6 The expressions "instinctual," "impulsive" and "abstinent," used in the following pages, in referring to the position of each parent within the critical semantics, does not mean I am accepting Freud's instinct theory. The use of these terms is intended simply as a tribute to Freud and psychoanalysis, whose contribution to this pathology is still essential, even for those who, like me, adopt a different position.

7 For example, Melanie Klein (1932) suggests that obsessive neurosis is an attempt

to deal with an underlying psychosis. I quote this theory to emphasize how authors from very different areas agree with the view that there is a split in obsessives between good and bad parts; these authors, of course, differ in their interpretation of this split.

8 Using Feixas et al.'s implicative dilemma concept the "self-assertion" pole—usually positive or at least neutral—implies the negative pole of good/bad construct which for obsessive organizations takes the higher position in the self construction.

9 Guidano, for example, states:

> The organizational unity of obsessive-prone individuals' emotional domain rests on a perceived ambivalent and dichotomous sense of self unfolding through antithetical boundaries of meaning oscillating in an "all-or-none" manner. Thus any disequilibrium in one's need for absolute certainty is immediately experienced as a total lack of control.

10   Eros desires contact because it strives to make the ego and the loved object one, to abolish all spatial barriers between them. But destructiveness, too, which (before the invention of long-range weapons) could only take effect at close quarters must presuppose physical contact, a coming to grips.
>
> (Freud, 1925, p. 122)

11 I use the terms "mortification" and "annihilation" to describe an emotional state or feeling (which tends to last over a period of time) as well as actual emotion (short-lived and of considerable intensity).

12 Note the following passages: "Here anxiety appears as a reaction to the felt loss of the object; and we are at once reminded of the fact that castration anxiety, too, is a fear of being separated from a highly valued object, and that the earliest anxiety of all—the 'primal anxiety' of birth—is brought about on the occasion of a separation from the mother" (Freud, 1925, p. 137). "In this case the danger is of being separated from one's genitals (...) The high degree of narcissist value which the penis possesses can appeal to the fact that that organ is a guarantee to its owner that he can be once more united to his mother—i.e. to a substitute for her—in the act of copulation. Being deprived of it amounts to a renewed separation from her ... " (*ibid*, p. 139).

13 See Chapter 1.

14 For an explanation of the concept of implogenesis, see Section 2.6.

15 Here I am using an expression of A. Miller (1983).

16 The original intersubjective context of this patient is reconstructed in detail in Section4.5. He is also mentioned at the end of Section 4.1.

17 This is the title of an essay by Freud (1912/1957).

18 The italics are mine.

19 See quotation at p. 150.

20 See p. 132.

21 Even afterwards Salvatore made no effort to improve his job situation. When I met him he was still an unskilled worker. Keeping this position was perhaps a way of blaming his parents for not letting him stay in the South.

22 "Far more than any other external member of the body, the genitals are subject merely to the will, and not at all to knowledge. Here, in fact, the will shows itself almost as independent of knowledge, [...]. By reason of all this, the genitals are the real focus of the will, and are therefore the opposite pole to the brain, there presentative of knowledge, i.e., to the other side of the world, the world as representation." (*The world as will and representation*, p. 330).

23 In Nagera (1976); the italics are mine.

5 THE SEMANTICS OF POWER: ANOREXIA, BULIMIA, AND OTHER EATING PROBLEMS

1 The hypotheses put forward in this chapter are relevant not only to anorexia and bulimia but also to obesity, which is currently excluded from the official nosography (*DSM-IV*). I will limit the term "anorexia," without further specification, to cases where thinness is reached only by not eating ("restricting type"), at least for the first months of the illness. As is well known, the majority of "restricting type" anorexic patients in the subsequent stages also use weight control "purging type" strategies and within two years of the onset of anorexia a high percentage of anorexic patients cross over to normal weight bulimia (Sullivan, 2002). I will use the term bulimia in cases where weight is controlled with self-induced vomiting and the use of laxatives ("purging type") or with physical exercise ("non purging type"), specifying when it fluctuates around values regarded as normal or even ideal. While taking account of the differences between the various symptoms referred to, I will adopt and develop the hypothesis, shared by most of the literature), that eating disorders area homogeneous group of psychopathologies.

2 Except in cases of mixed psychopathologies. For example, the combined presence of anorexia nervosa and obsessive-compulsive disorders is not infrequent among my cases. It is calculated that both diseases are present in between 15 percent and 30 percent of cases (Blinder, Cumella & Sanathara, 2006; Godart et al., 2003; Speranza et al., 2001). In the family context of these patients, in addition to the semantics of power, described in this paragraph, I have always found the "semantics of goodness," which are characteristic in obsessive-compulsive disorders.

3 The dilemma of organizations typical of eating disorders is that it is less suited than the other three psychopathologies to be described within the concept of implicative dilemma of Feixas et al. (Feixas & Saúl, 2004; Feixas et al., 2009). Precisely because within this organization the ongoing relationship contextualizes the self, the dilemma, in my view, cannot be described regardless of the other. Therefore, I limit myself to describing it as a strange loop.

4 This hypothesis has many points of convergence with the views of various cognitivist psychotherapists (Bara & Stoppa Beretta, 1996; Guidano, 1987, 1991). For example, Guidano (1987, p. 155) states: "The oneness of personal meaning processes in eating disorder-prone individuals stems from a blurred perceived sense of the self and organizes itself around deep boundaries that oscillate between an absolute need for significant others' approval and the fear of being intruded upon or disconfirmed by significant others.."

5 Skårderud (2007) also found these attitudes.

6 Several authors have highlighted the tendency for patients with eating disorders to hypercontrol the relationship. See, for example, Button, 1985; Button & Winter, 2010.

7 90 The onset of anorexia is more frequent between 15–19 years old, while for bulimia, between 20–24 years old (Hoek & Van Hoeken, 2003; Keski-Rahkonen et al., 2009; Keski-Rahkonen et al., 2008).

8 Selvini Palazzoli et al. (1989) have, in fact, found that instigation is a necessary component not only in anorexia-bulimia but also in "psychotic games." For my part, I suggest that instigation plays a crucial role in eating disorders and in the other diseases developed in contexts where the semantics of power dominate the conversation.

9 Sabina's onset of symptoms was described at the beginning of the first chapter.

10 See the following reviews Hoek & Van Hoeken, 2003; Keski-Rahkonen et al., 2009; Striegel-Moore et al., 2006.

11 We know very little about the spread of eating disorders outside the West, due to the lack of reliable epidemiological studies. However it seems that with globalization and the spread of Western culture in developing countries, abnormal eating *attitudes* appear, but not eating disorders that respect the *DSM* criteria and nor do organizations typical of eating disorders, characterized by a specific way of construing meaning, such as those described in this chapter (see for example Becker, 2004; Becker et al., 2002; Cummins, Simmons, & Zane, 2005; Keski-Rahkonen et al., 2008; Makino, Tsuboi, & Dennerstein, 2004. For a general discussion of this topic see: Nasser et al., 2001). As Gordon (2001) underlined "outside Europe and the United States, there is only one country in which eating disorders have been as well known in the second half of the 20th century as in the West, and that is Japan" (p. 5). It's not by chance that we are dealing with a country that has seen radical changes in traditional family structures in the post-war period.

12 Translation by R. Dixon.

13 Aristotle, *Politics*, II 1261 a.

14 Galatians ch. 3, v. 28.

15 The Divine Institutions: Bk. 5: ch. 15

16 Translation by R. Dixon.

6 DEPRESSION: DENIED BELONGING

1 The same can be said for psychotherapeutic treatment aimed at eliminating symptoms only.

2 I agree with Linares (2010) that dystymia has relational dynamics that are profoundly different from those of bipolar and serious unipolar depression.

3 See the analysis of the results of this research by Horwitz & Wakefield (2007, p. 171–174).

4 This is a placebo with side effects similar to those of SSRIs, therefore less easily identifiable by the patients. Seventy eight per cent of clinical tests using an active placebo do not reveal any significant differences between antidepressants and the placebo (Kirsch, 2010; Moncrieff, 2008; Moncrieff, Wessely, & Hardy, 2005). For a general analysis of the effects of SSRIs see Kirsch, 2010.

5 Mainly CBT studies. See, for example: Butler et al., 2006; Imel et al., 2008. See also some systemic studies: Seikkula et al., 2012; MacFarlane, 2003.

6 Involving thirty-three patients, fifteen of whom had been psychiatrically diagnosed as bipolar. However, my psychotherapeutic reconstruction of these fifteen patients did not reveal any full-blown manic crisis in the absence of drugs that were potentially capable of inducing them. I do not include any cases of dysthymic disorder. My cases for the above disorder are too few to allow me to reach any general conclusion.

7 This dilemma, like those described in the previous chapters for organizations typical of phobic, obsessive and eating disorders, shares the characteristics of the strange loops of Cronen et al. (1982). If we limit attention only to the depressed patient, we can compare it to the implicative dilemmas of Feixas et al. (Feixas & Sàul 2004; Feixas et al., 2009). Belonging—the positive pole of the "belonging/being excluded" construct—is associated with "being unworthy"—the negative pole of the "worthy/unworthy" construct. In the light of the model of Feixas et al., the second construct is superimposed on the first: the subject with a depressive organization, before entering the full-blown depression, generally prefers being excluded rather than being unworthy. On the other hand, being excluded, for the subject, means "being outside human society."

8 Translation by R. Dixon.
9 Andrea and Louise are Natascia's parents. See Section 4.6.
10 I have already mentioned part of her family history in Section 6.2.
11 For a reconstruction of the history of melancholy, see for example the anthology by Radden (2000).

7 FAMILY SEMANTICS AND THE THERAPEUTIC RELATIONSHIP

1 Cfr. Section 3.6, p. 264.
2 Cfr. P. 264.
3 There is not much material even now on individual systemic therapy (Boscolo & Bertrando, 1996; Telfener, 1991).
4 As is well known, one of the central concepts of Bateson's thought is the interconnection between mental phenomena and the social and natural environment, and the consequent rejection of the western cultural premise according to which the subject believes he/she is carrying out a "finalistic" action on an object. In other words, Bateson rejects the hypothesis—or rather the claim—that one part of a system can influence another in one direction alone. The idea of power, which for Bateson is at the root of many evils in the West, is based on this very claim. Awareness of the interconnection of phenomena, inspired by his encounter with cybernetics and with the East, assumes an ethical value in Bateson. The conflict between Bateson and Haley over ideas of power and control was not therefore the classic conflict between father and son: Haley actually "betrayed" one of the pillars of Bateson's thought.

BIBLIOGRAPHY

Adams, P. L. (1973). *Obsessive children*. New York, NY: Brunner/Mazel.

Ainsworth, M. D. S. (1979). Attachment as related to mother-infant interaction. *Advances in the Study of Behaviour*, 9, 2–52.

Anderson, S. A. & Bagarozzi, D. A. (Eds) (1989). *Family myths: Psychotherapy implications*. New York, NY: Haworth Press.

Andolfi, M., Angelo, C., & De Nichilo, M. (1989). *The myth of atlas: Families and the therapeutic stories*. New York: Brunner-Mazel.

Arciero, G. & Bondolfi, G. (2009). *Selfhood, identity and personality styles*. New York, NY: John Wiley & Son.

Aristotle. (1941). Metaphysics (W. D. Ross, Trans.). In R. McKeon (Ed.), *The basic works of Aristotle* (pp. 689–934). New York, NY: Random House. (Original work ca. 350 BCE)

Aristotle. (1941). Politics (W. D. Ross, Trans.). In R. McKeon (Ed.), *The basic works of Aristotle* (pp. 1127–1324). New York, NY: Random House.

Aristotle. (1962). *Nicomachean ethics* (M. Ostwald, Trans.). Indianapolis, IN: Bobbs-Merrill Educational. (Original work published ca. 325 BCE)

Aquinas, T. (2006). *Summa theologica* (Fathers of the English Dominican Province, Trans.) Raleigh, NC: Hayes Barton Press. (Original work ca. 1273)

Asen, E., Dawson, N., McHugh, B. (2001). *Multiple family therapy: The Marlborough model and its wider applications*. London: Karnac.

Augustine. (1998). *Confessions* (H. Chadwick, Trans.) Oxford: Oxford University Press. (Original work 397–398)

Augustine. (2003). *The city of God* (H. Bettenson, Trans.) London: Penguin Books. (Original work 413–427)

Bamberg, M. (1997). Positioning between structure and performance. *Journal of Narrative and Life History*, 7, 335–342.

Bara, B. G. (Ed.). (1996). *Manuale di psicoterapia cognitiva* [Manual of cognitive psychotherapy]. Torino: Bollati Boringhieri.

Bara, B. G. (Ed.). (2005). *Nuovo manuale di psicoterapia cognitiva. Vol. 2: Clinica* [New manual of cognitive psychotherapy. Vol. 2: Clinical conditions]. Torino: Bollati Boringhieri.

Bara, B. G. & Stoppa Beretta, S. (1996). L'organizzazione cognitiva di tipo psicosomatico [The psychosomatic cognitive organization]. In B. G. Bara (Ed.), *Manuale di psicoterapia cognitiva [Manual of cognitive psychotherapy]* (pp. 278–314). Torino: Bollati Boringhieri.

293

Bateson, G. (1949). Bali: The value system of a steady state. In M. Fortes (Ed.), *Social structure: Studies presented to A. R. Radcliffe-Brown*. Oxford: Clarendon Press.

Bateson, G. (1958). *Naven*. Stanford, CA: Board of Trustees of the Leland Stanford Junior University. (Original work published 1936)

Bateson, G. (1971). The cybernetics of self: A theory of alcoholism. *Psychiatry*, 34, 1–18.

Bateson, G. (1972). *Steps to an ecology of mind*. San Francisco, CA: Chandler Press.

Bateson, G. (1979). *Mind and nature*. New York, NY: Dutton.

Bateson, G., Jackson, D. D., Haley, J., & Weakland, J. H. (1956). Toward a theory of schizophrenia, *Behavioral Science*, 1, 251–64.

Beach, S. R. H. (2001). Marital therapy for co-occurring marital discord and depression. In S. R. H. Beach (Ed.), *Marital and family processes in depression: A scientific foundation for clinical practice* (pp. 205–224). Washington, DC: American Psychological Association.

Beardsley, R. K. & Smith, R. J. (2004). *Japanese culture*. London: Routledge.

Beck, A. T. (1967). *Depression: Causes and treatment*. Philadelphia, PA: University of Pennsylvania Press.

Beck, A. T, Emery, Greenberg, (1985). *Anxiety disorders and phobias: A cognitive perspective*. New York, NY: Basic Books.

Becker, A. E. (2004). Television, disordered eating, and young women in Fiji: Negotiating body image and identity during rapid social change. *Culture, Medicine and Psychiatry*, 28 (4), 533–559.

Becker, A. E., Burwell, R. A., Gilman, S. E. (2002). Herzog, D. B., & Hamburg, P., Eating behaviours and attitudes following prolonged exposure to television among ethnic Fijian adolescents girls. *British Journal of Psychiatry*, 180, 509–514.

Beebe, B., Knoblauch, S., Rustin, J., & Sorter, D. (2005). *Forms of intersubjectivity in infant research and adult treatment*. New York, NY: Other Press.

Bekker, M. H. J. (1996). Agoraphobia and gender: A review. *Clinical Psychology Review*, 16, 129–146.

Benazon, N. R. & Coyne, J. C. (2000). Living with a depressed spouse. *Journal of Family Psychology*, 14, 71–79.

Bentall, R. P. (2009). *Is our current treatment of mental illness really any good?* New York: New York University Press.

Berger, P. & Luckmann, T. (1966). *The social construction of reality: A treatise in the sociology of knowledge*. New York, NY: Anchor Books.

Berman, C. M., Rasmussen, K. L. R., & Suomi, S. J. (1994). Responses of free-ranging rhesus monkeys to a natural form of social separation. *Child Development*, 65, 1028–1041.

Bhagavadgītā. (1979). (K. W. Bolle, Trans.) Berkeley and Los Angeles, CA: University of California Press.

Biederman, J., Petty, C. R., Faraone, S. V., Hirshfeld-Becker, D. R., Henin, A., Rauf, A. et al. Childhood antecedents to panic disorder in referred and non-referred adults. *Journal of Child and Adolescent Psychopharmacology*, 15, 549–561.

Biederman, J. K., Rosenbaum, J. F., Hirshfeld-Becker, D. R., Faraone, S. V., Bolduc, E. A., Gersten, M., et al. Psychiatric correlates of behavioral inhibition in young children of parents with and without psychiatric disorders. *Archives of General Psychiatry*, 47(1), 21–26.

Bifulco, A., Brown, G. W., & Harris, T. O. (1994). Childhood experience of care and abuse (CECA) : A retrospective interview measure. *Journal of Child Psychology and Psychiatry*, 35(8), 1419–1435.

Biral, A. (1991). *Per una storia della sovranità* [For a history of sovranity]. *Filosofia Politica*, 5, 5–50.

Blake, W. (2008). The marriage of heaven and hell. In D. V. Erman (Ed.), *The complete poetry & prose of William Blake* (Rev. edn, pp. 33–44). Berkeley and Los Angeles, CA: University of California Press. (Original work published 1790–1793).

Blinder, B. J., Cumella, E. J., & Sanathara, V. A. (2006). Psychiatric comorbidities of female inpatients with eating disorders. *Psychosomatic Medicine*, 68, 454–462.

Bögels, S. M. & Brechman-Toussaint, M. L. (2006). Family issues in child anxiety: Attachment, family functioning, parental rearing and beliefs. *Clinical Psychology Review*, 26, 834–856.

Boscolo, L. & Bertrando, P. (1996). *Systemic therapy with individuals*. London: Karnac.

Bowen, M. (1966). The use of the family theory in clinical practice. *Comprehensive Psychiatry*, 7(5), 345–374.

Bowen, M. (1978). *Family therapy in clinical practice*. New York, NY: Aronson.

Bowlby, J. (1969). *Attachment and loss. Vol. 1: Attachment*. New York, NY: Basic Books.

Bowlby, J. (1973). *Attachment and loss. Vol. 2: Separation: Anxiety and anger*. London: Hogarth Press.

Bowlby, J. (1979). *The making and breaking of affectional bonds*. London: Tavistock.

Bowlby, J. (1980). *Attachment and loss. Vol. 3: Loss: Sadness and depression*. London: Hogarth Press.

Bowlby, J. (1988). *A secure base*. London: Routledge.

Brandchaft, B. (2001). Obsessional disorders: A developmental systems perspective. *Psychoanalitic Inquiry*, 21, 253–288.

Bråten, S. (Ed.). (2007). *On being moved: From mirror neurons to empathy*. Philadelphia, PA: John Benjamins.

Brown, G. W. (2002). Social roles, context and evolution in the origins of depression. *Journal of Health and Social Behavior*, 43(3), 255–276.

Brown, G. W., Harris, T., & Copeland, J. R. (1977). Depression and loss. *British Journal of Psychiatry*, 130, 1–18.

Browne, T. (1835). Pseudodoxia epidemica. In S. Wilking (Ed.), *Sir Thomas Browne's* (Vol. 3, pp. 1–374). London: Pickering. (Original work published 1646)

Bruch, H. (1973). *Eating disorders: Obesity, anorexia nervosa, and the person within*. New York, NY: Basic Books.

Bruch, H. (1978). *The golden cage: The Enigma of Anorexia Nervosa*. New York, NY: Vintage.

Bruch, H. & Touraine, G. (1940). Obesity in childhood V: The family frame of obese children. *Psychosomatic Medicine*, 2(2), 141–206.

Bruner, J. (1990). *Acts of meaning*. Cambridge, MA: Harvard University Press.

Buber, M. (1958). *I and Thou* (R. G. Smith, Trans.). New York, NY: Scribner. (Original work published 1923)

Butler, A. C., Chapman, J. E., Forman, E. M., & Beck, A. T. (2006). The empirical status of cognitive-behavioral therapy: A Review of meta-analysis. *Clinical Psychology Review*, 26, 17–31.

Button, E. J. (1985). Eating disorders: A quest for control. In J. Button (Ed.), *Personal construct theory and mental health* (pp. 153–168). London: Routledge.

Button, E. J. & Winter, D. (2010). A personal construct perspective on control in eating disorders. In S. Sassaroli & G. M. Ruggiero (Eds), *Cognitive therapy of eating disorders on control and worry* (pp. 29–42). New York, NY: Nova Science.

Byrne, M., Carr, A., & Clark, M. (2004). The efficacy of couples-based interventions for panic disorder with agoraphobia. *Journal of Family Therapy*, 26, 105–125.

Campbell, D. & Groenbaeck, M. (2006). *Taking positions in the organization*. London: Karnac.

Carr, A. (2009). The effectiveness of family therapy and systemic interventions for child-focused problems. *Journal of Family Therapy*, 31, 3–45.

Caspi, A., Sugden, K., Moffitt, T. E., Taylor, A., Craig, I. W., Harrington, H., et al. Influence of life stress on depression: Moderation by a polymorphism in the 5-HTT gene. *Science*, 301, 386–389.

Castiglioni, M., Faccio, E., Veronese, G., & Bell, R. C. (2013). The semantics of power among people with eating disorders. *Journal of Constructivist Psychology*.

Caughlin, J. P. & Huston, T. L. (2002). A contextual analysis of the association between demand/withdraw and marital satisfaction. *Personal Relationships*, 9, 95–119.

Clayton, A. H., Pradko, J. F., Croft, H. A., Montano, C. B., Leadbetter, R. A., Bolden-Watson, C., et al. (2002). Prevalence of sexual dysfunction among newer antidepressants. *Journal of Clinical Psychiatry*, 63(4), 357–366.

Colangelo, L. (2005). Il disturbo borderline di personalità come esito di un processo di costruzione sociale [The borderline personality disorder as a result of social construction]. *Terapia Familiare*, 78, 53–82.

Compton, A. (1992a). The psychoanalytic view of phobias. Part I: Freud's theories of phobias and anxiety. *Psychoanalytic Quarterly*, 61, 206–229.

Compton, A. (1992b). The psychoanalytic view of phobias. Part II: Infantile phobias. *Psychoanalytic Quarterly*, 61, 230–253.

Compton, A. (1992c). The psychoanalytic view of phobias. Part III: Agoraphobia and other phobias of adults. *Psychoanalytic Quarterly*, 61, 400–425.

Compton, A. (1992d). The psychoanalytic view of phobias. Part IV: General theory of phobias and anxiety. *Psychoanalytic Quarterly*, 61, 426–446.

Coyne, J. C. (1982). A critique of cognitions as casual entities with particular reference to depression. *Cognitive Therapy and Research*, 6, 3–13.

Coyne, J. C., Thompson, R., & Palmer, S. C. (2002). Marital quality, coping with conflict, marital complaints and affection in couples with a depressed wife. *Journal of Family Psychology*, 16(1), 26–37.

Cozzolino, L. J. (2006). *The neuroscience of human relationships*. New York, NY: Norton.

Craske, M. G. & Zoellner, L. A. (1995). Anxiety disorders: The role of marital therapy. In A. S. Gurman & N. S. Jacobson (Eds), *Clinical handbook of couple therapy* (pp. 394–410). New York, NY: Guildford.

Cronen, V. E., Johnson, K. M., & Lannamann J. V. (1982). Paradoxes, double binds and reflexive loops: An alternative theoretical perspective. *Family Process*, 20, 91–112.

Crystal, S., Sambamoorthi, U., Walkup, J. T., & Akincigil A. (2003). Diagnosis and treatment of depression in the elderly medicare population: Predictors, disparities, and trends. *Journal of the American Geriatric Society*, 51, 1718–1728.

Cummins, L. H., Simmons, A. M., & Zane, N. W. S. (2005). Eating disorders in Asian populations: A critique of current approaches to the study of culture, ethnicity and eating disorders. *American Journal of Orthopsychiatry*, 75, 553–574.

Currin, L., Schmidt, U., Treasure, J., & Jick, H. (2005). Time trends in eating disorder incidence. *British Journal of Psychiatry*, 186, 132–135.

Dare, C. & Eisler, I. (1997). Family therapy for anorexia nervosa. In D. M. Garner & P. E. Garfinkel (Eds), *Handbook of treatment for eating disorders* (pp. 307–324). New York, NY: Guilford.

Dare, C., Eisler, I., Russel, G., Treasure, J., & Dodge, L. (2001). Psychological therapies for adults with anorexia nervosa: Randomized controlled trial of out-patients treatments. *British Journal of Psychiatry*, 178, 216–221.

Davila, J. (2001). Paths to unhappiness: The overlapping courses of depression and romantic dysfunction. In S. R. H. Beach (Ed.), *Marital and family processes in depression: A scientific foundation for clinical practice* (pp. 71–78). Washington, DC: American Psychological Association.

Davila, J. & Bradbury, T. N. (2001). Attachment insecurity and the distinction between unhappy spouses who do and do not divorce. *Journal of Family Psychology*, 15, 371–393.

Dell'Aversano, C. (2009). *L'analisi posizionale del testo letterario: Lettura di W;t di Margaret Edson* [Positioning analysis of a literary text: A reading of W;t by Margaret Edson]. Roma: Aracne.

De Ruiter, C. & Van IJzendoorn, M. H. (1992). Agoraphobia and anxious-ambivalent attachment: An integrative review. *Journal of Anxiety Disorders*, 6, 365–381.

Dickens, C. (1848). *Dombey and Son*. London: Penguin Books.

Doi, T. (1971). *The anatomy of dependence*. Tokyo: Kodansha International.

Doise, W. & Mugny, G. (1984). The social development of the intellect (A. St. James-Emler, N. Emler, & D. Mackie, Trans.). New York, NY: Pergamon Press.

Doise, W., Mugny, G., & Pérez, J. A. (1998). The social construction of knowledge: Social marking and socio-cognitive conflict. In U. Flick (Ed.), *The psychology of the social* (pp. 77–90). Cambridge: Cambridge University Press.

Dostoevsky, F. M. (1993). *The brothers Karamazov* (D. Mc Duff, Trans). London: Penguin. (Original work published 1880)

Dostoevsky, F. M. (1995). *Demons* (R. Peaver & L. Volokhonsky, Trans). New York, NY: Vintage. (Original work published 1873)

Dozier, M., Stovall-McClough, K. C., & Albus, K. E. (2008). Attachment and psychopathology in adulthood. In J. Cassidy & P. R. Shaver (Eds), *Handbook of attachment: Theory, research, and clinical application* (2nd edn, pp. 718–774). New York, NY: Guilford Press.

Dumont, L. (1970) *Homo hierarchicus: An essay on the caste system* (M. Sainsbury, Trans.). Chicago, IL: The University of Chicago Press.

Dumont, L. (1986). *Essays on individualism: Modern ideology in anthropological perspective*. Chicago, IL: University of Chicago Press.

Eisler, I. (2005). The empirical and theoretical base of family therapy and multiple family day therapy for adolescent anorexia nervosa. *Journal of Family Therapy*, 2, 104–131.

Eisler, I., Dare, C., Hodes, M., Russel, G., Dodge, L., & Le Grange, D. (2000). Family therapy for adolescent anorexia nervosa: The results of a controlled comparison of two family interventions. *Journal of Child Psychology and Psychiatry*, 41, 727–736.

Elias, N. (2000) *The civilizing process: Sociogenic and psychogenetic investigations* (Rev. edn) (E. Jephcott, Trans.). Oxford: Blackwell. (Original work published 1939)

Eliot, T. S. (1922). *The waste land*. New York, NY: Boni & Liveright.

Elkaim, M. (1997). *If you love me, don't love me: Undoing reciprocal double binds and other methods of change in couple and family therapy*. New York, NY: Aronson.

Ellis, A. (1962). *Reason and emotion in psychotherapy*. New York, NY: Lyle Stuart.

Esman, A. (1989). Psychoanalysis and general psychiatry: Obsessive-compulsive disorders as paradigm. *Journal of the American Psychoanalytic Association*, 37, 319–336.

Fairburn, C. G., Cooper, Z., Doll, H. A., & Welch, S. L. (1999). Risk factors for anorexia nervosa: Three integrated case-control comparisons. *Archives of General Psychiatry*, 56, 468–476.

Feixas, G. & Saúl, L. A. (2004). The multi-center dilemma project: An investigation on the role of cognitive conflicts in health. *Spanish Journal of Psychology*, 7, 69–78.

Feixas, G., Saúl, L. A., & Àvila-Espada, A. (2009). Viewing cognitive conflicts as dilemmas: Implications for mental health. *Journal of Constructive Psychology*, 22, 141–169.

Fergusson, D., Doucette, S., Glass, K., Shapiro, S., Healy, D., Hebert, P., & Hutton, B. (2005). Association between suicide attempts and selective serotonin reuptake inhibitors: Systematic review of randomised controlled trials. *British Medical Journal*, 330, 396–399.

Ferreira, A. J. (1963). Family myth and homeostasis. *Archives of General Psychiatry*, 9, 457–463.

Ferreira, A. J. (1966). Family myths. *Psychiatric Research Reports*, 20, 85–90.

Festinger, L. (1954). A theory of social comparison processes. *Human Relations*, 7, 117–140.

Fiske, S. T. (2004). *Social beings: A core motives approach to social psychology*. New York, NY: Wiley & Sons.

Fivaz-Depeursinge, E. & Corboz-Warnerey, A. (1999). *The primary triangle*. New York, NY: Basic Books.

Focht-Birkerts, L. & Beardslee, W. R. (1996). "Speech after long silence": The use of narrative therapy in a preventive intervention for children of parents with affective disorder. *Family Process*, 35, 407–422.

Focht-Birkerts, L. & Beardslee, W. R. (2000). A child's experience of parental depression: Encouraging relational resilience in families with affective illness. *Family Process*, 39, 417–434.

Fodor, I. G. (1974). The phobic syndrome in women: Implications for treatment. In V. Franks & V. Burde (Eds), *Women in therapy* (pp. 132–168). Oxford: Brunner/Mazel.

Fontane, T. (1967), *Effi Briest* (D. Parmée, Trans.). London: Penguin Books. (Original work published 1895)

Fournier, J. C., DeRubeis, R. J., Hollon, S. D., Dimidjian, S., Amsterdam, J. D., Shelton, R. C., & Fawcett, J. (2010). Antidepressant drug effects and depression severity: A patient-level meta-analysis. *Journal of the American Medical Association*, 303, 47–53.

Franklin, J. A. & Andrews, G. (1989). Stress and the onset of agoraphobia. *Australian Psychologists*, 24, 203–219.

Freud, A. (1976). Foreword. In H. Nagera, *Obsessional neuroses: Developmental psychopathology*. New York, NY: Aronson.

Freud, S. (1955). Beyond the pleasure principle. In J. Strachey (Ed. and Trans.), *The standard edition of the complete psychological works of Sigmund Freud* (Vol. 18, pp. 7–64). London: Hogarth Press. (Original work published 1920)

Freud, S. (1955). Notes upon a case of obsessional neurosis. In J. Strachey (Ed. and Trans.), *The standard edition of the complete psychological works of Sigmund Freud* (Vol. 10, pp. 153–319). London: Hogarth Press. (Original work published 1909)

Freud, S. (1957). On the universal tendency to debasement in the sphere of love. In J. Strachey (Ed. and Trans.), *The standard edition of the complete psychological works of Sigmund Freud* (Vol. 11, pp. 177–190). London: Hogarth Press. (Original work published 1912)

Freud, S. (1959). Inhibitions, symptoms and anxiety. In J. Strachey (Ed. and Trans.), *The standard edition of the complete psychological works of Sigmund Freud* (Vol. 20, pp. 77–174). London: Hogarth Press. (Original work published 1925)

Freud, S. (1961). The Ego and the Id. In J. Strachey (Ed. and Trans.), *The standard edition of the complete psychological works of Sigmund Freud* (Vol. 19, pp. 1–308). London: Hogarth Press. (Original work published 1923)

Freud, S. (1963). Introductory lectures on psycho-analysis. In J. Strachey (Ed. and Trans.), *The standard edition of the complete psychological works of Sigmund Freud* (Vols. 15–16, pp. 9–496). London: Hogarth Press. (Original work published 1915–1917)

Freud, S. (1964). An outline of psycho-analysis. In J. Strachey (Ed. and Trans.), *The standard edition of the complete psychological works of Sigmund Freud* (Vol. 23, pp. 139–207). London: Hogarth Press. (Original work published 1940)

Fry, W. F. (1962). The marital context of an anxiety syndrome. *Family Process*, 1, 245–252.

Gallese, V. (2001). The "shared manifold" hypothesis: From mirror neurons to empathy. *Journal of Consciousness Studies*, 8(5–7), 33–50.

Gardner, R. & Price, J. S. (1999). Sociophysiology of depression. In T. Joiner & J. C. Coyne (Eds), *The interactional nature of depression* (pp. 247–268). Washington, DC: American Psychological Association.

Gergen, J. K. & Gergen, M. (2004). *Social construction: Entering the Dialouge*. Chagrin Falls, OH: Taos Institute.

Gilbert, P. (1992). *Depression: The evolution of powerlessness*. New York, NY: Guilford Press.

Gittelman, R. & Klein, D. F. (1984). Relationship between separation anxiety and panic in agoraphobic disorders. *Psychopathology*, 17, 56–65.

Glauber, L., Copes, N., & Bara, B. G. (1996). L'organizzazione cognitiva di tipo fobico [The cognitive phobic organization]. In B. G. Bara (Ed.), *Manuale di psicoterapia cognitiva* [Manual of cognitive psychotherapy] (pp. 213–247). Torino: Bollati Boringhieri.

Godart, N. T., Flament, M. F., Curt, F., Perdereau, F., Lang, F., Venisse, J. L., & Fermanian, J. (2003). Anxiety disorders in subjects seeking treatment for eating disorders: A DSM-IV controlled study. *Psychiatry Research*, 117 (3), 245–258.

Goffman, E. (1959). *The presentation of self in everyday life*. New York, NY: Doubleday.

Goodstein, R. K. & Swift, K. (1977). Psychotherapy with phobic patients: The marriage relationship as the source of symptoms and focus of treatment. *American Journal of Psychotherapy*, 31, 284–293.

Gordon, R. A. (1990). *Anorexia and bulimia: Anatomy of a social epidemic.* Cambridge, MA: Blackwell.

Gordon, R. A. (2001). Eating disorders East and West: A culture-bound syndrome unbound. In M. Nasser, M. A. Kazman & R. A. Gordon (Eds.), *Eating disorders and cultures in transition* (pp. 1–16). Hove: Brunner-Routledge.

Grebe, P. (1963). *Etymologie: Herkunftswörterbuch der deutschen Sprache* [Etimology: Dictionary of German language]. Mannheim: Bibliographisches Institut.

Greenberg, G. (2010). *Manufacturing depression: The secret history of a modern disease.* New York, NY: Simon & Schuster.

Grossmann, E. K. & Grossmann, K. (1981). Parent-infant attachment relationship in Bielefeld: A research note. In K. Immelmann, G. W. Barlow, M. Main, & L. Petrinovich (Eds), *Behavioral development: The bielefeld interdisciplinary project* (pp. 694–699). New York, NY: Cambridge University Press.

Guardini, R. (1925). *Der Gegensatz: Versuche Zu Einer Philosophie Des Lebendig-Konkreten [The polar opposition: Essay for a philosophy of the living concrete].* Mainz: Der Werkkreis Im Mattias-Grunewald.

Guidano, V. F. (1987). *Complexity of the Self.* New York, NY: Guilford.

Guidano, V. F. (1988). *La complessità del Sé* [Complexity of the Self]. Torino: Bollati Boringhieri.

Guidano, V. F. (1991). *The self in process: Toward a post-rationalist cognitive therapy.* New York, NY: Guilford.

Guidano, V. F. & Liotti, G. (1983). *Cognitive processes and emotional disorders.* New York, NY: Guilford.

Hafner, R. J. (1977). The husbands of agoraphobic women and their influence on treatment outcome. *British Journal of Psychiatry*, 131, 289–294.

Hafner, R. J. (1979). Agoraphobic women married to abnormally jealous men. *British Journal of Medicine Psychology*, 52, 99–104.

Hafner, R. J. (1984). The marital repercussions of behavior therapy for agoraphobia. *Psychotherapy: Theory, Research Practice*, 21, 530–542.

Haley, J. (1963). *Strategies of psychotherapy*, New York, NY: Grune & Stratton.

Haley, J. (1967). Toward a theory of pathological systems. In G. H. Zuk & I. Boszormenyi-Nagy (Eds), *Family therapy and disturbed families* (pp. 11–27). Palo Alto, CA: Science and Behavioral Books.

Halmi, K. A., Sunday, S. R., Strober, M., Kaplan, A., Woodside, D. B., Fichter, M., & Kaye, W. H. (2000). Perfectionism in anorexia nervosa: Variation by clinical subtype, obsessionality, and pathological eating behavior. *American Journal of Psychiatry*, 157, 1799–1805.

Hamilton, B. E., Jones, M., & Hammen, C. (1993). Maternal interaction style in affective disordered, physically ill, and normal women. *Family Process*, 32, 329–340.

Hammad, T. A., Laughren, T., & Racoosin, J. (2006). Suicidality in pediatric patients treated with antidepressant drugs. *Archives of General Psychiatry*, 63, 332–339.

Hammen, C. (1999). The emergence of an interpersonal approach to depression. In T. E., Joiner & J. C. Coyne (Eds), *The interactional nature of depression* (pp. 21–35). Washington, DC: American Psychological Association.

Hand, I. & Lamontagne, Y. (1976). The exacerbation of interpersonal problems after rapid phobia removal. *Psychotherapy: Theory, Research, Practice*, 13, 405–411.

Harré, R. (Ed.). (1986). *The social construction of emotions.* Oxford: Blackwell.

Harré, R. & Moghaddam, F. M. (Eds) (2003). *The self and others: Positioning individuals and groups in personal, political and cultural contexts.* London: Praeger.

Harré, R. & Van Langenhove, L. (1999). *Positioning theory: Moral context of intentional action.* Oxford: Blackwell.

Harré, R., Moghaddam, F. M., Cairnie, T. P., Rothbart, D., & Sabat, S. R. (2009). Recent advances in positioning theory. *Theory & Psychology,* 19, 5–31.

Healy, D. (2004). *Let them eat prozac: The unhealthy relationship between the pharmaceutical industry and depression* New York, NY: New York University Press.

Heene, E., Buysse, A., & Van Oost, P. (2005). Indirect pathways between depressive symptoms and marital distress: The role of conflict communication, attributions and attachment style. *Family Process,* 44, 413–440.

Heene, E., Buysse, A., & Van Oost, P. (2007). An interpersonal perspective on depression: The role of marital adjustment, conflict communication, attributions, and attachment within a clinical sample. *Family Process,* 46(4), 499–514.

Henin, A. & Kendall, P. C. (1997). Obsessive-compulsive disorder in childhood and adolescence. In T. H. Ollendick & R. J. Prinz (Eds), *Advances in Clinical Child Psychology* (Vol. 19, pp. 75–131). New York, NY: Plenum Press.

Heraclitus (1954). In G. S. Kirk (Ed.), *Heraclitus: The cosmic fragments.* Cambridge: University Press.

Heraclitus (1972). In E. Hussey, *The presocratics.* New York, NY: Charles Scribner's Sons.

Heraclitus (1987). In T. M. Robinson, *Heraclitus: Fragments.* Toronto: University Press.

Herring, M. & Kaslow, N. J. (2002). Depression and attachment in families: A child-focused perspective. *Family Process,* 41(3), 494–518.

Hinde, R. A. (1982). Attachment: Some conceptual and biological issues. In C. M. Parks & J. Stevenson Hinde (Eds), *The placement of attachment in human behavior* (pp. 60–76). London: Tavistock.

Hobbes, T. (1968). *Leviathan.* Harmondsworth: Penguin Books. (Original work published 1651)

Hobbes, T. (1998). *On the citizens* (R. Tuck, Trans.). Cambridge: Cambridge University Press. (Original work published 1642)

Hobbes, T. (2004). *The elements of law natural and politic.* Whitefish, MT; Kessinger. (Original work published 1640)

Hoek, H. W. (2006). Incidence, prevalence and mortality of anorexia nervosa and other eating disorders. *Current Opinion in Psychiatry,* 19, 389–394.

Hoek, H. W. & Van Hoeken, D. (2003). Review of the prevalence and incidence of eating disorders. *International Journal of Eating Disorders,* 34(4), 383–396.

Hoffart, A. (1997). Interpersonal problems among patients suffering from panic disorder with agoraphobia before and after treatment. *British Journal of Medicine Psychology,* 70(2), 149–157.

Holmes, J. (1982). Phobia and counterphobia: Family aspects of agoraphobia. *Journal of Family Therapy,* 4(2), 133–152.

Hoover, C. & Insel, T. (1984). Families of origin in obsessive-compulsive disorder. *Journal of Nervous and Mental Disease,* 172 (4), 207–215.

Horowitz, A. V. & Wakefield, J. C. (2007). *The loss of sadness: How psychiatry transformed normal sorrow into depressive disorder.* New York, NY: Oxford University Press.

Hudson, J. & Rapee, R. M. (2001). Parent-child interactions and anxiety disorders: An observational study. *Behavior Research and Therapy*, 39, 1411–1427.

Hussey, E. (1972). *The presocratics*. New York, NY: Charles Scribner's Sons.

Ibsen, H. (1992). *A doll's house*. New York, NY: Dover. (Original work published 1879)

The *I Ching* [Book of changes] (1951) (Wilhelm/Baynes, Trans.) London: Routledge & Kegan Paul.

Imel, Z. E., Malterer, M. B., McKay, K. M., & Wampold, B. E. (2008). A meta-analysis of psychotherapy and medication in unipolar depression and dysthymia. *Journal of Affective Disorders*, 110 (3), 197–206.

Joiner, T. E. & Coyne, J. C. (Eds). (1999). *The interactional nature of depression: Advances in interpersonal approaches*. Washington, DC: American Psychological Association.

Jung, C. G. (1970). Mysterium Coniunctionis (R. F. C. Hull, Trans.). In H. Read, M. Fordham, & G. Adler (Eds), *The collected works of C. G. Jung* (Vol. 14). London: Routledge & Kegan Paul. (Original work published 1955–1956)

Jung, C. G. (1971). Psychological types (R. F. C. Hull, Trans.). In H. Read, M. Fordham, & G. Adler (Eds), *The collected works of C. G. Jung* (Vol. 6). London: Routledge & Kegan Paul. (Original work published 1921)

Kahn, A., Leventhal, R. M., Kahn, R. S., & Brown, W. A. (2002). Severity of depression and response to antidepressant and placebo: An analysis of the food and drug administration database. *Journal of Clinical Psychopharmacology*, 22 (1), 40–45.

Kahneman, D. (2011). *Thinking, fast and slow*. New York; NY: Farrar, Straus and Giroux.

Kant, I. (1929). *The critique of pure reason* (N. Kemp Smith, Trans.). London: Macmillan. (Original work published 1787)

Kaye, K. (1982). *The mental and social life of babies*. Chicago, IL: University of Chicago Press.

Kelly, G. A. (1955). *The psychology of personal constructs* (Vols. 1–2). New York, NY: Norton.

Keski-Rahkonen, A., Raevuori, A., & Hoek, H. W. (2008). Epidemiology of eating disorders: An update. In S. Wonderlich, J. E. Mitchell, M. De Zwaan, & H. Steiger (Eds), *Annual review of eating disorders. Part 2* (pp. 58–68). Radcliffe Publishing: Oxford.

Keski-Rahkonen, A., Hoek, H. W., Linna, M. S., Raevuori, A., Sihvola, E., Bulik, C. et al. (2009). Incidence and outcomes of bulimia nervosa: A nationwide population-based study, *Psychological Medicine*, 39 (5) 823–831.

Kierkegaard, S. (1978). Autobiographical, Part One, 1829–1848. In H. V. Hong & E. H. Hong (Eds. and Trans.), *Søren Kierkegaard's journals and papers* (Vol. 5). Bloomington: Indiana University Press. (Original work published 1835)

Kirsch, I. (2010). *The emperor's new drugs: Exploding the antidepressant myth*. New York, NY: Basic Books.

Kirsch, I., Moore, T. J., Scoboria, A., & Nicholls, S. S. (2002). The emperor's new drugs: An analysis of antidepressant medication data submitted to the U.S. Food and Drug Administration. *Prevention & Treatment*, 5 (1), art. 23.

Kirsch, I., Deacon, B. J., Huendo-Medina, T. B., Scoboria, A., Moore, T. J., & Johnson, B. T. (2008). Initial severity and antidepressant benefits: A meta-analysis of data submitted to the food and drug administration. *PloS Medicine*, 5 (2), 260–268.

Klein, M. (1932). *The psycho-analysis of children*. London: Hogarth Press.

Kleiner, L. & Marshall, W. L. (1985). Relationship difficulties and agoraphobia. *Clinical Psychology Review*, 5 (6), 581–595.

Kohut, H. (1977). *The restoration of the self*. New York, NY: International Universities Press.

Koskina, A., Van den Eynde, F., Meisel, S., Campbell, I. C., & Schmidt, U. (2011). Social appearance anxiety and bulimia nervosa. *Eating and Weight Disorders*, 16 (2), 142–145.

Krueger, J. I. (2012). *Social judgment and decision making*. New York, NY: Psychology Press.

Kundera, M. (1999). *The unbearable lightness of being* (M. H. Heim, Trans.). New York, NY: HarperCollins. (Original work published 1984)

Lacasse, J. R. & Leo, J. (2005). Serotonin and depression: A disconnect between the advertisements and the scientific literature, *PLoS Medicine*, 2 (12), e392.

Laing, R. D. (1961). *Self and others*. New York, NY: Routledge.

Laing, R. D. (1965). *The divided self: An existential study in sanity & madness*. London: Pelican.

Laing, R. D. (1969). *The politics of the family*. London: Tavistock.

Lane, C. (2007). *Shyness: How normal behavior became a sickness*. London: Yale University Press.

Lao Tzu. (1963). *Tao Te Ching* (D. C. Lau, Trans.), London: Penguin Books.

Laughlin, H. P. (1967). *The neuroses*. Washington, DC: Butterworths.

Lawrence, D. H. (1996). *Women in love*. New York, NY: Barnes & Noble (Original work published 1920)

Leibowitz, M. & Klein, D. F. (1982). Agoraphobia: Clinical features, pathophysiology, and treatment. In D. Chambless & A. Goldstein (Eds). *Agoraphobia: Multiple perspectives on theory and treatment* (pp. 153–181). New York, NY: Wiley & Sons.

Lewinsohn, P. M., Pettit, J. W., Joiner, T. E. jr., & Seeley, J. R. (2003). The phenomenology of major depressive disorder in adolescents and young adults. *Journal of Abnormal Psychology*, 112 (2), 244–252.

Lichtenberg, J. (1989). *Psychoanalysis and motivation*. Hillsdale, NY: The Analytic Press.

Lilenfeld, L. R. R., Wonderlich, S., Riso, L. P., Crosby, R., & Mitchell, J. (2006). Eating disorders and personality: A methodological and empirical review. *Clinical Psychology Review*, 26 (3), 299–320.

Linares, J. L. (2010). Depressione e distimia: Basi relazionali e guide per l'intervento [Depression and dysthymia: Relationalbasesand guides forintervention]. *Terapia Familiare*, 94, 79–94.

Linares, J. L. & Campo, C. (2000). *Tras la honorable fachada*. Barcelona: Paidós Ibérica.

Lloyd, G. E. R. (1966). *Polarity and analogy: Two types of argumentation in early Greek thought*. Cambridge: Cambridge University Press.

Lloyd, G. E. R. (1991). *Methods and problems in Greek science*. Cambridge: Cambridge University Press.

Lock, J., Le Grange, D., Agras, W. S., & Dare, C. (2001). *Treatment manual for anorexia nervosa: A family-based approach*. New York, NY: Guilford.

Lorenzini, R. & Sassaroli, S. (1992). *Cattivi pensieri: I disturbi del pensiero schizofrenico, paranoico e ossessivo* [Bad thoughts]. Roma: Carocci.

Lorenzini, R. & Sassaroli, S. (1998). *Paure e fobie* [Fears and phobias]. Milano: Il Saggiatore.

Loriedo, C. & Jedlowski, M. (2010). *Aspettative totalizzanti e relazioni familiari nella depressione* [Full-embracing expectations and family relationships in the depression]. *Terapia Familiare*, 94, 60–78.

Lyons-Ruth, K. & Jacobvitz, D. (2008). Attachment disorganization: Genetic factors, parenting contexts, and developmental transformation from infancy to adulthood. In J. Cassidy & P. R. Shaver (Eds), *Handbook of attachment: Theory, research, and clinical application* (2nd edn, pp. 666–697). New York, NY: Guilford.

MacFarlane, M. M. (2003), Systemic treatment of depression: An integrative approach. *Journal of Family Psychotherapy*, 14 (1), 43–61.

MacIntyre, A. (1981). *After virtue: A study in moral theory.* Notre Dame, IN: University of Notre Dame Press.

Makino, M., Tsuboi, K., & Dennerstein, L. (2004). Prevalence of eating disorders: A comparison of Western and non-Western Countries. *Medscape General Medicine*, 6 (3), 49.

Manicavasagar, V., Silove, D., & Curtis, J. (1997). Separation anxiety in adulthood: A phenomenological investigation. *Comprehensive Psychiatry*, 38 (5), 274–282.

Manicavasagar, V., Silove, D., Curtis, J., & Wagner, R. (2000). Continuities of separation anxiety from early life into adulthood. *Journal of Anxiety Disorders*, 4 (1), 1–18

Manicavasagar, V., Silove, D., Wagner, R., & Hadzi-Pavlovic, D. (1999). Parental representations associated with adult separation anxiety and panic disorder-agoraphobia. *Australian & New Zealand Journal of Psychiatry*, 33 (3), 422-428.

Marcaurelle, R., Bélanger, C., & Marchand, A. (2003). Marital relationship and the treatment of panic disorder with agoraphobia: A critical review. *Clinical Psychology Review*, 23 (2), 247–276.

McGuire, M. T., Raleigh, M. J., & Johnson, C. (1983). Social dominance in adult male vervet monkeys: General considerations. *Social Science Information*, 22 (1), 89–123.

Meltzoff, A. N. (1995). Understanding the intentions of others: Re-enactment of intended acts by 18-month-old children. *Developmental Psychology*, 31 (5), 838–850.

Meltzoff, A. N. & Moore, M. K. (1977). Imitation of facial and manual gestures by human neonates. *Science*, 198, 75–78.

Meltzoff, A. N. & Moore, M. K. (1999). Persons and representation: Why infant imitation is important for theories of human development. In J. Nadel & G. Butterworth (Eds), *Imitation in infancy. Cambridge studies in cognitive perceptual development* (pp. 9–35). New York, NY: Cambridge University Press.

Miller, A. (1983). *For your own good: Hidden cruelty in child-rearing and the roots of violence* (A. Miller, Trans.). New York, NY: Farrar, Straus and Giroux.

Miller, M. & Pumariega, A. J., (2001). Eating disorders: A historical and cross-culture review. *Psychiatric: Interpersonal & Biological Processes*, 64 (2) 93–110.

Minuchin, S., & Barcai, A. (1969). Therapeutically induced family crisis. In J. H. Masserman (Ed.), *Science and psychoanalysis* (pp. 199–205). New York, NY: Grune & Stratton.

Minuchin, S., Rosman, B. L., & Baker, L. (1978). *Psychosomatic families: Anorexia nervosa in context.* Cambridge, MA: Harvard University Press.

Minuchin, S., Montalvo, B., Guerney, B. G., Rosman, B. L., & Schumer, F. (1967).

Families of the slums: An exploration of their structure and treatment. New York, NY: Basic Books.

Moncrieff, J. (2008). *The myth of the cure chemical: A critique of psychiatric drug treatment.* Basingstoke: Palgrave MacMillan.

Moncrieff, J., Wessely, S., & Hardy, R. (2005). Active placebos versus antidepressants for depression. *Cochrane Database of Systematic Reviews 2004,* 1.

Mugny, G. & Carugati, F. (1987). *Psicologia sociale dello sviluppo cognitivo* [Social psychology of the cognitive development]. Firenze: Giunti.

Muris, P., Meesters, C., & Spinder, M. (2003). Relationships between child- and parent-reported behavioural inhibition and symptoms of anxiety and depression in normal adolescents. *Personality and Individual Differences,* 34 (5), 759–771.

Muris, P., Merckelbach, H., Wessel, I., & van de Ven, M. (1999). Psychopathological correlates of self-reported behavioural inhibition in normal children. *Behaviour Research and Therapy,* 37 (6), 575–584.

Muris, P., Merckelbach, H., Schmidt, H., Gadet, B., & Bogie, N. (2001). Anxiety and depression as correlates of self-reported behavioural inhibition in normal children. *Behaviour Research and Therapy,* 39 (9), 1051–1061.

Nagera, H. (1976). *Obsessional neuroses: Developmental psychopathology.* New York, NY: Aronson.

Nasser, M., Katzman, M. A., & Gordon, R. A. (Eds) (2001). Eating disorders and cultures in transition. New York, NY: Brunner-Routledge.

National Institute for Clinical Excellence (NICE). (2004). *Eating disorders: Core interventions in the treatment and management of anorexia nervosa, bulimia nervosa and related eating disorders.* Retrieved April 27 from http://publications.nice.org.uk/eating-disorders-cg9

Needham, R. (1987). *Counterpoints.* Berkeley, CA: University of California Press.

Neimeyer, R. A. (2009). *Constructivist Psychotherapy.* New York: Routledge.

Neimeyer, R. A. & Raskin, J. D. (Eds). (2000). *Constructions of disorder: Meaning-making frameworks for psychotherapy.* Washington, DC: American Psychological Association.

Nierenberg, A. A., Leon, A. C., Price, L. H., Shelton, R. C., & Trivedi, M. H. (2011). Crisis of confidence: Antidepressant risk versus benefit. *Journal of Clinical Psychiatry,* 72 (3), e11.

Ogden, C. K. (1932). *Opposition: A linguistic and psychological analysis.* London: Kagan.

Olson, J. M., Herman, C. P., & Zanna, M. P. (Eds). (1986). *Relative deprivation and social comparison.* Hillsdale, NY: Erlbaum.

Osgood, C. E., Suci, G. J., & Tannenbaum, P. (1957). *The measurement of meaning.* Urbana, IL: University of Illinois Press.

Parks, T. (2009). Semantic polarities in the works of Thomas Hardy and D. H. Lawrence. *Merope,* 53–54, 5–46.

Parrott, W. G. (2003). Positioning and the emotions. In D. Harré & F. Moghaddam (Eds), *Positioning individuals and groups in personal, political, and cultural context* (pp. 29–44). Westport, CT: Praeger.

Pettit, J. W. & Joiner, T. E. (2006). *Chronic depression: Interpersonal sources, therapeutic solutions.* Washington, DC: American Psychological Association.

Plato. (1966). *Phaedo* (H. N. Fowler, Trans.) London: Heinemann. (Original work ca. 387–386 BCE).

Plomin, R., De Fries, J. C., McClearn, G. E., & McGuffin, P. (2001). *Behavioral genetics*. New York, NY: Worth Publisher.

Procter, H. G. (1981). Family construct psychology: An approach to understanding and treating families. In S. Walrond-Skinner (Ed.), *Developments in family therapy* (pp. 350–366). London: Routledge and Kegan Paul.

Procter, H. G. (1985). A construct approach to family therapy and systems intervention. In E. Button (Ed.), *Personal construct theory and mental health:Theory, research and practice* (pp. 327–350). London: Croom Helm.

Procter, H. G. (1996). The family construct system. In D. Kalekin-Fishman & B. M. Walker (Eds) *The construction of group realities: Culture, society, and personal construct theory* (pp. 161–180). Malabar, FL: Krieger.

Procter, H. G. (2007). Construing within the family. In R. Butler & D. Green (Eds), *The child within: Taking the young person's perspectiveby applying Personal Construct Theory* (2nd edn, pp. 190–206). Chichester: Wiley & Sons.

Procter, H. G. (2009). The construct. In R. J. Butler (Ed.), *Reflections in personal construct theory* (pp. 21–40). Chichester: Wiley & Sons.

Procter, H. G & Parry, G. (1978). Constraint and freedom: The social origin of personal constructs. In F. Fransella (Ed.), *Personal construct psychology 1977* (pp. 157–170). London: Academic Press.

Radden, J. (Ed.). (2000). *The nature of melancholy: From Aristotle to Kristeva*. Oxford, NY: Oxford University Press.

Rado, S. (1959). Obsessive behavior. In S. Arieti (Ed.), *American handbook of psychiatry* (Vol. 1, pp. 224–244). New York, NY: Basic Books.

Raleigh, M. J., McGuire, M. T., Brammer, G. L., & Yuwiler, A. (1984). Social and environmental influences on blood serotonin concentrations in monkeys. *Archive of General Psychiatry*, 41 (4), 405–410.

Raskin, J. D., Bridges, S. K., & Neimeyer, R. A. (Eds). (2010). *Studies in Meaning 4: Constructivist perspectiveson theory, practice and social justice*. New York, NY: Pace University Press.

Rasmussen, S. A. & Eisen, J. L. (1992). The epidemiology and clinical features of obsessive-compulsive disorder. *Psychiatric Clinics of North America*, 15 (4), 743–758.

Reiss, D. (1981). *The family's construction of reality*. Cambridge, MA: Harvard University Press.

Ricci, C. (1986). Interactional complexity and communication. In M. S. Palazzoli (Ed.), *The hidden games of organizations* (pp. 159–169). New York, NY: Pantheon Books

Rivett, M. & Street, E. (2009). *Family Therapy: 100 key points and techniques*. New York, NY: Routledge

Rizzolatti, G., Fogassi, L., & Gallese, V. (2001). Neurophysiological mechanisms underlying the understanding and imitation of action. *Nature Review Neuroscience*, 2 (9), 661–670.

Ruesch, J. & Bateson, G. (1951). *Communication: The social matrix of psychiatry*. New York, NY: Norton.

Salzman, L. (1966). Therapy of obsessional states. *American Journal of Psychiatry*, 122, 1139–1146.

Santor, D. & Coyne, J. C. (2001). Evaluating the continuity of symptomatology between depressed and nondepressed individuals. *Journal of Abnormal Psychology*, 110 (2), 216–225.

Sapolsky, R. M. (1989). Hypercortisolism among socially subordinate wild baboons originates at the CNS Level. *Archive of General Psychiatry*, 46 (11), 1047–1051.

Sapolsky, R. M. (2005). The influence of social hierarchy on primate health. *Science*, 308 (5722), 648–652.

Sassaroli, S., Lorenzini, R., & Ruggiero, G. M. (2005). Le fobie e il loro trattamento [Phobias and their treatment]. In B. G. Bara (Ed.), *Nuovo manuale di psicoterapia cognitiva. Vol. 2: Clinica* [New manual of cognitive psychotherapy. Vol. 2: Clinical conditions] (pp. 61–92). Torino: Bollati Boringhieri.

Schembri, C. & Evans, L. (2008). Adverse relationship processes: The attempts of women with bulimia nervosa symptoms to fit the perceived ideal of intimate partners. *European Eating Disorders Review*, 16 (1), 59–66.

Schopenhauer, A. (1966). *The world as will and representation* (Vol. 1). (E. F. J. Paine, Trans.). Mineola, NY: Dover Books. (Original work published 1819)

Schopenhauer, A. (2007). *Parerga e paralipomena: A collection of philosophical essays.* (T. Bailey Saunders, Trans.). New York, NY: Cosimo Books. (Original work published 1851)

Scott, R. L. & Cordova, J. V. (2002). The influence of adult attachment styles on the association between marital adjustment and depressive symptoms. *Journal of Family Psychology*, 16 (2), 199–208.

Seikkula, J. & Arnkil, T. E. (2006). *Dialogical meetings in social networks.* London: Karnac.

Seikkula, J., Aaltonen, J., Kalla, O., Saarinen, P., & Tolvanen, A. (2012). Couple therapy for depression in a naturalistic setting in Finland: A two-year randomized trial. *Journal of Family Therapy.*

Selvini Palazzoli, M. (1974). *Self starvation: From individual to family therapy in the treatment of anorexia nervosa* (A. Pomerans, Trans.). London: Caucher.

Selvini Palazzoli, M. & Viaro, M. (1988). The anorectic process in the family: A six stages model as a guide for the individual therapy. *Family Process*, 27 (2), 129–148.

Selvini Palazzoli, M., Boscolo, L., Cecchin, G., & Prata, G. (1978). *Paradox and counterparadox: A new model in the therapy of the family in schizophrenic transaction.* New York, NY: Aronson.

Selvini Palazzoli, M., Boscolo, L., Cecchin, G., & Prata, G. (1980). Hypothesizing-circularity-neutrality: Three guidelines for the conducer of the session. *Family Process*, 19 (1), 3–12.

Selvini Palazzoli, M., Cirillo, S., Selvini, M., & Sorrentino, A. M. (1989). *Family games: General models of psychotic processes in the family.* London: Karnac Books.

Shean, G. D. (1990). Interpersonal aspects of agoraphobia: Therapeutic implications. *Psychotherapy in Private Practice*, 8 (3), 101–122.

Shilkert, C. (2002). The role of unconscious pathogenic beliefs in agoraphobia. *Psychotherapy: Theory, Research, Practice and Training*, 39 (4), 368–375.

Shively, C. A., Laber-Laird, K., & Anton, R. F. (1997). Behavior and physiology of social stress and depression in female cynomolgus monkeys. *Biological Psychiatry*, 41 (8), 871–882.

Shorter, E. (2009). *Before Prozac: The troubled history of mood disorders in psychiatry.* New York, NY: Oxford University Press.

Siegel, D. J. (2012). *The developing mind: How relationship and the brain interact to shape who we are* (2nd edn). New York, NY: Guilford Press.

Skårderud, F. (2007). Eating one's words: Part III. Mentalisation-based psychotherapy for anorexia nervosa. An outline for a treatment and training manual. *European Eating Disorders Review*, 15 (5), 323–339.

Sluzki, C. E. (1981). Process of symptom production and patterns of symptom maintenance. *Journal of Marital Family Therapy*, 7 (3), 273–280.

Speranza, M., Corcos, M., Godart, N., Loas, G., Guilbaud, O., Jeammet, P., & Flament, M. (2001). Obsessive compulsive disorders in eating disorders. *Eating Behaviors*, 2 (3), 193–207.

Stam, H. J. (1998). Personal-construct theory and social constructionism: Difference and dialogue. *Journal of Constructivist Psychology*, 11 (3), 187–203.

Stead, C. (1979). *The man who loved children*. Sydney: Angus & Robertson.

Steiger, H., Gauvin, L., Jabalpurwala, S., Séguin, J. R., & Stotland, S. C. (1999). Hypersensitivity to social interactions in bulimic syndromes: Relationship to binge eating. *Journal of Consulting and Clinical Psychology*, 67 (5), 765–775.

Stein, D. J. & Stone, M. H. (1997). *Essential papers on obsessive-compulsive disorders*. New York, NY: New York University Press.

Stern, D. N. (1985). *The interpersonal world of the infant. A view from psychoanalysis and development psychology*. New York, NY: Basic Books.

Stern, D. N. (1999). Foreword. In E. Fivaz-Depeursinge & A. Corboz-Warney (Eds), *The primary triangle* (pp. xi–xii). New York, NY: Basic Books.

Stern, D. N. (2003). *The present moment in psychotherapy and everyday life*. New York, NY: Norton.

Stern, D. N. (2008). The clinical relevance of infancy: A progress report. *Infant Mental Health Journal*, 29 (3), 177–188.

Stojnov, D. & Butt, T. (2002). The relational basis of personal construct psychology. In R. A. Neimeyer & G. J. Neimeyer (Eds), *Advances in personal construct psychology: New directions and perspectives* (pp. 82–110). Westport, NY: Praeger.

Stoler, L. S. & McNally, R. J. (1991). Cognitive bias in symptomatic and recovered agoraphobics. *Behaviour Research and Therapy*, 29 (4), 539–545.

Stolorow, R. D. & Atwood, G. (1992). *Contexts of being*. Hillsdale, NY: Analytic Press.

Stone, M. B. & Jones, M. L. (2006). *Clinical review: Relationship between antidepressant drugs and suicidality in adults*. Retrieved from http:www.fda.gov./ohrms/dockets/ac/06/briefing/2006-4272b1-01-fda.pdf

Stratton, P. (2003). How families and therapists construct meaning through anticipatory schemas. *Human Systems*, 22 (2), 563–576.

Striegel-Moore, R. H., Franko, D. L., & Ach, E. (2006). *Epidemiology of eating disorder: An update*. In S. Wonderlich, M. de Zwaan, H. Steiger, & J. Mitchell (Eds), *Annual Review of Eating Disorders*. (Part 2, pp. 65–80). Oxford: Radcliffe Publishing.

Sullivan, H. S. (1956). *Clinical Studies in Psychiatry*. New York, NY: Norton.

Sullivan, P. F. (2002). Course and outcome of anorexia nervosa and bulimia nervosa. In C. G. Fairburn & K. D. Brownell (Eds), *Eating disorders and obesity* (2nd edn, pp. 226–232). New York, NY: Guilford Press.

Sullivan, P. F., Neale, M. C., & Kendler, K. S. (2000). Genetic epidemiology of major depression: Review and meta-analysis. *American Journal of Psychiatry*, 157, 1552–1562.

Süskind, P. (2001). *Perfume*. New York, NY: Vintage. (Original work published 1985)

Suzuki, D. T. (1968). *The essence of Buddhism.* Kyoto: Hozokan.

Suzuki, D. T. (1969). *An introduction to Zen Buddhism.* London: Rider.

Tajfel, H. (1981). *Human groups and social categories: Studies in Social Psychology.* Cambridge, MA: Cambridge University Press.

Taylor, C. (1991). *The malaise of modernity.* Concord, ON: House of Anansi Press.

Telfener, U. (1991). La terapia individuale sistemica [Individual systemic therapy]. In M. Malagoli Togliatti & U. Telfener (Eds), *Dall'individuo al sistema: Manuale di psicopatologia relazionale* [From the individual to the system: Manual of relational psychopathology]. Torino: Bollati Boringhieri.

Thomas, C. P., Conrad, P., Casler, R., & Goodman, E. (2006). Trends in the use of psychotropic medications among adolescents, 1994 to 2001. *Psychiatric Services,* 57, 63–69.

Tocqueville, A. (2003), *Democracy in America,* London: Penguin Books. (Original work published 1835–1840)

Trevarthen, C. (1979). Communication and cooperation in early infancy: A description of primary intersubjectivity. In M. Bullowa (Ed.), *Before speech: The beginning of interpersonal communication* (pp. 321–347). Cambridge, MA: Cambridge University Press.

Trevarthen, C. & Aitken, K. J. (2001). Infant intersubjectivity: Research, theory, and clinical applications. *Journal of Child Psychology and Psychiatry and Allied Disciplines,* 42 (1), 3–48.

Trevarthen, C. & Hubley, P. (1978). Secondary intersubjectivity: Confidence, confiding and acts of meaning in the first year. In A. Lock (Ed.), *Action, gesture and symbol: The emergence of language* (pp. 183–229). London: Academic Press.

Ugazio, V., Fellin, L., Pennacchio, R., Negri, A., & Colciago, F. (2012). Is systemic thinking really extraneous to common sense? *Journal of Family Therapy,* 34 (1), 53-71.

Ugazio, V., Negri, A., & Fellin, L. (2011). Meaning and psychopathology. The semantics of phobic, obsessive-compulsive, eating disorders and depression. *Quaderni di Psicologia Clinica* 2 (pp. 69-100). Bergamo: Bergamo University Press.

Ugazio, V., Negri, A., & Fellin, L. (2012). The conversation with phobic, obsessive, eating, and depressed clients is dominated by freedom, goodness, power and belonging semantics? Manuscript submitted for publication.

Ugazio, V., Negri, A., & Fellin, L., & Di Pasquale, R. (2009). The family semantics grid (FSG): The narrated polarities. A manual for the semantic analysis of therapeutic conversation and self-narratives. *TPM. Testing, Psychometrics and Methodology in Applied Psychology,* 16 (4), 165-192.

Ugazio, V., Negri, A., Zanaboni, E., & Fellin, L. (2007). La conversazione con i soggetti fobici è dominata dalla semantica della libertà? [Is the conversation with phobic patients dominated by semantics of freedom?]. *Quaderni del Dottorato in Psicologia Clinica* 1 (pp. 103-133). Bergamo: Bergamo University Press.

Valenstein, E. S. (1998). *Blaming the brain.* New York, NY: The Free Press.

Van Brakel, A. M. L., Muris, P., Bögels, S. M., & Thomassen, C. (2006). A multifactorial model for the etiology of anxiety in non-clinical adolescents: Main and interactive effects of behavioral inhibition, attachment and parental rearing. *Journal of Child and Family Studies.*

Vandereycken, W. (2002). History of anorexia nervosa and bulimia nervosa. In C. G.

Fairburn & K. D. Brownell (Eds), *Eating disorders and obesity: A comprehensive handbook* (2nd edn, pp. 151–154). New York, NY: Guilford Press.

Van IJzendoorn, M. H. & Bakermans-Kranenburg, M. J. (1996). Attachment representations in mothers, fathers, adolescents, and clinical groups: A meta-analytic search for normative data. *Journal of Consulting and Clinical Psychology*, 64, 8–21.

Van Son, G. E., Van Hoeken, D., Bertelds, A. I., Van Furth, E. F., & Hoek, H. W. (2006). Time trends in the incidence of eating disorders: A primary care study in the Netherlands. *International Journal of Eating Disorders*, 39 (7), 565–569.

Veronese, G., Romaioli, D., & Castiglioni, M. (2012). Attachment styles and construction of self in a clinical group of aerophobic: A pilot study. *Psychological Studies*, 57 (3), 303–309.

Vetere, A. & Dowling, E. (2005). *Narrative therapies with children and their families.* New York, NY: Routledge.

Villegas, M. (1995). Psicopatologías de la libertad (I) : La agorafobia o la constricción del espacio [Psychology of freedom (I) : Agoraphobia or the constriction of space]. *Revista de Psicoterapia*, 6 (21), 17–40.

Villegas, M. (1997). Psicopatologías de la libertad (II) : La anorexia o la restricción de la corporalidad [Psychology of freedom (II) : Anorexia or the restriction of body]. *Revista de Psicoterapia*, 8 (30–31), 19–92.

Villegas, M. (2000). Psicopatologías de la libertad (III) : La obsesión o la constricción de la espontaneidad [Psychology of freedom (III) : The obsession or the constriction of spontaneity]. *Revista de Psicoterapia*, 11 (42–43), 49–134.

Villegas, M. (2004). Psicopatologías de la libertad (IV) : Anorexia purgativa y bulimia o el descontrol de la corporalidad [Psychology of freedom (IV) : Purging anorexia and bulimia or the loss of body control]. *Revista de Psicoterapia*, 15 (58–59), 93–144.

Vygotsky, L. S. (1962). *Thought and language* (E. Hanfmann & G. Vakar, Trans.). Cambridge, MA: MIT Press. (Original work published 1934)

Wagner, K. D., Berenson, A., Harding, O., & Joiner, T. (1998). Attributional style and depression in pregnant teenagers. *American Journal of Psychiatry*, 155 (9), 1227–1233.

Walker, I. & Smith, H. J. (2001). *Relative deprivation: Specification, development and integration.* Cambridge, MA: Cambridge University Press.

Walsh, F. (Ed.). (2003). *Normal family processes.* New York, NY: Guilford Press.

Warren, S. L., Huston, L., Egeland, B., & Sroufe, L. A. (1997). Child and adolescent anxiety disorders and early attachment. *Journal for the American Academy of Child and Adolescent Psychiatry*, 36 (5), 637–644.

Waters, T. L. & Barrett, P. M. (2000). The role of the family in childhood obsessive-compulsive disorder. *Clinical Child and Family Psychology Review*, 3 (3), 173–184.

Watzlawick, P., Beavin, J. H., & Jackson, D. D. (1967). *Pragmatics of human communication.* New York: NY: Norton.

Watzlawick, P., Weakland, J. H., & Fisch, R. (1974). *Change: Principles of problem formation and problem solution.* New York, NY: Norton.

Whaley, S. E., Pinto, A., & Sigman, M. (1999). Characterizing interactions between anxious mothers and their children. *Journal of Consulting and Clinical Psychology*, 67 (6), 826–836.

Whiffen, V. E., Kerr, M. A., & Kalloss-Lilly, V. (2005). Maternal depression, adult attachment and children's emotional distress. *Family Process*, 44, 93–103.

Whitaker, R. (2010). *Mad in America: Bad science, bad medicine, and the enduring mistreatment of the mentally ill*. New York, NY: Basic Books.

Winter, D. A & Viney, L. L. (Eds). (2005). *Personal construct psychotherapy: Advances in theory, research and practice*. London: Whurr.

Wolpe, J. (1976). *Theme and variation: A behaviour therapy casebook*. New York, NY: Pergamon Press.

Wood, D. J., Bruner, J., & Ross, G. (1976). The role of tutoring in problem solving. *Journal of Child Psychology and Psychiatry*, 17, 89–100.

Wood, J. J., McLeod, B. D., Sigman, M., Hang, W. C., & Chu, B. C. (2003). Parenting and childhood anxiety: Theory, empirical findings, and future directions. *Journal of Child Psychology and Psychiatry*, 44 (1), 134–151.

Wonderlich, S. A., Lilenfeld, L. R., Riso, L. P., Engel, S., & Mitchell, J. E. (2005). Personality and anorexia nervosa. *International Journal of Eating Disorders*, 37, 68–71.

Zachrisson, H. D., Vedul-Kjelsås, E., Götestam, K. G., & Mykletun, A. (2008). Time trends in obesity and eating disorders. *International Journal of Eating Disorders*, 41 (8), 673–680.

Zahavi, D. (2001). Beyond empathy: Phenomenological approaches to intersubjectivity. *Journal of Consciousness Studies*, 8, 151–167.

Zuk, G. (1969). Triadic-based family therapy. *International Journal of Psychiatry*, 8, 539–556.

INDEX